C000154155

UNDER the SPREADING CEDAR TREE

School life at SPRING GROVE HOUSE, Isleworth
As seen through the eyes of the pupils 1924 to 1959

At Isleworth the school occupied a building that had been the home of Andrew Pears and, before him, of Sir Joseph Banks.
The atmosphere of a 'home' persisted during our period of occupation and staff and pupils worked together like members of one large family.
The red brick house, set in its well-kept grounds, always seemed to be a friendly place but a school is more than just a building.
The Spring Grovian virtues of happiness and friendliness continue to flourish as of old.

An unattributed view of a senior pupil in the "Spring Grovian" in 1960

i

http://www.fast-print.net/bookshop

UNDER THE SPREADING CEDAR TREE
Copyright © Ray Pearce 2015

A catalogue record for this book is available from the British Library

ISBN 978-178456-236-6

First published privately 2011.

This edition published 2015 by
Fast-Print Publishing of Peterborough, England.

THE SPREADING CEDAR TREE

My husband was reading the story about the tree and remembered that his aunt, Elsie Titchen, made a drawing of the front of the school when she was a pupil. She is mentioned in the Old Spring Grovian Magazine, Vol 1, No. 1, in an article by J.L.Davidge [see Page19] and was therefore probably one of the first intake from 1923 - 29. She is still with us, aged 97, and lives in a retirement home in Bristol. His uncle, Frank Marston, was also one of the 1923 - 29 pupils, he too is still alive and lives in Toronto.

I enclose a copy of the drawing showing the original tree and the house. (reproduced below)

Brenda Standivan '51 2009

The enormous mature Cedar tree, pollarded with large chains, which stood at the South West Corner of Spring Grove House, was a feature in the memory of every pupil of the school until 1951 when it collapsed under a weight of snow. The photo below with the snow laden fronds was taken a few days before the collapse.

Contents

Chapter 6 - 1950 - 1955   119

Introduction

Spring Grove House was first used as a school in 1923. The school's association with Spring Grove House finally ended when it moved to Lampton Road in 1959.

Newsletters and journals were produced to keep the pupils informed of what was happening at the school. During and immediately after the 2nd World War there was a thriving Old Spring Grovian Association that organized social, recreational and sporting events for former pupils.

In 2000 several OSGs started to try to engender some enthusiasm into past pupils to revisit their schooldays. John Hore ('46-'51) and John Bloomfield ('49-'54) started websites and Pam Neal (Isom) and Avril Acott (Cutting) (both '48-'53) started to try to find some of their class mates.

In Pam's words:- "It all began some years ago - Avril and I had often talked about our desire to find the friends with whom we had shared our school days. Talked yes, but done nothing! With some unexpected spare time on my hands, late in the year 2000, I put an advertisement in "SAGA" magazine. The first phone call came from the late Mike Stacey and the first letter from Glenys True. Heather Campbell gave me John

Founders - Pam Neal and Avril Acott

Hore's phone number. My call to John coincided with him setting up his web site and between us, the numbers grew. The "friends-reunited" web site also brought in some new contacts."

John Hore became the webmaster and the websites were amalgamated as www.springgrovegrammarschool.org.uk. He joined Pam and Avril in the organization of a reunion to be held at Spring Grove House. The "reunion club" was aimed at Spring Grovians who had spent all or part of their time at Spring Grove House. Over 300 former pupils contacted Pam and John and were able to get in touch with each other via the SGGS website. Of these, 120 were able to come to the first reunion at Spring Grove House on Wednesday 19 Sept, 2001.

The newsletter "Spring Grovian Report" was started the following year.

Ray Pearce '53, was unfortunate enough to sneeze just as John Hore asked for a volunteer to edit the newsletter and so got the job. By 2010 the SGR was being sent to over 700 OSGs on every continent of the world Their 5th years at the school ranged from 1932 to 1960.

Ray Pearce has compiled this book from pupils' memories recorded in the Spring Grovian Reports and extracts from previous Spring Grove newsletters and articles relating to the school, the house and the district, Heston and Isleworth.

Acknowledgments

Most of the material in this book is the recollections of the former pupils at the school. 112 OSGs have sent their recollections of their schooldays for publication in the Spring Grovian Report newsletter and they constitute the bulk of this book. Which also means that, sadly, over 600 of the OSGs we are in contact with, had insufficient memories to fill a foolscap sheet to share with us.

The only consolation is that, reading through past copies of the School and OSGA newsletters, persuading people to contribute was always a problem.

For the historical research all have made use of the local history department of the Hounslow Library and we are all grateful to the knowledgeable and helpful staff there.

Two OSGS must be singled out for their efforts in researching the past of SGH and SGG/SS.

John Bloomfield, '54, launched the first website dedicated to Spring Grove Grammar School, it was established on Thursday 24 May 2001. The objectives were to create a focal point for pupils and staff of the school, to encourage communication, and in time provide a picture gallery, a chronicle and other interesting features. OSGs were invited to submit details and information about their connection with the school.

John undertook considerable research into SGH and its inhabitants using the West Thames College and Local Historical Archives. His research was available on the website. In 2003 John amalgamated his website with John Hore's ('51) reunion website, www.springgrovegrammarschool.org.uk, and his research can now be found there.

Peter Salter, '58, made a great effort to compile a definitive Roll of Honour of the OSGs who fell during the World War II. Peter also researched the life and times of Joseph Banks.

Finally thanks must go to Bud Cutting, '44, who has spent many hours poring over the proof copies of the SGR newsletters over the last ten years and again has spent time to ensure that this copy is word perfect.

We hope that one or two of the readers get satisfaction from finding the deliberate mistakes that Bud has left in.

Further copies of this book may be obtained by downloading the order form from the website:- www.springgrovegrammarschool.org.uk

THE SPRING GROVE HOUSE SCHOOLS

1

Extract from the Borough of Heston and Isleworth Souvenir Handbook for Education Week; June 28 to July 4 1936 :-

The end of the century brought great changes. The Board of Education Act of 1899 established one control authority, and the Balfour Act of 1902 placed Elementary and Secondary Education within the scope of the Board and Local Councils, thus laying the foundation of our national system. The British and Foreign Schools Society now relinquished its control of the "Isleworth Upper School for Boys" and it became the "Isleworth County School for Boys." The girls were provided for by the establishment of the Green Secondary School for Girls at Busch Corner in 1906. This school was a development from the Green Elementary School, its endowments now being used for the Secondary School. The Duke of Northumberland generously made himself responsible for the cost of the school, to accommodate 120, and leased it to the Trustees for £8 a year.

To help in providing and training teachers a Pupil Teachers' Centre was established in the Hanworth Road (1905-1909) with Mr. C.A.Wood as Principal.

The Middlesex Education Committee moved the Polytechnic classes from Hanworth Road to larger premises in the Spring Grove House in September, 1922, thus starting the Spring Grove Polytechnic.

In the following January, a Mixed Secondary School was opened in the same house with 40 pupils, a number which rapidly increased.

Spring Grove Grammar School. Isleworth

SGH - Spring Grove Grammar School 1950

2006 SGH dwarfed & enclosed by 1960s concrete blocks - West Thames College

1923 -   Spring Grove Secondary School established
1946 -   School renamed Spring Grove Grammar School
1959 -   SGGS moves to new premises in Lampton; Spring
          Grove House becomes Isleworth Polytechnic
1967 -   Rebuilding of Isleworth Polytechnic is commenced,
          involving demolition of NW section of house.
2007 -   Refurbishment of West Thames College
          Work includes the demolishion of the 1960s blocks and
           their replacement by blocks which are sympathetic to the
          style of SGH and allow the house to be seen from several
          vantage points on the perimeter of the grounds.
2011 -   Refurbishment completed. On time!

Above: NE View from Main Gate - Oct 2008; '60s concrete blocks demolished:
Below: WIP: NW View from Harvard Rd.- Oct 2010 new main Block & SGH

Historical Dates and Events

A Short History Of Spring Grove School up to 1958

The following historical narrative was prepared by the **Heston & Isleworth Schools' Local History Society,** *published in the* **Middlesex Chronicle** *in 1958 and provided to us by the* **Hounslow Library Local History Collection.**

SPRING GROVE GRAMMAR SCHOOL

Newest of the grammar schools, and the only co-educatonal school in the borough, Spring Grove Secondary School, as it was then known, opened with a meeting of the future scholars in January 1923, in a building and on a site rich in history, which will be dealt with in a later article. Twenty-one attended the first roll call - "Fifteen young gentlemen and six young ladies," to quote from an article in an old school magazine. There were only two members of staff, Mr C.A. Wood M.A., the Headmaster, and Miss I Bonnett, and the varous subjects (75 per cent gardening) were divided between them. The school was officially opened on April 25th, 1923.

The grounds were described by one of those original pupils, John Davidge, in a 1939 edition of "Old Spring Grovian" as "Very wild; heavy undergrowth and many trees, since cut down, made them ideal for the pupils to lead the caretaker, Mr Stowe, a dance, when they stayed after school in the evening. The top pitch was divided down the middle by a high wall and there were orchards in each part. The vinery had a really fine vine in it and in the first two years many dozens of bunches were grown.

Many of the rooms have been altered, but the biggest change has been in the Banksian Room, which originally was like a hothouse at Kew and had all kinds of vines, trees and plants growing in it, and also an aquarium. Today there are few traces left of the grotto-like room of 1923.

On Wednesday, December 17th, 1924, the new Assembly Hall was opened by the Right Hon. Sir W. Joynson-Hicks, Bart, M.P., the Home Secretary, on the first "Speech Day."

In 1927 Aleck Westrupp gained the first Matriculation and the annual prize distribution on December 8th, 1928 was reported in the "Middlesex Chronicle" under the heading "Six Years' Steady Progress! Excelsior!" The school now contained more than 450 pupils and many societies already flourished.

Many will remember the old black and white uniform of those days, the "Men of the Trees," and the pageants and exhibitions in connection with which we recall the name of Mr. Fendick, then History Master, now a Director of Education.

Above:- The Banksian Room   Below :- The Music Room

The school continued to flourish, and there is nothing specially noteworthy to report, apart from Mr Wood's retirement and the arrival in January 1935, of Headmaster, Mr L.T.Brown, M.A. Cantab, under whom Spring Grove made so much progress in numbers, in the widening of outlook and in academic achievements. At the outbreak of war it seemed possible that the school would cease to function, as it was taken over by the Office of Works, but their stay was a brief one, and the school was soon able to carry on its normal activities, after a short period during which the County School gave it accommodation.

War naturally affected the conditions and smooth running of the school in many ways, but fundamental principles remained unchanged. The school remembers, with pride, the many pupils who gave their lives. Among the early casualties was John Rhys, the first Spring Grovian to qualify for the medical profession. We cannot list all the tragic losses, but might be forgiven for singling out Hazel Batten, who joined the W.R.N.S. and was drowned, and two brothers, Leslie and David Barden, in remembrance of whom their parents give annually two greatly appreciated prizes for French and Geography.

Although war brought dislocation of routine, many obtained the General Schools Certificate. Teachers and pupils worked under difficult conditions; often work was interrupted for long periods and had to be continued orally in the air-raid shelters.

The school survived the lively bombardment experienced during the war years and although a number of bombs fell dangerously near, the damage was fortunately superficial. Some of the present staff still remember their fire-watching days and how they escorted pupils home at the end of a day if an air-raid was in progress.

In 1948 the whole school celebrated its 25th anniversary and the last week of the summer term was noteworthy not only for Speech Day, but for various educational, athletic and social activities. There was an Open Day on which displays of pupils' work was added to the exhibition of boys' physical training, of country dancing and the finals of the tennis competition. An excerpt from "A Midsummer Night's Dream" was presented by the Dramatic Society.

On the third evening of the week there was a grand reunion of the staff and Old Spring Grovians; next day the senior concert. A staff v pupils tennis tournament and a cricket match between the School XI and the Old Spring Grovians on July 24th ended the week's events.

Speech Day during that week was honoured by the presence of the Dowager Marchioness of Reading, the widow of one of India's greatest Viceroys, as well as head of the W.V.S. and governor of the B.B.C. It was especially marked also by the Headmaster's report, containing news of the sporting achievements of Sylvia Cheeseman and Doris Batter, and of six University successes, four being honours degrees gained by former pupils. The school has been honoured by many other distinguished speakers since the war, including Miss

Pictures from the 1930s
Above :- Room 2 ; Below :- The Gymn

Florence Horsbrugh, C.B.E., M.P., Minister of Education, Sir Frank Tribe, the Comptroller and Auditor General, Canon C.V. Raven, the Queen's Chaplain, and the Very Reverend W.R. Matthews, Dean of St. Paul's.

From the subject of distinguished visitors to "Spring Grove" which ended the first article, our thoughts turn to outstanding members of the staff. The first Headmaster was C.A. Wood M.A., whose death in 1952, at the age of 80, ended a remarkable career and caused sadness to many. He was a very active man with wide interests, among them Natural History and Sir Walter Scott's works; not only was he a great lover of books, but he showed a truly remarkable encyclopaedic knowledge which made him a singularly interesting and effective teacher.

The school has been most fortunate to have as members of staff several of outstandingly long service, such men as Mr. A.H. Aldersly (Chemistry), and Mr. A.C.P. Handover (Mathematics). In 1941 these two much-loved and respected masters died. Their services to the school are commemorated by a plaque in the main entrance hall and by the Aldersly-Handover Prizes given annually to a Fifth Year boy and girl for outstanding perseverence (sic) . Mr. Handover's enthusiasm on behalf of the Royal Lifesaving Society received world-wide recognition. Mr. Cross, who taught woodwork and P.T. and took a great interest in the Parents' and Teachers' Association at Spring Grove for 24 years, retired in 1947; Miss Nash also left, after more than 20 years teaching Biology, to join the staff of the Cty of London School for Girls where she still is.

In 1949-50 came the resignations of Mr. Trevor Owen, still so well known in the borough, and Mr Corby, whose death, so soon afterwards, was a great blow to his many friends, as was that of Miss Bromwich in 1953. Miss Bromwich who had taught cookery, needlework and baby-craft to so many girls in the Old Cottage, now the caretaker's home, left in 1949, followed in 1951 by Miss Walters who taught art here for 29 years before she also retired to a Suffolk village where she still lives. Bernard Joy, well-known sports reporter, played association football for Arsenal and England and was a member of the Olympic Team while on the Spring Grove staff

Three even more outstanding members of staff must now be mentioned. First, Miss Griffin, who retired in 1948 after 23 years' service as Senior Mistress and teacher of French. In his address, the Headmaster paid warm tribute to her as a most helpful colleague, praising her amiable temperament and friendliness, while stressing the fact that, while she could be severe in dealing with misdemeanour, she was always eminently just in her administration. A former pupil wrote: "Her individuality inspires leadership in others, together with the will and the zest to lead full and useful lives to the utmost extent of their capabilities." She married and now lives in a Dorset village.

Mr. F.W. Brown, who joined the staff in 1925 remained here for 30 years, 13 of which were spent as Senior Master. When he succeeded Mr. Snaith in his

Above:- Room 4
Below:- Woodwork

post in 1941, he maintained a remarkable level of efficiency as a teacher and organiser of the Mathematics Department. He was a man of wide cultural interests; among them music and chess. When he retired in 1953, it seemed impossible to imagine the school without this kindly "tower of strength." His death in 1956 brought a sense of loss to all who knew him. A pastel portrait of him, executed by the art master, Mr Bullough, hangs in the school library, a lasting tribute to him from the staff.

 The most recent member of these distinguished three to retire was Mr. R.L. Callow, who had spent thirty years at the school as a Geography and Scripture Master, the last four as Senior Master in succession to Mr. Brown. For many years he arranged the annual school outings and he also showed great interest in the Christian Union Society which was founded in September 1954.

The school has many societies covering a very wide range of interests. In these societies the pupils are able to extend their interests in their favourite subjects under the expert and enthusiastic guidance of the staff. A special feature is the School Council, consisting of the staff and prefects, who are elected by staff and sixth year pupils. New entrants receive a pamphlet describing this and other aspects of school life.

The goal of a grammar school should be academic success and we could produce a long list of those who have won great success at the University, but it would be invidious to single out few from so many.

Organised games play a large part in the life of the school and many successes have been gained in this field too. In individual sportsmen and sportswomen our school has an outstanding record in producing three Olympic athletes, Lorna Frampton (Swimming 1936)and Sylvia Cheeseman and Doris Batter who both ran in the 1948 Olympic Games; Dorothy Saunders was a member of the English team in the Empire Games in Sydney in 1930.

When pupils leave Spring Grove they go into all walks of life and all parts of the world. But they are all linked, all who wish to be, by the Old Spring Grovian (sic) Association - the link between the past and present generations at Spring Grove. For many years the staff and pupils have been awaiting the erection of a new school building; although the present one (condemned in 1935!) may be called unusual and picturesque, situated in undeniably pleasant grounds, it is not suitable for use as a school, despite various modifications, such as the building of a canteen, where the pupils now dine instead of in the basement, and a small school library and new Domestic Science Department replacing the caretaker's original quarters. 1957, however, actually saw the begining (sic) of a new school building near the Great West Road. Generations of Old Spring Grovians, some of whose children are now pupils, together with the many staff who have loved "the old place" while recognising its deficiencies, will hope that the new Spring Grove at Lampton will carry on the best traditions and make still better citizens.

The school moved to Lampton in 1959 and in 1969 changed its name to Lampton School. In 2010 Spring Grove House is the administration centre for West Thames College. Wide bodied passenger jet aircraft thunder overhead, a few minutes apart, at 600ft on final approach to land at London Heathrow Airport.

West Thames College: 2010

- West Thames College has approx 7000 students each year – most are from the local west London area, but many come from overseas to study at the college.
- The college has two campuses – the main campus in London Road Isleworth, plus the Feltham Skills Centre (a smaller centre specialising in practical, vocational skills such as construction, catering, Engineering and motor vehicle maintenance).
- The Isleworth Campus is currently undergoing a three-phase - £70 Million rebuild - funded by the LSC. In September 2008, the new Nursery was opened and the professional hair and beauty salons were completely refurbished. New purpose-built makeup studios and dance studios were also completed.
- In April 2010, the Atrium building opened with a three storey Learning Resources Centre, the Endeavour Theatre and performance spaces, a sports hall and gym, two common rooms and canteens. The college now also boasts a state-of-the-art media and music recording and editing studios including a TV studio, multimedia suites and photographic studios.
- By September 2011, the Sir Joseph Banks Building will open, consisting mainly of high-spec classrooms for teaching and learning. Key areas of Spring Grove House will also be carefully restored and refurbished whilst new outdoor sports pitches will be laid along with the complete landscaping of the college grounds.
- The college has one of the highest success rates of the 34 FE Colleges in the London region and had a very good Ofsted inspection in 2007.
- The college offers a wide range of courses for the whole community – from basic/introductory level courses right up to degree level higher education courses – for school leavers, adults and employers.
- The college specialises in vocation courses – students have access to excellent, industry-standard facilities, workshops, salons and studios.
- Teachers are industry professionals who pass on their knowledge, skills and contacts to the students.
- West Thames College is the largest provider of higher education provision in the local area and runs courses in partnership with Thames Valley University and Kingston University.

THE EARLY YEARS

2

Early Days at Spring Grove

Mr. R.L.Callow

Reminiscences of a master at the school for 38 years, 1924 – 1962. He will be remembered by all Spring Grovians. This article was written for the Old Spring Grovians' Association shortly after his retirement - 24th Dec 1962.

When I was appointed, in September 1924 the school was small, and had less than two hundred pupils. Only the first two floors were used, the top floor being used by a day continuation school, under the control of Mr. Handover. This school was the last of its kind and closed in December 1924. The following term Mr. Handover joined the Spring Grove staff.

Many of the forms were small, and thirty represented the maximum. There was only one form II, no form I and no form VI. The senior pupils, those in form V, were fourteen plus. Pupils came from a very much wider area than at present, some coming from Putney, Ealing and westwards beyond Harlington. There were four houses, named Robins, Seagulls, Swallows, and Skylarks. Pupils who failed persistently to conform to the school rules, were removed to a Cuckoo house.

When I arrived, the Chemistry Laboratory was brand new as also was the hall. I can still remember the wood shavings on the laboratory floor, when I first started to teach chemistry there.   I also taught geography throughout the school and also some mathematics with several periods of games to fill up my time-table. There were no external exams to worry about, and so for internal school exams, academic work proceeded at a leisurely pace.   House tea parties were quite easy to arrange when there were only about 50 pupils to each house. The number of staff was small - the headmaster was Mr. C.A. Wood, Mr. Snaith (Physics, Maths), Miss Blair Smith (French), Miss Edith Taylor (English), Miss Casselden (Botany), Mr. Fendick (History) and Mr. Cross (Woodwork and P.T.).   Visiting staff included Miss Quelch (Art), Miss Cook (Needle-work), Miss Jones (Girls' P.T.) and Miss Bonnett (Music).

Hours were from 9 to 12 and 2 to 4.   Only a handful of pupils stayed to lunch, which was served by the caretaker and his wife and eaten, in the basement, in silence.

The Headmaster at the time was very keen on keeping the grounds in good order. Each pupil had a small plot, and Mr. Cross, the woodwork master, more often than not was out in the grounds supervising the pupils - so much so, in fact, that his complexion suggested that he had only just returned from the South Seas.

My form, in those days was VB - a prize collection of doubtful academic ability, but easy to get along with.   We inhabited Room 2 (later the Commercial Room).

1930 Staff:- Back Row:- W. Lineham;O.Jones; Miss Bromwich; J.F,Cross; T.V. Watts;
Middle Row:- H.W.Howes; Miss E.M.Richards; W.O.Corby; Miss B.D.Stubbs;
A.C.P.Handover; Miss Heather; G.W. Barrett;;Miss B.D.Potts; A.H.Aldersley:
Front Row :- R.C.Callow; Miss B.D.Nash; T.G.Fendick ; Miss E.H.Griffin;
C.A.Wood; Miss M. Scupham; G.L.Snaith; Miss E.P. Walters;F.W.Brown:

The Headmaster was also intent on keeping his staff trim and physically fit.
In the summer term of 1925, we all turned out to play tennis, and the grass
courts, whilst never up to Wimbledon standards by the end of July, showed
more than a superficial resemblance to the Sahara. The male staff was expected
also to play cricket and I became a vital member of the staff team.

We had a part time music teacher and so it fell to my lot to play the piano for
morning assembly.   The Headmaster required music for pupils to march into
and out of the hall; Percy Grainger's "Country Gardens" was a special favourite.
Morning Assembly frequently went on so long that first lesson was cancelled.

The caretaker, Mr.Stowe, was as so often happens, "a character", and always
ready with advice on the running of the school; he invariably wore a straw hat
with his official overalls, whatever the weather.   There was also a groundsman,
who had to look after the "school horse", which was used for pulling the rollers
and the mower.   When the groundsman retired, the horse disappeared also.

The original stabling or coach houses, with a little alteration, became the physics
laboratory and gymnasium and the coach yard between them, when roofed
over, became the School Hall, which was officially opened at the first Speech
Day in December 1924, by Sir Joynston Hicks (later Lord Brentford), Home
Secretary and M.P. for Brentford.

Many changes took place in the considerable period that I spent at Spring
Grove - The Great West Road was in process of construction and large areas
South of the Southern Region railway-line, and West of Thornbury Road were
still market gardens. There was no fire station or cinema, and Harvard Road was
just a rough track and houses in The Grove were just being built.

It would be nice to go back and relive those 38 years, but as this is impossible,
the next best thing is an armchair before a blazing fire and an invitation to
reminisce.

Football Team (Juniors).

Football Teams 1924/5

Football Team (Seniors).

In the Beginning

J. L. Davidge, '29.

This article was first published in the Old Spring Grovian Magazine Vol. 1 No.1 published in Spring 1939.   It describes the first years of the school at Spring Grove House.

Sixteen years ago is a very long time, but I can still remember quite clearly the opening day of the School. The scholars met in the room opposite the main entrance.   It has had various names among them being the " History Room " and " Room 2 " which is its official name according to the illustrated brochure issued about 1926. The actual date eludes me, but it was early in January, 1923 and there were 21 of us at the first roll call, 6 young ladies and 15 very assorted young (?) gentlemen. There were only two members of the Staff—Mr. Wood our Head and Miss I. Bonnett and the various subjects (75% gardening) were divided between them. Not long after the School opened, Miss Blair-Smith came and took French and English. Those early days were more holidays than schooldays, as the grounds were in such virgin state that they needed and received much attention.

It is difficult to visualise the grounds as they were, but the boundary at the front ended at the hockey pitch, a wooden fence separating the bushes and grasslands from some allotments which stood where the football pitch now is, and the only tended grass was that outside the Art Room. The grounds were very wild, heavy undergrowth and many trees since cut down made them ideal for the lawless pupils to lead the caretaker, Mr. Stowe, a dance, when they stayed after school in the evening. The top pitch was divided down the middle by a high wall and there were orchards in each part. The Vinery had a really fine vine in it and in the first two years many dozen bunches of grapes were grown. It was later cut down, I forget the reason, but I think it had something to do with the boys coveting them! The boundary fence went a few feet west of the Pavilion—the hard court was not part of the School grounds then—it was added a year or two later as the authorities failed to see why the pupils should have to climb a fence each time they wanted cherries or raspberries.

Many of the rooms have been altered but the biggest change was in the Banksian room, which originally was like a hot house at Kew and had all kinds of vines, trees and plants growing in it and had an aquarium. But things were gradually altered until it reached its present state, far removed from the beautiful grotto-like room of 1923, but probably more useful to the school. The physics and chemistry laboratories were built some time after School opened, as was the Main Hall, originally a stabling yard. The gymnasium consisted of two barns, upper and lower. After the School opened the floor of the upper room was removed and the place converted into the gymnasium.

In the first few terms each pupil had a vegetable plot and some fine crops were raised, although the boys from Sipson and Harlington seemed to produce far better crops than those from Brentford and Isleworth.

All hopes of record marrows were dispelled for after the summer holiday of 1924 we returned to find it all ploughed into the ground prior to removing the wall and preparing the top pitch.

It is interesting to recall our efforts at competition with other Schools at Soccer. Our first match was played against Hampton Grammar in Winter term 1923 and we lost 8-1. Lawrence, A. Lee, Skipper, Knott, G. Payne, Clarke and Grant were amongst those who took part in that match. We held the Hampton team (I'm not sure whether it was the 3rd or 4ths) to 1-1 at half time, but in the second half the team went to pieces and Hampton did as they liked. Later in this season we played Isleworth County 3rds at Busch Corner and believe it or not we lost 22-0. The half time score was 15-0. Isleworth had some very strong teams at that time and several of the team that day went on to form the nucleus of some of their best School and Old Boys elevens. The team improved as it got older and the boys became used to each other's play. I believe our first win as a School was against Crosby House, a Southall private school (and not a school for Crooners!) The teams improved from season to season and it was not many years before we held our own with the 1st elevens of the rival schools. Owing to the small number of girls, hockey against other schools did not start until 1924/5 season, and Ena Uncle, Margaret Potter and " Bill " Stronach were among the stalwarts of the early teams. Netball also came into its own with Elsie Titchen as star goal shooter.

So the School has grown from that small beginning in 1923, with Mickey Trowell as the number one pupil, until in 1930 there were over 500 pupils. So they have grown up and gone their way to different parts of the globe — Collins and Charlie King in Australia, Batten in Canada, Murray and Freeman in Palestine, " Ran " Saunders in India, and many others --but there will always be the bond between us all — we are Old Spring Grovians.

Above : The banksian room in 1902 and below as the science room in 1924

THE 30s

3

Pre War Spring Grove School

Doreen Boddy, '38

Doreen recalls the teachers who influenced her during her
years at the 'Black and White" school

Does anyone else remember Mr Handover cycling to school with his stiff leg and fixed pedal, holding his umbrella over his head on rainy days? ....and he wore a bowler!
We were post war babes in my generation – although none of us realised it. Just as the word "teenager" hadn't been coined nor had the phrase "post war babe" - "war time babe" yes, but not PWB. I don't think any of us realised how recent the Great War was. Time is different when you are young. I remember hearing my father and his brother talking about the war when I was a child and wondering why they remembered it so often. We live and learn, as I found out when we had a war of our own!

A result of being so near to the Great War was that we had other teachers who had been involved and who had their war injuries. Mr. Watts had lost his right hand and had it replaced with by an odd cylindrical perforated thing through which he could push a pen and write as quickly as anyone else. However we had a lot of young teachers too, although I don't think we realised how young they were. You could tell to a certain extent by the newness of their gowns which were always worn. I remember one had the back in shreds – was it Mr Snaith? - an oldie! Of course they all had respectable ones for speech days when they sported their hoods too.

In my first year Mr Woods was the headmaster – a gentleman. I had just one lesson with him. We spent the whole time discussing the first paragraph in a book. He weighed up the meaning of each word most carefully, questioning whether it could have meant this or that. Mr. Lineham taught in much the same way in English Lit. classes. I remember him discussing when we were reading Silas Marner just what it was that marked the character as a gentleman. Was it his britches? Labourers could wear britches. Was it his voice? No, he wasn't speaking, was it this or that? Was it his whip? Yes, but only partly. It was the way he swiped his whip in the ditches that marked him as the squire's son. Little did I know that I'd just had my first lesson in body language.

Mr. L.T. Brown took over as headmaster at the start of my second year. He was a good head I believe.

Miss Ransom, was a legend in her own time, took us on a school trip somewhere near to Worthing – the place to which Mr. Wood had retired. He invited us to visit him. We walked there in a crocodile. I can't remember what did happen when we were there, but the word "strawberries" comes to mind – surely a gaggle of schoolgirls didn't get given strawberries? Does anyone else remember?

Then there was Mr. Varney. His "stage" name was Trevor Owen. He sang and a welsh name was a better one to have. He brought a lot into our lives that was new. His enthusiasm was huge and apart from various concerts, he produced a Gilbert and Sullivan opera "the Gondoliers ". This set me off on a love of G & S for ever. I'm sure other people must have been touched in the same way. The opera was performed in the assembly hall – the only time that I can remember the curtains in use. On Friday afternoons for the last two periods all the pupils in the first and second year were together in the Hall singing French songs – "Frére Jacques" etc. which shook the building.

Names of the teachers crowd into my mind and their images too. Miss Griffin our female head teacher who did her best to make us be more ladylike each week at the girls assembly. Miss Taylor, who, when asked a date (in History) would start somewhere and then mutter a whole series of numbers until she reached the right one. Miss Bromwich, of the apple cheeks and somewhat fearsome manner, who was straight out of an Angela Brazil book.

Then there were the men, Mr. Callow who was so much fun in the school concerts; Mr Aldersley, who wheezed – Chemistry; Mr. Fendick - a really brilliant history teacher who left us for some exalted post in the midlands to be replaced by Mr. Bernard Joy who played centre-half for Arsenal and England for the princely sum of £8 a match; Mr. Tomlinson, who always raised his eyes to heaven and said "Hope springs eternal".

Mr. Davey – a super, super teacher who taught me the French I've used in France for many years and I've blessed him for his insistence on pronunciation. Some years ago I was in France with my husband and adult son. We stopped at an auberge in the middle of nowhere for the night. Deciding to catch the last of the sunshine, we sat outside and fell into conversation with another couple. It transpired that the husband had been to Isleworth County and played in the cricket team with my older brother and the wife was in my year at Spring Grove for about five weeks before her father had to move. Over dinner he mellowed and confided in me that he had always heard that "Black & White" girls were a bit of "goers." When we finally took our leave, he kissed me soundly and said, "I've always wanted to kiss a girl from the "Black and White". His wife was not amused! I wondered if I looked like his idea of a "goer".

In the sixth form were some whose names became quite famous:- Maurice Moisiewitch wrote a series for the BBC about the legendary Henry Penny of Acacia Avenue. Leslie Miller became head of Borough Road College. Jennie Cassini became a well-known pianist. Dorothy Saunders a runner and Lorna Frampton, who swam back stroke in the 1936 Berlin Olympics.

I loved Spring Grove very much and have many treasured memories tumbling round in my head.

A German Holiday

Doreen Boddy, '38
Doreen wrote this for the Spring Grovian 1939

One rather warm Saturday afternoon at the end of July our small party of about twenty gathered together at Liverpool Street station, all very excited at the prospect of a fortnight's vacation in Germany. Eager as we were to be off, we found it very difficult to locate our reserved compartment in the train. After rushing from one end to the other to find our seats, we were finally settled just as the train was starting, though some were nearly left behind.

It was an uneventful run down to Harwich, and we spent most of the time in getting to know the person who was to be our guide. He was a German, but spoke English very well (having learnt it from an Irishman). We arrived at Harwich at about five o'clock and, having passed through the Customs, we embarked immediately, and none too soon, as the boat left at about 5.10 p.m

It was a glorious sunny afternoon, and when the boat had started most of us went up on to the sun deck and made ourselves comfortable. Gradually the shores grew fainter and the sun went down. It seemed hours before we sighted the coast of Belgium. Ostend soon stood out plainly—a riot of bluish lights which outlined all the buildings along the front. It was half-past eleven before we reached the harbour at Vlissingen and saw the Dutch men and women standing on the wooden quay. Then we were fortunate enough to see a very unusual sight, although none of us realized it at the time. Myriads of minute, phosphorized organisms had appeared in the water near the shore, a phenomenon which occurs only in hot weather, and they made the water appear full of glowworms.

Dozens of the Dutch people were clopping up and down the quay, in spite of the late hour. We went quickly through the Customs building, which was very clean compared with our Customs-houses. Not long afterwards we were speeding across Holland and then Germany on the Swiss Express. It was about 3.30 a.m. when we arrived at Munchen Gladbach, after having our cases inspected by Germans on the train. From there it was only a short journey by coach to Dusseldorf, where we arrived at the hotel so early that we had to wake up the proprietor to let us in.

The next day we were formally welcomed to Dusseldorf by the Mayor's representative at the town hall. While we were in Germany we were privileged to visit many interesting places of the Rhineland. We went by boat to Cologne and visited its beautiful Cathedral. On another day we went by coach to the Ahr valley and to the Seven Mountains, and to Wuppertal, where we rode on a suspension railway. We spent one very happy afternoon playing skittles in an old inn, with a group of old people, who were out on some excursion, looking on and encouraging us. The fact that we could not speak each other's language did not make the game less exciting. Another interesting trip was to ruined Kaiserwerth, where the "eternal" flame of the Hitler Youth movement burns. Every year members of the movement pay one pfennig to keep the flame alight. On a later occasion we visited a youth hostel and saw how the German youth spend their holidays, and really had to admire the organization of the colossal hostel.

A fortnight later the same party met again, this time at midnight, in the magnificent entrance to the new Dusseldorf station. Tired but happy, we started off for home. We returned by train to Munchen Gladbach and then had a wait of three hours for the express. This time we were able to see a little of Holland in the early morning light. When the boat sailed we had a fine view of the great sand dunes on the Dutch coast. In a short time we were once again back on the train rushing from Harwich to London.

So ended a delightful holiday. We are all extremely grateful to those who organized it and to our German friends who had been so kind to us.

1A 1937 Mr R Callow

Spring Grove 1929 – 1935

Grace Mitchell, '35

Doreen's article prompted this response.

With regards to Doreen Boddy's "Down Memory Lane" I well remember Mr Handover – especially also for plunging nearly the length of Hounslow Swimming Pool. I belonged to Hounslow Swimming Club with Lorna Frampton (who is still a great friend of mine) and we gained our Bronze Medals and Bars for The Royal Life Saving with him.

I joined Spring Grove in 1929 when my parents moved from London to Heston. I used to cycle along the Great West Road to school. In bad weather I caught a train from Hounslow West Underground station to Osterley and walked down Harvard Road.

I remembered all the staff that Doreen mentioned. I loved sport, played netball and hockey and ran for the School. We played against the Green School for Girls (Isleworth), Gumley House and Twickenham Grammar schools. Mrs Phillips our games mistress took us and we had cocoa and buns afterwards. My last year was in form 5A with Miss Taylor our form mistress. I still have a photo of us all taken in front of the school. It was a lovely school and I was honoured to be a pupil where Sir Joseph Banks lived. It was in the early part of 5A that I became a prefect – my black and white badge was presented to me in assembly by the Headmaster Mr Wood.

Also while I was there I joined the British Red Cross Middx 246 detachment and passed my exams and did 96 hours nursing at West Middlesex County Hospital, Isleworth.

After I left school I became a Civil servant in the Ministry of Health in London and when the Second World War was declared, we were evacuated to Blackpool in January 1940. I didn't like it very much so while there I enrolled in the local hospital and did some more nursing, still with the BRC. Eventually I left Blackpool and returned to West Middlesex County Hospital and joined the "Civil Nursing Reserve". I think many of the pupils in my year joined up. It was our age group! Our nurses' home was in Syon House at that time and we used to go over on the ferry to Kew Gardens when off duty.

It was during my nursing that I met Sergeant Pilot Stan Walton who was to become a Flying Officer Spitfire Pilot and we were married in Southport, Lancashire in 1942.

15th January 2003

How I Made It into 3c

George Childs, '37

When the time came for me to take the eleven plus, I was in bed with measles. Instead of sweating over exam papers I read and reread Swiss Family Robinson, my favourite book at the time. The downside was that, as soon as I looked a little better, I was hauled out of bed to stagger along for the resit. I failed. I then took the examination for a place in a Central school and ended up in Spring Grove Central, just down the road from Spring Grove Grammar but, seemingly, on a different planet. I spent two years there before getting a place in the Grammar School and it is from this that I feel able to say why we all look back on our days there with such loving affection. The culture there expected thoughtfulness, tolerance, good nature and good humour, and that was what we had. I was never aware of any bullying.

Not so in the Central school. The culture there was one of discipline (when people say "they need more discipline", they really mean "they should do what I say and without question"). The headmaster, Mr. G. E. Bates, was always impeccably dressed. A well cut suit, carefully pressed, shirt and tie and spats! He also wore very special shoes which allowed him to walk in absolute silence like a cat, shoes which were later known as 'brothel creepers'. He would prowl around the school, ready to pounce, a look of disapproval permanently on his face. We nicknamed him "Tabby". Discipline there was, and bullying too.

My arrival at Spring Grove Grammar in the third year was a shock for me and a problem for the school. Where were they going to put an unknown quantity from a central school? They decided on 3C. I spent a year in 3C before I was kicked out and up into 4B because I got too many marks, and I am not sure whether to say, "Look what it did for me" or "Look what it did to me!" I will tell you about it.

On my first arrival at the school the secretary, Miss Ashbrook, took me up to the 3C classroom and as we entered there were shouts, screams and wolf whistles from the 3C girls. The 3C girls would wolf-whistle almost anything in a   pair of trousers. They were street-wise, sex-wise and all there. I was naive, over-sensitive and terribly embarrassed. I gave them encouragement by flushing to the roots of my hair, and thus it was that I missed out on learning many interesting things that I could have learnt about in 3C. Some of the girls met their boy friends, usually from the fifth or sixth year, down in the spinney. Are you wondering where the spinney was? Well, in my day there was no fire station but twenty or so trees and many bushes, all affording a great deal of privacy. When I explored the place with my friend Len, our imaginations ran riot on what went on there and I regret that even in the 6th form I never got around to meeting girls in the spinney, but, by that time, I was madly in love with a girl in the 5th year whose loveliness inspired me to write poetry which I was too shy to show to her. Then later, the council had the fire station built there and a wonderful co-educational opportunity was lost for ever!

Let me come back to 3C. It is obvious, is it not, that if you are going to stream an intake, you put the bright ones in the A-stream, the dullards in the C-stream and the in-betweens in the B-stream. Not a bit of it. As a rare specimen who sampled all three streams, I can tell you that some of the brightest people I met were in the C stream!

They were just not interested in academics, a teacher's yardstick for ranking their charges. Here I met people who had no inclination towards history, geography, languages, mathematics and all those things, and must have been pulled into the grammar school by their performance on Cyril Burt's I. Q. tests. There were boys who were radio hams and built their own radio sets. Another would strip down a car engine at the weekend, de-coke it and grind in the valves. Two others were expert shop-lifters and always had a selection of very saleable goods at half the high street price. I have since come to the conclusion that the factor deciding which stream people went into was academic inclination rather than intelligence, which was why, at the end of the year, I was kicked out of 3C and up to 4B. I had an academic streak! When, later, I joined 5A I became one of the few to sample all three streams at Spring Grove. The Q stream was not in place in my time.

Mind you, 3C had more than its share of odd balls too, but that is another story.

Girls end and Boys end 1935 Roll-up Photo

Hindsight

Peter Rance, '38

As an eighty-year-old Spring Grovian I have never forgotten my 1933 view of the entrance hall to Joseph Bank's Spring Grove home with its stained glass and abundance of carved wood in the lower classrooms and corridors. In those days the whole 18th Century environment of our school simply oozed an intellectual and physical atmosphere that influenced everyone's formative years.

The view from Mr. L. T. Brown's sunlit study overlooked my favourite class-room i.e., - the football pitch where Bernard Joy [History - and Arsenal's 1939 Centre Half] taught me how to take and give hard knocks without losing my temper. London's largest plane tree lorded it over the great cedars that shielded our school's west wing with its glass domed Art Room alongside Miss Nash's Biology Lab with its ivy covered walls. Mr Snaith's Physics Room with its row on row of flaming gas taps, always excited my youthful imagination, little Mr. Lineham [English] daily scanned our faces at the 'Pupil's' back entrance, located beside the Main Hall where Mr. Trevor Owen [Music] thumped out England's national songs, while our sixth-form pianist, Ray "Awkward" Orchard, often encouraged us to sing wartime 'radio hits' in the same hall after school.

In that sun soaked summer of 1940 many Prefects sneaked out to sit on the school's wooden air-raid shelter, to watch the Battle of Britain being fought among the fluffy clouds overhead. As most pupils slept in their beds each night, surrounded by shot and shell, this daytime adventure seemed relatively tame by comparison.

During the previous autumn we had been told to stay at home before being instructed to visit our teachers' homes each Monday to collect our homework for the following week.   However, once the school shelter was built in 1940, lessons restarted. Miss Dolly Ransome and Miss Richards [French, Geography and Maths] again ruled our lives. Mr. Barrett [Cricket - my best subject]- and Maths were well taught. Mr. Callow attempted Latin - and how not to keep discipline in a classroom. Mr. Cross [Muzz] demonstrated Woodwork and Glue, which became a School Cert, subject for the first time in that year. Miss Kate Klarner - and her 'Fire Watching' companion of the Tennis Court Pavilion - called Mr. Hemming - taught English next morning with sleepy eyes.

The last Spring Grovian Magazine conjured up many vivid 'mind pictures' for me. Angela Goatcher, who played 'mixed' hockey like a fiend. Her hockey stick belaboured every part of my body before she 'flicked' the ball between Ron Price's eyes, and he collapsed on the rear hockey pitch as if pole axed. This was no mean feat, as the school's tough 'first-eleven' football team had previously beaten the local Fire Station with ease.

Then there was Valerie Gunn, the startling strawberry blonde and her red headed soul mate - Iris Fudge - from whom that spiteful war dragged me north to build airfields in 1941. Who remembers happy Myrtle Atkins, who made us laugh when 'time bombs' exploded around school during the daylight hours? What happened to the ever-cheerful blond, Joan Lane, who lived near Osterley Station and Freda Holman [Freddie] who became a Librarian? She restored my faith in human kindness by sending me letters as I trudged southwards beside the Irrawaddy River. Patriotically, we created peacetime 'normality', by holding our Annual Swimming Galas where the well-endowed, Peggy Percy, always won the Breast Stroke for the 'Swallows'.

Even after school was hit by small bombs and shells, our curvaceous lovelies continued to take their turn at nightly Fire Watching. They were a brave lot. Later they became the post-war Mums, who brought up their children while coping with shortages of every kind. As a wartime soldier, such women have long earned my admiration and respect for their courage and fortitude, both on, and off the field of battle. Slowly the war faded as Britain grew richer, due to the nation's hard work and perseverance, while our middle-aged wives learnt to drive ever-larger family cars. The age of the 'School Run' had arrived!

Like Cecil Field, I have often wondered if it was our Willie Fleischer who became Germany's post war Chancellor. Was it he who started a school mag with adverts, to pay for our 'free admission tickets' to Southall's Odeon

Peter Rance is far right of the back row next to Mr. Fendick

cinema? Does Dr. Peter Brown, who became the Medical Officer of Health on the Isle of Wight, remember dismantling one of the previous night's unexploded incendiary bombs just prior to Mr. 'Basher' Brown's maths lesson and then build small explosive bombs at home from the chemicals stored in his father's garage? Who said children cannot teach themselves? Who realises that 'Jacko Jackson - the famous post-war forensic officer at Scotland Yard', was a classmate of Johnny Wynne in 1939?

Brave Bernard Braden, Class of 1937, died as a Captain in Burma, just before I arrived to replace him in 14th Army to chase the Japs from Kohima Ridge to Rangoon before entering Thailand to rescue our P.O.W.s. My years of warfare were rough but very interesting.

By 1946 'Young' Bob Swash became a very successful second 'Muzz', and just preceded me into Loughborough University when at twenty-two I was being 'demobbed' from the British, Indian, and Burmese Armies. Eventually peace taught us to forget the war, especially after we discovered that many of our school girl friends had married local lads or gone off to America as blushing brides.

How do humans learn to walk and talk? I truly believe, "No one can 'teach' anything! Indeed, the only possible process is that human beings 'learn'. Thus, it is only when we have interesting subject matter, presented to us in an attractive manner, that we fully strive to comprehend. Is this the real educational secret our talented prewar teachers taught us within their enlightened surroundings? In the 1970's I published the first books about child centred education - I only mention this because L.T. Brown's Spring Grove philosophy was to encourage his pupils to follow their natural talents when trying to construct a useful life.

Girls, lady staff members and L.T.Brown - 1935 Roll-up photo

Sir Joseph Banks Estate

Yvonne Roberts (1932-37)
has some unique memories

The headings above and the following article appeared in Popular Gardening magazine, March 22 1980. The article and the photograph were handed to Pam Isom at the October 2004 reunion. It certainly captures the feelings many of us had when we returned in recent years.

Reference is often made in 'Popular Gardening,"PG", to Sir Joseph Banks, and the Banksian roses which were named after his wife. Thus I thought you might be interested in a few memories I have of his estate.
The house that Sir Joseph Banks leased in 1779 and continued to live in until his death in 1820, was called Spring Grove. After Lady Banks died in 1825, Spring Grove changed hands over the years and eventually passed to Andrew Pears, the great-grandson of the founder of Pears' soaps, and remained in that family until 1903.

During the First World War the house was used as a hospital for army officers. Eventually the Middlesex County Council bought it, and in 1923 it was opened as an experimental co-educational grammar school.

I attended this school some years ago and have very happy memories of the school, the building and general atmosphere, and of its historical associations.

The large and rambling grounds were a delight, thanks in no small measure to the plantings of Sir Joseph. Many of his specimens are still flourishing — or their progeny! Several plants were seen in this country for the first time at Spring Grove — paeonies from China, hydrangeas, American cranberry. Sir Joseph also cultivated an apple known as the Spring Grove Codlin and possessed the finest grapevine in the country.

Although much of the grounds had latterly been given over to football pitches, tennis courts, etc., there were also many unspoiled and wild areas where the school gardeners were constantly kept busy. It wasn't difficult to find a quiet little haven if one felt like being alone for a while.

I think we all loved the large cedar trees. There were several, and I can remember a tree surgeon being called in when a large branch was damaged in a gale. An archway of hops — what an aroma on a sunny day! — led through to a vegetable garden which was cultivated by pupils, under supervision of course!

During the summer months art classes were held in the grounds where we sketched or painted any quiet, picturesque corner which took our fancy.

A small portion of the grounds was sold off while I was there. 'The spinney', which fronted the main London Road, was lost to a fire station and more recently the front lawns were built on.

I remember Spring Grove as a house with immense character. Parts of the interior were lovely. Without a doubt the best and most unusual room of all was known as the Banksian Room, in which, for obvious reasons, biology lessons were held. Looking back now I feel we were highly privileged to have had access to such an environment for our lessons. I doubt whether there has ever been another school in the country with a biology room quite like it.

The Banksian Room probably started life as a large conservatory. It was a long room constructed almost entirely of glass, with a domed glass roof. It was a very light room, cold in winter, hot in summer of course. On low shelves were large glass cases of stuffed birds, mainly birds of prey, and small mammals. Desks were placed where there was room, for the focal point of this room was a large rockery built up to about 3 ft. high at one end and slowly descending to near ground level.

At the highest part of the rockery was a small fountain. A waterfall tumbled down the rocks forming tiny pools on the way, and eventually the water flowed into a large pool at the bottom. Small fish swam in the lowest pool and frogs lived happily in and around the rockery on which grew plants of various kinds. Small aquatic plants grew at the water's edge.

To complete this picture of natural harmony birds flew in and out through openings in the roof, to splash in the pools and dance under the fountain. (These roof openings were inconvenient, and when it rained some of the desks had to be moved to avoid a drenching!). I often wondered why the birds bothered to come indoors for their ablutions when there was a statue and a perfectly good fountain outside, but I suppose they just preferred the Banksian Room. They

The Banksian Room Circa 1902
The glass structure that forms the left-hand half of this
view of Spring Grove House from across the West lawn.

were mostly sparrows which came inside. Occasionally, during a lesson someone would have to duck to avoid the obvious, but it merely caused a giggle and a welcome diversion.

Progress being what it is, Spring Grove Grammar School is now a comprehensive school and has moved to a modern building. A few years ago I went back down 'memory lane', nearly always a fatal mistake, and re-visited the old place. When I saw what was left of our lovely Banksian Room I could have cried. The fountain no longer pumps its sparkling water down into the lively little pools. Gone are all the birds, the frogs, the fish, the plants. The hundreds of glass windows were grimed with dirt and algae inside and covered with trailing weeds outside. The Banksian Room was stacked with old chairs and tables and used as a store. I cannot explain my feelings on seeing this vandalism of my dreams of gentler and happier days. But one thing is certain - we who passed through that school, who took our lessons in the Banksian Room were richer for the experience.

Sir Joseph, do not weep! And, of course, we have the living memorial of your roses.

The previous article was published in SGR 6 and asked who the writer, Yvonne Roberts, was. Jean (Langton) Rhodes ('38) answered the question and forwarded a letter which Yvonne had written in January 1981 to Barbara Nash, a teacher from her era at the school, who had written to Yvonne having read the PG article. An abridged version of Yvonne's letter is published below

Little did I know when I wrote the letter to Popular Gardening what repercussions it would have!   Especially as it was not really intended for publication, but mainly because I thought the Editor might be interested in the content.

My maiden name was Moyle, and I don't imagine many of the staff of that era would be likely to forget Yvonne Moyle in a hurry! Certainly not Mr. Snaith who thought I was a pain in the neck!

I was at Spring Grove from about 1932 to 1936/7. (I was transferred at the age of 12 yrs. when we moved to the area). Although I was a year ahead of them (I often asked myself why, because I wasn't particularly bright) I went around mostly with Elsie Naylor, Ethel Pitts, Vera James and Joyce Rushbrook, and in my form my main friends were Emily Miller, Kathleen Blake and Muriel Davis. The reason we all stuck together was because we all lived in the Cranford/Harlington area and consequently travelled together. We were a lively bunch who believed that life should not be taken at all seriously! But they were happy days and I especially loved Spring Grove because I had come from a strict all girl school in Putney (Mayfield) and this was so completely different.

A great deal of water has flowed under the bridge since those days. I met and married a young policeman who spent four years abroad during the war in the army, and finished up as a Detective Superintendent. Elsie Naylor and I have remained firm friends. She is married with two brilliant daughters, both of whom passed for Cambridge. Recently they moved to Cheltenham but up until then they had lived all their married life in Heston. They have all spent several holidays with us, and we have stayed with them on a number of occasions. Whenever we meet the years just roll back and we find we are laughing at all the idiotic things we used to do years ago! Elsie keeps in touch with Joyce Rushbrook and Vera James intermittently. They both married. Vera married a local lad whose farming family lost all their land to Heathrow Airport (as did Vera's parents, who owned a smallholding). Vera and her husband bought a farm in Sussex and had several children; they have now retired.

Kathleen Blake married a Leslie Gaydon, who I believe went to S.G., but before my time. They had three girls. Early in their married life they moved to Bexhill and we corresponded as time permitted. We last met when we were both at Cranford visiting our respective parents. Eventually, though, Kathleen failed to answer my letters, and though I used to visit her parents when in the area and get news of her, she never did write again.

Muriel Davis, also in my form, was the dark Welsh girl with the lovely soft Welsh lilt to her voice. Most of the time she was the quiet one of the bunch - the one to sit back and enjoy the fun with an infectious giggle. She has gone far - to Australia. She went into catering management and did very well. She has practically travelled the world - mostly on her own and has remained single. She has visited us twice when on holiday in U.K., and usually at Christmas I get a letter and card from her. Muriel never believed in being on time for anything, and many's the time the gang of us have held up an early morning bus while she panted and puffed her way up the road (That wouldn't be possible these days - no driver would wait that long). Needless to say, Muriel has lost all her shyness and I have found her a most entertaining person with tremendous wit.

Do you remember those Terrible Twins - George Spiers (Pimple) and Herbert Hunt? They were a real couple of live wires but there wasn't a scrap of harm in them. I don't know what happened to them but I understand that John Kipps is married and still living in Heston.

I certainly didn't know that the rocks in the Banksian Room were made of lava from Mt. Hecler. How interesting. I wish I had taken more notice of them. I wonder what happened to them, or if they are still there.

And lastly, there was another spin-off from my 'publication' when David Parker (younger than me by several years) saw it in P.G. and asked Elsie Naylor if it was written by "our Yvonne". Elsie didn't know anything about it but assumed it must be. I had no idea so many people read Popular Gardening!

The "Scholarship" Exam

Tony Evans ('34)

Tony Evans ('34) explains the origins of the Scholarship, later to become the "11+". This has been extracted from Tony's book "Betty" commemorating the life of his wife Betty Corby (OSG '38).

Until the middle of the 19th century learning had been the privilege of the very few, the relative aristocracy whose families had been able to call on the necessary funds to purchase it, but from that time onwards Churches, Sunday Schools and various charitable organisations began to set up schools for "children of the diligent poor" usually for a fee of a penny or twopence per day.

Development then followed rapidly with an Education Act of 1870 setting up School Boards and making it compulsory for all children between the ages of five and eight to attend school and the upper age was gradually extended to thirteen by the end of the century. School Boards were soon absorbed into Local Education Authorities and an Act of 1902 took the almost revolutionary step of requiring those Authorities, usually through the County Councils, to provide Secondary Education for those who were considered to be likely to be able to benefit from it.

The division between the sheep, who were considered likely to benefit, and the goats, who were not, was decided on a single day when pupils who were between ten and eleven years old were required to undergo tests in English, Arithmetic and General Knowledge. The process was known as "The Scholarship" but, whilst the tests themselves may well have been concentrated into a single day, concern about them most certainly was not and, indeed, they tended to become the be-all and end-all of the School. What would normally be called Years 5 and 6 in a modern Primary School were known as the Pre-Scholarship and the Scholarship Classes!

Secondary Education meant the provision of Arts, Sciences and Languages at levels well beyond those that were attempted in the Elementary Schools but they also meant paying a fee, giving a parental undertaking to remain at school until the age of sixteen and providing many extras, the most obvious of which was a school uniform. All of these meant considerable sacrificial contributions from the budget of a family at a time when the average working man's wage was £2.12.6 (£2.62) a week and where in many cases a cut was imposed by the "Geddes Axe" between 1931 and 1934.

Be an Athlete and See the World

Dorothy Saunders, '31
Written for the Spring Grovian in 1939

I lived in Isleworth and went to Spring Grove Infant & Junior school and from there passed the eleven plus and went on to Spring Grove Grammar (Black and White). I was into all sports and played hockey and tennis for the school and won the girl's races on sports days.

I remember many of the teachers who were at the school in my time; Mr C A Wood was headmaster.

I passed my matriculation and was encouraged to go on to Goldsmiths' College at London University to become a teacher. I think two of Spring Grove's men teachers had been to this college. Whilst I was at college (1934-36) I took part in athletics for London University and became their chief woman sprinter. I went to Budapest in 1935 and a few other places representing the University.

I became a fully qualified teacher in 1936 and went to teach at Marlborough primary school at Busch Corner. I continued my athletics and in 1938 I was chosen to run for England in the Empire Games to be held in Australia. Middlesex granted me leave of absence for four months *with no pay and loss of 4 months superannuation.* My ability as No1 Woman sprinter took me to many places to run for Britain - Paris, Berlin, Bonn, Vienna, Monte Carlo to mention but a few. "Be an athlete and see the world," I might say, with apologies to the famous recruiting poster.

In August of 1935, at the end of my first year at Goldsmiths' College, I was selected to run for the British Universities in the World Students' Games at Budapest in Hungary. This was a grand trip, and one I shall ever remember. I was second in the 100 yards to Stella Walsh who was the World Record holder for the distance.

At the beginning of August, 1937, I ran for Great Britain in an International match in Berlin. At the end of August I represented the British Universities once more in the World Students' Games, which were held this time in Paris. I won the 80 and 200 metres. I hope I shall be able to defend those titles in the next Students' Games which will be held in Vienna this year.

Then came my greatest trip of all. I was selected to run for England in the British Empire Games. The Games were held in Sydney as part of the National Celebrations of the 150th Anniversary of the founding of Australia.

I obtained the necessary four months leave from school and sailed for Australia on the 4th December, 1937, accompanied by teams from Scotland, Wales and Northern Ireland. The combined teams numbered 91, 72 being English, 10 Scotch, 6 Welsh and 3 from Northern Ireland. The women in all the teams (21 in all) were either athletes or swimmers, the men were to take part in athletics, swimming, boxing, cycling, rowing, wrestling and bowls.

On the outward journey the majority of the teams took part in a P.T. class held by a member of the English Team, who was a P.T. instructor. The athletes were met at each port of call and taken to a running track for a work out.

Our ports of call were, Gibralter, Toulon, Naples, (here we were able to pay a visit to the ruins of Pompeii), Port Said, Aden, Colombo, Fremantle, Adelaide, Melbourne, Burnie and Sydney. On our homeward journey we also called at Hobart, Bombay, Malta and Marseilles.

On January 13th, 1938, we arrived at Sydney, and the Australian Organising Council met the teams with a fleet of motor cars and conducted us to our quarters, the men to the Empire Village on the Agricultural Show Ground, and the women to an adjacent hotel. During the journey across the City great enthusiasm was shown by the onlookers.

On reaching the village, the flags of England, Scotland, Wales and Northern Ireland were hoisted with ceremony and short addresses of welcome were given by our Australian hosts. In like manner were received teams from British Guiana, Canada, Ceylon, Fiji, India, New Zealand, Rhodesia, South Africa and Trinidad.

After settling down we commenced serious training. The climate was exceptionally trying as there was a wave of extreme heat and humidity.

On the 26th January, the great pageant depicting the history of Australia took place in glorious weather. There were 150 floats in the procession, and among these was one of Captain Cook landing in Australia and with him was his Botanist, Sir Joseph Banks. The competitors from the countries of the Empire marched in the procession and our appearance evoked a wonderful display of patriotism. Such cries as " Do you know the Smith's of Manchester? " or " I come from - Street in Leeds," etc. made us realise we were 13,000 miles from home, but we were going *back,* and most likely some of the people that had emigrated to Australia, and were calling to us, had said goodbye to England for ever.

The Games began on 7th February, on the famous cricket ground, the opening ceremony being performed by the Governor of New South Wales, Lord Wakehurst, who read the message of goodwill from H.M. The King, after which an Australian athlete proclaimed the Oath of Allegiance on behalf of all competitors and officials, who were in line behind their respective National Flags.

Then followed a week of remarkable sport, much to the enjoyment of approximately 250,000 spectators, amid sunshine and weather which could not be excelled, and which contributed no doubt to the many new records set up.

The games were over on the Saturday, and we sailed for home the following Wednesday.

During my stay in Sydney, I met Vic Collins, another Old Spring Grovian, who has been in Australia for the past ten years.

Our journey home was much less energetic than going out, although a few of us took advantage of another series of P.T. classes, with the hopes that we should be fit enough to compete in the Indoor Championships at Wembley. These Championships were due to take place a fortnight after our arrival home. These P.T. classes, together with plenty of Deck Tennis must have kept me fit, for at this meeting I broke the 60 Metres British Indoor Record.

In July, 1938, I became the National 200 Metres Champion of Great Britain, and also joint holder of the 60 Metres British Record (Outdoor). As a result of this, I was chosen to represent Great Britain in the European Championships in Vienna.

We just managed this trip in time, as the Games took place a week before the German—Czech crisis.

I can now say that I rank fourth best 100 Metres sprinter of Europe, and fifth best 200 Metres sprinter. The winner was Stella Walsh, World Champion Record holder. Any Old Spring Grovians that know me, will realise the strength of foreign competitors in International Competition when I say that I was the *smallest* finalist in the 100 Metres. (I am 5ft. 8 ½ ins.).

The more places I visit, the more determined I feel to carry on with athletics and try to be chosen for British Teams. I think my next aims will be to go to Vienna for the World Universities Games this year, and then to Finland for the Olympic Games in 1940. I might be in the running for the next Empire Games in Canada, but 1942 is a long way off at the moment.

SPRING GROVE SECONDARY SCHOOL, ISLEWORTH.

Form 1B.   September 1936.

Those Were the Days

As remembered by

Alfred [Jack] Stammers '37

It was the announcement in the magazine "YOURS" of the reunion 6th. October 2007 that caught my sister's eye and resulted in the very warm welcome from Pam Isom, who kindly sent us copies of former years' reports. At our request, she is sending further copies to my sister's form mate, Doris Everard [nee Barry], who has lived in New Zealand for 50 odd years now.

The wonderful experience of exploring the old school once again, made up for not finding anyone from our years, but to our surprise, we met up with Brian Martin '52, who had been a good friend before we moved away from Heston some 20 years ago - without being aware that he is an OSG! Previous contributors to Reports have described the familiar features of the old house which, thankfully, helped us to overlook the horrible buildings of the college that occupy so much of the former grounds. I remember the earlier violation in losing the Spinney to the Fire Brigade along with the horse trough and drinking fountain, from the junction of Spring Grove Road ! However, much worse was to come during and after the war.

As for memories of the Staff, during my time Mr. L.T.Brown took over headmastership from Mr. Wood, and I have a vivid memory of meeting L.T.one day in the Covered Way, to be asked if I would be good enough to fetch something or other that he had left behind. Pleased to be of service, my response was "Right-ho Sir"! only to be restrained with the quiet advice that is would have so much better if I had said "very good sir"! Our education included much besides lessons and homework.

There was a slip in discipline one prize day, with the whole school in the assembly hall, standing in silence as the staff and important visitors entered in file to mount the platform. As the last of the visitors came into view, there was what amounted to a cheer[quickly subdued] for a former teacher, namely Mr. Fendick - such was his popularity. I remember his history lessons, which he illustrated on the blackboard with "matchstick men" engaged in some ancient battle. Pictures are certainly stronger than words.

On another occasion, the whole school sat enthralled by a virtuoso performance from the renowned pianist Benno Moiseiwitsch [whose niece, I believe, was a Spring Grove pupil]. From my seat close up to the stage, my view was limited to the reflection from the open lid of the grand piano, of his hands at he keyboard. That was a "polished" performance I shan't forget !

Perhaps this is the time to confess to my form's devious behaviour during a particularly cold winter, in diverting the attentions of the caretaker's assistant from his morning distribution of coal for our fires. One of us quickly emptied an extra bucket full into a spare desk, so that we could stoke up.

My most satisfying memories are of Miss Walters' art classes in probably the warmest room owing to it's previous purpose as a conservatory.

I wouldn't know how many years the custom was maintained; it did not cease with the onset of World War II, as my sister's year '42 can confirm. I refer to the annual opportunity for those about to sit their GSC/Matric exams, to attend a professional performance of the Shakespeare play featured in that year's English Literature paper.

I have forgotten which London theatre hosted it in my year '37, but it was large enough to seat most, if not all, such pupils of the London area. On the other hand, I would surmise that the cast performing "Julius Caesar" on that occasion would prefer it to fade from memory!

We were all following the development of the play to the point where Mar Anthony is about to address the crowd, starting with the famous words which are familiar to everyone. I imagine he must have been bracing himself to deliver them as the bier bearing Caesar's body was being carried round to the strategic position on the stage. The four anonymous characters engaged in this were then meant to merge into the crowd, I'm sure. As it happened though, three of them followed the script; but the fourth had not noticed he had trapped his toga under the bier and, try as he might, could not free it until at last it tore away!!

You will understand that I cannot recall how the company recovered from the mishap since, along with the hundreds of teenagers present, I was 'rolling in the aisles' – and that's not much of an exaggeration.

In the anecdotes prompted by attending my first reunion with my sister, I failed to remark on the marvellous collection of photographs that had been assembled. They represent an invaluable archive for OSGs and, although I was unable to recognise myself among them (!) there was one of a close friend of mine featured in the football team. If I am honest, there are few names I could put to those of my form as shamefully, I have not kept in touch with any of them for many years. Of the girls, there are only two I'm sure about; one was Elsie Diamond with whom I vied for top marks in mathematics; and the other was Irene Illsley who suffered my clumsy efforts in the ballroom dancing that was arranged, I suppose, to provide us with some social grace! Amongst the boys are some I can only give surnames to; Wyatt, Dodds and Graham, for instance. But, Kay Bearne I remember (mentioned by Jean Langton in SG Report No.9), I coveted his Raleigh bike, mine being a Hercules. I don't think touring holidays such as I learn Miss Ransome led were on offer then; but there was a one-day trip to Boxhill for the cyclists that comes to mind. Who arranged it, I have long forgotten. Apart from the scenery and the view, it was the return journey that is imprinted on my mind. As a result of my brakes failing down a steep hill, I had to resort to hanging on to my nearest fellow rider!

The football player I mentioned, who became captain and also of Cricket , was Alfred Hughes, one of three loyal companions of mine. We would all meet up weekends, and play badminton, or patronise the brand new swimming baths at Heston. Winter evenings were often spent with Alfred's family, playing cards – only '21' as it was called. On these occasions, his name was Alfie One, while I was Alfie Two (too, get it?).

Summertime, we four enjoyed cycling to Shiplake, a place on the Thames upstream from Henley. Free wheeling down Remenham Hill could be hair raising! We got to know the lock keeper there, who let us borrow his punt; exploring the Lodden tributary was fun. We took picnic lunches with us, and maybe had a swim; then it was time for the 'grind' back home – a round trip of about 60 miles. We could recite, in correct order, the names of all the pubs we passed en route – yes, passed!

Another was Doug Snelling; his bike had a hub dynamo (or was it a brake?) ultra modern anyway. His father actually built his own micro-light aircraft; they were known as flying fleas! The fourth 'musketeer' was Peter Rogers; he and I became prefects together and, later he was head boy; his sport was running. He lived in Whitton, near Kneller Hall, and most lunch-times I rode along with him, chatting away, and then turned to head for my home, close to Hounslow Heath. It didn't leave me too much time for eating.

Our careers had only just begun when World War II overtook us. Alfie had started in a Patent office, but I imagine he made a greater impact as a pilot of a Lancaster bomber, he was a steady type. Doug, I'm not sure about; I heard he trained as a fighter pilot. Peter followed his eldest brother into dental surgery and, after qualifying, entered the Navy in that capacity. I hadn't planned my job with the Borough Council's Electricity Dept., but had 'found my feet' before breaking off to do my bit in the Fleet Air Arm.

It's all such a long time ago now. My classic 'Gillot' bicycle, acquired later hangs in my garage, ready for use when my bones let me.

On reflection, I enjoyed lessons at the old school, which is by no means supported by my Pupils Reports Book judging by teachers remarks! My excuse is that only certain aspects of a subject caught my attention; which is no basis for sitting examinations. For instance in English, recognising and analysing clauses in complex sentences had fascination for me. Miss Klarner had only to glance in my direction for the response of "Zeugma"! from me if she had quoted some poetical phrase using it (look that one up!). But to write an essay had me gazing at the ceiling for inspiration, regardless of choice in subject. History and Geography were about times and places that required sorting into the right order, no matter how colourful each may have appeared. Curiously though, later in life I developed a deep interest in maps; and a wish that I had found employment with the Ordnance Survey.

After a slow start, Mathematics became my strongest subject, only competing with Art for enjoyment. In both of those I 'blossomed' to score 'Distinction', but only secured a School Certificate by managing a Pass in French. Miss Walters, I know, thought I should go on to Art school, but I "made her day" in producing (with her assistance) two items of calligraphy - on vellum, with illuminated initials (embellished with gold leaf!) which, after framing, finished up in L.T. Brown's study on either side of the fireplace. These were the two prayers used at assembly on the last day of the school year - when some pupils departed, to be replaced by 'fresh' ones next term.

School Life 1931-1937

John King, '37

I was a pupil at Spring Grove from circa 1932 to 37. My younger brother Peter King followed on four years later, I think he was a Swallow. I was a Skylark and an occasional Cuckoo!! but I really did enjoy those days and have always mentioned the School with pride. My brother Peter, now living in New York put me wise to the main website for Old SG's and I am delighted with the pictures and history. My remembrances are of the swimmers Mary Cutter and Lorna Frampton. The pianist Xenia Moseiwitch (I don't know whether I spelt that right), Mr Corby and Mr Callow doing the "Southern Brothers " take off of the Western Brothers, for which my father lent one of his Southern Railway caps. The School end of term parties, Mr Varney, alias Trevor Owen, who taught me to sing properly and produced a lovely boy soprano voice that my mother spoke of with pride.
I would really like to know what happened to some of the crowd that I was at school with. I did find myself sitting next to a soldier in the Metro Cinema in Cairo in 1942 who turned out to be Len Hunt who was in my Class. I was serving in the RAF at the time and we were both on leave. Others in my class that I remember were Bobby Knapton, Robby White, Len Small, Gwen Stephens (daughter of one of the master's), Joan Luke, Marjorie Whiteman, Joyce Robertson to name a few but in those days everyone treated their school classmates with respect and friendship was very deep within the school. Of course I was one of the sporting crowd who were delighted when the England Amateur joined the Staff and quite probably me more than some for we travelled to School each day on the same train from Hounslow to Isleworth.
I am 86 years young, but as my only form of transport is a bus pass only valid in the Principality, I would find it difficult to join in the reunions although my heart would be with you. Lovely to be able to contact the seat of learning that gave me a wonderful start in a very active and varied life. I have just had a look at my CV and the actual dates I have for my schooling at Spring Grove

were 1931 to 1937. Looking at my CV has made me realise what a chequered life I have led since leaving the School. Serving 8 years in the RAF, surviving the war, during which I was stationed in many stations abroad and on very special assignments, many of these places would have made Mr Callow's mouth water! (I believe he taught us Geography) When I first went to the School dear old "Sammy Wood" was Headmaster. I think he knew every pupil in the school by name, form and qualifications. He ruled the School with Gentle Discipline and was respected by all and if you saw him frown you knew you had done something wrong! I believe Mr Snaith was deputy head. There were then the back stairs and right at the end of the corridor very impressive doors leading to the main entrance on the left hand side with I believe a Secretary's office in the vestibule and facing you the "Holy of Holies" The Headmaster's study. Then, on the right, the entrance from the frontage and views of the sports ground, cricket pitch, the London Road boundary and views of the trams going from Bush Corner to The Bell at Hounslow. As you turned round you saw the magnificent main stairs leading to the first floor and a balustrade round three sides of the area. This was really impressive. By the left hand side of the stairs you could proceed to the Art Room passing I believe the entrance to the Music Room and a large class-room. The Music Room and The Arts Room were as elaborate then as the photos on your website are today and were a joy to be in. Miss Walters queened over the Arts Room and she was a charmer. Mr Varney (Trevor Owen) was the ruler of the Music room and taught me a lot about music that has been very useful in life since for I am now a very qualified musician playing organ and piano.   My school days, although very happy ones (and certainly there were some things in school education that must have affected my future life) were not very exciting except for the fact that during one term, I hit the tops with 13 detentions and became a 'Cuckoo'. As part of my punishment, I was told that I had to stand out in the front at assembly but I don't think it had the result that it was supposed to have, for it was my week to stand in for Mr Callow at Assembly and play the piano. I am sure that some of the pupils who were there in 1934/35 will recall me going up the stairs to play for the march in, then back to the front and then up again to play for the hymn and down again afterwards. My stay in this position lasted one day only and then I was advised to stay at the piano for the rest of the week but I would remain a 'Cuckoo' for the remainder of the term. They felt I had suffered enough humiliation, but I think it had the reverse effect for at least in my own class I became a tiny bit of a celebrity for having beaten the system!! I'm not really proud of my achievement but it certainly caused some hilarity amongst the pupils.

Tuck Boxes and Coal Scuttles

Dennis Collins, '38
Dennis remembers pre and post war Sporting Occasions

In 1936 the County Council decided to sell the bit of our front grounds to the west of the main gate on the London Road in order to build a much wanted new fire-station for the Borough. When it was finished it looked really impressive with its tower for the drying of hoses and our first eleven football team invited a team from the Fire Service to a game; the invitation was accepted and what turned out to be a very enjoyable game was finished off by them inviting us to their new station for a cup of tea, a look over the place and a game of snooker to finish. 1936 was an Olympic Year and perhaps that is the reason why our School Athletics were coming on by leaps and bounds. By then Mr. Wood had retired and his place had been taken by Mr. L. T. Brown who was really keen on all sports and for a reason best known only to himself he arranged for a javelin thrower to come along during one of Mr.Corby's free periods. He took me up to the North Pitch for some javelin practice but this time we had a proper javelin. Standing about fifty yards away from me and just about to light his pipe, Mr.Corby suddenly looked up and then jumped rapidly out of the way because the javelin that I had just thrown was heading straight for him. It seemed as though I had got the technique right for that one particular throw! Before leaving my comments about Spring Grove School I should not forget to mention the caretakers, Mr. and Mrs. Archer who appeared at every break time near the bike sheds with a box full of goodies for us to buy. We always had clean and tidy classrooms but they were heated by coal fires; what a job the Archers must have had lugging the coal scuttles up the stairs and round to all the classrooms. Alas, only about a year elapsed between the end of our school-days and the outbreak of war and, when 1 think back on it, it seems strange that the only serving Old Spring Grovian that I saw and recognised during the whole of those war years was Betty Corby as we were both in the RAF at Chicksands. Finally, with the war over, I found myself in the Old Spring Grovians Football team which had got back into action. One Saturday afternoon we were playing against another team in the Old Boys' league when we were surprised, but yet delighted, to see Mr. L. T. Brown on the touchline. We had quite a chat at half-time and I think that he went away as pleased as we were.

Memories of Spring Grove 1935-1939

Stan Wheeler , '39

I joined the school in April 1935 at the start of the summer term, having spent two terms at Acton County before my family moved to Cranford. Having received a copy of the compilation issue of numbers 1 to 4 of the Spring Grovian, memories of nearly seventy years ago came flooding back on reading items by Leo Lewis and Tony Young.

I started in form 1(Rowans) with Miss Nash in her Banksian Room and I remember French with Miss Griffin in her 1 Beta class. She soon shunted me off to Miss Ransom as I was farther advanced than her class. This was compensated by my having no Latin at all, as the policy at Acton County was not to start that until the second year, and I was soon moved out of the Latin class.

History was with Miss Taylor, whose usual ending of the description of a battle was "all was bloodshed and confusion" pronounced "BLUTTSHETT AND CONFUSSION". This was eagerly awaited by the pupils and there was disappointment on the rare occasions when it did not come.

English was taken by Miss Kate Klarner, who was one of the most popular of the staff. I was very interested to learn that she later married one of her fellow teachers who joined the school after I left.

The sciences, Mr Aldersley (I think), Chemistry, and Mr. Snaith (who seemed very old at the time), Physics, did not manage to leave much of their knowledge with me.

Muzz Cross was a real character, who I think must have been a quite a gymnast in his day. Much timber was used for making boxes for shoe cleaning brushes and table lamps. I never graduated to the metalwork class.

Domestic Science was not a subject for boys so I did not have much contact with Miss Bromwich. However I had it on good authority that it was she who put the kibosh in the mixed net ball game that was organised by some of us who stayed on for school dinners - it was held in the court outside her cottage and only lasted for two days!

I well remember Mr Handover with the fixed wheel bicycle with only one pedal. This was because he could not bend one of his legs and the fixed-wheel kept the pedal turning full circle. He was a brilliant teacher and I can remember him once putting a column of figures four wide and about six deep on the blackboard, placing three fingers on the top row, sliding them gently down to the bottom and writing in the total. It was years before I recalled the incident and wondered whether he had fixed it and known the total before he started.

Sport was my favourite subject. I have vivid memories of Bernard Joy who had a BA degree, taught history (although not to me) and to the best of my recollection Latin. As well as being an excellent cricketer and tennis player Bernard Joy played centre half for a high class amateur football team called Corinthian Casuals in the Isthmian league, as well as the England amateur team. He subsequently played as an amateur for Arsenal and the England professional team. We met again after we had both left the school, I believe in 1940 - it was certainly in the 1940-41 football season. I had joined the RAF in January 1940 as a sixteen year old apprentice and he had joined the physical education branch as a pilot officer. At Ruislip, where I was stationed, two corporal PT instructors arrived, who happened to be George Male and Eddie Hapgood ,the Arsenal and England full backs. Bernard Joy was serving at the time in Uxbridge and we met when he came to Ruislip to visit his team mates. At that meeting he promised to arrange a match between the school XI and the Ruislip apprentices, which he duly did. The match was played at the school's pitch at Vicarage Farm Road and afterwards we all went to the restaurant in the Ambassador Cinema at Hounslow West for high tea - which was much appreciated by the apprentices who were always starving! The game was won by Ruislip, who were too strong for the school, some of the lads being eighteen years old. I was much too junior to get a place in the team, but I was allowed to watch, meet old friends and eat the tea! I learned from the magazine that Mr. Joy did not return to school after the war, but I did know that he had become a sports journalist for a London evening newspaper.

Almost all the other teachers that I remember have been mentioned in previous issues. Mr Varney a.k.a. Trevor Owen whom I avoided whenever possible as I have a singing voice like a corncrake, and was very sensitive about it. One of his stars was Margaret Taylor, a particular friend of mine in my form who had a marvellous contralto voice.

I have enjoyed writing my memories, which are still remarkably vivid, I just hope there are not too many inaccuracies.

Boys and male staff - 1935 Roll-up photo

Whatever Happened to the Fifth Form?

Jean Langton, '38

Secretary of the OSG Association for many years from 1938, Jean sent a cutting with this article from the Daily Mirror published in 1948 featuring her
SGSS 5th Year 1938.
Jean says she can identify most of those mentioned ....but didn't!

DAILY MIRROR   **Tuesday August 3rd 1948**

**They left school in 1938. War came before Life had
given them a break.   Today we tell you—**

By CECIL FIELD

S o many people natter so much about today's late twenties. "It was only to be **expected**," they say. "Pushed Into the Services without learning a job. Made officers before they'd learned to be office boys. ... Of **course** they've gone off the rails."

So many mugwumps expected young men and girls out of the Services would go off the rails, and take it for granted they have. But— **have they** ? I found the answer at the former pupils' reunion of a London secondary grammar school, one typical of scores all over the country, except that it's co-educational.

I took couples from the dancing in the gym, teachers from coffee in the music room, to ask them: **" Do you remember —— ?"** and I traced the tracks of the Fifth Form of 1938, the twenty-sixes of today.

The Fifth Form of 1938 at that school, as it happened, was one of the sort that a teacher likes to remember. "It was one of those forms," I was told, "that happen every few years. When it does, you're glad you're a teacher."

The Fifth was a form with personality plus. The girls were a pretty bright lot, and pretty. too, some of them.

There was a handful who were quiet, purposeful, and there was one girl who was a handful in herself.   She had brains, she had looks— rich dark auburn hair and blue eyes with a gleam in them.

And she had a wild temperament. When a teacher talked to the class about stability, the need for self-discipline, he talked at her. When a mistress said of her, " I wonder what will happen to her when she leaves," she said it fearfully.

But the boys ?   Ah, there was a bunch who made the form master swagger in the common room and talk about them like a man with his first baby.
Six of the school's first Soccer eleven,   including the captain, were in that form of sixteen-year-olds, easily outclassing big chaps in the Sixth.

They were not just footballers. Some of them were in the cricket first eleven. One was the record javelin thrower, one of the best six tennis players of the school. All were pretty good at their school work, too.

Energy, initiative, brain, muscle—that group had everything. The rest of the form were good sound types, but that group would go far. Well, where did they go ?
To begin with, the mugwumps are hardly right in saying they were " pushed into the Services." They rushed in - into the RAF in 1940. Eleven of the sixteen boys in the Fifth Form of 1938, five out of the six of the athletic group   went   into the RAF.

FOUR of that form were killed. All were RAF aircrew men. All were from that little group. Four out of the six.

The two who came back were a pilot, who is now a teacher, and an Army NCO, who is back in the council offices where he served a few months before joining up.
Ten others — what has happened to them? Nothing spectacular, but — this is the important point — **not one has gone off the rails.**

There was one whose post-war career the mugwumps must have watched with confident pessimism. His RAF career hit the headlines at a time when the spectacular was commonplace. One of his exploits was to make his way through the enemy lines, dressed as an Arab, after his plane had come down in the desert.

" A man like that won't find it easy so settle down in a London suburb," they said. He will tell you: "It wasn't too easy.   But, you know, we had some not-so-easy jobs in the Service."Anyway, he's done it. He's a sales clerk, married , living happily on a weekly wage he'd have spent in a night at a Cairo celebration. " I'm not beefing," he says. " I came back. I've got a grand wife. I'm on the way up."

Of the rest, two have stayed in the Services, one is a lawyer, one a marine insurance man doing rather well, one a decorator, a couple are teachers, and four are get-ting by on £5 10s.to£8 10s. a week, as clerks and salesmen.

So much for the boys of the Fifth Form of 1938. What about the girls? "Everyone knows" that the suburban teenagers lost their heads during the war, found it difficult to get husbands, and have gone to hell. Here are the facts:—
Only five of the sixteen are unmarried.
Two of them are teachers. (One of them is an art teacher who is doing well—she has just had a book published.)
Another is in the Foreign Office. (She came home on leave recently from Moscow, and is now in Brussels.)
One is in a bank, and the other in the Civil Service.

Maybe the pessimists would like to know about the married ones? Two are married to Americans — quite happily, thank you very much.

One married a farmer, another a lieutenant-colonel who is now an accountant, another an artist, and the others engineers, clerks, minor executives. None of them married anyone who went to the same school.

But the wild beauty, the girl with the auburn hair and the gleam in her eye? Well, she's still got the gleam in her eye, and people still talk at her when they talk about stability.

She married before she was seventeen, had a baby, went on the stage—she was in a recent West End musical success—and is now divorced.

And that, in 1948, is the Fifth Form of 1938. Not so bad

Sisters at Spring Grove School

Atkins Sisters '33, ' 37 & '43

Marjorie Atkins, the eldest of three sisters, arrived at Spring Grove when she was fifteen. She transferred from Wembley County which was a very strict school. Their mother insisted they attend a co-educational school as they had no brothers. At the time, Mr. Tomlinson was her form teacher, whom she liked very much.

She remembers Mr. Fendick who taught History, and was studying Law. Miss Stubbs taught Art, assisted by Mr. Maylott, who had degrees in Art and Science. She recalls Mr. Handover, who presented quite an image as he cycled to school on an upright bicycle, with one stiff immobile leg and holding up an umbrella in the rain, wearing a tall black hat. Strapped to the carrier on the back was a black Gladstone bag.

One of her contemporaries was Maurice Moiseiwitch who wrote the Mr. Penny series for the BBC when he was still in school.

An incident she remembers most vividly was being outside the classroom which faced Harvard road. Her History text book had been tossed out through the window, so she crawled out onto the porch roof to retrieve it. Unfortunately, the class teacher arrived before she could get back, so she was stuck. No rain, no harm done, and she wasn't missed. However, a nosy parker in one of the houses facing the school telephoned Mr. Woods, the headmaster, to inform him that one of his pupils was playing on the roof. Apparently, nothing much happened afterwards, as far as she can remember.

Miss Bromwich, who was quite young in 1933, taught housewifery. This involved tidying cupboards, cleaning windows, and staining the wooden floors in Miss Walters' cottage. Using a pad on a stick dipped in Permanganate of Potash, the purple liquid was applied to the wood floor. This stained the floor a dark brown and hands and knees if one wasn't careful. A section of the grounds, near the London Road entrance, was set aside in small lots for the students to garden. These were called "Beds of Natural Order". Could she have really meant weeds?

She loved the stream in the Banksian room, and remembers the fountain outside in the grounds, which worked on a few occasions.

She remembers the following staff:

Mr. Varney, who sometimes sang on the BBC, taught Handwriting as well as Music. His stage name was Trevor Owen.

Mr. Snaith taught Physics, called magnetism and electricity in those days.

Mr. Callow - Geography (he lived in Brighton and never taught last thing on Friday's because of his need to travel).

Miss Phillips - Gymnastics.

Mr. Cross - Wood working - (he travelled across America by train in 1938, and told us of his experiences with multi cultured races - M).

Miss Taylor - History

Mr. Aldersley, who had a bad cough, but taught Chemistry.

Mr. Woods was the headmaster before Mr. L. T. Brown

She knew Dorothy Saunders who was an Olympic runner. She thinks Dorothy and Bernard Joy, another History teacher competed in the 1936 Olympic games. Was Mr. Joy playing soccer for England?

Mary Cutter was another student - a great swimmer and diver. She could climb the ropes in the gymnasium while upside down, from the bottom to the top. Marjorie and Mary played hockey for the Old Spring Grovians and Mr. Watts was the referee.

Mr. and Mrs. Archer, the caretakers, lived in the school basement and were very strict. No-one was allowed to run on the stairs or in the corridors.

After her Matriculation, she studied Commerce under Mr. Tomlinson, and passed the Civil Service Entrance examination, after leaving school in 1933.

The second Atkins sister, Joan, followed Marjorie. She too, remembers Miss Bromwich. The cottage was decorated and painted by the girls. On one occasion a student stepped off a step ladder and put her foot into a bucket of whitewash. More clean up! They also used to cook lunches in the cottage kitchen, and had to consume the results. Miss Bromwich retired to Norfolk, where she drove a pony and trap!

She remembers a school visit to Hemel Hempstead where the group stayed on a farm, slept in the barn and enjoyed long walks. Until recently, she still had the tin plate she used at the camp with her name, J. V. Atkins, scratched on the bottom. She played tennis on the courts outside the cottage and hockey on the North pitch. Music was taught by Mr. Varney who produced "The Gondoliers" and sang "Take a Pair of Sparkling Eyes". Another production was "The Bohemian Girl" with a favorite number "I Dreamt I Dwelt in Marble Halls" (which was the gypsy girl's dream) sung by Audrey Priest.

Joan also wrote and produced a form play. The girls dressed as ghosts to frighten the boys, and vice versa. Then, the real ghost appeared. The students were particularly pleased with the giant ghost - one student sitting on another's shoulders and both shrouded in black - which created a huge impression on all. She left school in 1937, passed the Civil Service examination and worked at the Ministry of Labour offices in Edinburgh. From there, she volunteered for the W.A.A.F. and was stationed in the Met Office at Carnforth. Weather observations were made hourly, and collated every six hours in the regional R.A.F. Stations. As radio communications were non existent, weather conditions were transmitted to operational stations throughout the country by teleprinters, which ran continuously.

I, Myrtle, entered Spring Grove in 1938. I still remember feeling very proud to wear my school uniform which was a blue blazer and a pinafore dress over a biscuit coloured blouse. This was quite a change from the usual navy blue gym tunic. In winter we wore gabardine macks which kept us warm but which became sodden in the rain. Walking back and forth to school with cold feet induced chilblains, which were the bane of our lives, and, I suppose, a mild form of frostbite.

During the war, we sat at least one school certificate examination in the basement. I remember when the shelters in the school grounds were used for refuge. Miss Nash taught us to crochet. The boy sitting next to me, whose name I can't recall, became quite an expert! Two of my more vivid memories of this time are not school time related. First, I remember my mother calling me in from the back garden where I was trying to turn somersaults on the garden swing ropes with my friend Vera Harvey. It was September 1940, and we were admiring the vapour trails being generated by the planes flying overhead. She felt that falling debris was best avoided. Then at nights during air raids, when we were forced to escape our house and go to the Anderson shelter, buried in the garden, I was more concerned at having to accept the sound of large spiders plopping down from the roof onto the linoleum floor. We were very reluctant to go there to sleep. A refuge under the kitchen table was preferable to those things.

Unless relocating to the laboratories, the pupils remained in their classrooms throughout the school day. The building just could not accommodate 500+ bodies on the move at one time. Staff transferred from classroom to classroom for their assignments. We ate sandwiches in the school hall at lunch time and school dinners were served in the basement. Tapioca with jam in the middle was a dessert I didn't care for, but the cooks made enormous efforts to create nutritious meals from wartime allocations.

Swimming and running were my main pursuits. The Hounslow Swimming Club team, coached by Mary Cutter, travelled to Kingston and other local towns for competition. Once or twice I was included in the Spring Grove running team along with Enid Shepherd, Elna Goddard and Sylvia Cheeseman. It was wonderful to have Sylvia as the relay team anchor, as we often came in first.

During the war, unexploded bombs were both a nuisance and dangerous. One was buried somewhere along Spring Grove Road. Avoiding this hazard meant a detour of at least a mile on the walk to school. At first, pupils dutifully walked the extra distance to avoid an explosion, but soon gave up and ran the gauntlet, forever hoping the bomb was inert. This went on for a number of days until the bomb squad arrived to dismantle the fuse.

Looking back on my school days, I feel my mother was correct in having sent her three daughters to a co-educational school. I enjoyed the friendly interplay between girls and boys and appreciated being taught by men as well as women. Although I believe the County Boys' School had some women on the staff, I don't think men were on the staff of the Green School.

THE EARLY 40s

4

Spring Grove Revisited

Eric Beale '40

In the autumn of 2004, I made my last trip to the Old Country, but not quite for the sole purpose of a visit to my "Alma Mater". I had also received an invitation to visit Tarrington in Herefordshire, because Tarrington in Victoria is where I live and the two Tarringtons had been E-mailing each other, and I was seen as the obvious go-between.

But about Spring Grove. After a lapse of 64 years since my last scholastic days, I experienced both joy and sadness. Lovely to see the old Art and Music rooms again, to feel the atmosphere of the panelled corridors and the grand old staircase we ran up and down as often as we could without getting caught. But there it all ended. Where was the rest, and why was this remnant all boxed in by ugly modern rectangular constructions? What would Joe Banks and Arthur Pears have thought, could they have known where their dreams would finish up?

I was at Spring Grove from 1935 to 1940.

In 1935, I sat at a desk in the second - floor classroom, idly watching the trams as they clanked along the old London Road. I was there at Spring Grove for the sole purpose of sitting the Scholarship Examination, later called Eleven-Plus, and I had finished the paper half an hour early. The trams clanked by with a fascinating monotony that harmonised perfectly with the haze of that early summer's afternoon.

The night before, sleep had eluded me. I had to get that scholarship, for I was one of six children, and I knew my parents could not afford to pay fees. And I had to get to Spring Grove, the old "Black and White" as it was called. I've no idea why I was so keen on Spring Grove. Everybody told me I should go to Isleworth County, the "County High", explaining that it was a better school, better at work, better at sport, indeed better at everything. The only thing the County High lacked was girls, but at the age of eleven that was hardly relevant. But I desperately wanted to go to Spring Grove and nowhere else, and the scholarhip was vital. It had seemed to go on for ages, starting way back in February, when we did a "Mock Scholarship" at Heston Primary School. There were three papers, English, Arithmetic and General Knowledge. On top of that we had old exam papers from everywhere! Oxford, Nottingham, Scotland , the West Riding of Yorkshire - to name a few, and we did the lot!! So, by the time it finally got round to fronting up at Spring Grove for the real thing, I had been turned into a total examination freak.

Despite that sleepless night , I got through the exams in record time checked and double-checked, and then spent the last half - hour tram spotting. I could not relax, confident that I had not let my parents or anybody else down but there was still one last hurdle to get over, the feared interview with the Headmaster, L.T . Brown himself.

I handled it rather badly, Persons in authority always made me nervous no matter how nice they tried to be. "Did you find the entrance examination easy?" the great man asked. No, it wasn't easy, but it wasn't hard either, but I couldn't find words to express myself and muttered some stupid reply- The interview went from bad to worse, I was sure I had failed and went home in a bit of a mood.

The letter arrived.... I hadn't failed and so I turned up in September 1935 to start a new life in fantastic surroundings, arriving on the last of those clanking trams.

I look back nostalgically to the 'thirties as a dream-time, a time of peace and tranquillity. Spring Grove was more than a school. In fact, it didn't even look like a school, more like a stately mansion in a beautiful garden setting. We didn't want to think about war and the nasty guy over there in Germany. Our impression of Hitler was of a raving lunatic, a view we shared with Charlie Chaplin. But we did get a jolt when we received our first refugees in 1938, one of whom was Wilhelm Fleischer (we called him Villy) who had a few tales to tell. I heard that Villy, like me, finished up in Melbourne after the war and changed his name to Forbes. I had his address but never got round to meeting up with him.

My first impression of the Head Master, Mr L.T. Brown M.A. (Cantab), was of a quietly spoken man, who chose his words with care and made his points with the utmost clarity. At all times, he commanded attention and nowhere was this more apparent than at morning assembly. We would all be sitting quietly in the hall, boys on the left, girls on the right, when Mr. Snaith, the Senior Master would rise from his table on the stage and press his bell. It happened the same time almost to a second every Monday, and immediately everybody would stand, and a deathly silence then ensued as we listened to the slow staccato footsteps sounding along the covered way and approaching the hall entrance. It seemed an eternity before Mr. Brown at last materialised at the back of the hall, then walked with measured stride to the stage and ascended steps. Mr. Callow gave us an intro. on the piano and we sang the opening hymn. Then prayers would be said, the head prefect would read a lesson, then perhaps another hymn, after which we could all sit down to await the great man's words of wisdom.

Who was this L.T. Brown, that he could exact such instant obedience, yet be remembered by nearly all with such fondness?

First, he was devoutly religious, and I recall well his 'Scripture' lessons he gave us one period every week in Form Five. Being the last period of the day, most of us were tired, but nothing of what he said was dull or boring. A great classical scholar and seemingly a master of all the humanities, his lessons ranged all the way from ancient history to current affairs. His accounts of Bible stories usually found a parallel with our modern lives. He was essentially a man of peace, but recognised we were heading inevitably towards war and branded the Nazis as "absolute fiends". He was also scathing in his criticism of aspects of modern living he considered foolish or frivolous.

The curriculum of Spring Grove reflected his concept of education, being broadly based and covering a wide range of subjects.

Every student learnt at least one foreign language and studied at least one science subject, all the way up the school. Even music, art, manual training and physical education were well catered for. The teachers of French, History and Music, namely Miss Griffin, Mr. Bernard Joy (the great centre-half), and Mr. Varney gave me a life-long love of these subjects. I should mention Miss Richards (Maths and Geography) too. It was indeed a truly liberal education. Some educationists criticised L.T. on the grounds of conservatism, and one or two considered him a reactionary. Nothing could be further from the truth. He certainly believed in the Secondary Grammar, or High School as some called it, as opposed to the Comprehensive idea. No doubt he looked askance at the policy of Social Engineering as applied to secondary schooling and thought, as I still do, that it can only be achieved at the expense of academic excellence.

Even so, L.T. was not opposed to experiments in education. In my time at Spring Grove, the "Q" system was in operation. I don't know if it was his idea, but he certainly gave it his full approval. Briefly, it meant that Form One would be divided into three streams; namely, 1A, 1B and 1Q, standing for Quick. A and B would proceed up the school year by year, but the Q stream would jump straight from Form One to Form Three, thereby taking their School Certificate exams one year earlier than the others. That it worked was proved by the number in my Form Five who gained Matriculation Exemption (about one-third). But the scheme had its demerits too, and was soon abandoned. L.T. was nothing if not human. At Spring Grove we were not all that good at team games. I remember one occasion when our first eleven lost twelve-nil to Isleworth County. What made it worse was that Mr. Brown, accompanied by the Isleworth County H.M, Mr. Thurston, was watching the match. You can imagine what he said on the following Monday. A man with his superb command of the English language would not take such an insult to his pride lightly.

So, to sum up, how much influence did this man have on our subsequent lives? I would say, an enormous amount. He ran the school his way; he presided over a highly qualified and dedicated staff; his scholarship, his philosophy, his integrity and his enthusiasm passed to nearly all his charges. Much of what I have managed to achieve could be due to the vision and inspiration I absorbed from the Headmaster and Staff at Spring Grove.

Being the Principal of any school is no easy task. Teachers are intelligent, well-qualified and usually individualistic, and to combine their various talents into a smooth-running and efficient organisation needs a person of exceptional ability at the helm. I believe L.T. Brown was such a man.

I left school in 1940, but my friend John Morris stayed on for his Higher School Certificate, and we still meet occasionally. With the fall of France, we all finally realised that Hitler was something more than a clown and it was going to be a long war. At home, politics became important, especially when Germany invaded the Soviet Union. Many young people became communists or, at least sympathisers, Anglo-Soviet Societies sprang up everywhere and almost everybody was involved in "Aid to Russia". Admiration for the tenacious and heroic Russian resistance to the common enemy gave rise to lots of meetings and debates everywhere, including Spring Grove.

I attended one meeting chaired by Mr. L.T. Brown himself, in which there was a speaker from the Soviet Union. In school, debates were held and my friend earned himself the sobriquet of "Red Morris", nothing to be ashamed of in those days. Actually, we all expected that after the war the Allies would build a new world, in which things like war, depression and injustice would be non-existent, a hope that springs eternal but is never realised.

To get back to the 2004 Reunion, it wasn't only the topography that saddened me. I didn't meet one person from my year or even the following year. Where had they all gone? Was I to be the sole survivor, or was it on their part just lack of interest? Having come ten thousand miles for this event, you may forgive my pique. Apart from these regrets, I thought the organisers did a wonderful job, and I did meet several delightful personalities.

Towards the end of my visit, I went down to Hereford as the guest of the Tarrington Brass Ensemble. The people of this picturesque rural outpost gave me a magnificent welcome and made me guest of honour at a concert given in the Ledbury Church. The next year, my hosts came to Tarrington, Victoria, and we were able to reciprocate. Tarrington here is also a tiny rural community, but it boasts a wonderful brass band of which I have the honour to be the long serving Musical Director. Music has been my life, and some of my inspiration was derived from Spring Grove, from a certain Mr. Varney, aka Trevor Owen, aka Owen Jones. What a complicated character! But he loved music, sang beautifully and made music a living language for us.

Thank you, Spring Grove, for everything.

" The Dubble, Dubble Beat of the Thuundering Druum"

Leo Lewis '42

The report on Pre-War Spring Grove by Doreen Body rang several bells with me. Mr.Handover of stiff leg, waxed moustache and 28 inch upright bicycle frame actually spent much time trying to teach me maths. He was, to my mind, a real gentleman. "Bill" Lineham, an obvious Yorkshire man was such an enthusiast for his subject of Literature. His resounding rendition of "The dubble dubble beat of the thuundering druum cries:- HARK" the foes cuum!!" had to be heard to be believed. It worked!!! I remember the words but what is the piece taken from?? Mr.Snaith taught Physics. In my time he was even older. I seem to recall in his lecture on electricity he started by explaining that the current flowed from positive to negative.... or negative to positive!!! yet another subject I failed to conquer!! Mr. Brown was Headmaster in my time. A position he held together very well. There was another Mr. Brown who taught maths, we called him "Basher" Brown to differentiate. The Head had occasion to deal with one of our classmates who, on two? or three? consecutive days unrolled the toilet rolls and blocked all the toilets in the boys outside loos. He administered a beating and dismissed the lad. The only occasion when such an event occurred. (Was his name Clothier??? I apologise if that was an innocent member of our year!!) "Dolly" Ransome is a name I recall easily. She never taught me but still the name lingers, was her subject French? Trevor Varney was a most flamboyant character. When my voice broke during rehearsals for the Annual "big" concert - Tales from the Vienna Woods he swapped me from Contralto to Tenor. I believe that is why my voice has never been useable since. Miss Griffin, wow, French teacher extrordinaire, sweeping into the room with "Bonjour mes eleves", acknowledging our reply of "Bonjour Mademoiselle" with a command of "Asseyez vous", because we all stood up when a teacher entered the room. We were taught French, by her; initially we wrote it phonetically. I was absent some 30 days in the first term after losing three teeth and breaking an arm when a motor cycle ran into my bike on the way to school. During the time off the class swopped to "normal" spelling, another poor start to a new subject. Miss Taylor I recognise as a history teacher. We also had a Miss Richards who taught Geography. Miss Bromwich was, I felt, a most unreal character. Probably because we boys did not study "Domestic Science"?? However her "Laboratory" backed onto the "Manual" room of Muzz, Mr.Cross. His name arrived because sideways on his profile was a dead ringer for Mussolini the Italian leader who was a figure of some ridicule to us in pre and early war days. Our "Muzz" was aware of this and cut the shape from a plank of wood whilst joking about his "nickname". He was also the school "detective". When, as often happened, something went missing, he would approach each boy in turn. Whispering confidentially in your ear he would say. "I know you took it lad, let me have it back and nothing more will be said". There was the occasion when a set of metal taps and dies was "lost". Muzz finally found them "Scattered all over the North Pitch" (the hockey field). Our first year project under his tuition was to each make a wooden table lamp. A square piece of deal was carefully planed and chamfered. Another similar but slightly smaller square was equally lovingly created and was glued on top of its larger counterpart. Lighting the gas under the glue pot was another opportunity for Muzz's imitation of Hercules Poirot. Appealing to the whole class he would say "Has any lad got a match?" The unfortunate who replied yes, and produced the box, was greeted with a forth-right...... "Gottcha lad, smoking again eh?" The upright member of the lamp was made by grooving two long pieces of deal and gluing them together to produce a square wooden tube. The end was filed to a round shape. A hole was drilled with a hand brace in the middle of the two previously prepared square pieces. We were not very tall. Holding the squares in the wood working vice and struggling to use the brace and bit produced, for me, a hole which left the upright member very far from truly perpendicular. Pisa was not comparable to my leaning member. I produced another two bases with equally bad results. The war was by now well under way and Muzz advised we could not get the wood for me to continue. I therefore converted to metal work. Mainly this consisted of making scoops from old empty tins for him to use when dishing out the food to his rabbits at home. Muzz had been a gym master in his younger days. Pictures of his carefully mounted "human pyramids" were on the walls. His instruction was that when jumping down from a height "Always land at full knees bend, lad". We converted this to his jumping off Snowdon and landing at full knees bend. We all made fun of him but with respect and great admiration for one who was the greatest adult "character" I had ever met until then. Preparing for the General Schools Certificate we had to cut two pieces of brass plate an eighth of an inch thick. I was sent to the Central School for the material. All they had was a sixteenth thick. "Muzz" got me to solder the material together with lead solder. Unfortunately the project was to make a small catch. The brass was hard. Because of the lead solder I could not anneal it. When trying to bend it at right angles, to form the sides of the catch, it split into two separate sheets as the solder gave up. Another failed subject! I often wondered what the examiners made of the pieces of sixteenth material covered in lead solder? Mr. Callow fitted his name quite well, I remember him as a teacher of Geography. His article mentions a Miss Taylor whose name seems to ring a bell somewhere. The house names of Robins, Seagulls, Swallows and (my own allocation) Skylarks. We had brown as our house colour I recall. Then we changed to Rodney, Drake, Nelson and ? However I resolutely remained a Skylark!! Mr. Davey was a fiery language teacher. Once, as our form teacher, he swept in to say he had left his mortar board on the desk. As I was prone to do, I used a saying in current vogue on the radio something like "Takeitaway". His response was to hurl the wooden black-board cleaner at me. Fortunately I ducked.   Bernard Joy was a "God" to all the boys but I had no idea he taught History. During the war he was in the Air Force and returned at least once in his full officers kit.   Miss Nash was a favourite teacher of mine. We had our form room in her glass roofed biology lab (The Banksian room). Not a good place to be in during Air Raids!   Mr Hemming was our sports master after Bernard Joy. Not universally liked.   He had a habit of handing out punishments of three strokes of the slipper. Administered after "the next" P.T. session through those terribly thin shorts we wore in those days. I found this a trifle sadistic. Some reports I read after the war in the Telegraph(?) were from a Mr. James Hemming Sports Psychologist. The same chap?

Having, as forecast, failed my General Schools in every subject except English Literature, I started the next term after the summer holidays in form 6 Commercial under Mr.Tomlinson, was it? He ran Spring Grove Polytechnic, from the school premises, as a night school. Within a month he produced an opportunity for me to join Carriers as a diamond mounter. Feeling my life rescued from the scrap heap I leapt at the chance. I have very fond memories of Spring Grove. A place where I was allowed to grow up and mix with other developing boys and girls. I have mentioned only the fringe of our activities.   There was the Banksian cycling club a group of us formed to tour extensively all year round but especially in the summer holidays. In 1942 we Youth Hostelled round North Wales calling in on the girls' harvest camp en route in Gloucestershire??   Remember that, during the War all road sign posts and the like were removed for National Security reasons.   We became better map readers as a direct result of that. Having actually walked up Snowden we then doubted Muzz's ability to leap off the mountain and land at full knees bend!   The boys' harvest camps were held in Herefordshire. Thus we helped the wartime food production. Not only that, much of the crop in Hereford was hops!!   From memory I found difficulty in absorbing any of the subjects with which we were ably presented. Most staff obviously recognised me as a challenging case. Very few gave up on me and, except for Mr. Hemming, I acknowledge the influence they have had on my life. However that is a different story not to be told at this juncture.

I note mention of Mary Cutter who married John Leslie Barden. He came back to teach himself Japanese. I repeat, to teach HIMSELF Japanese. The acknowl-edged leader of our "Banksian Cycle Club" was Ernie Mills who lived on the Council Estate close to the Vicarage Farm Road Junction with the Great West Road.   I knew his family well and respected Ernie. He continued in the Army,after the war, gaining a commission, but died on an expedition in the snowfields of Norway. I forgave him his acquired "posh" accent as a necessary "self defence" mechanism. My own Mancunian pronunciation was similarly "lost" much earlier. I could not be the only one talking of "Jam butties" in pre-war West London!

Recollection after a First Reunion

Marjorie Stammers '42

My brother and I headed for the Oct.07 reunion as first timers, very excited about the opportunity of visiting the grand old house again after more than 60 years, even though we were aware that "horrible things" had happened to it and the grounds as we remembered them.

It seemed strange to enter by the main door facing Harvard Road, as we remembered this being the Staff entrance, leading to Miss Ashbrook's office and the Headmaster's study. We [the pupils] always used the front South Pitch entrance or the Covered Way door at the rear. However, once inside, memories came flooding back as we gazed at the oh ! so familiar entrance hall and grand staircase leading up to that magnificent stained glass window, on the half landing. The stairs up to the top floor reminded me of an incident during my first days at school. I was climbing these stairs to reach my form room [Room 15] when a group of 6th formers came out of the Boy Prefects' room. I recognised one of them and said "Hello", only to be told later that is was not done for a 1st former to speak to Prefects in school buildings, even if he happened to be one's brother! On peeping into the Headmaster's study. I recalled Latin lessons in there, taken by L.T.Brown himself with us seated on his pale green suite, which made us feel very privileged indeed.

Through to the Music Room, still crowned by its mirrored Adam fireplace, minstrel's gallery and surrounded by framed panels dedicated to composers. I remember their portraits hanging on long cords in these panels, although my brother says they were plaster reliefs of the great men, not paintings, in his time. Whose recollection is true? Or were they changed ? I sat my Matriculation Exams. in front of Beethoven, my favourite composer. None of them are in position any more, of course.

How wonderful to be in that elegant Art Room again and to find the mosaics in the alcove still intact and just as colourful as in the past. It was interesting to discover the original fountain site in the floor [it had obviously been obscured by equipment before]. In Sir Joseph Bank's time the Winter Garden must have been a truly magical place. It was good to see potted plants and ferns on the double bench decking around the room instead of as it was in our school days, a dumping place for all our satchels, where "Amicus", Miss Bromwich's dog, would craftily try to nose his way in to our lunch bags !

Naturally we missed the dear old Cedar tree, the West Lawn Elms and the irreplaceable Banksian Room and all the other familiar buildings and places that are sadly long gone, but they will stay forever in our mind's eye, as part of that unique school - Spring Grove -surely in a class of it's own !

What is it about "Spring Grove" that the magic remains so positively in our memories, even though parts of the buildings and grounds are no longer there?

Each reunion we enjoy at the old school, thanks to the warm welcome we receive from the West Thames College, and the sterling efforts of Pam, Avril and the team, in organising them, giving us another chance to relive more of the magic.

This year after our 'fix' at the reunion, I'm on a 'high' remembering all sorts of little incidents regarding what is still there and <u>not</u> (all of which I had not mentioned in my previous writings to the magazine).

My time at Spring Grove began in 1937, with Mr Joy as my form master in room 15 on the top floor, he was of course the well known Arsenal centre-half. My brother also remembers directing the team manager to Mr Joy, when he called at the school one day to see him. On clear days we could see Richmond Hill and the North Downs quite clearly from our windows, tempting our attention to wander from the lesson. To my shame, I recall on more than one occasion, Mr Joy scoring a direct hit on me with a well aimed piece of chalk (I doubt if it would be approved of nowadays, but it was very effective I can assure you!).

My second year was marked by English teacher Miss Kate Klarner doing a year's teaching swap with Miss Sara M. Light of the USA. She was a very different lady from Miss Klarner, who was always dignified and sensible dressed wearing her gown on duty at all times. Whereas Miss Light was a 'Thoroughly Modern Millie' American. A small slim figure, teetering into class on very high heels carrying all her books in front, with handbag on top under her chin to steady the pile. We always expected her to trip over something! She told us we were well ahead of her class back home in America which was nice to pass on to Miss Klarner when she returned the following year (1939).

I have mentioned taking Latin lessons in the Headmaster's study before, but now also recall his subtle sense of humour. On the occasion of our first lesson when he translated our Christian names from the Latin, but the nearest to Marjorie was Margaret which meant 'Pearl of great price!' From thereon he referred to me by that phrase accompanied by a little smile.

A trip up the back stairs brought us to "Kipper Hemming's" tiny staff room where it was quite usual to find steam rising from rows of soggy football socks drying on his fire guard around yet another coal fire after wet days on the playing fields.

Wandering down into the basement, just at the base of the staircase was where Mrs Archer (the caretaker's wife in my time) held a 'Tuck shop' at breaktime during the war. I can't quite remember how she coped with sweet rationing!

Occasionally I had to stay to dinner at school. This was not something I particularly enjoyed as Miss Griffin, Headmistress presided at the head of the table and insisted on us using French in conversation. I was unusually quiet – a rarity for me as my report book records!

Now, a few cameos into things that are not there now.

Miss Bromwich's cottage was so familiar to us girls, where in spite of the wartime shortages, under her 'eagle eye' we learnt how to keep house, 'make do and mend', and cook. Although we were surprised at her using a whole double period showing us how to produce potato crisps, when it was still possible to buy Smith's crisps for 1 or 2 old pennies!

Alongside the cottage was the hut where Mr Varney encouraged us to sing and appreciate good music. I remember one year he helped us to produce a wonderful performance of "Tales from the Vienna Woods" held in the hall.

The Banksian Room was the one place that should have been preserved, it being the sole connection with Sir Joseph. My two years in the Banksian Room with Miss Nash as form mistress was my favourite time, even when she had us dissecting those dreadful smelly dogfish! Such a remarkable classroom, grotto-like at one end with rocks, waterfall, pools of fish and birds flying in through the glass roof during lessons; surely in 'a class of it's own'!

Out in the grounds, the grand row of mature Elms on the West lawn, out of bounds in the winter because of branches falling, seemed as if they would be there forever, as did the wonderful old Cedar tree with its platformed seat around the bottom of its huge trunks where we would gather to chat and hastily finish off our homework before the bell rang.

My time at the School began two years before the war, when the fire station was quite new. Our form room was room 15, on top floor with a fine view of the rear of the station. Just imagine the excitement of young boys (1st formers) to see firemen sliding down the pole when the alarm was sounded! They would rush to the windows to get a good look, leaving poor Mr Callow, red faced to the roots of his blond hair, desperately trying to get them to return to their seats.

Another time Mr. Callow became the target of our disobedience was at morning assembly As someone has already mentioned – he used to play the grand piano in the hall to accompany the hymns. On this morning (after the war began) he had unfortunately chosen the tune to the German National Anthem and we all flatly refused to sing, much to his embarrassment. (We all felt he should have known how patriotic we would feel!)

Getting to school proved to be difficult sometimes during the days of the blitz. Some of us were actually bombed out, and were taken in by friends and neighbours, but most spent the night in shelters, only to be faced in morning by a tedious journey to school, detouring around Hounslow High Street, where fireman's hoses filled the carriageway making the road impassable

And so the war continued, fire-watchers were organised and anti-litter teams formed to keep the grounds tidy and we girls bought lots of little brass coloured shapes like Spitfires that we fixed to our handbags etc. in aid of the Spitfire Fund (I think the prefects ran this). There was a time when we all thought the lovely old wrought iron front gates would have to be melted down as materials for the war effort, but thankfully they are still with us.

In the early war years (I think about our 3rd) the Head Master asked our year to welcome Vere Faktor a Czhechoslovakian girl, who we assumed had escaped to England with her family but didn't like to ask as she was very quiet. A clever girl who went on to do well in Matriculation, gaining a distinction in her own language, I believe. Does anyone know what happened to her?

Who remembers Stephanie Thomas(?), who on rainy lunch times, would respond to our pleading with a performance of her examination pieces, with great panache on the piano in the hall.

Once a year we were trusted (in groups) to walk "with decorum" to the Dominion Cinema in Hounslow, to hear a concert performed by a full symphony orchestra – my memory tells me the conductor one year was Sir Malcolm Sargent. Certainly for me, they were a wonderful experience showing the importance of the conductor and leading to my life long love of good music, courtesy of Spring Grove.

For those of us having memories like mine compelling us to return each year, this unique seat of learning certainly holds magical qualities.

Spring Grovian 1942

Peter Cottrell '43.

I regret missing last year's get-together but certain flaws at "foot and knee" make life difficult on occasions and make long distance commitments (is that right) very difficult. As somebody who will not be remembered at Spring Grove for his academic brilliance I am mightily inspired by the Spring Grovian Report.

I do not know when the Spring Grovian first started but an attempt to start it came about in 1942. John E (Ginger) White was the driving force and a group of us got together in John's small garden shed in Heston and put something together using a John Bull printing set!! As I was considered to be semi illiterate my contribution was extremely modest. There was an injection of dynamic talent soon after and the whole thing got on the road. I stayed involved as I was attracted by the Friday night trips to the Dominion Southall.

Willi Fleischer was the "Mr Fix-it" behind this and sometimes as many as twenty of us would arrive and after a brief conversation with the manager (he stood no chance with Willi) we were ushered into our seats in the circle.

John E White was Jimmy Hemming's agent when he stood for Parliament; he "backed the wrong one". We should have put up Willi who would have made us all millionaires. Could go on as I moved into garrulous old age about five years ago and realise it can be very boring. Please excuse my typing and numerous errors but my handwriting is impossible to read much to my shame, however I did confess to being semi Illiterate and that situation hasn't changed over the last sixty years - no fault of Spring Grove which did its best,

The Tintinnabulation of the Bells

Dorothy Lovibond '43

Transferring from Heston Junior School to Spring Grove was such a contrast, Heston being almost brand new and SGGS old, beautiful and full of History. To say that I was impressed would be an understatement. I was in 1A with Mr. Hayley, young and good looking, the girls' dream boat, he taught Maths.

Our first task was to fit a padlock onto our desks because all our books and possessions were kept there – no lockers. The desks were wonderful, big and heavy, with lots of carving from previous owners. Our classroom , No. 10 had an open fire which the caretaker had to attend towith coke in the winter. We also had a wonderful view of the grounds as we were on the first floor. That winter was very cold with snow and we were waiting outside for first bell to be allowed in. I fainted and came to in the Banksian Room with Miss Nash, she was so kind and an excellent teacher of Biology.

Bernard Joy was my form master in the second and third forms, he also taught History but was best remembered as an Arsenal footballer. He broke his nose and the whole form went to his home to offer our condolences. His beautiful wife gave us chocolate biscuits. He took part in a spelling bee on the radio and was caught out with disestablishmentarianism and the blackboards had it written on them all over the school the next day.

Miss Light and Miss Klarner taught English and I remember the Children of the New Forest, The Moonstone, Macbeth and Henry IV, V & VI. I became an ardent fan of Shakespeare. Miss Ransom was very nice with great enthusiasm for french travel and life itself which was catching. In 1939 she helped take a party to Southampton Docks to go over a huge liner. I think it was called the Aquitania or it could have been the Mauritania, anyway it was very interesting and I was very impressed by the work going on in the dry dock near by.

I must mention Mr. Lineham (poetry) " the tintinnabulation of the bells, the bells, the bells" and Mr. Varney (music), he made us all sing solo at times , which actually did us good and gave us confidence. I sang Tales from the Vienna Woods in the choir and loved it so much that I drove them mad singing it at home. Miss Walters taught Art and Miss Bromwich Domestic Science in the cottage. We did cooking and sewing and also chimney sweeping and how to blacklead the grate. Both were formidable ladies, frightening but, I found out later, with a soft centre.

The war came and we had a wait for the shelters to be dug. They were lit but not enough for us to see our shelter work. Some of us knitted squares to be made into blankets for the WVS to distribute to bomb victims. We did have extra homework to try to make up the time lost. I'm amazed that the school kept going. I look back to school days and the school buildings with great affection. I am so glad that some of it has been saved and is put to good use.

We Were Just Friends

Maurice Baguley '42

I received my copy of Issue No 9 this morning and when I read the article written by Alan Pinch, it brought a lump in my throat and a tear to my eye. The Pinch family lived just around the corner from me in Hounslow West and I was friendly with Frank and Evie and also knew their parents very well, although I cannot remember Alan. I frequently attended the discussion group that Mr & Mrs Pinch used to organise and the meetings always ended with a bit of a tea party.

The air-raid incident which Alan mentioned, I feel sure, is the bomb which fell during the 1940 blitz and hit the house opposite mine! The son of the family opposite was also a pupil at Spring Grove, in the same form as me. His name was Peter Hanson and he and his parents survived the bombing by sheltering beneath the staircase and they emerged from the rubble covered in brick dust. There was a man walking past our house at the time of the impact and he was mortally injured. He crawled a few yards along the road into our alleyway, where he sadly died. Our house was badly damaged, but liveable after temporary repairs and we survived the bombing by sheltering beneath the sturdy dining room table. There were many neighbours helping at the scene and I am sure Frank Pinch was one of them.

Alan's sister Evie was a lovely girl and very pretty too! She had a boyfriend called Moggie Morgan (I can't remember his proper first name), also a pupil at Spring Grove, where I think the romance began. Moggie joined the Merchant Navy as a radio officer and I recall meeting them both at Evie's house, when he was on leave. I took Evie out several times before the Moggie association got serious. However, after the war, I think they parted company and Evie used to call round to my house from time to time for a chat and a cup of coffee. I was between girl friends at the time, so I looked forward to Evie's visits. Then I became friendly with a girl tracer in the drawing office where I was working in 1947, but we only met about twice a week at first, I think it was Wednesdays and Saturdays. So when Evie called to see me one Tuesday, I think it was, I made her welcome and did coffee for the two of us. After a while, there was a knock at the front door, which couldn't be Lynne (the new girl friend's name) as it was not her night. When I opened the door I nearly passed out, because there was Lynne, all made up the to the nines saying that she thought she'd surprise me! She did that all right. Then I took her into the sitting room and tried to explain what this pretty girl was doing, all cosied up in an armchair by the fire, with a cup of coffee. Evie saw my embarrassment and assured Lynne that we were just friends and had been so for many years. I did eventually convince Lynne, but it took several days before the air cleared. We married in November 1948 and sadly, I lost her due to cancer in March 1983, but she reminded me many times during our 35 year marriage, of the Evie Pinch incident and I'm sure there was always a lingering doubt in her mind.

I loved Evie and was very sad this morning when I read of her sudden death in 1990 and she could have only been in her early 60's. She was a few years younger than me and I was 64 in 1990. The last time I saw her was a chance meeting in London. I was working as a design engineer for a firm in Brompton Road and at that time, had bought a house in Bexleyheath, Kent. I used to travel early to Charing Cross station and walk from there to the office in Brompton Road. One morning in the early 50's, probably 1953, I walked past the Ritz Hotel and as I got to the park gate near Green Park station, a voice said, "hello Maurice". It was Evie. She told me that she had been staying in Toronto, with the family where Frank was billeted when he did his RAF training in Canada. I cannot recall whether she told me if she had married at that time, but I do remember that she looked very drawn. That was the last time I saw her.

Class 6a of 44

Top row:-
    1 Derek Millett, **2.** Ian Macfarlane, **3.** Bill Osterburg, **4.** David Mitchell,
    5.Jim Hughes, **6.** Graham Clarke, **7.** Bob Goldsmith, **8.** David Salvage,
9.Reg Lindall, **10,**Des Chaplin. **11.** Chas Cracknell, **12** Sid Reynolds
Middle row
    13 ?, **14.** Beth Young, **15.** Myrtle Atkins, **16.** Audrey Rogers,
    17. George Barrett, 18. Jean Stark, **19** ,Anne Lusher, **20.** Elna Goddard
  Bottom Row
    21 Gerry Swettenham, **22** Jim Winslade, **23** Norman Dixon,
    24 Ray Harwood, **25** Bud Cutting, **26** Alan Burrows.

Sixty Years Backward March

Michael Mason '42

I suppose that in any memoir of schooldays we recall particularly those teachers who took the most trouble to help us win all the honours that we possibly could. On my own Roll of Honour I include L.T. Brown the Headmaster for his quiet dignity and authority, his sense of humour and wise scholarship; together with Bill Lineham, Head of English, who used to bring me out front all too often for my comfort to read or recite passages in drama, and thus pull me from my introspective existence into the glare of publicity. Because of this I became a schoolmaster in England and a Professor of English in Southern Africa and Canada. Miss Klarner (Mrs. Hemming) was also encouraging in this respect, as were two other ladies who seem to have slipped out of many OSG memories after so many years: Miss Gay and Miss Hollwey. Miss Gay was a blonde goodlooker who was known outside the school for distributing Leftwing literature to the general public. Miss Hollwey taught Shakespeare to a trio of us in the Sixth Form, and on one occasion hosted us at her home, quite a rare event in those days of rationing.

Outside the English Department Mr. Callow — "Doughnut" to some imaginative students - fostered my interest in Geography, and Miss Taylor that in History, displaying a remarkable ability to identify with the hardships of English soldiers in France six hundred years before. Mr. Barrett and F.W. "Basher" Brown tried hard to teach me Maths, and "Pop" Aldersley did his best in Chemistry. Little Miss Ransom for French I remember as the most popular as well as perhaps the kindest personage on staff. Mr. Cross (Muzz) was a famous personality in the Manual or Woodwork Building, with his harrowing stories of boys who in careless moments had run themselves through with chisels or other sharp implements. Many years after the war he came into my Osterley neighbourhood to canvass "for my brother, who's standing for re-election to the Middlesex County Council." He had no recollection of me as he rumbled away about this; and for the only time in my life in any continent I voted Conservative. He got in, by the way.

We seem to have got into anecdotes. Miss Bromwich I encountered in First Year only. This was for Gardening, which in fine weather meant weeding our class plots outside the Art Room somewhere or dropping the odd worms down the girls' necks. In winter some instruction went on in the classroom, from which nearly seventy years later I recall the following exchange:

Miss B: Skipper! Where do you plant wallflowers?

Skipper: In the ground, Miss, same as any other plant.

Miss B: Skipper! I knew you were not paying any attention! [And so forth for some time.]

I've come to see this as a classic example of a straight question thought to be a trick, and a straight answer received as insolence.

We came to know many members of staff much better because of firewatching duties. Mr. Corby I knew already, since he'd introduced me to shorthand and typing during my brief session in the Commercial Sixth. I knew him for a time shortly after the war, when he came to fish in Osterley Park, where I lived; and he had vivid memories of his army experiences in 1914-1918. "The quietest place to be in the whole war was the front line of the trenches — because every sound meant something!"

Miss Walters was our ever patient Art Mistress, but I think that some of us were more accustomed to Miss Quelch, a mildly eccentric lady whom I remember especially for her cheerful classes frequently studded with remarks such as "You will take a thousand lines!" Fortunately, as their production was never demanded, this sort of imposition was soon accepted as only a conversational contribution.

Other people I respectfully remember include Mr. Davey (French), who eventually transferred to Woolwich Grammar School, which was nearer home, an important consideration in wartime; Miss Nash (Biology), the lady of that most attractive of staff habitations, the Banksian Room; Miss Griffin (French and Senior Mistress), strict but friendly; the Sports Master, Mr. Hemming, who was an excellent Latin tutor; Mrs. Rochford (Latin), who years later recalled that "You could never remember the accusative-infinitive construction;" and Mr. Joy, whom I saw play for Arsenal. He joined the RAF; as did Mr. Hayley, another athletics master, who gave me the only gold star I ever received for that kind of activity.

To me more peripheral figures include Mr. Beynon — did he write science fiction? — and Mr. Maylott (General Science). There was also Mr. Snaith (Physics and Senior Master), who was determined to complete his farewell address to the School. Dave Barden, Head of School, rose from the back row:

Barden: School! Three cheers for ~

Mr. Snaith: Wait a minute! I haven't finished yet!

A few general features of school life occur to me. Among them was the Catapult. This operated briefly from the Boy Prefects' Room, was fastened to either side of the sash window, and fired over the South Front to as far as the London Road. It had more power than accuracy, and was easily dismantled; but it was discontinued as a diplomatic gesture to civilisation because staff were liable to drop into the room without notice.

The Courier magazine was another interest for the students in our final years. It owed much to the enthusiasm of Willy Fleischer, our refugee from Austria. A tolerant school administration allowed what amounted to a semi-official opposition as part of our education under war conditions. Often scurrilous, it included identities such as Gatecrasher — I confess that was me ~ who wrote about our lives in wartime.

Finally the last straw, as you might say, was the departure of many of us to the farm camps in August-September 1942. From there I went on to a university and its air squadron, and returned to the school in the following years only as a visitor. However, something happened at the Marlow camp which has become for me a symbol of both the school and its significance in later life, so much that long afterwards I wrote a poem about it which appeared in the magazine English. We were taking a rest at the end of the day until the last load of wheat for the season was brought in by the team gathering it. At this moment Farmer Emmett, who was sitting with us in the field, said to us: "Look up there. You'll never see a sight like that again." On the crest of the hill, and surrounded by some of us and his own people, a horse drawn wagon was receiving the last sheaves; and there was almost no movement because of the height the pitchers were stretching to reach the loaders waiting on top. The entire group was silhouetted against the sunset; and a minute later they were rolling home to the rick, and the day of harvest was over.

Farmer Emmett had been a true prophet. Fare well with you all!

The Waggoners - ENGLISH published in Autumn 1972 by OUP

How shall we remember, after mechanization, Harvests gathered in the older style?
For there's in them a kind of glory. Not needing any touches of glamour,
Deserving the plain truth merely, They ask an enduring symbol, wrought
Through a celebration in rhyme: Rhyme, on which the returning past,
Like a waggon with a full load In the time of the fall and the garnering,
Draws to each one of us, in the evening, His harvest, its wealth and its weeds together.

Lurching, rolling, juddering, grumbling Slowly through stubbled fields,
Rearing up the finest wheat That land in good heart yields—
While gripping on hard, its men aloft Ride high over the distant plain—
Bound for the rick, its horses hauling, A wagon jolts under swaying grain.

Alongside; comes the heavy swish Of the glittering fork that heaves
High and swift, as the rickmen wait In their nests for its tightbound sheaves;
Then clash and scrape of glinting steel; A breath; again the prongs bite deep,
Thrusting down to find and hook New victims for their upward sweep ...

Until men pause, for a moment only, Cease the long swings of strength—
Heavily leaning, dour, not speaking,On each haft's work-polished length;
Their gaze into the shadowy evening, Far across the plundered land,
Turns where the highest glow of summer Silhouettes a group that stand
Black on the white rim of the world— Their emblem, under coming night.
Waggon, men, horses, bent in toil, Impress, crown, crest with life the light.

And now this last load, rumbling home, Towers far above the hurrying team;
Highest of all, upon the dome Of that great burden, rests the moon.

Michael Mason '42

Spring Grove Farm Camps 1942/3

Terry Hibbs '42

Harvest Camps were organised at the Government's instigation to assist farmers who were suffering from wartime labour shortages. The Black and White eagerly participated in this scheme by arranging for 5th and 6th Formers, both male and female, to help with the more mundane and labour intensive tasks on farms, for a period of 4 weeks during the school summer break. In keeping with the morals of the period, separate camps were arranged for girls and boys!

We were to be billeted in the small village of Ashperton in Herefordshire. Our efforts were so successful that the same location was chosen for the following year. My memories have been meshed together by the passage of time, so the following jottings are a combination of events during those times. A party of about 20, were instructed to meet at Paddington Station on Saturday morning with clothes (including gloves) and bicycles (most important!). A few brave souls, led, I believe, by George Griffith, had opted to cycle to Ashperton overnight on the Friday, leaving the Ambassador cinema at Hounslow West at 7.0 p.m. They should have arrived before the train, but they lost their way crossing the Cotswolds and Malvern Hills, because of the blackout and the removal of all village and town names. I believe that they cycled an extra 40 miles before arriving in a somewhat distraught condition. As one of the travellers by train, my particular memory of the journey relates to the boy sitting next to me who had been given an accumulator to carry for the "wireless" at the camp and he placed it in the netting luggage rack above the seats. A small quantity of acid from the accumulator dripped onto the back of the seats and severely damaged the back of my brand new sports Jacket, completely ruining it. I felt extremely upset, as my mother had saved both her money and her clothing coupons for this jacket, to ensure that I wouldn't disgrace her.

On arrival at the Village Hall, our first job was to fill our palliasses with straw, for our makeshift beds on the Hall floor for the next 4 weeks (our first shock!). The next was to be shown the rudimentary washing and very primitive sanitary arrangements. A meal was provided and we were told that a local farmer was cutting grain in a nearby field, so some of us cycled there and our job was to kill the rabbits attempting to escape. What a sadistic lot we were! We armed ourselves with sticks and had only just started the chase, when one of our number (Ken Styan, I believe) was mistaken for a rabbit, and received a crack on the head from one of the boys. We halted immediately.

Mr. Davey, whom I regarded as a superb French teacher and Form Master, accompanied us, but I cannot remember anybody who assisted him. I believe that breakfast consisted of porridge and cereal washed down with gallons of stewed tea. We were given sandwiches to take to our jobs, and an evening meal was available on our return. I have to say that Mr. Davey's accomplishments as a teacher did not extend to the culinary arts. The porridge one morning being so lumpy that it was inedible: not to be wasteful, this was reheated the following morning only for it to be lumpy and burnt! You can imagine the hoots of derision emanating from the boys, released from the strictures of school discipline.

Each morning, we would cycle to our allotted farms, there to participate in our sometimes strenuous endeavours. Such duties included the following: Stocking the sheaves of grain. Moving hay for the building of haystacks. Fruit picking e,g apples and plums. hop picking.

Some personal observations of these; building haystacks was performed by the experienced farm workers and we were only used to transfer the collected hay to the stack. Apple and plum picking were enjoyable, apart from the hazards of being at the top of the ladder without someone at the base to steady it. Hop picking is surely one of the most boring occupations known to man!

Together with the sandwiches for lunch we were also given a bottle of water One day was hot and we had been working hard. I was thirsty and my water. bottle was empty, I was sitting on an empty cart being towed by the farmer to collect more hay. I spied a brown bottle on the cart and took a swig, expecting it to be water, but, to my horror, the bottle contained petrol! You can imagine my surprise and discomfort. Needless to say, I did not participate in the evening meal, consuming nothing but lots and lots of water. Insult was added to injury, as the farmer chastised me for wasting his petrol ration!

Working till late on the fine days, we were too exhausted to think about socialising but the local pub was situated almost directly opposite the Village Hall and they served some very palatable local "scrumpy". Those in charge of our activities were fairly lenient regarding our drinking at the pub, recommending a maximum of one pint of the scrumpy per evening. There were a few sore heads on occasions. I started chatting to one of the elderly locals at the pub, who told me that we were doing a grand job and asked me what it was like in 'Palm Springs' !

Normally we worked on Saturday mornings, but, if the weather the previous week had been bad a few of us would work Saturday afternoon and maybe Sunday. Those not engaged normally piled on the bus to Hereford to visit the cinema, have a meal or just wander around. We had to be aware that the last bus left early and there was no Sunday service. In one instance a few of the lads missed the bus, and they had to resort to walking the 14 miles, arriving at the Hall at about 3.0 a.m., very footsore and weary.

We were visiting a cinema one Saturday afternoon, when one of the group suddenly leapt up and raced towards the toilet. I knew that he had been picking plums so was not too disturbed. He returned about 10 minutes later, looking rather crestfallen. He said he felt fine medically, but the reason for his dismay was that no toilet roll or other paper was available, and he had been forced to utilise his precious and irreplaceable sweet ration coupons!

There are many other memories of my two attendances at the Farm Camps, but those detailed above are the most vivid. Did I enjoy them? I don't think that I would have volunteered to return for a second visit if I hadn't enjoyed the 4 weeks in 1942. I know that I consider these periods to be among the most pleasurable and memorable of my young life. Why else would I remember them after more than 60 years?

ASHPERTON HARVEST CAMP

Number of boys—26.;   Number of hours worked—5,570.
Total Earnings—£215 5s.;   Pocket Money—£117 2s.

According to the newspapers, the Kent farmers have stated that the boys sent to them for the harvest were "bone lazy," Hereford farmers could not make the same complaint against the Spring Grove boys the who came to their assistance. It was sheer hard slogging from early morning until dusk.

It Wasn't all Work. Three weeks of glorious sunshine spurred everyone to get in the harvest while the going was good, and right well they did it. It wasn't all work; week-ends were free, and then swimming, trout fishing (with or without permission), cycling, rabbiting, &c., were the orders of the day. At least three foxes will not play havoc with the poultry this winter.

One disappointment was met—the late frosts had ruined the orchards, and there was very little fruit to be picked. Fancy Ashperton without plums!

The menu on some of the farms was wonderful after the strict London rationing. One heard of "Eggs always fried in butter," "Chicken between two," "The farmer keeps heaping bacon on to my plate until I have to push it away," "We had real cream and plenty of it," ₁&c.

The month went all too quickly, and many boys decided to stay longer. Four of them took the Government warning, "Keep away from London," very seriously, and stayed long enough to pick hops. Rumour has it that they earned so much that they offered to buy the farm before leaving.

Some farmers have invited the boys to come and spend Christmas with them. One lad, when leaving the farm for home was heard to address the finest turkey in the yard, "Au revoir, old son. Hope to see you later."

Impressions of the Herefordshire Harvest Camp

R Ackary '42

This article was first published in the Spring Grovian magazine; Autumn 1942

T he Herefordshire camp was a great success. Valuable help, which was greatly appreciated, was given to the farmers. We had plenty of physical exercise, since everyone was up to the neck (unwashed) in farm work at all times of the day.

The situation of the camp—Ashperton. The size of the place-negligible. The importance of this inhabited locality can best be illustrated by the following conversation.

Spring Grove Harvest Worker : "Which is the way to Ashperton, please?"

Native : "Turn right, and it's about a couple of miles to the `Box Bush.' "

S.G.H.W. (irritated): "I don't want the `Box Bush,' I want Ashperton."

Native (laconically) : "The `Box Bush' is Ashperton."

Now for general information : Box Bush is not another name for Ashperton or anything of the sort. No, it's just the name of a milk bar, or anyhow we'll call it that.

Sleeping quarters were at the Village Hall, and there we arrived on a sunny Saturday afternoon. The first night found us in rather a jolly mood, and since we were somewhat crowded together, sleep was difficult if not impossible. The next day being Sunday, however, this did not matter very much. Some of us went swimming after finding the river, which needed quite a bit of doing, as its dimensions were rather on the small side. Others went to Hereford or Ledbury, others again to Church. Something which everybody did was to try the cider.

The evening was spent partly in writing home to our dear ones and to our relatives. This was followed by a general sing-song, where we heard for the first time that great composition of E. Sach, namely, "Drinks all round . . ." Space, however, does not permit me to delight you with the various verses of this unique song.

On Monday we started work, but I shall not tell you how to build up a stook so that it looks all right but falls down during the slightest breeze, nor how, if working in a group of three, it is possible for the other two fellows to do the total work without noticing it.

Nor will I tell you how to exchange baskets at convenient moments while plum-picking, nor any of these details which make a farm-worker. Talking about plums, let me warn future generations of farm-workers and give them some sound brotherly advice, namely, "Don't touch them." If this is not enough, consult D. Chaplin, Va. Space again does not allow me to go into details, so I will try to confine myself to the highlights of the camp. Here, of course, Eric Sach springs to mind with his celebrated version of a Roman Emperor of about 20-40 A.D.

Every Monday was pay-day, and we all collected in front of two desks, behind one of which was seated Mr. Hemming, with a book containing the hours worked, and behind the other Mr. Corby (or later, Mr. Davey), with a huge pile of money. The boys, divided into groups of five, received a pound note per group; overtime money, 3D, was paid out in full. The fellows with the pound notes could be seen filing out with a string of juniors behind them anxious to obtain their four shillings.

There was little chance to spend money at Ashperton, except while going to work through Bosbury, where one could obtain last week's newspaper, chocolate, or some freshly-made bread which was still hot and had some unfortunate after effects. The only other chance to spend money was by going to Hereford on Saturdays. Hereford possesses the usual qualities of an English provincial cathedral town : a cathedral of considerable age, a high street with the indispensable Woolworth's, Marks & Spencer's, etc., a pleasant park, and two or three picture houses. Hereford is much the same as any other town except that it is crowded with troops of many nationalities and possesses a river, the Wye, which is conspicuous by the clearness of its water, through which the bed of the river can easily be seen. The countryside, of course, is very different from that of London and the suburbs. There are many hills, and on clear days the Black Mountains can be seen in the distance. There are one or two roads which were built by the Romans, and some of us worked on Bunker's Hill, where many years ago the Romans gave battle to the Britons of that day. The people of Hereford are fortunate in getting considerably better water than Londoners; their water is obtained from Malvern. They speak a weird and wonderful language, the language of some labourers seeming to resemble Welsh more than English. Farm labourers usually have a very limited vocabulary consisting of three words which are very much overworked. `

As we were coming home one Saturday night from Hereford town, a thunderstorm of such intensity overtook us that it made walking and cycling impossible. Very heavy rain continued for hours, interrupted only by thunder and lightning, and before long many fields in the valley were flooded. About ten boys were trapped in Ashperton Railway Station, and got home at about 2 o'clock. Two senior boys, however, were worse off, as they were caught on the Ashperton-Hereford Road; the visibility was soon reduced to practically nil, and so they searched for shelter, which they at last found in the shape of an old barn, not, however, before having spent about half-an-hour in the rain, so that they arrived there wet to the skin, but were lucky enough to find some old sacks which they used for cover. Eventually they a r r i v e d home shivering and infested with a rural odour. One evening, as we were going peacefully to bed, Mr. Hemming announced Matriculation and Higher School results, so that was another night's sleep lost. Evenings were usually spent playing table-tennis, arranging soccer matches that were never played, writing letters, and once holding a debate. At ten o'clock we trooped slowly to bed and proceeded to change apple-pie beds into ordinary ones. Lights out followed at ten-thirty. Having removed our right neighbour's foot from our ear (I mentioned we slept somewhat close together), and stuffed a shirt down the other neighbour's throat to prevent him snoring, we settled down. Peace at last reigned and all was quiet.

THANKS

On behalf of all those who were at the Ashperton Camp I would like, as an epilogue to Ackary's light-hearted account, to extend the thanks to Mr. and Mrs. Evans, Mr. and Mrs. Saznwells, and to Mrs. Richardson and her daughter for their incredibly hard work keeping us fed; to Mr. Hopkins, the W.A.E.C. Liaison Officer, who helped us in every possible way; and to the Ashpertonians in general (especially the Lauries of "Box Bush") for their generous friendship and unfailing kindness.

Bouquets also to Sach and Penton, for catching a deserter, winning much local respect thereby; and to the "workers" themselves for the high spirit of service they showed in putting the needs of the country and of the camp before any purely personal considerations.

James Hemming

Girl Prefects 1944

Back row, - Ena Sutton; Doris Berry ; ? ? ;   Myrtle Atkins; Pam Crook
Front row, - one of the Fox twins? ; ? ? ; ? ? : Jeanne Lewis

Wartime Schooldays at Spring Grove

Tony Young '42

In September 1939 war was declared and schools could not re-open until suitable air-raid shelters were provided. At Spring Grove, these were excavated on the south pitch near to the house and occupied the space used by the girls for their hockey pitch. The football pitch, nearer to the London road was unaffected. The cloakrooms and rooms in the basement were also used as shelters.

For the whole of the first autumn term of the war, pupils attended for one morning a week for an hour or so. This was to receive an assignment of work to be completed and brought back the following week. The main subjects were English and maths and not a lot of ground could be covered. From January 1940 the whole school was in regular attendance. Lessons were often interrupted by the wailing of the sirens and all would traipse to the basement or the south-lawn shelters. This disturbance to routine meant that staff found it difficult to settle a class and continue the lesson in the shelter. There were frequent night-time air raids during the blitz and disturbed sleep in garden Anderson shelters. If the raid was still on after midnight pupils were allowed to come in later the next day, missing the first lesson.

The school survived the lively bombardment experienced during the war years and although a number of bombs fell dangerously near, the damage was fortunately superficial Paper had to be used sensibly and not to be wasted. Red ink was used to highlight an unused line in an exercise book or a whole line used for the date or a short heading or title to a piece of work. Ruling a margin was also frowned on!

Merchant shipping was targeted by German U-boats and this blockade meant that many things were in short supply. Softwood generally was available only on licence. Educational needs had a pretty low priority and manual training lessons (i.e. woodwork) with Mr.Cross (known as Muzz for his likeness to Mussolini) were geared to using small amounts of wood per pupil. In spite of the rationing, shortages, bombing and disturbed nights, life, school and homework went on and the best was made of things.

Many pupils cycled to school. Tyres and inner tubes were in short supply and, when obtainable, were 'war grade' i.e. made of substandard ersatz rubber. New bicycles had no chromium plating on wheel rims, pedals or handlebars. A young Oxford graduate named Mr.Cox who started at Spring Grove in September 1937 left the staff early in the war. There was also much sadness when there was news of any casualties to staff or ex-pupils either by word of mouth or official announcement.

Incendiary bombs could start devastating fires unless spotted and dealt with early. Senior students in the sixth form could volunteer for fire-watching duty and this was an heaven sent opportunity for agile youths to explore the whole of the building and discover places normally out of bounds. Or perhaps enjoy a game of table tennis in one of the basement rooms. The practice was to bed down in the basement and only get up to patrol if there was an alert. It was rumoured that on summer nights James Hemming and his wife-to-be, Kate Klarner, would move their camp beds out on to the west terrace and sleep under the stars.

Overseas school trips to France and Germany were no longer possible but the school organised month long summer holiday harvest camps. In 1942 there was one at Marlow and another at Hereford. These were staffed by our teachers. At Marlow accommodation was in a school, the dormitory in a classroom. Each day pupils cycled out to different farms to help with the threshing or stacking the sheaves of corn in the fields. Poor Miss Bromwich, in charge of the catering, was reduced to tears on one occasion because there was some kind of complaint about the food.

The senior pupils formed a school social club, which provided various after-school and out-of-school activities. The cycling section arranged trips out to the surrounding countryside. Often as many as forty would meet at The Bell on a Sunday morning and wind their way out to the open roads beyond Leatherhead. It was an ideal time to be on the roads because they were so empty. Very few cars because of strict petrol rationing meant that the only traffic likely to be met was the occasional army convoy.

In spite of the rationing, shortages, bombing and disturbed nights, life, school and homework went on and the best was made of things.

There was laughter and cheerfulness which helped to lessen the hardships and difficulties which were experienced by so many.

Formation of Spring Grovian Cadet Force

Spring Grovian - July '42

Spring Grove has now its own Cadet Force. Much to the surprise of everybody, certain members of the 3rd, 4th, 5th and 6th Forms have been seen strolling round the School sporting a complete khaki battle-dress, boots, anklets and all. Also, if you had chanced on certain evenings to enter the School Grounds between 7 and 9.30 p.m. you might have heard the stentorian roar of a sergeant-major's voice, or seen those self-same Cadets sitting, and listening intently to a lecture on map-reading or some such topic. The Commanding Officer is Mr. (now Captain) Corby. So we have now two sources of consolation : we cannot lose the war, and the School is sure to be safe in the event of invasion.

Spring Grove Army Cadet Force

Alwyn Davis '45

The School formed its own Army Cadet Force unit in the early part of the war and it was open to 3rd formers and above to join – boys only, of course. Mr Corby, who I remember taught history as well as gardening, became overnight its Commanding Officer, Captain Corby.

The first meetings (parades) were interesting to say the least with some of the prefects peeved that they had not automatically been made sergeants! In due course our battledress uniforms arrived complete with forage caps, army-issue boots, webbing belts and webbing gaiters – but alas no weapons. We became 'A' Company, 7th Cadet Battalion, Middlesex Regiment and received our Middlesex Regiment cap badges. We were then instilled with some of the regiment's long history from Capt. Corby who was in his element. The exploits of the regiment in the Peninsula War and in particular the story of how they gained their nickname, the 'Diehards' remains in my memory to this day.

Tuesdays, or maybe it was a Thursday – my memory is not really that good – was parade day and we discarded our school uniforms for the day and took on our military garb. Sporting our new uniforms we attended lessons with carefully pressed knife-edge creases in our battle dress trousers, with our webbing carefully blancoed (Khahki Green No 3), our cap badges lovingly polished to a high sparkle, our boots starting to take on a polish acceptable to the RSM - and our hair cut and tidy. We must have presented quite a sight; far removed from that of the usual schoolboys in their drab wartime school uniforms. My recollection is that the girls were totally unimpressed!

The battledress uniform trousers were terminated at the ankles by the wearing of webbing gaiters that covered the upper part of the boot. The trousers were then tucked into the gaiters to form what can only be termed as an inside-out turnup. To ensure that the trousers were overlapping the gaiters correctly it was necessary the stamp ones feet down smartly on the floor. Naturally, it took very little encouragement to convince young lads to go around stamping their feet to make a noise just ensure that they were correctly dressed.

The fun came when, at the end of lessons, on rising from our desks prior to leaving the classroom; we stamped our feet in the regulation manner to ensure our trousers were being worn correctly. The problem, as most of us will remember, was that the school building was wooden-floored and was noisy at the best of times. The 'thunder' created enthusiastically by the Army Cadets, out of sheer devilment and high spirits, made the most of the opportunity of winding up the teachers. The game, however, was short-lived as the staff went into 'black-mark mode' which, in the circumstances, was considered to be not in the spirit of war-time Britain.

Parades were also held on Sunday mornings and who would possibly have believed that we would have been prepared to attend, or even defend, the school on Sundays. On one occasion we took part in an exercise with the Home Guard, monitored we were told by 'two officers from Hounslow Barracks' – we were suitably impressed. The aim was for the Home Guard to capture the old tennis pavilion on the West Pitch and for the Army Cadets to put up a defence to prevent an easy walk-over for the more 'senior' troops. It didn't quite work out that way! We, of course, knew the geography of the school grounds and they didn't, we were faster on our feet and they were not, we didn't play by all rules and they, monitored by Hounslow Barracks, did. Just imagine our sheer enjoyment of creeping through the bushes, jumping over the walls on the West Terrace and generally turning the school grounds into playground without prefects to stop us. In the event somebody had the bright idea that we would declare to the umpires, but not to the Home Guard, that we had 'figuratively' surrounded the Pavilion with heavy barbed-wire. The Home Guard subsequently attacked, oblivious of the obstacle before them, and their action was discounted as ineffectual by the military observers. 'A' Company of the Spring Grove Militia had won! I don't remember the Home Guard ever inviting us again to take part in an exercise with them.

The training had, however, a serious role and eventually some cadets reached the standard where they attended Hounslow Barracks and were taken through their paces by real NCOs and officers. If successful they were awarded a 'War Certificate A' which would, when they joined the army as conscripts or National Service, almost automatically lead them onto a War Office Selection Board (Wasbee) course for a potential commission.

Eventually the Spring Grove Army Cadet unit moved out of the school and formed the basis of a larger unit, under Territorial Army control, meeting in the Drill Hall in Hanworth Road. Thus, to some limited extent, Spring Grove had played a part in the Defence of the Realm during the war – and we had had a lot of fun.

Spring Grove Under V-Bombs

Graham Clarke '45

I am fortunate still to have a copy of my Spring Grove Report Book, as it shows details which I would hardly have been able to reconstruct. It charts my somewhat devious progress through the school, but records all of the staff names as signatures, along with comments.

I say *devious* progress because in late summer of 1938, during a short stay on the south coast, I suffered severe sunburn followed by a devastating skin condition. The only treatment appeared to be a potent chemical TCP (whose full 34 letter name I still know by heart) which was so pervasive that people could not be expected to be in the same room with me. As a result my first term clocked up 68 absences, the second 52, the third 38. My Report for some reason has no entry at all for the last term of 39, which I assume was something to do with the outbreak of the war on 3rd September, though I don't remember the school closing because of it.

I do however clearly remember the first sirens wailing on that day. I was on the way with my brother to Richmond Ice Rink, and along with many others we scuttled underneath the Twickenham Rugby Stadium, and cowered there for some hours, not knowing what to expect. Nothing happened (I believe it was a false alarm), and indeed this was the pattern for most of 1940. Air raids of significance didn't start until after Dunkirk. By this time we all had "Anderson" shelters in our gardens, and most families spent almost all the nights in these cramped quarters. 'Fire-watching' involving two pupils and two staff was instituted at the school, but luckily west London never received the attention that central and east London received. I can still hear the tinkle of shrapnel from anti-aircraft shells hitting the ground as I went about my paper-round and am sorry not to have preserved some of the (still hot!) samples I collected. On one occasion I looked down a 6-inch hole in someone's driveway and, passing there later, found it surrounded by bomb disposal people attempting to extract an unexploded shell!

Previous articles in earlier Spring Grovians have mentioned many members of the staff who taught in this era, and I heartily endorse the high esteem which we had for characters like "Muzz", "Dolly" Ransom, Wally Maylott, the maths. masters George Barrett and "Basher" Brown, and of course headmaster L.T.Brown. Miss Ransom's outings were taken up with enthusiasm, and I clearly remember one to the Youth Hostel at Jordans, where I forgot to take any food or money and was kindly rescued by some of the girls present. She also ran one which I have not seen mentioned, to Ventnor in the Isle of Wight.

Sport was well organised by "Kipper" Hemming. I am not sure if this nickname was universal, or where it came from. It may have been derived from his habit of sleeping on the west veranda during fire-watching, or from a play on his surname resembling "herring". We had football on the south pitch, hockey on the north, cricket on the west, and tennis on the hard courts to the east. There was an outstanding tennis player in our time in Bill Osterburg who qualified for Junior Wimbledon after the war, but had the misfortune to be ill and never got there. I never heard of him in later years.

Discipline in the school never seemed to me to be severe. One or two of the teachers adopted an unusual tactic. Miscreants were told to leave the class and stand outside L.T.B's office. One of three things then happened. a) he never appeared (or wasn't there) and one escaped at the 'bell' with relief, b) he came out rushing off somewhere else and gave only wag of the finger and a scowl, or c) he beckoned us into his office to quiz us on the misdemeanour and suitably chastise us. We all however feared the dreaded Mr.Tomlinson, who taught commercial at the Poly. Occasionally he had classes during the day, and on one occasion was in the next room while we had an English class, held by Frances Gay (a temp?) who was young, pretty, and inexperienced. It took only a few mischievous students to generate chaos and bedlam at her classes. As things reached a crescendo, the door flew open and Tomlinson appeared. An instant hush descended and everyone froze like statues. His satanic eyebrows went down and he growled just two words into the silence- "That's enough", then scanned his steely eyes across the room. Those standing collapsed back into their seats as if machine-gunned. With a nod to Miss Gay he left the room and the class continued in silence thereafter.

By 1943 there had been time enough to recover from my missing first year and passing "G.S.C with Matric Exemption" (as it was in those days) proved not a problem. Then one of those chance happenings took place which can have a dramatic influence on one's future. We had in the school a German boy Willi Fleischer, who I think had escaped from Germany somehow, sometime. He was perhaps a year or two ahead of me, and one day said to me "what are you going to do about being called up?" Conscription at that time was mandatory with few exceptions, and I had not even thought about it. But he had discovered that if one had a guaranteed place at a university in a science subject before one reached 18, then one was exempt! How could this help me? I was already 16 and had two years to complete Highers, by which time it would be too late. His answer was "..jump a year, and then do scholarship work. Go and ask the staff". Hardly believing this would be considered practical, I did so. The answer was to give me much toil. I was told that if I took all the necessary books home for the long vacation, and reappeared with enough groundwork done to enter the second year Highers class, they would let me try.

The class was due to be evacuated to Hereford for the duration of the holiday, where we were to toil in the fields to support the war effort, and be largely safe from enemy action. I well remember how we were billeted in the village hall at Ashperton, near Ledbury with Mr. Hemming in charge. I visited the area a few years back, and it is still there unchanged, as was the village pub down the road.

Here, although not allowed to enter at our tender age, we were often plied with the local cider, which didn't help studying much. There were some odd consequences of studying new subjects alone. In particular I had with me the first book for calculus. This of course makes great use of Greek letters (delta, sigma etc.) and I had no idea how to pronounce the funny symbols before me. Mr. Brown was most amused at my examination on return, when I used phrases like "squiggle x by squiggle y" for differentiation and so forth. He and Mr. Barrett were most supportive and devoted much their free time to coaching me to enable Highers to be completed in 44 and scholarship work to be undertaken.

1944 was Invasion of Normandy year, and also marked the arrival of the V weapons. V1's (doodlebugs) droned overhead and when the engine stopped, dived to the ground and exploded. On one occasion walking back from the Odeon with Rog (no.16 in the photo), towards her home at Osterley, one 'stopped' just ahead of us, and it was with some relief we got back to find it had come down elsewhere. We were never really aware of the V2 rocket at the time, as the current story was always that a "gas main had exploded", though a house vanished in my road in Hounslow undoubtedly as a result of this weapon.

I still have a detailed diary of that year (and that year only) which is quite difficult to read, as not only has handwriting never been one of my strong points, but much of it is in pencil and on now brownish paper. However it is extremely repetitive and the entry for any day can virtually be composed by choosing from a few phrases. E.g. "worked most of day/evening, rang/met Rog /took Buster (her dog) for walk, went to Odeon/Dominion, had/didn't have/ row, happy/not happy". It also records my first interest in photography which came via Alan Burrows (no.26 in photo), a very switched on character whose range included being a member of the Young Communist Party! Luckily Russia was our ally at that time. He introduced me to the Richmond Photographic Society. This derived a huge advantage from the fact that some Americans were members, and they contributed photographic materials which only they could obtain. There were also superb studio facilities, which I used to make portraits of school members, some of which I still have. The diary also records playing chess with David Sobell and Reg Lindall (no.9) which surprises me for I believed until I read it, that I didn't start chess till much later. (It is now almost my only "sport").

Willi Fleischer's scheme did indeed work, and I ended up with a choice of scholarships.

Even so we were all interviewed at Cambridge by military officers who, not put off by the fact the we couldn't be conscripted, asked us to state which service we would have preferred if we had had to choose! The war had ended by the time I got there, and inevitably the student population (and staff!) had a high proportion of servicemen whose studies had been interrupted. They covered a huge range of ages and of course worldly experience. But that takes us outside the scope of the Spring Grovian.

Spring Grovian Ramblers Club

Gordon Harvey '45,
muses on life at Spring Grove in the
immediate Post War years.

I cannot really recall any specific celebrations at the school at the end of the war – though this may, perhaps, be due to my memory rather than their absence. Certainly several of us were in Trafalgar Square for the VE Day celebrations and there were, of course, OSG Dances from time to time in the Main Hall.

A group of us participated in an exchange scheme in 1946 making our first post-war visit to the continent. This was to Amsterdam and we certainly enjoyed the experience and, of course, welcoming Dutch students into our homes and to the school.

After the war too Miss Ransom left for a while to go to Central Europe on relief work – a further instance of her dedication. A performance of "A Quiet Week-end" was given at the School and the proceeds sent to this cause. Some of those on the 1945 class photo on the website were later in this production– I had just left by that time. Incidently the girl on the right of the photo, Jean Harvey, (no relation) came to the school in about the fourth form, I think, and clearly had aspirations to be an actress – she had in fact a lead role in a TV soap some while back. Others in the cast were Sheila Griffin, Eleanor Bilton, Barbara Rothery, Doreen Ellis, Pamela Jones, John Lawlor, Geoffrey Stone, Douglas Benham and others acting and contributing behind the scenes – all in a photo in the 1947 Spring Grovian which I still have.

In December 1946, according to the School magazine, the school leapt into the new technological age and acquired a 16mm sound projector – a far cry from the facilities with which current schools are endowed. The laboratories during the war must have been maintained on a shoestring and it is a credit to the staff that the science courses were successfully provided. Physics courses had magnetism experiments (cheap?) – which could always be frustrated when the less dedicated in class walked round the lab with strong bar magnets up the sleeve.

The Chemistry lab. Bunsen burners were fuelled by coal gas from the gas works at Brentford long since gone. The coal gas was of quite low pressure and it was possible to blow into a rubber tube on a gas point at the back of the lab and successively extinguish all the other burners! Certain resourceful would-be 'chemists' soon discovered the recipe for producing a light powder which produces a loud "crack" when touched. This, associated with the fact that the female staff toilet was situated next to the boy prefects room and the

VIth form room, resulted, on one occasion, in the hasty explosive exit of one unfortunate occupant.

The boy prefects' room was located at the centre of the top floor facing the front. At that time model aircraft, pre-dating the petrol driven upmarket developments, were powered by ¼in. wide elastic "engines". It was found, by certain other 6th. Formers, who shall be nameless, that this material, when stretched across the open window produced an effective missile launcher and thus various items subsequently appeared on the front pitch following a range competition.

Meanwhile I think an OSG Committee was formed and organised various social events with reports in the School Magazine (of which I have a couple of copies) and also produced a paper "The Echo" though I do not know the outcome of this venture.

National Service was of course in force throughout the war and continued for several years after so that was the immediate post school destiny for most of us, effectively removing us from active OSG involvement for a while. It was possible to obtain deferment for a secured University place but for many of us the call-up papers arrived rather more promptly than the university acceptance so, in practice, it was the latter that was, in reality, deferred. Thereafter the effectiveness of our dedicated school study was challenged by such chastening barked comments as "yer minds is all clotted up wiv education yer can't fink straight!". After the initial trauma, nevertheless, most of the more resourceful of us managed to carve a little niche somewhere and were often able, as I did, to go abroad.

A broadening experience unaccompanied by conflict danger was of considerable value before returning to university.

Class 5L 1945

Fourth from the left of the photo is Margaret Martin, later Dr. Margaret Rule who was the senior archeologist responsible for the lifting and preparation for preservation of the "Mary Rose" at Portsmouth.

THE LATE '40s

5

Spring Grove During the War

By Peter Wotton '46

Because of the war, repairs and maintenance at the school were neglected and items such as blackout curtains did not add to the decor. The effects of a bomb which had fallen nearby were evident and I have been told that, in the year before I arrived, the woodwork classroom could not be used. Apparently some lessons were held at the home of the handicrafts master, "Musso" Cross.

However, I was much more impressed by the rambling building with its odd corners, hidden rooms and unexpected staircases and I ignored dirty or peeling walls. Some of the senior boys spent nights at the school fire-watching and I thought that would be fun but the war ended before I got to that stage. In the early days we always carried gas-masks but, as the threat of poison gas receded, it was no longer necessary to carry these. However, we were supposed to bring them to school for inspection on appointed days. I was always forgetting to do that and received black marks and even a detention as a result. Some people still carried the containers but, instead of gas-masks, they held packed lunches.

It was always cold at Spring Grove during the winter. The classrooms were heated by open fires but rationing meant that supplies of the low grade fuel were meagre. During breaks between lessons there was always a scrimmage around the fireplace of students trying to get warm. Education could be interrupted by air-raid warnings when we would move to the underground shelters where the teachers would try to continue lessons while we preferred to play cards or tell feeble jokes. Late in the war came the V1 flying bombs known as "doodle-bugs" with their characteristic throaty roar. One fell in the road where I lived a few seconds after my mother, a Spring Grovian named Johnny Lawlor and I dived under the dining room table. Five people were killed and over fifty were injured but, although our house was badly damaged the only injury was to my face which had a confrontation with some flying glass. After the "doodlebugs" came the V2 rockets which would arrive without any warning. Being British, I thought this was very unsporting as it gave us no chance at all of taking cover.   For reasons unknown to me, there was a news censorship on the rockets and they were not referred to on the radio or in the newspapers. Our joke was that the explosions were caused by defective gas mains. During one lesson there was a shattering explosion when a rocket fell on a factory in the Great West Road. After the noise died away there was complete silence in our class until the tension was released by a voice at the back of the room drawling, "It is about time they did something about those confounded gas mains!"

I remember various VE/VJ celebrations - there was a street party in Priory Road, Hounslow and effigies of Hitler were burnt in Douglas Road, just off Hounslow High Street, and in Murray Park Whitton and elsewhere but I do not remember any events at the school.

Remembering those days and looking at the state of the world one wonders if humankind will ever learn to live in perpetual peace.

Extracts from the First Letter from a German Pen-Friend.

Sent by IRIS BEWLEY, '46? to the Spring Grovian Magazine, 1946.

Last week I received your nice letter, and I am pleased to have you as a pen-friend in England. I hope that through our mutual correspondence I can correct my knowledge of English.

My name is Gert Langer. I am 18 years of age, and I now attend the seventh class of a Secondary School here in Dresden, the capital of Saxon . Next summer I'll finish my training at school; that means that I may take my leaving Exam and afterwards I intend to study at the University.

Our school is like a ruin; it is burnt, has neither glass in the windows nor a roof, and two storeys are destroyed. In winter it is so cold inside that we pupils can't stay in it. During the last two winters our school was closed because of the too great cold and the teaching was removed to a factory because our school had no coal.

I am living in the outskirts of Dresden in a little house. My parents and I inhabit three little rooms. Our dwelling is not greater than fifteen square metres (3 ft. = 0.91 metres). The house stands in a little garden which is covered with vegetables. The greatest part of the population of Dresden lives in such bad flats as we. The whole city is destroyed by bombs. All the houses are ruins and burned. Hotels, churches, hospitals and schools - all are gone. In the outskirts and suburbs are many burned houses too. The population of the city which survived the great air aggression and war lives now in the outskirts. The lodgings in it are crowded.

It is hoped that you have no difficulty in understanding my very simple English. In my next letter there will be more about me and my hard fate. I will also try to give you a little description of our bad food situation and my conditions of living. I am ready to help you in clearing up your doubts about Germany.

Only such a correspondence brings the feelings of the different nations of one another nearer.

The understanding between the youths of the different nations is one of the principal matters to contribute to world peace.

(Form 5 Remove).

Three Little Boys

Phil Marshall '46

Three little boys, Noel Adams, Neville and yours truly on the westbound platform of Isleworth railway station. The first fall of snow of winter 42/43 formed its carpet whilst we had struggled with the afternoon periods; that is what we called the lessons then. We had had fun on the way and now awaited the train for Hounslow, preceded by the chugging steam locomotive goods train some eighty plus wagons long. Nobody ever threw anything at the sacred loco, but the wagons were fair game. We decided to compete, giving the guard's van as many snowballs as we could — no ill intent - just 13 year old boyish fun. As the guard's van trundled into range, we gave it everything we'd got. As it passed and the rear drew level, so the old guard, just like Del's Uncle Albert, came into view resting on the rear rail of the verandah, immersed in another world enjoying his hard earned, and scarce in the wartime years, pipe of baccy. He got a couple of doughboys before we reacted in dread of immediate retribution and stood rooted in fear, but then realising that he was riding gently into the sunset, we curled up with laughter as he waved his fist saying words for which we could only guess the meaning. As we waved him goodbye, so our gaze turned to the eastbound platform where, opposite, two pairs of glaring eyes that were not there before, drilled a hole straight through us. If only the earth could have swallowed us as Miss Saur and Mr Davy transmitted their silent and unmistakable message. I was the one that got ticked off, very nicely, by the gentle Miss Saur, to whom I did not even attempt to explain that we could not possibly have known the guard was out of his cage! In the summer that followed, the loco stopped for the signal at the station. We were admiring the fine beast when the Engine Driver took us on to the footplate and let us have a hand to drive it along to Hounslow. What a gent to make our day and, yes, we raised caps to thank him and his stoker as we jumped off. No, we did not tell him about the guard!

The Muzzery under the watchful eye of Mr Cross (by name and nature) was ruled with a rod of ash, the age of which was hotly disputed. At last, my chance to shine, only to fall at the first fence when red stuff came pouring out of a halving joint in the making. It was a swift plea of guilty there being no chance of a cover up, but at least it gave the lesson a novel twist as Muzz ("Gather round me lads.") demonstrated the art of binding two bits of thumb together. He lived at 246, Nelson Road in Whitton which struck me as a dark and homely abode with all his hand made furniture; french polished of course. Mrs Cross was both a skilled pianist and violinist - they were just nice people with a kind streak.

The first two years at SGSS were misery for me; always bottom of class whilst fumbling to try and get a grip of things. Dative, nominative cases, the Bard with asses and fairies did not make sense to me then or now. Art in a green house, freezing in winter and boiling in summer all added up to doom, relieved only by the occasional visit by the overhead Hun. I had **wante**d to go to Spring Grove Central which was more of a head and hands school, but best parental intentions had put that idea out of reach from the off. Worse, Mum and Dad always referred to SGSS as THAT school so, alongside my own abysmal performance, I had to offer up praise for the school quite unsupported by any academic evidence on my part. One of the best moves made by LT. was the abandonment of class positions for the report book in December 42; this opened a few more channels for ingenious ways to say just how well I was doing as the book was duly signed by my mother; I have a suspicion she was really shrewd enough to know the score.

Third form saw the turn of the tide and the act started to come together both at school and outside. Mr Maylott, affectionately Wally, was the our form master - a real smoothie with the art of keeping us firmly in place in a nice way. Our form room was opposite the physics lab. with the grandiose hearth and roaring coke fire during winter. Edna Cathcart, poor thing, came in frozen to find all the boys hugging the fireguard. She complained bitterly and, sympathetically, I and another sat her up on the mantelpiece. As Wally walked in, we scattered leaving Edna on her perch pretending not to be there. As cool as a cucumber, he said, "Two boys, remove that." Fait accompli.

In reply to the question, 'Why does the jam burn the tongue and not the pastry.' John Stratford put down, 'The pastry has no nervous system.' Wally was not amused even though John was right on the ball.

On one occasion, the whole school trooped down to the Odeon cinema at the end of Harvard Road to see the film Henry V. Cinema managers always seemed to be little fellers with ducks' disease and I can see him now as he took centre stage and, throwing out his chest, announced, "I have pleasure to present to you, Henry Vee." There was an audible titter and my thought was that it was a good job it was not Henry vee eye eye eye.

In the war years if you had a pair of hands and a head, 13 or over, traders and workshops would all but hijack you from the street and the variety of available jobs was without limit. Broadway Motors (arms production), Marriot Scott (lift makers -demoted to making jam boxes for Wm. Poupart and on Sundays you could make anything you wanted using their superb machinery), Stanley Cycles, Post Office Xmas rush, paper boy, grocer's boy, BHS, Board of Trade Osterley (took early retirement there!), to name just a few. I simply enjoyed working, the experience and, of course, the money.

Holidays were in those times austere and the ATC (Air Training Corps) provided joys and a reasonable margin of discipline on operational airfields. I think that the RAF bods were glad to have our younger company and we gofers enjoyed going on training and proving flights with the crews.

It was a time when purchases of tools and simple manufactured goods could only be made with that valuable docket from the appropriate ministry. Toys had to be hand downs or made by resourceful hobbyists using scrap wood or material. Rolls of film were just not made as industry was geared to the armed services only. However, a quantity of cut film was available as RAF cameras had progressed to better things. I made a dead blacked frame to fit in a Kodak Brownie camera, loaded the cut film in the dark room, (ie. blackout curtain drawn) and then took just one photo before unloading in the dark room, developing and fixing the same with bicycle rear lamp and pudding dish technology. The first such picture was that of Peter Wotton posing under our plum tree in the back garden. Thinking, quite justifiably, that it would never work he had put on the most ridiculous grin he could muster. Much to his embarrassment, the picture came out very well and after printing the first 20 or so he asked me to lose them and, being a loyal friend, I did, or maybe there might be just one, somewhere.

It was, I think in 1959, when there was a ceremonial farewell gathering at the School where most of the staff that I knew were in attendance. When it was over, we were chatting and Miss Klarner asked what I was doing for a living (from previous experience, she could understandably have taken it for granted that I would be on National Assistance!) On admitting to being a policeman, James Hemming clutched his jacket and, shrinking rearwards, remarked, 'We shall have to be careful what we say here.' That set the pace for comments about honest and upright teachers that set us on the road to our working life etc etc. The repartee developed with innuendoes to the point that I expressed mock horror and surprise that Miss Taylor could wander from the straight and narrow path; it was the one and only time that I ever saw this lady curl up with laughter. We owe them a lot, but the pity is that we (meaning me) do not take that on board until it is too late to tell them. What would have happened had I gone to Central? Never will know as we just get one shot at life; there is no rehearsal, but for sure, we could not have had a better crew to look after us through that part of the

1945 Election

Dennis Olney '46

Mr Hemming standing for Parliament ? I remember it well. Jim Hemming stood as Commonwealth candidate for the constituency of Carshalton and Banstead. He had a large and battered but gaily painted motor car with his election poster plastered on it. It bore a large megaphone on the roof and was used for announcements at the school sports day in 1945 which was held on Greenhams field. Most amusing for all of us.

Up here in Lincoln we have a public complex known as "The Lawn", originally built in the 1820s as an asylum. It is now a centre for public recreation and contains a restaurant, concert hall, shops, museum and a Banksian room, a large greenhouse for tropical plants which brings back shades of my old Alma Mater.

"M'am, The Baby's Arms and Legs Have Fallen Off!"

Margaret Sears '47

I attended Spring Grove Grammar from September 1942 until October 1947. My first form room was the delightful Music Room. I was in Nelson house, the others being Rodney and Drake. I remember we did spend a lot of time in the brick air raid shelters where lessons were almost impossible as for some time there were only a couple of oil lamps at each end of the building.

"Dinner" was served in the basement where it always smelt damp and musty, watery semolina with a blob of jam in the middle was often served for dessert, also tapioca. I have never liked either of those since!.

I remember Mr May the caretaker walking through the corridors with his red setter Lassie. In the fifth form we had Mothercraft lessons. One of the bedrooms in Miss Bromwich's cottage where we had domestic science was fitted out as a nursery. We had a baby doll which had to be called by name and we took it in turn with a friend to bath her. We did not dare miss out any of the stages as Miss B used to pop in to see how we were doing. Imagine two giggly girls trying to compose themselves to go down and confess very seriously "Please Ma'm, the baby's arms and legs have fallen off". This caused a great deal of merriment for the rest of the class and a lot of relief too as they could not be called upon to bath. Three cheers for rotten elastic. I wonder if Rene Northwood remembers that day.

We also had social club one evening a week after school where we practised our ballroom dancing. A lady who had a dancing school along the London Road did come for a few weeks to give us some lessons but I do not remember her staying the course very long. I think perhaps we all had our own ideas. Sid Reynolds, sadly no longer with us, used to be up in the minstrels' gallery playing the records. Stan Garnet was a great partner for a quickstep and Andy Williams was a super foxtrot partner. Where are they now? We girls were frowned on if we had the slightest trace of face powder or lipstick. Not like today.

I left in 1947 and at the end of term concert that year Ron Daniels and Pat Brown played the Alligator Crawl in the middle of the Ritual Fire Dance to gasps from the audience and the next morning Mr Callow, without a change of expression, played the hymns for assembly when the piano sounded Honky Tonk due to newspaper having been put in it.

After I left school I was an active member of the OSG Dramatic society with Brian Woodruff, Valerie Vidler (Bishop), David John, Pamela Jones, Victor Flexon and others and David Owen became our producer when Miss Johnson gave up.

I was also on the committee of the Old Spring Grovians with Johnny White, John Blandford, Valerie and Les Bishop, Don Cutting and others.

I look forward to renewing acquaintance with old friends at the reunion.

Filtered Memories of SGGS in the Early 40s

David John '47

Recollections of days at school, 1942-1948, are filtered in the memory, yet given substance by the 2004 reunion where contemporaries recall other incidents and schoolboy humour. I remember Basher Brown; an avuncular man and his daily immortal phrase; "Lead on from the front and the back", spoken each day at the conclusion of assembly.

Does anyone remember Mr. Hemming standing for Parliament at the 1945 General Election? He stood for the Commonwealth Party, a brainchild of Sir Richard Acland, a public spirited man with sufficient money to finance what turned out to be a political investment which bore no fruit. There was a notice in chalk in the wooden side door of the hall with the slogan: "Vote for Hemming. There's nothing fishy about a kipper". The uninitiated will need to know that "Kipper" was Mr Hemming's nickname. ....

Mussolini's death triggered a notice on the covered way board. It went something like this:- "Owing to the recent demise of an Italian dictator, it will be necessary to re-invent a name for the woodwork master. Muz is no longer appropriate."

One day, during assembly, Mr L.T. Brown had something serious to bring to our attention. It had been discovered that in the boy's toilets lavatory paper had been festooned, rather like, we imagined, paper chains at Christmas. What struck me at the time was Mr. Brown's verbal emphasis on the word "festooned", surely "le mot juste" for the circumstances.

Since my registration with the OSGs, I have been told of events unrecalled by me. My apologies, in particular, go to a female classmate who has reminded me that I took her to the cinema on more than one occasion, and even sent her my photograph when serving in the R.A.F. in Singapore. Mea culpa and all that!

The school dramatic society occupied much of my attention. Organised and driven by Miss Johnson, I trod the boards in a number of plays, and in "Quiet Wedding" I was able, quite legitimately, to kiss the lovely Heather Gunn as the curtains closed. Miss Johnson was an enthusiast about drama, and she did have the wild eyed look of a Bohemian, prone, poor lady, to the occasional epileptic fit which bothered us from time to time.

Kate Hemming, to me, was an inspirational teacher, and the catalyst which inspired me to complete a B.A. degree at the Open University. I discovered her home address, and then in my fifties, I called at her home in Teddington. Her appearance had hardly changed since school, and she greeted me by name before I spoke. Husband James (Kipper) was summoned, and the two of them made me very welcome. I stayed for one year in the sixth form, where the gentle Dickie Callow tried, unsuccessfully, to teach me Latin. Hardly any of us stayed on that year, and I became friendly with those in the fifth, a year well represented at the 2004 reunion.   What a pleasure it was to return and attempt to recognise people not seen for over fifty years.

Reflections on Spring Grove 1945-1949

Mike Sloman '48

There are some things in life, when looking back, you know you enjoyed, there are some things you know at the time that it is special and enjoyable. My time at Spring Grove was one such time for me. That grand old building, with all its faults, a marvelous staff group led by the greatly admired L.T. Brown, all helped to create that very special Spring Grove atmosphere.

I came late to the school; my early teens' education was severely disrupted during the war years. The School had a number of iconic figures, among them, Sylvia Cheeseman, and Bill Osterburg. Alan McGowan was Nelson House captain; little did I think that I would be following in his footsteps, in three years time. Compared with my previous schools, the staff- pupil relationships and the approach to learning, were very different. The only concession to corporal punishment was 'Kipper's slipper, Kipper being Mr Hemming the PE instructor and the slipper he used to hurry up those who did not get changed quickly enough after games sessions. That stopped when he left after my first year.

The School philosophy was based on trust, opportunity, good relationships, a code of conduct and a quiet discipline, "Hands out of your pockets", "No eating in the street", "Punctuality", "Keep noise levels within reasonable limits" (High spirits were ok but shouting was taboo). Rudeness to others, particularly staff was very frowned upon and yet the heaviest punishment was to report to the head. Standing outside his study was an experience that was rarely repeated - it seems the ridicule of one's peers was a powerful remedy. For lesser crimes staff and prefects awarded detentions. I believe that persistent serious offenders were asked to leave the School, but this did not seem to happen that often - I think L.T.B, would have felt he had failed anyone falling into that category.

The staff commitment to the pupils out of hours was amazing; there were so many activity clubs to choose from, groups of four to twenty or more. The School drama productions were superb and not just restricted to serious works. One memorable variety show with E Hawkins, miming an Al Jolson classic particularly springs to mind. There were many sports opportunities as well when J T Short joined the staff. I can't remember basket ball or hockey for the boys being available until then, but it seemed every day offered another sporting choice, gymnastics, boxing, hockey, cross country, athletics training, tennis.

JT Short (Jim) a Loughborough graduate I think, was an all round sportsman, with as I recall considerable physical courage - I remember him receiving a very severe blow from a wayward discus, and his response was to quietly admonish the field sports group with " please keep your equipment in your designated area". On another occasion at a school swimming gala, he demonstrated a high board dive, missed his take off and hit the side of the pool before entering the water. There was a stunned silence as he climbed out of the water a huge bruise already appearing on his thigh, he went back to the top board and carried out his demonstration dive again, this time without incident.. I always felt that he favoured the potential champions among the pupils, but I have since learned of many examples of his encouragement to the less able pupils, a man to be admired. I have strong memories of the school, even today, I can recall the smell of polished woodand chalk dust, which in that old building was quite distinctive. The slightly damp atmosphere of the Bankesian Room with its smell of Formaldehyde once the dissecting jars were opened. The great old cedar tree with those massive chains supporting the lower boughs. The endless and rather pointless lunch time walks around the school, after having not really enjoyed the meal served in the basement, or a quick dash to the small pie and cake shop opposite the school in London Road. The very noisy Main Hall which was opened when the weather was in inclement. The piano playing duo Widdington.and Browne who gave impromptu concerts on the wet days. They were greatly admired, had their very own fan club, but may not have been aware of it.

The formidable female staff led by Miss Griffin, the Misses Taylor, Klarner (later Mrs. Hemming) Coultard and Clothier, although in reality, each in their own way were sympathetic to their charges. Their severe exterior often hiding a kindly nature or sense of humour. Shakespeare with a broad Yorkshire accent in Bill Lineham's class. Peels of laughter from Dicky Callow's classes (not always appreciated by him) when somebody had tried a practical joke - Mr C was not the strongest on class discipline but for those who were prepared to listen he was a fount of knowledge. The quiet school, shortly after 9 o'clock, then the steady measured steps of L T B, along the long corridor from his study, through the covered way to the main hall. His quiet smile but without any comment when things did not go according to script. On one such occasion Mr. Callow started the first hymn, and the piano sounded like a harpsichord a red faced Mr. C. extracted several sheets of paper from the strings before he could start again. Not a word from LTB.

Staff pupil relationships were close but most seemed to know where to draw the line. However one Monday morning I recall on the main flagpole on top of the tower, there was displayed an upturned jerry-pot and a black flag flying freely, this turned out to be a masters gown. Mr May the school Caretaker (who was always followed by a red-setter dog) was complaining about having to remove the offending objects. The master concerned had not been at the school that long, but his approach to his pupils was overly friendly including a quiet smoke with the boys, out of sight of the main building, with the result that some took advantage. By September that year he had left. I suppose he paid the price.

The school did not seem to produce winning teams but many personalities. At cricket I recall the speed and accuracy of Jimmy Powers bowling, the elegance of Widows batting, the captaincy of my good friend Doug Lygo and the meticulous scoring of David Andrews. The outstanding athlete was, my long term friend, Micky Balls who sadly died at the early age of 60. His very competitive races over 440 yards against Walsh, who's school was that place up the road , were a feature of Middlesex Schools athletics over several seasons. Other athletes of the time were Wiggins, John Blight and Peter Martin. I recall the many hours of training at the Alperton Track of Thames Valley Harriers, for those of us who were to represent the School. The outstanding talent at football was again Micky Balls who later turned professional, for a short time, before following a career in accounting. On the hockey field Martin, Lygo, Hawkins, Hamblin, Crook and Isaac, were all good players. We played together in club hockey in later years. Many O.S.Gs played for Heston Mixed Hockey Club. The school was a constant supply of new players to the club.

In the summer of '48 a group of fifth year boys carried on a school tradition from the war years and attended a harvest camp in East Sussex. It was hard work but great fun. Perhaps it is best if I gloss over the fun part, except to say that the local cider was much more potent than was anticipated.

In my last year at the school, I enjoyed the freedom of being in the sixth form with all the personal space, as well as the responsibility, of individual study. I have many happy memories of the prefects' room on the top floor. It was very small for nine, but it gave status, admittance was respected by all, including teachers. This "private" space was often the nucleus for some abuses of privilege - mostly light hearted, for example, at the time of the general election the social club amplifier was used for political purposes from the top floor window. The broadcast could be heard as far as Greenham's field, the only reaction from LTB was a brief note - "I trust undue bias will not be shown to either party". This was enough to bring an abrupt halt to proceedings. As part of my studies in the sixth, I had the good fortune with four others, to have two tutorials a week with the Head, studying psychology. We all came to appreciate the intellectual stature and the sense of humour of this very kindly man who has influenced the lives of so many of us as we passed through his school.

In the summer of '49 a group led by 'Dolly' Ransom enjoyed an extended holiday in the Austrian Tyrol and Germany. For many of us, it was our first trip abroad. 'Dolly had been working with UNICEF and she was obviously highly respected in the areas we visited. Another valued part of our Spring Grove education.

The school social club was exclusive to the fifth year and above. We gathered in the Music Room on Thursdays after school, dancing to a variety of recorded music; responsibility was with the seniors present. The club had links with Bell Road Youth Club. O.S.G's for many years enjoyed Saturday evenings there, widening their social contacts. Another feature of the social life of the school was the annual Christmas Eve dance which many attended for years after they had left the school. These were happy reunions with traditional singing of carols afterwards at the Milford Arms; the singing always became more robust as the evening progressed.

Much of the above will be familiar to many. I really did enjoy my time at Spring Grove and I do believe, as do many others, that the experience had a real influence on my life.

Send in the Clowns!

A Composite article from three '48-ers reunited at the last reunion.

Exhibit "A" from Colin Tuffield.

Exhibit "B" from Dennis Hoare, aided by Kenneth Munday.

Exhibit "A"...... I first learnt of the OSG association while spending time on the web, and starting with "Friends" gradually found the school site – and spent hours reading all I could find on the site and in the magazine. Gradually more and more information was gathered and assimilated which led inevitably to making contact with several colleagues from the same year, which in turn naturally led to acceptance to attend the 2004 reunion.

Living in Australia since 1964, I had been back to Europe and the UK many times, thanks to my employment with QANTAS Airways, but with so many of my relatives still living in England I had little time for other ventures.......until now!! Although I am no longer with Qantas, I do part-time unpaid work with a travel agency and so still have recourse to cheaper seats.

Having made e-mail contacts with Vera Heath (Newton), Doug Lygo, Rick Holt, Dennis Hoare, Ken Munday (erstwhile head honcho of the Tong Men), Mike Whillock, Hugh Rhys amongst others, numerous electronic messages were whizzing their way around the globe, re-establishing relationships in a way we could not have imagined in our time at school!

Having made my acceptance firm, anticipation fought with nervousness right up until 1 week before, when Rick Holt hosted, with his supportive and ever-patient wife May, a mini-reunion at his home. The excellent company, the memories, the tempting food and mellowing wine soothed the savage breasts - and mine as well! No more hesitation, go forth and enjoy what lies in store.

Cometh the day, cometh the school! What a shock! To see our magnificent school reduced to a shell of its former splendour, and dragged down by the ghastly erections (Too awful to dignify them by "buildings") around it, no magnificent avenues of trees, no playing fields or netball courts. Someone has already written of the reduction in the size of our school by the increase in our years – how true! How sad! However; all is forgiven – we had our reunion, we met, we embraced, we shook hands, maybe a tear or three were shed. We talked, we questioned, we ate and drunk and talked and talked – at times the noise level did remind me of school classes before the teacher made an appearance!

And so the day, my first school reunion, drew all too speedily to its inevitable close and the welcoming hugs and kisses were exchanged for farewell hugs and kisses and promises to meet again soon, not to lose touch again. A memorable, unforgettable day, old-become-new chums, laments for those unable to be there and frequently expressed hopes to meet again.

I have always remembered my old school with fondness and affection; I am not sure now just how I feel having seen it in its horrid modernity, but my memories and feelings engendered over 50 years ago, will always be with me – untarnished and renewed. It would be remiss, having talked of the joys of the reunion not to give thanks to those who did so much to ensure the OSG meetings continue and who give so freely of their time and energy to keep us all in touch and make the meetings the joy they truly are. One memory remains untrammelled and un-bowed by the years and their changes: for me he was and is the stand-out man of my life, the Head, Mr L. T. Brown MA. Always in control of himself and all around him, he possessed an aura that kept me in total awe and admiration, which exists to this day. A great and wonderful man who epitomised the qualities he espoused for OUR school.

It was for me, and I suspect, many others; a magical day – our 48'ers reunion. Thank you for all those who attended, bad luck on those who were not able to make it – as the song "Send in the Clowns" has it:- **"Well – maybe next year"**. **Exhibit "B"**......AH! Memories!! What a wonderful and evocative day the Oc-tober 2004 reunion turned out to be. My first day at school was a nervous one, especially as being "Weeds" we were herded to stand in line outside the tennis court. We subsequently found out this was a prank instigated by a 1st or 2nd form member and was quite unofficial!

On summer afternoons, when the wind was right, the windows of our class-room on the first floor west corner would be opened and the distinctive scent from the Isleworth brewery would come wafting in. This was not a particularly attractive aroma but even now whenever I catch THAT smell, I am transported back over 60 years to THAT classroom.

The South Pitch evokes another particular memory, that of an Autumn after-noon football match, when we played against the S.G. Central School during school time. I can only recall one other team member, Ken Munday, playing at inside left, with me at outside left and I can't quite recall if it was the under 15's or the first team. Now my memory slips into fantasy mode but I'm pretty sure there were hundreds of spectators, the majority being girls and screaming like mad! Okay, okay, let me down lightly please any one of the dozen or so people who were the crowd! I think it may have been their extra detention period, and I think we won!! But we still remember those cheering girls............

At the reunion, we discussed various staff members of our time but I recall Mrs Metcalfe – we didn't get to talk about her. She was our Spanish teacher but I think only for a fairly short time, maybe a couple of terms. I do recall that she seemed to be the answer to a schoolboy's dreams of a teacher – she was always smartly dressed and wore make-up! Someone (and I honestly don't know who) boasted for weeks about the time he had sat next to her on the 657 trolleybus coming to school – even though there were plenty of empty seats!!

Finally, I remember the many lessons we had in the brick air-raid shelters which were situated to the East side of the main building, which prompts this question: does anyone else recall a Summerhouse to the west of the Chem.Lab. or is my memory having yet another "Senior moment"? **"Yeah - make it next year!!"**

10 Wickets for 3 Runs - Memories of a '48er

Vera Newton '48

Attending the 2004 and 2005 reunions brought back many memories. I was not even aware that there was an OSGA until Ken Munday telephoned me and it was great to eventually meet up with him, Rick Holt, Den Hoare, Doug Lygo and Colin Tuffield at a mini reunion in September 2004.

One of the biggest surprises was meeting up with Hazel and Myrtle Smith (the ginger twins!) We were evacuated together in Suffolk and had a wonderful time for nearly four months. No school! I think they did try to get us into Framlingham Girls School but obviously they did not fancy three evacuees from the London area. Not that we minded.

I so enjoyed seeing the old building again despite all the changes that have taken place and some of the faces 1 saw did not seem to have changed at all.

It is strange how selective memories can be. Doug Lygo mentioned, in a previous article, the social club and dancing lessons which I don't remember at all. From my early days I do remember my first nickname - and all that followed were equally derogatory! The first was Idris - who remembers the advert with the squashed lemon sitting on top of a wall? Later it became Battleaxe which upset me a bit as we always used to call Miss Bromwich "Battleaxe", and I did not think I was a bit like her!

In later years several of us used to meet up most Saturday mornings at the Green Parrot cafe in Hounslow High Street for coffee and general chit chat.

I recall being escorted halfway home from school by a certain person (on our bikes) and we would stand chatting for ages under the bridge at Osterley Station before going our separate ways.

When I was in 6C a group of us offered to repaint the old pavilion during the summer holidays, but we spent so much time larking about and puffing on the odd cigarette that we got very little done. Eventually the school got someone in to do it.

Swimming was one of my least favourite activities and Shirley Powley and I regularly used to bunk off home. Unfortunately we had to get by the archway in the netball courts on the way out and one day got caught by Miss Phillips. We were sent to Miss Griffin who gave us detention. She did tell me that she knew Shirley was a bad influence on me! I shall never forget the smell of the hops from the brewery, on the way to Isleworth Baths. It used to make me feel quite sick.

Geography was another bugbear. Following an 'F' for my GSC Miss Richards wrote on my report - a result that was not unexpected!

Everyone now knows how good I am at finding my way around having arrived at the 2005 reunion at 1.45 pm after leaving home at about 9.15 am.. I think I went round Woking, Weybridge and Walton-on-Thames about four times!

Cricket was a favourite and we played many matches, travelling round with Miss Johnson to various schools. I once took 10 wickets for three runs and the boys were very disbelieving and said that all the opposing team must have been blind. Mind you they were not very good and Myrtle Woolley was not playing that day otherwise she would have got most of the wickets - she was a much better bowler. One very embarrassing situation comes to mind. In Five Blue I used to sit right at the back with Shirley Powley and Sue Lomax and never paid much attention in Miss Griffin's scripture lessons. But one day, goodness knows what part of the bible it was, she suddenly mentioned the word fornication and in my ignorance I put up my hand and asked the meaning. To give her her due she gave an explanation but I don't think I heard much of it as the boys were giggling too much and I just wanted to sink into a hole in the floor. Needless to say it was a very long time before I was allowed to forget that.

All in all school days were a wonderful time in our lives although I don't think we always realised it at the time.

Memories of the Social Club in the late 1940s

Doug Lygo '48

In the 5th or 6th Form was the entitlement to membership of the Social Club.This provided music and dancing in the Music Room plus table tennis during the winter on Friday afternoons whilst in the Summer additional pursuits included tennis and cycle rides. The highlight of the year was the Grand Social Club Dance held in the Hall and open to members past and present.

On the surface goodwill abounded but unknown to the rank and file, there were tensions which the extract from the Minute Book shockingly illustrate.

We have been lucky to obtain the following manuscript of the Club Committee meeting.

The minutes of the Committee meeting held in the Boy Prefects Room and reported in THE SPRING GROVIAN - Spring 1949.

The hard-working committee: Lygo, Fletcher, Sloman, Shepherd, Heather Gunn and Vera Newton, and our very keen and efficient Treasurer, Andrews, and last of all the backbone of the whole group you, the members

H. RHYS, Hon.Sec, (Upper 6a).

The Secretary's modesty does not permit him to mention his own efforts, which have been considerable. Many thanks must be accorded him for the smooth running and success of the Social Club Dance, and it was with regret that the

Committee accepted the resignations of Rhys and Andrews, whose Polytechnic studies do not allow them to attend the Social Club on Friday evenings.

D. LYGO,(Upper 6a).

MINUTES OF SOCIAL CLUB MEETING

The meeting opened with Rhys announcing that the minutes book had been lost; an announcement that met with subversive derision. The question of the Social Club Dance to be held in February was the next item on the agenda. The Chairman, Lygo, invited suggestions from the girl members, but was met with such encouraging results that the invitation was withdrawn. From the incoherent hubbub which was steadily rising to a roar, it became apparent that Sloman was proposing something. The challenge was taken up and order reduced to a shambles. Fletcher criticised Shepherd, Shepherd criticised Sloman, Sloman criticised Rhys, and Rhys criticised everybody. The girls banded themselves into a compact and powerful unit and pulled everyone's arguments to pieces. Andrews buried himself amidst pages of figures, while Lygo, after three or four attempts to restore order, gave up and retired to a corner to survey the proceedings.

Shepherd then proposed that the Secretary be reprimanded for not keeping the minutes book up to date and for the Secretary's English style. The Secretary hotly defended his style and made some derogatory allusions to his (Shepherd's) style of English, stating that he (the Secretary) only put down what they (the Committee) said. It was said in the Secretary's favour that he (the Secretary) had been very busy with school work of late and that would account for the defects in recent information. The Committee was still undecided when Fletcher asked the Secretary if he felt he ought to resign, but the Secretary did not feel it incumbent on him to do so.

Vera Newton suggested that the Secretary could not remember an accurate account of the proceedings without taking notes. The Secretary interpreted this as a challenge and accepted it with alacrity, giving his reason for not taking notes as having no time to argue with the others if he did so. The business concerning the Secretary was then dropped.

As there was no other business, the swains and wenches went their various ways.

(Signed) D. G. LYGO,(Chairman).

Note to the Secretary.

Would the Secretary please draw up, in future, minutes which are worthy of the fine tradition of the Social Club Committee?

D. G. LYGO.

Spring Grove Recalled

Daniel Goldblatt '48.

In August of 2005, motivated by nostalgia, I made the return journey to Spring Grove. The occasion was my first annual OSG Reunion. There was the old building as I remembered it, now vandalized by the addition of a hideously out of character modern block. Through half closed eyes, the graceful lines of the old red brick Georgian building were there to admire, while inside for rediscovery were the majesty of the panelled Main Staircase, the elegant Music Room where I took my General School Certificate examination all those years ago and the wonderful Conservatory, once the Art Room presided over by the talented Miss Walters. Hidden behind the new building was the old Summer Pavilion, now designated as a Store Room. I remember a large fountain stood nearby, now sadly gone, no doubt to make way for the new addition.

Scattered in groups around the Music Room and Conservatory were the elderly OSG's, dignified and courteous in polite conversation; perhaps I chose to see a mirror of myself in them. Back came a flood of memories of years long past; those unsophisticated but uncomplicated post-war years of austerity when our hopes and aspirations were unlimited and our horizons seemed boundless. The Russian Dynamo football team coming to England and the crowds chanting "Zatopek, Zatopek" at the Wembley Olympics and the horrors exposed at Belsen and Auschwitz were all of that vintage.

What other memories? Sports Day at the playing fields across the London Road, of Speech Day at the end of the Summer Term with the stately procession of the teaching staff, all bedecked for the occasion in their coloured academic hoods and the school, singing in unison " Lord dismiss us with thy blessing, thanks for mercies past received …".

Perhaps a more poignant memory for me happened a few years earlier when a chance snatch of music overheard on the radio and I was transported back to 1947 and once again I was a schoolboy, seated at my desk, with the warm sunlight streaming through the open wisteria framed window, and the lilting strains of the school choir rehearsing from somewhere below the Gavotte from Thomas's Mignon in preparation for the Summer Concert. How evocative music can be!

And, stimulated by the surroundings, memories return of the truly committed staff of teachers to whom we owe so much. Mr Lineham who taught English. Miss Griffin French, Mr F W Brown Maths, Miss Taylor History, Miss Richards Geography, Miss Nash Biology and the omniscient Mr Callow who taught almost anything. How much we owe them for their dedication and patience in imparting to us the joy of knowledge and of learning and for the preparation they gave us for the challenges that our futures would present. I miss them all.

The Three Virgins

Tony Fletcher '48

WARNING: This article has been given a 'C' for Caution rating because it contains sex, violence and bad language. (That should get 'em reading!)

1945 was a memorable year. First, there was VE Day, then there was VJ Day and then there was the Day I was frog-marched from a macho all boys school in Birmingham down to the dear old Black and White. A culture shock of the first order to the extent that, by morning break on the first day, I decided that No way, Jose, am I going spend my tender, formative post-puberty years under the influence of a gaggle of giggling school girls. Sorry, girls, but that's how I felt at the time. Mind you, I was a bit young. As it happens, I couldn't have been more wrong, especially about the 'giggling school girls' bit., as I soon found out the first time we played them at hockey. Their understanding of 'Sticks' was anywhere below head height. I'm still in therapy.

Then I thought, Hang on, Jose, look on the upside. First, I wouldn't have to dance backwards at music lessons. Then I wouldn't have to play Principal Boy in the school panto and wear those oh-so-tight tights. Still brings tears to my eyes just the thought of it. Put 'em on and it was 'Oh for the wings of a dove'. Get 'em off and it was 'Old man river.' But, above all, whereas up there all we talked about was the 'F' word, down here we debated the more important issues in life -($E = mc^2$, the 'Big Bang' theory, 'Do you think this makes my bum look bigger? -everything under the sun except 'football'. So I decided to give it another 24 hours, which turned into 26280 hours, give or take.

Bearing in mind that senility is setting in, let's see what else I can remember. Oh, yes... One of my first ambitions was to become a Thespian. I saw myself as another Laurence Olivier but with a Brummie accent. 'To be or not to be. That is the question, our kid.' Different! So, naturally, I jumped at the chance to play the lead shepherd in the school nativity play. Comes the time for my one and only, make-or-break line, "And, behold, they saw a great light..." and all the bloody lights fused. Scout's honour! No more Thesianing for me.

Oh, and I'll never forget that ridiculous school cap the boys had to wear - black and white triangles with, of all things, a silver tassle in the middle. The things we used to do with that tassle. Twirling it clock-wise, counter-wise, every which way. Reminded me a bit of an act I saw in some night club, but no more of that except to say I've never seen a woman with such muscle control on either wing.

Even now, whenever I get saddle-sore, I think back to those Sunday bike rides we used to go on. We went everywhere, man, - Box Hill, Devil's Punch Bowl and Leith Hill with its Silent Pool. Funny name for a pool, 'Silent'. I mean, I've heard of a raging river, a roaring waterfall, a babbling brook, but I've never heard of a noisy pool! Makes you wonder how they found it in the first place. "Shush!". "What?". "Thought I didn't hear something". "Must be The Silent Pool".

But one of my fondest memories was of those lovely ladies, Miss Coulthard and Miss Barr, known affectionately as the Little and Large of Academia. Miss C, BA (Oxon) taught French and had this ambition to be the first to get someone from the B & W to Oxford and I drew the short straw. I say 'short straw' because, having seen the film, 'The Confessions of...' all I wanted to be at the time was a window cleaner. Anyhow , all credit to her, I just scraped in. 'Course, I was pretty fluid with my 'la plume de ma tante', 'Frére Jacques' and 'Auf Wiedersehen, Pet' but I think what really swung it was that I was a bit of a dab hand at tennis.

Remember the old tennis court hidden way back in the backwoods and the games we used to play, including tennis? Just between the two of us, I was the first to invent that shot where, with your back to the net, you hit the ball back through your legs. Get it right and it was a match winner. Get it wrong and...but I don't want to go down that road.

But now, fasten your safety belts 'cos here's the bit you've all been waiting for -The Three Virgins. It all started when John (Wilf) Coppin and I somehow conned our way onto a summer course at the University of Grenoble, where, from our window just a spitting distance away, you could see these three mountains, all in a row, which were called 'Les Trois Vierges'. And the reason they were called 'The Three Virgins' is 'parceque aucun homme ne les a pas monte'...'til now.   For the Spanish and German class pupils... : 'because no man had mounted them'.

Well, I looked at Wilf and Wilf looked at me. A nod's as good as a wink! So, next morning after a bit of a lie-in 'cos we wanted to save ourselves for the 'mounting' bit, we set off at the crack of noon with flip flops and packed lunches.

As it turned out, it was a tad more than the spitting distance we first thought because by sunset we hadn't reached base camp. But, being British, we decided to soldier on and, if needs be, do our 'mounting' bit in the morning.

So there we were, just about to breast the last of the foothills and thinking to put our feet where no one had put theirs, when what did we bump into - a bloomin' bus stop.

Well, (TEETH CHATTERING), I said to (Wilf), aW..W..(W..Wilf), h..h..here we are, f..f..frozen s..s..stiff, s..s..starving, f..f..foot-sore and k..k..knackered. W..W...What do you r.r.reckon?" And, quick as a flash, (Wilf) said, "B..B..BLEEP IT)" So, we caught the last bus back. No excuse, but there are more things to life than mounting just mountains.

There again, having said that, little do those 'Trois Vierges' realise how close they came to having to change their name to les Trois Madames'.

A 66 Year Old Mystery Solved

John Blight '49

I have always believed that I had astounded myself and my junior school teachers by gaining a place at Spring Grove by achieving the necessary standard by passing the Scholarship examination; later known as the 11 plus. How wrong was this belief!

Recently, while researching my family history, I came across some relevant documents that destroyed this belief. In reality, I had been awarded a special place at a secondary school by the Middlesex Education Committee in accordance with their General Powers Act 1838. A clause was included which explained that special places were not a scholarship and that a fee of £15-0-0d per year was required towards the £40-0-0d year that was usually required. A further stipulation was that my father had to sign an undertaking to keep me at school at least until the end of the school year in which I attained my 16th birthday. Failure to comply could result in a fine of £15-0-0d. A provision was made for financial assistance towards the annual fee.

My father applied for this and had to submit a financial statement of the family's gross income per year on the form supplied, together with the number of wholly dependant children in his care. Applicants could identify if they qualified for the assistance by reference to a chart where consideration was given for salary bands rising from £275 TO £775 (in increments of £50), and a family having from 1 to 6 children. From this my father was not liable to pay towards the cost of my education because he was supporting a family of 3 on an annual salary of less that £375.

This was confirmed in July 1944 on an agreement form confirming the allocation of a special place for me at Spring Grove Secondary School – soon to become Spring Grove Grammar school under the 1944 Education Act. How lucky was I and how many other pupils were fortunate?

I think that I justified my place by obtaining 4 credits and a 2 passes in the General Schools Examination of 1949.

In 1944 I was the second member of the Blight family to benefit from an education at Spring Grove, having followed my uncle Anthony George who left about 1930. My sister Janet was next to start there in 1950 followed by twin cousins Gwendoline and Margaret in 1956.

Others followed after the school relocated to Lampton in 1959. My cousins Kathleen started in 1958, followed by Elizabeth in 1961 and Shirley in 1963, making a total of 8 – can any other family beat this?

Frank Pinch and Willie Fleischer '38

Alan Pinch '49

I am grateful to Heather Gibson (nee Campbell), a childhood friend, for putting me in touch and suggesting that I should receive your newsletter. I was the youngest of a family of three children, all of whom went to Spring Grove. I was pleased to hear news of old acquaintance. But it is not of my own time at the school that I want to write, but rather of my brother, Frank Pinch (1923-1944). He was nearly ten years older than me, and lost his life in an RAF raid on central France on the night of 7-8th May, 1944, a little while before I entered the school. If any of his school friends read these lines, I would like to tell them that a very vivid account of his last years - his own account in letters home to us - still exists. Frank was a bright, idealistic young man with wide interests and an ambition to write. He described vividly and in detail how he dealt with a bomb which narrowly missed our house (while Dad was absent), how he entered the RAF as a volunteer, his brief studies as an airman-student at Southampton, his training in Canada, the experience of flying and many person-alities he met on the way. In 1990 I produced an edited version of these letters, preceded by a brief essay on our family history. I did not offer it to a publisher, but had plenty of copies made privately for family and friends. If any of Frank's school friends want a copy I shall be very happy to supply one free of charge. (I gave a copy to Hounslow Public Library at the time).

Willi Fleischer, who is mentioned on page 7 of issue 6, was a friend of Frank's, and kept in touch with our family for some years afterwards; I can give some information about him. He definitely did not enter Austrian politics. Because he was Austrian the British army ignored his gifts and enrolled him in the Pioneer Corps, where many talented Europeans classed as "enemy aliens" had to dig trenches, since, very unfairly, a slight suspicion hung over them. Willi had a talent for science, and graduated, I think in physics, from London University, and went on to post-graduate study. He married a girl called Eileen Forbes, and, wishing to distance himself from antisemitic Austria, adopted his wife's surname. Those who wish to trace him might do worse than look through our science faculties for a Professor William Forbes. Willy was both talented and energetic, and is highly likely to have ended up in a university chair. My sister, Evelyn (Evie or Eve), unlike me a popular and social figure in the school, died suddenly in 1990 just before I could give her a printed copy of the letters she had cherished for so long. She married twice, but had, alas, no children. In later life she suffered more than her share of ill health. From being the carefree belle of the fifth form she became a very serious and dutiful woman.

We change, don't we? It is a very strange experience for me, still at heart the adoring kid brother, to read those letters which breathe the spirit of youth, and wartime 1940s youth at that, when I have been given so many more years than my wonderful brother had.

To Hire This Bus

Brian Tilbrook '48

I was so sad to leave Spring Grove in1948 to go to Art College that I did a complete and lingering walk around the whole establishment – talk about a heavy heart! I came back much later as qualified art teacher and met up again with Mr. Brown who was exceedingly welcoming. I had lunch with the staff, explaining with regret to Jim Short that St Nicholas only played rugby.

I had other links with some of the staff from doing the illustrations for what I think was Kipper Herring's first book through to regularly visiting Miss Walters for whom I had lasting affection. It was one of the great delights for my three children to visit Miss Walters in Suffolk and spin round on her revolving gazebo! Sadly as she was dying the message reached me too late to be there. She lived alone, was famous in the village for her pony and trap and sadly lost the company of Miss Bromwich soon after retirement from Spring Grove.

I also have a very vivid memory as a first or second former using the boys' toilet, a converted stable, when Miss Griffin strode in to lecture us on graffiti. Quite what she expected us to do as we stood there performing none of us were quite sure.

I have another strong memory of contributing to the school out of class activities by the back drop and scenery for "Twelfth Night" – one of Miss Johnson's excellent productions. It was notable for Malvolio coming through the door – and the door following him.

The ultimate "joy" was in the final scene. I had used London Transport bus indicator blinds to paint on. All went well until the caretaker, a large man who sold delicious buttered buns at break, switched on the outside lights. In the final magic moments of Twelfth Night the audience could see clearly repeated in the sky:-

"TO HIRE THIS BUS"   "TO HIRE THIS BUS"!

'47ers
Peggy Leake,
Marie Pryke and
Peggy Dansie
In 1946

Magic of Spring Grove

Judy Abbott '49

When I read other people's accounts, or speak to them about experiences at Spring Grove, I cannot help being struck by the feeling that the school seems to have had a 'magical effect' on us all.

Was it the building? When I enter the house, or look at pictures of it, all the happy memories of being there, in formative years of my life, come flooding back. There was no other school in the area that had those distinctive, atmospheric surroundings to learn in. That wonderful staircase and entrance hall, the elegant Music Room, the Art Room, the Banksian Room, - Miss Bromwich's cottage!

Was it the staff? So many amazing, dedicated characters, all determined, each in their own way, to teach their subject to the highest standard possible. I remember Miss Bromwich, she was my first form (1 Blue) mistress, rather daunting, in her long black dresses and the 'bun', but kind to anyone in trouble. Domestic Science in her cottage was 'something else'! Those block paper patterns for pyjamas that we girls had to make - very un-glamorous! And, I will never forget the stew we made in a double lesson and took home in jam jars. My poor dad very heroically ate every last mouthful.

Miss Walters, the art mistress, was a very quiet, gentle lady. I enjoyed the lessons, but didn't think of myself as an artist in those days. However, something must have rubbed off, as I ended up teaching pottery at one time and am now (in retirement) getting hooked on water colour painting and drawing.

I have grateful memories of 'Basher' Brown (I don't know how he earned that name, he always seemed a kind man to me) and Miss Richards, guiding me through the intricacies of mathematics. Other teachers that come to mind are 'Dickie' Callow (geography), Mr. Frid (chemistry), Mr. Maylott (physics), Mrs. Holman (biology), Mr. Featherstone (Spanish).

Then, there were the English teachers, Miss Johnson and Katie Klarner (she married Mr. Hemming), who introduced us to the niceties of the language. My love of singing was nurtured by Trevor Owen (Jones). I remember singing in productions of 'Merry England' and 'Hiawatha's Wedding Feast' and joining the 'Trevor Owen Singers' when I left school. Many years later, I joined another choir and met Mrs. Holman who had retired by then, but was still singing alto. She played the piano for the performance of 'Hiawatha's Wedding Feast'. I also met up again with John Short (sports master), when I started my teaching career. Or, was that 'magic something', all down to that wonderful, progressive headmaster L.T.Brown? Who led his staff and the pupils in such a way that everyone wanted to do well and be proud of the school.

What ever that magic was, I hope it still exists for the children who now attend Lampton School. Although, I was so glad that the powers that be did not get around to building the new school until well after I left Spring Grove; and I know those in my year all felt the same.

Recollections 1945 - 1950

Peter Hatcher formerly Barringer '50.

My transition from primary to secondary was not as smooth as I had anticipated, probably because of the change in status from being one of the senior children at the primary school to being one of the "weeds" as the first formers were called by the higher forms. Particularly those in form two who had so recently escaped the weed tag. There was also the change in the way the lessons were conducted. In the primary school one teacher taught all subjects and in the new environment we had different teachers for each subject. Some classes such as art and the sciences were conducted in rooms dedicated to that particular subject. If the truth be known I was also missing the friendships I had established at the previous school. The secondary schools took their students from a wide area of the County of Middlesex so children from different parts were thrown together in a strange environment.

After a month or two things settled down and the new subjects such as languages, German in my case, algebra, geometry, physics, chemistry, etc all presented their own challenges. Our form 1 Blue was located in room 4 on the ground floor overlooking the West Terrace. The form teacher was Miss Bromwich a rather formidable lady in the 50 to 60 years old bracket who lived opposite the school with the Art teacher Miss White. Miss Bromwich was the Domestic Science teacher and ruled her cottage in the grounds like a sergeant major. Her only role as far as I was concerned was to keep the class records for form 1 Blue and she also conducted the assembly for two of the first forms. This was done in the music room which was not so called because music was taught there, but that was the original purpose of the room when the house was built. The room was quite large and had a minstrel gallery above a very ornate fireplace. The gallery was out of bounds but that only made it a more attractive place to explore.

The ground floor of the house was very lavishly appointed and was not designed for use as a school, however, it gave the place an ambience that would have been entirely lacking in a purpose built school.

The entrance hall with the magnificent staircase, carved balustrade and parquet flooring had several oak doors giving access to the headmaster's office, classrooms 2 and 3 as well as the front and side entrances. I believe that this part of the building has been restored in recent years. The head was Mr LT Brown, he was a very competent and erudite leader of the school community who was held in the highest respect by all of the people I met whilst at Spring Grove. This compliment comes from someone who had to present themselves to him on one or two occasions for behaviour prejudicial to good order and school discipline.

The period immediately after the Second World War was a time of upheaval whilst the country was in transition from a war-time environment to one of peace. Not the least of these changes was the demobilisation of the majority of the services. This meant that many people were returning to their pre-war occupations. Amongst this group were teachers and it is hard to imagine a greater contrast from being in the services which were involved in fighting a war to administering a classroom in a government school. This situation created tensions all round; some female teachers who had been teaching to overcome the almost total absence of males from the teaching profession felt that their prospects were jeopardised by this influx of returned service person-nel. The returned people also had great difficulty in adjusting to civilian life from a situation where irrespective of rank you were in a very strictly control-led environment to one where all the decisions were on your own shoulders. Among the general populace there was an expectation that after the war everything would be rosy, the sun would shine, food and housing would be freely available and everyone would be prosperous. The reality was very different with food and petrol rationing sometimes more severe than when the war was in progress, housing was in short supply both due to the bombing and the fact that none had been built during the previous six years and the economy had not changed to peacetime conditions as quickly as people expected.

The point of this is that we were subjected to numerous teacher changes during our schooling which did not give much continuity of instruction. As an example for German we started off with Miss Ransom who got us off to a good start with her enthusiasm. She left to assist in the massive task of looking after displaced children in continental Europe as a result of the war. She was followed by a succession of teachers some of whom stayed for such a short period I cannot recall their names. Some were ex army officers who found controlling children a lot more difficult than issuing a few orders knowing they would be carried out. The situation in this subject reached such a low ebb that the headmaster took some of the poorest performers to try to overcome the lack of progress. I was one of these students but I did not manage to reach a satisfactory level. That is probably due to my lack of motivation as well as ability, motivation because a common feeling was that German was the last language one wanted to use.

I must have had an aversion to languages as the English teacher, Miss Johnson and I crossed swords constantly with the result that I did not spend much time in her classes, usually being told to leave shortly after the class commenced. The results of this depravation are probably already apparent to the reader but it is still my view that she concentrated on her interests rather than the syllabus. There was therefore an over emphasis on drama and literature and almost none on grammar or sentence analysis with the result that my writing is much worse than my reading.

All this must sound very negative but some of the teachers were inspirational with Miss Richards for Geography and in the early forms, Mathematics. I can still see her demonstrating positive and negative numbers by using the corner of the front desk and stepping forward for positive and backwards for negative when I was in first form. She had a very systematic teaching method and often had projects for us to complete. I managed to get one of my few gold stars for getting four "A" ratings in succession for some maps of Africa showing various features of that continent. In later years Mr. Barrett who taught the Beta group for mathematics encouraged me greatly with some of the higher mathematical concepts with which I was having considerable difficulty. He instilled a sense of self-belief and the knowledge gained in his classes stood me in very good stead with my future studies of electrical theory. The only fault I can find is that the applications of these mathematical processes was almost never discussed but was presented as something to be learnt without any reason why it might be useful.

One of the other teachers was Mr Maylott who taught Physics and with considerable ingenuity managed to demonstrate many of the concepts being studied. I think I was a bit of a surprise to him as he singled me out as being one of the better performers at the pre General School's Certificate examination conducted prior to sitting for the real thing at the end of Form V. I was disappointed by his professed low opinion of my potential but gratified that he recognized that some students are not what they seem on the surface. Mr Cross who taught manual instruction and his successor Mr Pollard along with a Mr Corby who taught nature study and other homely topics were three of the staff who did not possess University qualifications, but that did not stop them being some of the most commonsense people on the staff. I think in all three cases they had had the corners knocked off in the University of Hard Knocks. I am not sure about Mr Cross but both Messrs Corby and Pollard had served in the armed forces, Mr Corby in the army in France during the First World War and Mr Pollard on Russian Supply Convoys in the Navy during the Second. If those experiences did not make one grow up then you never would.

Miss Taylor was a very effective history teacher, which is quite an achievement, when history had such a low oomph rating amongst school children. She was quite often late for class and the inevitable rowdy behavior would be interupted by her arrival announcing that we were not fit to live in a democracy. Hence her nickname, at least in our class, of "Miss Democracy". I still remember the lessons on Sir Robert Peel and the Corn Laws to this day, so she must have done something right.

The woodwork room was often called the "Muzzery" which was a play on the nickname of Mr Cross which was Muzz and probably a corruption of misery as we called these sessions misery in the muzzery. This was not because it really was miserable but it was fashionable to claim it was. The power of peer pressure made it unwise to go against the accepted opinions.

'Horses Hooves and Matter'.

Stan Sach '46

Amongst my many happy memories of Spring Grove during the war years, was one of Headmaster L.T. Brown. Moscow Dynarno had arrived in England to play a friendly against Chelsea at Stamford Bridge and of course many of us sporting boys dearly wanted to see them (no television), so on the day, there were quite a number of empty desks for the afternoon periods. Next day, I was in a class being taught by L.T. himself and at the start of the lesson he said he hoped the boys had enjoyed their afternoon and found it worthwhile. He knew, as we did to our cost, that we saw very little of the match as fog obscured about two thirds of the pitch His remarks came from behind a very understanding smile. Nothing further was said.

Taking the odd afternoon off clearly is no new phenomenon as I recall a couple of occasions in the depths of winter, going with John Parslow to Osterley lake on of course the Osterley Estate. In really cold weather the lake froze over, and being a private lake, was the ideal setting for some serious speed skating. Both John and I had ice hockey skates and with a stretch of well over a quarter of a mile, we had a wonderful time, always that is, keeping a very weather eye open for the game keeper who was not averse to emptying one or sometimes two barrels of his shot gun at the disappearing rear of trespassing boys.

John Parslow lived above his father's shop in Heston Rd. Heston, where Mr. Parslow Snr. plied his trade as a cabinet maker etc. and John like his father was a very good worker of wood which made him a firm favourite of 'Muzz', Mr. Cross the woodwork master.

Of all the characters who taught at Spring Grove, Muzz was probably my No. 1. With his "Gather round this bench lads" when he wanted to impart something of general importance, more often than not, after he had seen a boy using a sharp tool in a less than safe manner. He would regale us with stories of how the last boy that had done that, had run the tool straight through some part of his body, and he described in detail all the blood and gore and how he had had to tell his parents how their son had ended up in hospital. The woodwork room always had the pleasant smell of sawn and planed timber, with the additional smell of 'Scotch glue' which Muzz frequently told us was made from 'Horses hooves and matter'. I never recall any punishment being meted out by Muzz, but we were always under threat of receiving a piece of four by two round our backsides !

This of course was war time, and as well as wood being in short supply for us boys to use, so was food, so one afternoon Muzz, who had managed to get a rabbit, sought to educate us in the art of skinning it. Fortunately, the lesson was conducted outside the woodwork room on an old bench, for whilst the skinning went according to plan, the next part of the operation, that of 'gutting' the animal was less successful. Muzz, using a sharp knife, managed to cut into the intestine and the stench was appalling, sending all the boys back inside to the more pleasant smells of scotch glue and wood, and leaving an embarrassed Muzz to clean up his smelly rabbit! I don't know what today's educationalists would have made of it but I still hold my wood working tools correctly as Muzz taught.

1946-7 Prefects
Sent by Margaret Sears (1947)

You'll find me in the contact list under 1946. I was Head Boy in 1947-8 as well as cricket captain in that year. I've recently been looking through a lot of old photos and came across 1946-7 Form 6A. I sent a copy to Peter Wotton who was in the same class as me. His reply to me was as follows: "Thank you for sending them. Apart from Mr Barrett and yourself, I have identified Andy Williams Keith Dennis, David Escudier, Alan McGowan and (I think) Pip Bono,Roy Jones and Ray Daniels. I cannot quite make up my mind whether Dennis Olney is in the photo. Amongst the girls I have placed Sylvia Cheeseman, Jean Davidson, Doreen Knott, PamJones, Daphne Smale and (I think) Molly Lambert and Doreen Leach. There were two identical twins Hazel and Myrtle Smith and one of them is in the photo."

I've also recently made telephone contact with two of my classmates, Andy Williams and Keith Dennis, who are both now in USA. Maybe they could be persuaded to contribute their life stories to the magazine. My story is pretty straightforward, I graduated in Mathematical Statistics at Imperial College in 1951 (Keith Dennis followed the same course the year after me) and worked for the same employer as a Scientific Officer in the Civil Service all my working life. I moved up north to Sheffield, working at the Safety in Mines Research Establishment. This later became the main research laboratory of the Health & Safety Executive. My speciality was spark ignition of flammable gases and the safe use of electrical equipment where there is a risk of explosion. Then in 1981 my part of the laboratory was moved to Buxton where we've lived ever since. Hope you find this of some use for the SGR.

David Widginton

1950 - 1955

6

Reading My Reports

Pamela Griffin '50

Having read with interest all the previous copies of the O.S.G. newsletter, I decided to put pen to paper and share some of my memories of my years at Spring Grove (1946—1950)—a very mixed bag I must confess! I had spent one year at Glendale Grammar School at Wood Green, when my parents decided to move to Cranford because of my Father's work. It wasn't easy changing schools at that time as everyone had made their friends during their First Year.

My Form Master was Mr. James Short, who I seem to remember was the P.E. Master. One of my memories is of standing up in front of class and opening my mouth as wide as possible to demonstrate what an "aperture" is. I was not amused! I seem to remember that lunches were served in the basement, and that our way of dealing with the bullet-like peas was to have a game of hockey with them!

I was looking through my report book recently—I don't really know why I've kept it, as it' s not something of which to be very proud! My Maths teacher, Mr Barrett,must have despaired of me and I quote some of his comments:

1)"Showing some awakening of ability—may yet surprise herself". 2) " Is a source of distraction to neighbours". (I don't think my parents were very amused at this!)   3)Still a long way from Pass standard, but is not hopeless. 4) General Schools Exam.B—This represents a very good performance. Well done. Thank YOU Mr. Barrett.   One of my better subjects was French and I owe a great debt of gratitude to Miss Coulthard who helped me achieve an A.

Other brief memories come to mind:

1)Domestic Science, taught in the cottage, by Miss Bromwich. One famous day we were making pancakes. One poor girl, who was left-handed was told to use her RIGHT hand—with disastrous results!

2)"Mothercraft classes"—having to bath a rubber doll which "leaked", caused much hilarity!

I do have very happy memories of lessons in the beautiful Art Room with Miss Walters.

Another occasion to remember was a concert performance of Edward German's "Merry England" directed by Mr. Jones. I think it was possibly partly due to him that I became a music teacher.

I also came across a certificate reminding me that in 1950 I broke the record for Senior Girls throwing the cricket ball—162' 6" Not much of a record by today's standards I'm sure! I remember many happy games of tennis with Beryl Whittaker. Does anyone remember the school uniform? It really was quite attractive I think -a mid- blue gym-slip with buttons on the side, a blazer of the same blue—BUT those awful hats! In the summer we wore blue and white check dresses which could be made to your own pattern-—within reason I'm sure!

The Remove Classes

Tony May '50

Mr. Odell, Headmaster of Spring Grove Central school, walked into 2A's history lesson one afternoon and after a brief, quiet word with the teacher he addressed the class. "Hands up all those of you who would like to be teachers." I cannot remember how many hands went up, but mine didn't. However for the rest of the afternoon I thought hard about it. I was well aware that my friend John, a year older than me, had experienced something similar the previous year and had been transferred to Spring Grove Grammar School. The Central, a selective school half way between an Elementary (later called Secondary Mod) and a Grammar school was alright but lacked the reputation of the "Black and White" as SGGS was known. I was a bit young to commit myself to a profession at that early age. They could hardly hold me to it. So after school I went to see Mr Odell and told him I would like to be considered. A short while later my parents received a letter from Mr L. T. Brown inviting me to interview at SGGS. My father accompanied me. I was impressed with the ambience of the place. What a difference compared with the Central school just down the road, stained glass windows, a beautiful staircase and a quiet serenity. (Obviously not lesson change-over time). It transpired that other schools had been contacted and we were told that there were 40 plus interviewees to be seen and 20 places available.

Later, talking to some of the other pupils who were successful it seemed that if a parent accompanied you to the interview you were in with a good chance . LT needed parental support because the plan was that we should join the school at the beginning of year three for a three year course to School Certificate. (Pupils already there would only have two more to do). Obviously it meant a year longer at school and I was nineteen when I left the sixth form after A Levels.

So in September 1948 twenty of us assembled in room 13 at the top of the building with our form teacher Miss Clothier. Other classes were given the suffix red, white or blue. To this day I do not know whether they were streamed or not. We were different. We were called 3Remove. 4Remove, with my friend John, had their classroom directly below us. I had read comics with school stories featuring "Remove" classes but could never understand why they were called that. Does anyone know? Eventually we went on to become 4 Remove and the following year dispersed into the regular red, white and blue classes. I don't know whether the practice continued of moving late developers into the school but I shall be eternally grateful to Mr Brown for giving me the chance.

What happened about the teaching bit which started this off? As it happened I did become a teacher and at a Borough Road College Reunion some years later, by which time I was a head teacher, I met Mr Odell again in his late nineties and was pleased to tell him about the outcome of his visit to our history class so many years before.

I enjoyed reading John Blight's recollections in SGR issue no.9 He remembered Miss Harding, his teacher at Chatsworth Junior School. He wrote that she had a poor opinion of his capabilities but that was true of most pupils of which I was one. She told my father that "I wasn't even good enough for the Bulstrode", which was a school for the "bottom layer" so I wasn't allowed to sit the eleven plus and had to wait until the beginning of year three when I left Spring Grove Central (a school midway between a secondary modern and a grammar) and joined 3 Remove at SGGS with nineteen other new pupils. Miss Harding was the worst teacher I have ever come across and I have known well into three figures during my professional life. I was grateful for the second chance which L T Brown gave me.

In his article John writes about meeting OSGs in far off places. You also meet them doing unexpected things. In the early seventies the PTA of my school in Kent used to hold fairly regular discos to raise money for school funds. On one occasion the Committee decided to use the school music system instead of hiring one in, somebody having offered to be the DJ and the money saved would be used to provide a cabaret. Accordingly one of the committee was authorised to contact a theatrical agency and make arrangements.

On the night in question a stunningly attractive woman arrived who looked very Middle Eastern and who turned out to be our cabaret, a Belly Dancer. She was superb. I have only seen three or four such dancers whilst on holidays but this one was a sensation. We were enthralled. Afterwards, talking to her, I asked her where she was from, fully expecting her to say The Lebanon or somewhere close, but no she said she was from England. I asked whereabouts. She said Isleworth. I asked where she went to school and yes you've guessed it she said Spring Grove Grammar. Wow!

John's reminiscences about his athletic career at Spring Grove reminded me of my own, similar in many ways except that I didn't start mine until the fifth year when I too represented Heston and Isleworth at the White City and then Middlesex in the National Schools' Championships at Port Sunlight and then in following years at Southampton and Bradford. At the last OSG reunion I learnt that my school 100 yard record had never been beaten. Certainly I expect my County one will have gone long ago.

I have a great fondness for Spring Grove Grammar School. I cannot exactly put my finger on it. Some teachers were great, others less so, one or two were very substandard. The building and the grounds were almost inspirational, certainly in the Music Room and the Art Room but some of the small classrooms with their open fires on the top floor were a bit of a trial . What other school had a fountain even if it wasn't working? It seems to be the whole ambience of the place and the relationships which were built up in a co-educational framework which makes it so special.

"O" Level Exams

Shirley Turner '51

Recently at Centre Parcs with my husband, two sons and daughters-in-law and my five grandchildren, we were talking about exams, as my eldest grandson Ben, is just taking his and I started to think about my own "O" level exams and decided to write this article for the school magazine!

I well remember starting at Spring Grove Grammar School (The black and White) in 1946. I contracted mumps which in those days had a six weeks quarantine, and as a result I had to sit the 11+ at just the age of 11, in an entirely empty school with just one teacher to adjudicate. To my amazement I passed and with fear and trepidation arrived for school in September 1946. My fears were soon allayed when I discovered Trevor Jones Esquire, was my form teacher, a delightful Welsh music teacher and professional singer, as music was most certainly my favourite subject. Sadly by the time I reached "O" level year, although music and art were two of my then favourite subjects, they were considered to be "interest subjects" and I was only allowed to take eight academic subjects. I often wondered how different my career would have been, had I been allowed to take them.

I remember the school etiquette of those days. Lunchtime strolls in the grounds of the school, full uniform had to be worn, hats and blazers, and we were only allowed to walk not run.

I went to school by bike, returned to Hounslow, lunch time, and at all times in full uniform, including hats which had to be held in place, cycling in a road where trolley buses also travelled!!! Religious Studies with Headmaster L.T. Brown with whom I disagreed so often. Miss Taylor, so strict, yet with a warm heart.

So many of the teachers come to mind. Favourite ones, Miss Johnson – Drama and History, Miss Walters – Art, Miss Ransom, some French, Mr Maylott – Physics. Biology was also a favourite but I was not one of Miss Holman's favourite pupils. Miss Bromwich, the domestic Science teacher put the fear of death into me, as indeed did Miss Barr in French lessons. English was a favourite but Miss Fleming was also Sports Mistress and she got angry because I would not play in her school hockey and netball teams as I just enjoyed sport and did not want to compete. I had to sit on the landing of Domestic Cottage where staff had their tea – as a punishment and tried to cream butter and sugar for a cake in a freezing cold domestic cottage!! The Banksian room (our 5th form room) was my favourite classroom because we had a pond in there with fish!

Drama was a favourite, especially the makeup department, and being "Charlotte" in Jane Austen's " I have five daughters". I still have the photographs of that.

I have a copy of the 1951 School photograph and remember the names of so many in my years 1946 – 1951. I remember cycling back to school to see the exam results paper hanging in the quadrangle and being amazed to find that I had five "O" levels.

Olympic Memories

Roy Bradshaw '51

I have just been reading a book called The Austerity Olympics, which I thoroughly recommend, if only because it brings back memories of Spring Grove, and also of one of our fellow pupils, Sylvia Cheeseman, who took part. As a pimply 13 year old I well remember seeing her flying round the track at some school sports event, and as she suggests in the book, looking attractively feminine; Fanny Blankers-Koen could have taken some sartorial tips, but when you are the best in the world perhaps it doesn't matter. I also remember going to the baths to see the Olympic swimmers training; many of them wore funny hats - it's all in the book.

For me school sports sometimes had a somewhat less attractive aspect as we ran round the sewerage works on the Cross Country course. I was never particularly good, usually being picked when no-one else was available. I actually played football for the school once - I guess there must have been a flu epidemic. I know it was very cold and by the time the match was over my hands were so frozen that I couldn't do my buttons up. Do you remember the changing rooms then? In the days of fly-buttons and braces I was glad I had ridden to school on my bike as I could then get home without my short trousers falling down. Another time I was picked to play football was when we, Nelson House, were playing Rodney. Rodney didn't have enough players so I was picked to play for them. The ball came to me somewhere just over the centre line so I simply booted it goal-wards. Much to the dismay I think of everyone, the ball landed in front of the Nelson goalkeeper and bounced over his head into the goal - this really wasn't the way to play football. Similarly, at cricket we all had to bowl. My effort landed somewhere about the middle of the pitch and trickled towards the batsman who took a terrific swipe, and missed; the ball rolled on gently into the stumps and the bails came off - that also wasn't the way to play cricket. I really don't know how the tennis match came into being or how I got involved, but once again I was taking part. It was the Pupils against the Teachers, my return hit the Teacher, definitely not fair-play. Another time we were being tested to see what athletic abilities we had. Jumping hurdles was certainly not my forte, but for some inexplicable reason I managed to throw the discuss. The trouble was that that was the one and only time, so picking me was a mistake.

I really enjoyed low level sports, playing football with a tennis ball on the netball courts, or handball up against the wall. Cricket on the North Pitch with a tree for a wicket, and, if it can be included, tuppenny-ha'penny football on the forms in the main hall. If I had any small ability it was due to cycling to school. Just recently I had been wondering if my memories of cycling to work in London once I had left school were being seen through rose tinted memory banks. I had always liked to think that it was ten miles from home to work, but was it really? Surely it was probably only seven. I decided to put the locations into Autoroute and was delighted to find the distance was twelve miles. Now I have done the same for home to school, and it comes out at over 4 miles. They were good days when we had the freedom to travel as we wished, meeting up with friends on the journey instead of being closeted in a car or crammed into a school bus. Mind you, we also had fogs - walking 4 miles home wasn't uncommon, and once I found myself adding a few hundred yards by walking all round the entrance to Heston Church. It does make today's School Run seem a bit of a nonsense.

I suppose it was a mixture of Family Interests - my father was keen on Photography and Radio, that's building them when radio was in its infancy - Tuition, I always found Physics more interesting than Latin, - and Army Training, I did my National Service in the Signals - that resulted in me spending most of my working life with the BBC. I also suppose this is why I frequently take my Video Camera with me wherever I go, and in 1994 I took it with me to the School Reunion. Some of you will have already seen the results of that visit through my DVD, but last year my daughter - also keen on photography - introduced me to a Website called Vimeo where you can upload your own videos, primarily to share with other users of the site, but also to make them available to friends etc. There has been a Link on the SGGS Website for a while, but recent conversations with other users has made me realise Broadband is what it says - a very Broad range of download speeds, and what works OK for some can be frustrating for others. So now I have created three versions, one for Dial Up, one for Low Broadband and one for Medium Broadband.

For those who may be interested, I use Final Cut Express HD on my Apple Mac Computer, and export a Quick Time Movie using Quick Time Conversion where you can choose your preferred compression. This Movie you simply upload though a link on the Vimeo site.

I don't know how other people's memory works, but mine seems to be a series of snapshots; instances in time that have no before and no after. I hope my memories will trigger off some of yours.

My first snapshot was probably on entering the school for the very first time. I had cycled to school and come through the side entrance. I am just approaching the turn to go round the back of the main building when I see two "blackbirds" in flowing black cloaks scurrying through the rest of the arrivals. These turned out to be teachers; I had never seen the like before. Round the corner was the Covered Way, for some reason this blurred snapshot seems to have a forbidding, or perhaps foreboding atmosphere, is it because it was there that our exam results were published? A much happier snapshot is of the great tree, in the front of the building, that was a natural meeting place for us all. Sadly, though fortunately, it collapsed one winter when we were all on holiday.

I was put in 1 Red with, well I'm sure he was called Mr Jones but I note in the list of teachers he was called Mr Varney, and as Trevor Owen he had a part in

The Desert Song at the Chiswick Empire. My next snapshot is of me standing up in class while Mr Jones played a chord on the piano. His idea of a music lesson was to get each of us to sing the various notes; this was one of the few things I was any good at. I enjoyed singing but why, later on in school, I didn't join the choir I don't know; just another time I couldn't be bothered to learn I suppose. I think the school put on Monsieur Beaucaire.

The First Formers had various duties and another snapshot is of setting up the forms in the Music Room for junior assembly; the trick was to set the legs so there was a good chance the form would collapse when students sat down. Another duty was to scrape the plates at dinnertime. I see myself standing at a table in the basement receiving piles of plates, a smelly exercise.

My next Snapshots all involve the Main Hall. Not all the school could be accommodated for dinners, so each year had to take a turn bringing sandwiches, which in cold weather we would eat while sitting on the radiators, or playing twopenny halfpenny football on the forms in the main hall. If we were lucky two of the older lads would play jazz duets on the piano. If it were really cold then the bottles of milk left just outside the hall would have 2 or 3 inches of frozen milk sticking out the top. The jazz duets were eventually stopped; perhaps it had something to do with milk bottles being pulled out of the piano at the start of morning assembly.

Another lunchtime pastime was playing handball with a tennis ball up against the wall on the netball courts. The school had a visit from a tennis racquet manufacturer, the P&M Racquet, after Fred Perry and Dan Maskell. I had one of these and eventually played in a match against the prefects and staff. Once again my "unsporting" ability showed itself as I managed to hit one of the prefects who took some offence at this. I assure you it was an accident. Still on the sporting theme there was Cross Country Running. I have a snapshot of myself, a lonely figure, coming in not quite last after circumnavigating the local sewage works.

As you can see, lessons don't seem to be playing much part in my snapshots, but I do have a few. PT with Mr "from there" Short. He had us doing forward rolls over a box. I lose my orientation when I do this and only remembered where I was when I hit the wall at the far end. Mr "Muzz" Cross, though he had lost his nickname by my time, had us marching round the Woodwork room with our thumbs over the top of our chisel handles to ensure we didn't hurt ourselves or each other – I never really understood that. There was the Art Room with its fountain and "painted parts". I volunteered as a model for the Life class. I was fully clothed, but one girl asked about the bulge in my trousers – it was a tennis ball! There was the Banksian Room with its stuffed birds, rooms with fires on which we toasted our sandwiches, and a room with an intriguing dumb waiter. Another room overlooked the girl's tennis courts. I failed to learn French there.

Who Destroyed my School?

John Sanders '52

I must confess that I feel a certain ambivalence to the old school buildings. I feel I haven't now got an "old school" to visit as it was destroyed by Government action forty odd years ago. I was always glad that I had left before Lampton School was built. I used to pass it regularly but never visited it. I always felt privileged to attend school at Spring Grove House. It was more like attending an historic Public School than a State Grammar School and I prefer to remember it as it was with its beautiful cedar tree in the at the SW corner. Miss Coulthard used to park her Fiat 500 under it. It was dwarfed by the trunks of the tree which must have been planted when the house was built. A great pity about the snowfall - Miss Coulthart had a very lucky escape as it happened at night.

I knew the ambience couldn't last of course- those dozens of open fires fed with coalite were lovely but were totally impractical.

Some years ago I visited the house on the bike and found a maze of Porta-cabins on the lawns. I couldn't get out of the place fast enough! It wasn't my old school any more. I know they've gone now but I don't want to see the place "tarted up". I remember a wonderful team of teachers of the "old school" type. I suppose I'm old fashioned but I much prefer academic gowns which most of them wore to jeans and T-shirt!

LT was a wonderful "head" with just the right amount of gravitas; I particularly remember Basher Brown, a wonderful applied maths teacher, who emphasised points by bashing the blackboard making a choking cloud of chalk dust – one didn't forget the point. He got me through the GCE with a distinction – I don't know how because I thought I was not good at maths; Bill Lyneham gave me lasting love of literature and Mr Hart imparted a lifelong love of music. Mr. Cockroft regularly took a party of us to the new Royal Festival Hall to hear the early evening recitals on the new organ there. They inspired a love of organ music that lasted to the extent of my becoming secretary of the BBC Organ Society for many years some time ago.

I still keep in touch with many of the "Old Boys". I occasionally see– Henry Russell, Spud Taylor and Jeff Piner – the last a cycling companion for many years. Finally I would like to pay tribute to another OSG, Victor George Knighton, lost when his aeroplane crashed into the English Channel in 1941. Sgt Knighton RAF(VR) is inscribed on panel 4 of the Runnymede Memorial. He was only 22. It is a very sobering sight to see thousands of names stretching into the distance – and this is only the British armed forces. Victor's parents were great friends of my parents and myself. They gave me his aviation books which helped me to become an aviation enthusiast They were lovely people, still mourning his loss many years later. He was probably one of four mentioned in the Cecil Field's article about the class of 1938. Had he lived he would have been welcomed at the old school as a hero and, unlike us, he would have had a school to return to.

My Favourite Teacher Dolly Ransom

Derek Norman '52

I look back on my days at Spring Grove (1947– 52), with satisfaction, gratitude, and many fond and happy memories. My satisfaction has come, over the past 50 or so years, from the realisation that, compared to many people I have met, we at SGGS appear to have received an excellent, very varied, all-round education, akin to that usually reserved for pupils of expensive private schools.   My gratitude is for the teaching ability of the teachers, and their dedication and enthusiasm for their subject.

I must begin by totally endorsing all I have read in SGR about L T Brown. What an amazing example he was.

Having read several previous SGR articles of memorable teachers, which brought back my own recollections of those people, there are a few more who, in my opinion, deserve a mention.

George Barratt taught me Maths from 3rd form till GCE. He was a very serious teacher, but had an ability to help us to understand what we were trying to learn, as well as giving lots of tips for remembering formulae etc, which I extended in studying for professional exams post SGGS. When we had finished sitting GCE, he came to each class armed with fun games, some conjuring with figures on the blackboard, others involving two of us, tied together with loops of string, and standing on top of a desk, trying to escape from each other. Life was meant to be fun too.

Kate Hemming was another teacher who took her subject very seriously, but when the moment was right, she displayed a very clever wit, and great sense of humour.

Wesley Frid was my 3rd year form-master, and Chemistry Master. He was a very kind man, but knew all about the tricks children get up to. He used to cycle to school every day, and one day he was knocked off his bike by a car. He was away from school for a few months, and we had a relieving teacher in his absence, who was not good at maintaining control in lessons. He would sit at his desk on the raised dais in the chemi-lab and tell us to form into groups, and do our favourite experiments from our books. One group of boys used to bring ingredients and make toffee at the back of the lab, a smell I shall never forget! Another group made chlorine gas, which, being heavier than air, crept along the floor making everyone cough, before reaching the level of the teacher's desk, when we were evacuated into the garden. The other trick, when he told us to turn off our Bunsen burners, was to play the flame onto the gas tap handle, so that he burnt his fingers when he came to switch it off himself!

Miss Clothier was another teacher, not normally held in high regard by all pupils, who saw her as small, serious and scary. It was all an act, as my wife Betty, (nee Cook) discovered in the 6th form, when she told Miss Clothier she was planning to train for teaching. Miss Clothier was very helpful, and said, "when you start teaching, screw the discipline down very hard, and gradually loosen it as you gain confidence in your ability to control them as you want to." (At least, that was the thinking then, but now………??)

I remember Miss Coulthard teaching us the latin words to various carols one year, like "Adeste fideles, ……etc" (O come all ye Faithful), "Personent hodie……etc", the French carol "Il est nee le divin enfant…etc.", and Miss Ransom teaching us the German "Stille nacht, heilige nacht…..etc" (Silent Night). Whenever I hear those versions sung at Christmastime, I am transported in my mind back to school. Likewise, whenever I see a ballroom with a large mirror-covered revolving ball on the ceiling , lit by spotlights, I remember the Christmas Eve dances in the school hall.

Enthusiasm for their subject was particularly evident in my favourite teacher, Miss ("Dolly") Ransom. Miss Ransom was a really lovely character, full of fun, with a smiling face, caring personality and a very good understanding of human nature. She came to us in Sept 1948, after returning from Europe, where she had been helping to repatriate "displaced persons", driven out of their homes and countries by the war.

She loved her subject, languages, and in my case, German. She did not just teach us grammar, as a stodgy "must do" chore, but tried to make it "fun". She encouraged us to try to speak to each other in faltering German, thereby creating our need to learn the grammar, without which proper conversation is impossible. She taught us so much about the life, customs, culture, geography etc of the country, and managed to pass on to me, anyway, the enthusiasm to be able to converse in another language.

Good results in tests would be rewarded with a German coin, postcard, postage stamp, or, on one occasion, a hiker's spiked walking stick, covered with metal place badges from the Tyrol. Each prize would be presented with an explanation to the class of the place depicted, the person shown on the stamp, or the origin and use of the walking stick.

I still remember the longest word she had ever come across.

Oberammergaupassionfestspielalperkreuterklosterdeliktatfrustuckkaseschnitzen It was on a café window in Oberammergau, at the time of one of the Passion Plays, advertising a special cheese sandwich, created to celebrate the occasion of the Passion Play. It obviously stuck in my mind, but that was the kind of passion she had for her subject.

In the summer of 1951,when I was in the 4th form, preparing for the GCE exams the following year, Miss Ransom took a party of 26 of us on a YHA cycling tour of Holland and Northern Germany. Of the 26, only 2 of us were in her German language class at school, so the two of us had two weeks of asking the way, doing group shopping, and translating at the youth hostels for our travelling companions. It was great fun, and we had no problems with the GCE oral exam in German the following year!!

Miss Ransom also organised weekend YHA cycling trips in UK, which were lots of fun, even the ride in pouring rain from Isleworth to The Isle of Wight, which eventuated in a great heap of soaking wet clothes in front of a large fire in Cowes Youth Hostel.

The love of languages, which I caught from Dolly Ransom, encouraged me to learn French, Spanish, and Italian, in the past 15years. Her method of making you try to speak in the language from day one, is now the fashionable method used in language courses, and is referred to as the "immersion method". For me, it is the only way that really works.

Miss Ransom was not very tall, and once demonstrated to us that she had short legs, and a long body, which meant she was shorter than most when standing up, but just the same height as others when sitting down. "Not a lot of people know that"!!   What there was of her though was all quality!

I shall never forget my days at Spring Grove, but most of all, I shall never forget "Dolly Ransom"

More Memories of Miss Ransom

Edna Seymour '52

Maybe other members of her German class will remember us all being given a cup and saucer each when she returned to Spring Grove having spent time working in Germany, helping displaced persons after the war. This would have been in 1947 or 1948.

The little hand-made "Good luck" card from her was on each of our desks in 1952 when we sat down to take our "O" level German exam, a lovely gesture and much appreciated at the time. My cup and card below.

In the 1980s my youngest daughter mentioned a really interesting little lady who was a regular customer at Lowe's Travel Agency where she then worked as a travel agent. As I listened to her description of this lady and of the places she had visited I suddenly realized who this sounded like and yes, it was indeed Miss Ransom, still globetrotting and helping others after so many years. What an inspiration. I feel quite ashamed of the times when I was less than attentive in class and with homework - but I did manage to pass the "O" level so perhaps the "Glu'ck Auf" did work.

Jottings from a Life

John Young '53

I am amazed at the total recall which many who attend our reunions at Spring Grove seem to enjoy. My own memories are much more sporadic. I do, however, look back at those not so far off days through rose coloured spectacles. It seemed to be a time of endless fun, pleasure and good companionship. The sun shone for a great deal of the time! Memories linger, most of them happy...

o   I recall my very first day at school in September 1948. I was late! That certainly *wasn't* a happy moment. I can still feel the rising panic as I wondered where I should be and what I should do next (a bit like the rest of my life, really!)

o   I recall endless games of football, both informal (at lunchtime) and playing for the school and house teams. I have a crooked collarbone to celebrate the daring dive which I , as goalkeeper, made at the feet of centre forward Ray Pearce. I am told that the crack could be heard a long way off on that crisp January morning.

o   I also recall visiting Ray's home to watch the Coronation on their TV.

o   I remember cycling into a milk float on my pre-school paper round. This happened during a snow storm and I can still feel my abject misery as I lay on the freezing road!

o   I recall numerous slices of toast, usually burned, in the Prefects' Room on the top floor.

o   I recall (may God forgive me) crucifying some of the weaker teachers.

o   I also remember the brilliance of some of the more inspiring ones. In particular I recall, as a turning point in my attitude to school work, the day Miss Johnson told me that she thought I should be in the 'A' form. As someone who lurked in the lower reaches of the Blue Form I doubt that she was right, but her confidence meant a great deal to me.

o   I recall the plays which she produced, and her liberated and liberating approach as she thrust teenage boys and girls together to change into their outfits. We boys, at least, enjoyed that enormously!

o   I am tremendously grateful for the hours of voluntary time given by so many teachers, especially J. T. Short, our P.E. master.

o   I recall my first kiss in one of the classrooms. Sadly, I can't remember which room, but I do remember which girl (and no, I'm not telling!).

o   I recall large numbers of us going off on long cycle rides. We seemed to be 'unclubable' in any formal sense − I lasted in the Cubs for all of 4 weeks. Perhaps we didn't need to be organised because we organised ourselves so effectively.

And so the years have slipped by...

In my late 20s I married Isabel and we have two daughters, both of whom are married and both of whom have produced a boy and a girl. They all live nearby and bring us great joy, as well as a great deal of hard work and a few headaches (the grandchildren, that is!)

But let's rewind the DVD (mixing my metaphors here!). I don't think I was a devout teenager, although I did enjoy morning assemblies. This was mainly due to the remarkable Mr. Hart, who was almost as strict as Mr. Foss, the Chemistry Master. Mr. Hart (I don't know his Christian name, but things didn't work like that in those days) encouraged us unlikely lads to join the choir and, provided I stood next to someone who could read music, I could belt out the bass or tenor line. A wonderful experience, for which I am tremendously grateful.

Indeed, music has a strong place in my memories. Above all, there were those excellent concerts in the school hall. What was the name of that brilliant oboe player – Michael? And, of course, Margaret Wilsher with her wonderful soprano voice was a star performer. It is a delight that Margaret and Barbara have been able to get to some of our recent reunions, despite family illness.

Having struggled with science and maths at school I realised, too late, that I should have stuck with the humanities. In my thirties I discovered that some people were not only interested in reading what I wrote, but were willing to pay for the privilege! Writing hasn't made me rich but I have seen more than a quarter of a million books/booklets sold out there in the marketplace and I have had work published in around ten languages, including Korean, Albanian, Italian, Chinese and Russian. If anyone is interested. www.yorkcourses.co.uk gives a few examples of the English editions.

From the dizzy heights of captain of the school football team to the not-so-dizzy depths of a Church of England clergyman. I've made that journey in an increasingly secular world which usually thinks fairly kindly, though not too highly, of clerics and their old-fashioned faith. Quite right too, for we're not a very impressive lot. But then, we're not in it for prestige, but because we believe it's true.

John Young and Ray Pearce

with (above) fellow '53ers, David Sansom and Reg Day in Trafalgar Square 1953 and left at the 2006 re-union at Spring Grove House

Jottings from a Parallel Life

Ray Pearce '53

Since John Young and I were classmates for eleven years until our "O" level year in 1953, and pretty much inseparable during the school day, I thought I ought to keep him company on the Spring Grovian pages too. I've known John from day one. Well, actually, it was my day two but his day one. We were delivered to the West Mid. Maternity unit within hours of each other. We both started at Isleworth Town in 1942. Also with us and to continue on to SGGS were Don McNeill, David Sansom, Roger Davies, Avril Acott, Shirley White and Celia Dargon. Pretty good memory huh? No, not really, I've been coached recently by Avril.

Our class teacher for the last year at Isleworth Town was Mr. Palethorpe. He was so impressed with our academic achievements that he announced to the whole class that "if Pearce and Young pass the scholarship I'll eat my hat." He was as good as his word and as we astonished ourselves by getting through to the "Black and White" he produced a pastry hat which he ate before us.

My earliest sporting memory is from Isleworth Town. It's of sitting on the pile of coats that served as the goal posts, having a good weep because I wasn't picked as goalie. Having got the place later on, I was dismayed to learn on day one at SGGS that Brian Green was also in the class. He had been the goalkeeper at Bulstrode Juniors and his father had played in goal for Spurs. I decided to become a full back! For me Spring Grove was a splendid sports club punctuated by a few lessons designed to allow the body to recuperate between serious physical endeavours. Every morning, regardless of the season, we boys would arrive at 8-30-ish, assemble on the northern basketball court and set to with a tennis ball football game. The school day ended with one of the many after school clubs, sports training sessions or just a visit to the Ice Cream Parlour opposite the main gate; then a wander in the rough direction of home chatting with somebody, John Young, David Sansom and Maggie Wilsher come to mind. I rarely got home before 7.00pm.

I was also a sea-scout at Isleworth, then graduated to the ATC at Hounslow where I, inevitably, ran, boxed and got to wear the leopardskin apron and carry the bass drum in the band for events like the Heston Carnival.

For the first four years at SGGS I lived in Isleworth and cycled to school. A cycling memory is of riding my brand new Armstrong Whitworth, fixed gear racing bike, purchased from the shop on the opposite corner to the Fire Station, to school, when a lady stepped out of the Post Office in London Road and started to cross the road. I applied my brand new front brake and flew over my brand new handle bars to lie at her feet in a crumpled heap surrounded by bits of brand new bike. Although a keen cyclist I didn't know about the cycling club and cycle outings. I realise now that that was because my sister, three years older than I, was allowed to join the Ealing Common Cycling Club only if she took me with her. So, as a 13/14 year old, my Sundays were spent riding to Ealing, meeting up with the club and setting off for the day's ride to Brighton or Southend or similar and back. Since starting to write this I realise that while we were close pals at school during the week and on Saturday mornings for school sport, outside that time we did little together. For my last two years at Spring Grove from Easter through to September my weekends were spent cycling to Hyde Park where I spent the day working on the boats on the Serpentine.

Saturdays in the winter were spent playing for the school in the mornings and the afternoons would see me at my regular spot on the terraces at Griffin Park supporting the Bees (Brentford) then a first division club. For the '52/3 season I played for Brentford Juniors in the London League. School game in the morning, Brentford game in the afternoon and Wembley to watch Ice Hockey in the evening. Sundays with the Heston Mixed Hockey Club, well represented by Spring Grovians, from a span of years. Now that **was** competitive sport and a very good social club. We were fit in those days - little teenage obesity then.

My memories are of football on the front pitch - so muddy in winter - and I have the video clip with sound in my memory bank of John Young trying to break my shin with his collar bone - I didn't even get a free kick for it!

Hockey on the North pitch in winter and athletics in the summer; a 220 yard running track? Jimmy Brown ('43) tells me there was a school rowing club at Isleworth once. Does anyone remember it?

Our Cross country runs started from Greenhams field then over the railway track and along the river to Twickenham Rugby Stadium and back (who showed us the way the first time?). I think it must have been 1953 when John and I found ourselves comfortably in the lead in the school championship and agreed on a dead heat - J.T. Short was not impressed. We also ran in the inter-schools meeting at Borough Road College in the days when cross-country meant just that with ploughed fields, rivers and oodles of mud.

Great days in the athletics season at Chiswick Stadium and Lampton for the Heston Carnival games and the big thrill of running at the White City, London's premier athletics track in those days. Life-saving training at Hounslow Baths and the annual gala at the Isleworth Baths. Gymnastics and Boxing were activities carried out in gym lessons. I too remember J.T. Short jabbing at us with a stuffed boxing glove on a stick.

During my last year I commuted by train from Ruislip and would often have lifts to school and back with Mr. Pollard in his Bedford van. He was quite keen that I should work toward professional boxing - just shows how the staff regarded my academic ability. I do remember having one of my not infrequent interviews with LTB and him commenting that if it wasn't for my involvement in sport there seemed little reason for me to continue at Spring Grove! I had to agree.

My learning at Spring grove was largely by osmosis, Maths and English were learned progressively by usage, these I could cope with, subjects requiring "swotting" I didn't do! I was amazed on my first visit to Spain in '68 ish to find

I could understand Spanish remarkably well considering I never got above 15% in an exam for "Ichabod" Barker.

My favourite teacher was Di Clothier. I know she frightened the life out of many but she always seemed to have a soft spot for me and a twinkle in her eye. I remember that she was delighted when I got my O level in Maths.

Then there was my own special study on the top floor above the main entrance where I did most of my homework - somewhat late - others called it detention! Could have had my own desk in there as I was such a frequent attender.

I too enjoyed the Dramatic Society - I remember standing on a table in a pub called the Three Pigeons and singing some ditty, was that in "She Stoops to Conquer"? Was the part Anthony Lumpkin? I also think I remember having some part in "The Admirable Crichton" but that could be the dodgy bit of my memory.

We enjoyed theatre outings to London for The Mouse Trap (its first year?) at the Ambassadors (?) and Porgy and Bess at the London Coliseum.

I left in June '53, never to return, as my family moved to Godalming.

In January 1954, following my Father's advice to "get a job with a good pension", I joined the Metropolitan Police as a police cadet and moved into a "section house" (single police officers' accommodation) in Fulham. In Aug '54, with National Service looming, I joined the Parachute Regiment and served in Aldershot, Cyprus and Suez. If you have to go to war - a seven day war against the Egyptians is probably one of the better options. Leaving the Paras, I spent four years travelling around the country as a sales rep. for various companies and then managed to convince Her Majesty's representatives that I should be allowed to fly some of her aeroplanes and spent 12 very enjoyable years doing just that.

My only known contact with OSGs in the 50 years from leaving SGGS in 1953 to my first reunion appearance in 2002, was four meetings with class mates, when I met John in '55-ish in Aldershot as he walked through the Para's Barracks; Stan Sulman in Hounslow High Street '58-ish; Norma Childs on Waterloo Station (late 50s?) and Merill Thewliss at a RAF Officers Mess Ball in Lincoln in '63-ish. Her husband was also a Vulcan pilot.. They were all very brief encounters.

Like so many of us I'm sure, I wish I had taken advantage of the education I was offered at SGGS. I shall never know what I could have done, had I heeded and eradicated those " could do betters" on my reports. It's probably a bit too late now to decide what I'd really like to do when I grow up - if I ever do.

Rona Hodkinson '53, tells me that after leaving I returned to Isleworth for a Christmas Dance at the school and that I had a very nice time - ungallantly, I have no memory of that. On the radio one day in the '70s I'm sure I heard a Rev. John Young on "thought for the day"...that name rang a bell?

So, we both left school and went our separate ways but strangely both ended up with careers connected to the heavens. I never got above 45,000ft, John's interest is obviously considerably higher....and he never told me about that first kiss!!

Bell Road Youth Club and SGGS Recalled

Pam Neal '53

Back in the '50's, the Bell Road Methodist Church youth club seemed to be an extension of Spring Grove school, so many pupils were members. My good friend and fellow class mate Jean Cameron spotted a notice on the information board, put there by Carol Buxey, inviting the more senior pupils to go along for an evening and see if they would like to join. I really only went in the first place to keep Jean company.

There were two halls in use - one for the Saturday evening dances and the other, for table tennis. There must also have been a kitchen, as I vaguely recall interval soft drinks [such innocent evenings !]

When I was a member [Jean and I joined on our first attendance], Carol Buxey and John Fairbanks were club leaders . There must have been some "outsiders", but the names Aileen Long, Marie Walker, Rene Horne, Naomi Willmott, Jean Cameron, Janet Griffiths, Tony May, Hugh Rhys, Derek Sheen, David Andrews, Dennis Robertson, Brian Shepherd, Margaret and John West, John Ward and Tony Fletcher spring to mind. There may have been more and if I have forgotten anyone, I apologise !

How far away some of those friends are now - Rene in New Zealand, Hugh in America and Jean in Switzerland.

Do you remember the records we danced to - the last waltz always being Mantovani's "La Ronde". I can't recall any "wallflowers".........

There were other social occasions too - I remember going on several car rallies, as well as to a few parties. A few of the boys actually owned cars and were never short of offers from hopeful crew members for the rallies!

Whether they began there or merely flourished, several engagements were celebrated and I know of seven weddings [some to the afore mentioned "outsiders"!!] The first one I attended was that of David Andrews and I was Matron of Honour when Hugh married. Hugh and John West are my son's Godfathers.

When we weren't at Bell Road, we seemed to appear en masse, at the Red Lion Hotel, on Hounslow High Street - dancing was definitely the "in thing" -[I wish it still was]- but again only refreshed by soft drinks!. Who recalls the "live band" and the crooner, who always gave a heartfelt rendition of "Jealousy"?

These happy evenings were often rounded off with a bag of chips for the journey home - the buses ran late and no-one felt unsafe being out at gone 11p.m.

What a lot today's youngsters, who find nothing better to do than hang around town centres, are missing!

Spring Grove wasn't even my first choice of school – it fell between the Green School and Gumleigh House. How often does second best prove to be the better option.

Can any of my fellow '53 year girls remember their first visit to Spring Grove ? Mine was an introductory meeting, held in the hall, for Mothers and Daughters, chaired by Miss Taylor. At the end of this talk, each Parent was handed an information leaflet, which included some basic "facts of life". I recall my Mum glancing at this piece of paper and then [thankfully I felt] handing it to me. Not so my friend Enid's Mother, who after reading the literature, tucked it hastily into her handbag. Needless to say, Enid and I escaped to read mine !!!! 11 year old girls were so innocent in those days.

Next stop was the Banksian Room. To view and possible purchase, items of second hand uniform. This before the more expensive job of visiting Messrs Abernethie's [?] in Hounslow, for the rest of the gear. Material for making up gym dresses and summer frocks was also purchased, the sewing of which must have fazed many a Mum- certainly mine. She handed the job over to an Aunt, who whilst an excellent seamstress, had absolutely no idea about young girls and fashion. Thus the birth of the sack dress.

I have no memories of my first few months as a new girl, not even of the first day. What does come to mind is the overwhelming fear of never being able to find my way around that great building. Even after five years, I never got to visit every room.

A more general impression is that of walking round and round the house or sitting on the front staircase, in good weather [we must have been allowed inside, when it was wet]. Lunch in the dim basement, country dancing in the loft, seemingly endless games of netball and worse, hockey in the mud. Then there were the swimming lessons at Hounslow Baths, under the watchful eye of the sadistic Mr. Fry – I still can't swim ! Two more pleasant memories are of visits to the Odeon cinema, to see "Scott of the Antarctic" and "Hamlet".

It isn't until later years that the pictures become clearer – dates added with the aid of old and faded diaries !

January 1952 – a trip with the Dramatic Society [joined early on and much enjoyed], to see "The Merchant of Venice" at the Old Vic.

At school, again in March, watching the inspired acting of Jose Rowden as a blind girl, in "In a Glass Darkly" [or should that be "Through a Glass Darkly!?"]. March again and another trip to London with the Dramatic Society, this time to see Ann Todd in "The Seventh Veil" – wonderful.

In July, visits to Chiswick and the White City stadiums, for inter school sports. London in November to see "Pygmalion" wound up the year.

February 1952 and a visit to an Exhibition of Danish Dancing [or so it says in my diary!]. in July, a trip to Whipsnade Zoo [now that I do remember...].

Also in July, the departure from the staff of a truly inspirational teacher – Miss Irene Johnson. She bought her subjects to life – history became like looking through a window at the past and her teaching of Shakespeare had the text making sense to even the most bored pupil.

Speech Day that October had the Honourable Florence Horsbrugh [possible Minister for Education ?] as guest of honour.

Once again the year was rounded off with a trip to London, this time to City Hall, Westminster, to see a Spanish film. Did you come along to that ?

February 1953, London again [we should have known our way there by then] to see "Julius Caesar" at the Old Vic.

Finally for me, the leavers' service at St. Paul's Cathedral, in July. Did I dream it, or did we go to two services, one at St. Mary's Church, in Osterley ?

Can anyone remember where the Film Society met and how often there was a meeting of the Social Club ? I see from diary entries, that I occasionally danced with one John Hore..........

I remember two early crushes – one "boy" now found, one still out there. One of those boys gave me his photograph, which I subsequently lost. There was also a later crush and this one is now also in touch.

I don't remember any nastiness- perhaps a bit of name calling and petty rivalry between gangs or more properly groups of girls. We respected and sometimes feared our teachers and were somewhat in awe of the prefects. Isn't it wonderful that we have now found Heather Gunn and Doug Lygo, our head girl and boy. How many of you were part of a group and are you still in touch?

My five years ended, like many of yours, with the dreaded O Level exams. and the anxious wait for the results. When the envelope was finally delivered, my Mum offered to open it for me and to soften the blow, if necessary !

I know there were OSG DANCES and a Christmas Party is mentioned in December 1952. I am reminded that as senior girls, we were trusted to play tennis on the grass court, away from the eye of Miss Phillips. Apparently we cooked a meal in the cottage and invited Miss Gregory and Miss Clothier to lunch [how trusting they were to accept!!]. We also served tea and biscuits to our Mums, who dutifully turned up for Parents' afternoons. I wonder, did any Dads attend these events?

In the later built canteen, the more senior pupils had to wait at table for the staff [I bet no-one made them clear their plates before being served dessert!]

I know I was pleased to leave school and it is only with hindsight that I wish I had stayed on. The old building still exerts its magical air and I love revisiting it. I can't yet imagine the day when I walk out of the door for the very last time – can you ?

I hope my ramblings have awoken some memories for you – reading this back, I see most of my "moments" have happened outside the actual school timetable! Looking at the now almost indecipherable writing in my old diaries, for weeks on end, Monday to Friday, it just says "School" I have forgotten so much and didn't have the foresight to write more detailed accounts.

Pam, centre row, right, below, surrounded at the Bell Rd. YouthClub

Carved from the Spreading Cedar

Digging around today I fell over the piece of the old SGGS Cedar of Lebanon that came down in January 1951 and remembered carving and painting it at the time.

I was a little nuts those days regarding aircraft, so I carved that sliver of wood (about 2 1/2 inches square x 1/4' thick) into the shape of a tailfin, painted some words on it and varnished it, still in perfect condition in 2011. You can see my artistic talents were severly limited.

I had a struggle photographing it but I would not think there are too many specimens of that tree wood around with similar provenance. I did not realise I had put my name across the 1/4' bottom.

Graham Wallace, '55

Confessions of a Pupil from 1948-53

Joan Watkins '53

Although I have occasionally thought back to my schooldays, it never occurred to me to make contacts. Recently, the issue of bullying in schools has been in the news and I thought how happy everything was at Spring Grove Grammar School with no bullying, to my knowledge. Even the Prefects didn't bully, they simply carried out their duties. These thoughts led me to Friends Reunited, from where Pam Neal "found" me.

From my very first day at Spring Grove Grammar, I loved the house and grounds so intensely that I dreamed of winning the football pools one day and buying it from the Education Authorities for a sum too good to refuse!

I rode my bicycle to school, which, in my fantasy world, was a beautiful, highly-strung, powerful horse, and the cycle sheds were stables. So my desire to own the house incorporated filling the grounds with grazing horses, and turning it into a riding centre, of which there were very few after the war years.

I was a very ordinary girl, inclined to sports rather than academia, but with a disobedient streak running through me. I remember the many black stars I received which, to be given four, meant a detention. I received some of these from Prefects when caught after school without my beret on. Remember the shop over the road from the main gates, which was like a tuck-shop to us? Younger pupils, who stayed for dinners, were not allowed to leave the school at lunchtime, but I could not resist the challenge, or my unabated hunger couldn't, and was sometimes caught by Prefects. Being cheeky to staff- Mr Callow in particular - would get me a detention. Once I had a double detention but cannot remember why, only that I must have warranted it! Far worse than detention though, was when I had to stand outside Mr Brown's door as a punishment. I genuinely felt terror as he opened his door and coldly bade me enter. Rebuke from a normally kind, quiet man was terrifying. So why did I push my disobedience to such limits? I think I hoped my mother would carry out her threat to send me to Boarding School if I did not behave. I was an avid reader of boarding school books, such as the 'Mallory Towers' series, and hooked on the idea that it must be a marvellous life, suited to my temperament.

There were areas which were strictly "out-of-bounds" to pupils. One was a tunnel, which ran underground from behind the Fire Station where it was rough, overgrown terrain, and ran to the exit that emerged a few hundred yards further along. I imagine the tunnel was left over from an air-raid shelter or may have been used in training by the firefighters. But, obviously, it was out-of-bounds because of possible danger. At the age of 12, it was so tempting to go down, especially when dared to do so by boys (no names disclosed!). It was pitch dark and most likely inhabited by spiders and beetles, so I actually did not enjoy the experiences.

Another "out-of-bounds" was the Temple, or Chapel, situated past the Pavilion. This was once a beautiful, circular, single-room building, which had deteriorated dreadfully over the years, with rubble and broken tiles on the floor. I had to go in to envisage how it had once looked when cared for.

As pupils, we were not allowed into the Minstrels Gallery in the Music Room. Again, as a no-no, for me it had to be a yes-yes.

I once spent a whole lesson in Room 3, hidden behind a screen in the half room used by the Adult Education for Life Art classes. I hadn't actually meant to stay there, but couldn't get back to my desk in time when the teacher entered the room.

I suppose I should feel contrite for my escapades but, in fact, whilst recounting my memories, I have a smile on my face. At least it enabled me to deal sensibly with my two daughters' teenage behaviour. I could think, "been there, done that, got the T-shirt"!

Lest I have given the impression I was a hopeless case who deserved to be expelled - not so. My close friend, Brenda Taylor (where are you now?) and I competed with each other to get the most gold stars for Drake House. Although not as successful as Brenda, I was nevertheless proud of my efforts.

Too much swimming and diving was my undoing, resulting in health problems which meant much time off school and daily visits for hospital treatment. The consequence being schoolwork suffered and I did badly in the Mock examinations. Sadly for me, this meant leaving early, before taking 'O' levels and finishing my education at a Secondary Modern school, which I hated. I missed SGGS so much but, with no turning back, I had to get on with life.

Perhaps my confessions will encourage other OSG's to own up to their misconduct while at SGGS. I am throwing down the gauntlet.

Joan, right, ready for tennis......

Cycling Club 1953

Girls 1st XI cricket team 1953
Heston Mixed Hockey Club 1953

Short Diary of a Spring Grovian

Eileen McLaughlin (Titcombe) '55

1 Red - My first form room, a tiny room at the top of the building. The front desks practically under the blackboard. In the right-hand corner a tall square table with high stool where Mr. Barker sat when taking the register. At one of the earliest assemblies Mr. L.T. Brown said he would give five pounds to anyone who hit a cricket ball from the front pitch through his study window.

2 Blue - Form teacher Mr. Bullough, can't remember the room. During a physics lesson on 6th February, 1952 Mr. Brown came in tell us that King George VI had died and that Princess Elizabeth was to become the Queen.

3 Blue - September 1952 only back a week feel ill. The middle of the month I am in the Isolation Hospital at Mogden with suspected polio, the next day I am in the Highgate Wing of Whittington Hospital with tubercular-meningitis. Miss next fifteen months of school.

4 Blue - January 1954 return to school - mornings only. Form teacher Mrs. Holman. Often given a ride to school from Bridge Road by the domestic science teacher, Miss Gregory. It embarrasses me. I wish she would not do it. Most teachers do not seen to be aware that I am not at school in the afternoons, I have to keep explaining why I haven't handed in homework because I've missed half the lessons. Have extra English and Scripture with Mr. L.T.Brown, no problems. History with Miss Taylor, I can't cope, she writes in my report "I expected better." I think Miss Taylor was paranoid I might be taken ill again and was forever insisting I should rest on the camp bed in her study where she stroked my forehead and wrists with a cooling cologne stick.

5 Commercial 1955 - Form teacher Mr. Howell B.A. The room near the foot of the stairs near Mr. Brown's office. Not far from the stairs that led down to the basement kitchen where wonderful smells rose when cakes were baking. Not far from the table where the bell stood waiting for someone to ring it. Those oh so uncomfortable office chairs took a bit of getting used to especially when I tried to be so grown-up wearing my new nylon stockings and suspenders. The clatter of fourteen typewriters often caused another headache and I would pray that Miss Taylor would not look in or I would likely end up in her study in bed again. The last day of term arrived, my very last day at school. The place that was so familiar, so comfortable, so secure, so soon to be history. Last assembly, into the hall, the fear, the wonder, the tears, the emotions were all awry. Then Mr. Brown tells us that no one is to leave, he has been informed that someone has pushed apple cores inside the exhaust pipe of a teacher's car and school will not be dismissed until the culprit comes to his office.

Eventually we walk the path to the outside world, someone whistles, he wants to carry my books home. Did I say the outside world, well he was one of the lads from Isleworth Grammar.

Reunion 2007 & the Real School Reports

Richard (Dick) Harris '55

I had to travel only 70 miles for the annual gathering at the school. This represented approximately 1½miles for every year since I was a pupil there. As I drove along in the car I travelled this time-line in my mind considering all the events that have happened. The kaleidoscope of events flashed into my mind and it felt like I was trying to imagine myself again as a teenager. It was going to be my first time back inside the house for over 50 years; I know I had changed in just growing older and been buffeted by life's twists and turns; but how had the house faired in that time.

Navigating through Hounslow High Street and past the bus garage where I used to get the 657 trolley bus to school; the changes seemed enormous. The shop fronts were now catering for a more cosmopolitan population and the whole world's ethnic groups seemed to be represented on the pavements. Just going home at night, if that had been the sight out of the bus windows it would have really brought reality to my geography homework.

As I neared the school the old familiar red doors of the fire station come into view and next to it are the wrought iron gates of the front entrance. They stand closed and defiant against the changed world in the area and the dominating new building standing on our old games field.

My mind tried to imagine life again as a first year boy in grey short trousers in awe of everything and every teacher. Desperately trying to put names to faces on my old school photo, I entered the house and paused in the entrance hall, wondering what to expect. But I felt an absolute feeling of calm and stillness as it used to be outside the headmaster's study. The house seems to say to me, never mind how life has changed outside, I am still here, unchanged and unbowed. It felt as if I was entering the inside of a giant mother's womb; saying, do not mind how life has dealt your cards, look at me, they have raped my beautiful grounds but I will be here forever. Then moving into the music and art rooms, old school pals made themselves known to me as I mentally took it all in. Like me they had grown older and each would have a lifetime's experience to tell but we were all united for those brief hours in a common bond, set in the past. The reception had been well organised and a credit to those who planned it. Even looking at the back stairs I imagined running full pelt down them with all those school books; responding to the hand bell declaring a change of classroom. I looked in vain for the covered way leading to the physics and chemistry labs and the hall, but none of them exist now. I bet someone has a story about the bike sheds, but they would not be sharing it I guess. All too soon it was time to go and I waved goodbye and set off into that changed world outside, this time getting diverted into parts of Hounslow, with such high tower blocks, I could have been in another city. Then I came across my old familiar Hounslow underground station, still looked the same. Opposite though was a building announcing that it was The

Karachi Palace. In my youth it was The Odeon cinema and I used to sit with my girl friend and enjoy the films. Day to day life is one of constant change, but thankfully my memory stays the same and so does the old school.

We all had a permanent aide memoire to our schooldays, mine is with me as I write this. It's still in its protective brown paper cover which we were encouraged to wrap around it in year 1. My father's handwriting is on the front and of course inside where our parents had to acknowledge having seen it at the end of term. Do you remember when they were handed out at the end of term? They were locked away at school for most of the time and only given to us for a few critical days for parental viewing. I would study mine on the way home when sitting on the 657 trolley bus, quickly trying to find any bad bits and thinking of the possible explanations. Generally mine were satisfactory though but not outstanding. I have the greatest regards for our teachers, who always gave encouragement where extra effort was needed. Opening the pages I can now match the academic remarks and achievements with how I was feeling as I grew through adolescence. I loved being at the school and there were some tears as I passed through those lovely front gates for the last time. However what it does not report are these more social experiences we were all going through at the time. As I became more self aware, for instance in the fifth year, having to stand up and go through an aural French test in a mixed class was terrible and not because I did not necessarily know the words. Who remembers waiting to be called into one of Mr. Maylott's physics lessons? He always started with a written test of 20 questions on things you should have learnt from the last lesson. This called for a lot of last minute bookwork in the queue on formulae. Oh! The stress of it all. This would come after having had a late lunch because of older pupils getting priority in the lunch queue. Then there was the passage from reasonable soprano to poor tenor in Mr. Hart's choir. Just another thing to be dealt with. Mr. Short would say on one games report, fair progress. I would have said, absolutely marvelous as I was overweight through comfort eating and usually had insufficient cash for the correct football kit. The scripture lessons with Mr. Callow were a respite from the stresses of the day, only occasionally marred by elastic band and paper battles. I remember the smells of the gas in the Bunsen burners in the chemistry lab, the smells from the biology room of preserving fluids. I feel again the high humidity in the Art Room conservatory in high summer. The smells and the heat of the coke fires in winter, where I tried making toast, on a fork, before lessons first thing in the morning. I imagine again the long silences in the detention hour and the solemnity of the entrance hall outside Mr. Brown's study. Ah! This beloved school long may it remain there. Just why I was absent 22 times in 3 white and 30 times in 5 white is a mystery. I am so proud of having been to the school, appreciate now its core disciplines and many types of lessons which were enjoyable and stress free. No, the report is only one side of the experiences I was going through as I grew up, but I am proud of the record book and my later academic achievements, as would my teachers, if they knew, I feel sure.

Spring Grove the Beat Group Legacy

Tom Hanlon '55

The 1950's increase in consumer spending among teenagers created a Teenage Market for popular music. With the cessation of National Service, many teenagers who had formed skiffle/rock'n roll groups saw a real possibility of actually making a living from what had initially been a hobby or just a way of 'impressing the girls.' From about 1958 onwards the Grammar Schools in the South West London suburbs supplied a steady stream of musicians to various beat groups. For example, 3 of the 'Who' came from Acton County Grammar & some of the 'Yardbirds' were ex pupils of Hampton Grammar and in this respect Spring Grove were no exception.

Perhaps the most illustrious was Frank Alien of the Searchers group known to the staff at SGG as Francis McNeice (1955 -1960). Frank cut his teeth as 14 year old guitarist in the 'Ambassadors' a fledgling Skiffle Group almost entirely composed of existing or Old Spring Grovians namely Jonathon (Taff) Evans (1950 -1958), John Botterill (1949 -1956) & 'yours-truly'.

Somehow we managed to get ourselves a 'gig' providing the interval entertainment at the 1957 Old Spring Grovians Christmas dance at the school premises. We were a pretty shoddy outfit but we must have been a stark contrast to the dance group, the rather staid & jazzy Tony James Quintet. We were even photographed in the Banksian Room and a print is included in Frank's hugely entertaining book Travelling Man' How's that for posterity ?

The group metamorphosed into a rock'n roll group called the 'Raiders' gaining another Spring Grovian drummer Richard Thomas (1951 -1956) who sadly took his own life in the early 70's. We lost the banjo player, the folksy John and also Taff who was finding rock'n roll a bit difficult to cope with on a tea chest base. I eventually realised that I would have to take my studies to be a chemist more seriously to prevent H M forces from tapping me on the shoulder and in 1959 the group dissolved. Frank being 5 years younger had no such problems and went on to join a high profile Uxbridge band called Cliff Bennett & The Rebel Rousers when he turned professional and found himself gigging in Hamburg where British Beat Groups were much in demand. It was here that he became somewhat marginalised with 3 of the Searchers (also in Hamburg) as just about the only home bred musicians there who were tee-totallers. Thus he was already well acquainted with them when the offer came to join them in 1964 as bass guitarist. Now in his 40th year as a member he continues to front the band on appearances all over the world.

One of Frank's fellow members of the Cliff Bennett combo was yet another Old Spring Grovian David Wendells (52-58). A very proficient guitarist, Dave went on to have a sojourn with Lulu's backing group and is now believed to be living in Los Angeles.

From a later period 1960 -1965 keyboard player Ian McLachlan found himself a niche in the Small Faces of 'Itchycoo Park' fame who eventually mutated into the Faces and became associated with no less than Rod Stewart.

Finally we come to the joker in the pack, Vince Taylor the leather jacketed star of the 50's tele show 'Oh Boy' who was discovered in the legendary Two Ts' coffee bar in London's Soho. The publicity blurb had us believe that he was a pucker American, the genuine article who had come to the UK to make it 'big '. Later it transpired that he was actually born in 1938 in Isleworth as Brian Holden and emigrated to the US in 1945. Well, he didn't cross the Atlantic until 5 years later because I'm pretty sure he was the same Brian Holden who was a classmate of mine in 1 Blue for the autumn term 1950. Indeed, he did actually tell me that he must leave at the end of that term, because his family were emigrating to the US in the new year of 1951. This has never been mentioned in any references to Vince Taylor. We were quite friendly & we would board the 657 trolley bus to Hounslow garage after school. I thought he was a bit 'flash' and he certainly had more pocket money than me. And Taylor the rock'n roll star? Well, although he lacked nothing in showmanship, he couldn't really sing, neither did he have much sense of rhythm. He did however subsequently become quite a big name in France, but drink & drugs ruined him and he died in the early 80s from a heart attack while working as a porter at Geneva airport.

Dick Pearce (51 - 58) is in possession of a group photo of the 1st year soccer eleven of that 1950 autumn term and the goalkeeper is Brian Holden. I'll bet that would be worth a tidy sum to collectors of Vince Taylor ephemera

The Ambassadors

Prefects - 1951

Social Club Cyclists - High Wycombe - 1953
? ? ; Eddie Bennet; Don Curtis; David Sansom; Malcolm Harvey;
? ? ; Joan Lainson; Wendy Spring; Geraldine Seybourne

1955 - 1958

The Last Years at SGH

7

Three-Scimitar Badge -Sept. 1952

David Helsdon '57

I started at Spring Grove Grammar in September 1952. I can clearly recall those first few days, as a somewhat overawed 12 year old, getting to grips with the rambling geography of the school building and grounds, the names of fellow pupils and teachers, and not least a timetable which mysteriously spanned a six day working week (A day to F day).

On day one the new intake of, I guess, some 80 plus pupils assembled by the Harvard Road entrance. We all looked like tailors dummies, kitted out in full new uniform - never to be seen so clean and pristine again. Boys wore the black blazer with white three-scimitar badge while the girls were in either blue check summer dresses or pinafore dresses with blue blazers. Despite the marked colour differences of the sexes the school tended to be known by many locally as the Black and White school - echoes of inequality?

New pupils were assigned to one of three intake forms, 1 Red, 1 Blue and 1 White. I was assigned to 1 Blue based in Room 3 overlooking the South and West Pitches with Miss Phillips as our form teacher. As I recall she taught Scripture (RE) and English and was the girls' games mistress, being usually attired in a blue sports blazer and sensible skirt. First year assemblies were held in the Music Room. At the time I presumed the arrangement was devised on the premise that we were not yet considered ready for the big assembly. However I later learned that it was simply that the Hall could not accommodate all the new erks.

Even in the first few weeks the school had a fascination for me with its country house appearance and atmosphere, and well decked gardens. We became acquainted with exotic locations such as The Temple, The Pavilion, The Banksian Room, The Music Room and The Art Room. These contrasted with such pedestrian sites such as The Hut and The Loft. The latter was an unheated and largely unlit building where boys changed for soccer in winter, struggling with numb fingers to do up shirt and fly buttons in stygian gloom and icy cold.

Summer was certainly the best time to appreciate the school's qualities. There were opportunities at break and lunchtime of lazing on the grass or ambling round the grounds with one's chums or in pursuit of girls in which us boys were beginning to show an increasing interest. Winter was quite a different picture. Many of the classrooms had only old style fireplaces as the form of heating. While ornate they were quite inadequate for heating large classrooms and one either roasted to a frazzle or froze depending on where you sat. Distance now lends some enchantment to this scene.

Teachers made their mark upon us, none more so to me than the Headmaster, L. T. Brown. L. T. had had a classical education, was an intellectual and of deep religious convictions. To many of us however he was first and foremost a kindly man with an acute sense of humour. He had some favourite phrases, oft repeated, and some still come to mind.

"We are a Grammar School not a Crammer School".

This remark was sparked possibly because of the superior results often achieved by our neighbouring and rival school, Isleworth Grammar. That said L. T. did sincerely believe that a key role of Spring Grove was to turn out well-rounded and balanced individuals able to cope with the realities of the world rather than producing remote eggheads.

"Being vulgar is doing in public what should only be done in private".

This remark was usually triggered by L. T. seeing or having reported to him a pupil eating in the street on the way to or from school. With so much eating and drinking on the hoof now days this particular remark epitomizes a past world.

"The three P's" In seeking to drum some religious teaching into pupils L. T. liked to refer to God as the three P's which he then defined as Perfect Wisdom, Perfect Love and Perfect Knowledge. This phrase means more to me now than it ever did as a callow teenager.

Another teacher who made his mark was Keith Stuart Hart, the music master. I can see him now sweeping into the classroom with his crimped hair, immaculate suit showing just the right amount of shirt cuff, and the steel rimmed spectacles. He exercised a firm hold on any class from the moment he came through the door and woe betide anyone not paying proper attention or giving a wrong answer. Detentions or black stars were freely given for minor misdemeanors, and boys could also be at the receiving end of a clip round the ear. We were all in awe of him but he did succeed in inculcating an interest for many in serious music by playing records of classical pieces. I much preferred this to struggling to read or write music or sing off key. Mr Hart's female counterpart was probably Miss Clothier, a Maths teacher. Despite her diminutive size she had the ability with her razor tongue to reduce the bravest and biggest of pupils to slobbering wrecks.

In the hierarchical structure prefects were seen by us twelve-year-olds as not much lesser beings than teachers. Individuals such as Cutting, Bush, Isaac, Crook, Hore, Marion Brunt and Margaret Wilsher come to mind. For my part those who were particularly good at sport were especially regarded, though most of us young boys were star struck by the good looks of the head girl Marion Brunt. Then they seemed distant grown up figures. Seeing some of them now at our recent reunions the mysteries of time appeared to have drawn us closer together.

Though Old Spring Grovians are rightly aggrieved as to what has happened to much of our school and grounds it is probably fair to say that the demolition of the Hall did not stir too many passions.

Set apart from the main House and approached by either a covered walkway or a cobbled stone pathway (probably stabling in Andrew Pear's day) the hall skirted the gymnasium on one side with the Banksian Room and the Physics Laboratory bordering the other.

Yet despite its lack of architectural grandeur the Hall did represent the hub of school life at Spring Grove. Assemblies, prize days, concerts, plays, dances and meetings all took place there. If I try hard I can hear the steps of L T Brown approaching along the covered way, see him begowned entering the hall, ascending the stairs to the stage to set another assembly in progress. As you will recall L T sat centre stage on an elegant wood carved throne-like chair with the Senior Master and Mistress flanking him. Set behind were the choir led by Stuart Hart on one side, with prefects on the other.

In my time at Spring Grove the Senior Master position was held in turn by Fred "Basher" Brown, Dicky Callow, George Barrett and Bill Lineham. Miss Emily Taylor was the Senior Mistress followed later by Kate Hemming. These eagle eyed individuals were very adept from their lofty positions on stage to espy any misbehaviour amongst a vast throng of pupils who were supposed to adopt a silent and reverent pose before assembly began.

Daily school assemblies of the type that we experienced with hymn singing and bible readings are largely defunct nowadays in the state system. Then however prefects took turns to read lessons and I well remember one poor individual whose legs shook so badly that his trousers flapped as if in a force ten gale. I was more sympathetic later as a prefect myself when I had to read the lesson - I did try to keep my legs braced to avoid trouser flapping! L T, bless him, always praised a prefect on his or her first reading no matter how garbled the presentation might have been through nerves.

Another memory that comes to mind is the singing of the hymn "Lord Dismiss Us With Thy Blessing" on the last day of term. Whilst this was a joyous time for most, the odd school leaver, including certain prefects, could be seen singing with moistened eyes and quivering lips. For some perverse reason I can still remember all the words of the first verse of that hymn.

Naming and shaming was one feature of our assemblies. The names of individuals amassing the greatest number of black stars were read out, as were the names of two boys who nearly burnt the school down by lighting a fire in the Basement. We were also frequently lectured on the vulgarity of eating in the streets on the way to and from school. I also remember much being made of the shame of a particularly heavy soccer defeat at the hands of our arch rivals, Isleworth Grammar.

It was not all gloom and doom however. I recall the Headmaster telling us with much pride and delight one morning that Dicky Pearce had secured 100% in a maths exam - a particularly remarkable achievement from my perspective as someone who struggled with the subject and just scraped an

'O' level. On other occasions I remember announcements that Mike Worsfold and Jim Young had secured places at Cambridge University. Great achievements indeed for a school that was seen by some as not being at the same academic level as certain nieghbouring establishments.

Prize Day was a key date for some. Though not a regular attender I never ceased to be amazed by the vast quantity of potted plants that arrived to bedeck the Hall, only to disappear magically by the next day. To ensure a smooth running event rehearsals took place in the Hall before Prize Day. Would-be prize winners had to practise a measured walk across the stage, their bow or curtsey and hand shake. Miss Taylor often acted as the V I P at these rehearsals. On the actual days V I P's came from a broad spectrum - church, arts etc. - but the only name I can remember now was of the actress Sonia Dresdel. The prizes were invariably books, and although the titles did not always seem that exciting then I am sure that many are treasured now and even read!

Plays and concerts were also performed in the Hall. I recall "The Importance of Being Ernest" starring David Taylor, Gordon MacMillan, Pat Jeffries and June Clarke. In concerts Malcolm Harvey and Margaret Wilsher made a harmonious singing duet, while Michael Gardener was a very professional oboe player. Others coming to mind were Jean Usher as a solo vocalist and Audrey Minihane on piano. Capping it all however was Stuart Hart who as the need arose conducted in his own inimitable and flamboyant style.

There was one activity in the Hall which I cannot comment on, namely Girls' Assembly. What on earth did they talk about? Perhaps someone will tell me at the next reunion, or perhaps I shouldn't know!

Nowadays it seems the majority of students go on to university and grapple with such thorny subjects as media studies etc. Back in the 50's however the reverse was true with the majority leaving school, grammar or secondary modern, at sixteen. This was the expectation partly encouraged I am sure by a very healthy and varied job market at that time.

I was one of the few staying on at SGGS for two years. While some of my sixth form friends clearly had their sights set on eventual university placements I was still not sure what to do with the rest of my life, and the sixth form allowed me to "buy time". So in 1957 I "signed on" for "A" level studies in French, English and History – a somewhat lonely life for a male student as the rest of the male sixth form joined the Science side.

By a mixture of luck and design staying on turned out to be a good move. First and foremost school life seemed easier having got into the sixth form. Teachers treated you with greater respect and appeared more relaxed, and lessons became more enjoyable accordingly. Mr Leitch, our History master, smoking an aromatic tobacco in his pipe during lessons (probably breaking all school fire regulations) took us through subjects such as the English Civil War in the manner of a benevolent uncle. Miss Barr and Miss Coulthard invited our French "A" Level Group to their flat in Hounslow one evening where we drank wine and ate nibbles while undertaking some perfunctory and limited French conversation. Our English "A" level group went up to London to see the Tempest and Hamlet – a great way to better appreciate the written text.

Once a week we had an extra-curricular German lesson with the Head Master in his elegant study. We found L T Brown could be easily diverted from the subject in question and we enjoyed listening to him expounding on his student days, the differences between the Catholic and Anglican churches, and so on – occasionally we read a little German.

On a more mundane level we had free periods with access to private study rooms on the top floor (the ex-servants' quarters). These small rooms, well heated by open fires in the winter, provided much comfort and seclusion albeit little incentive to study. The rooms did however afford a good view on to the courts below and I confess I spent part of my time "studying" some of our shapely girls in their gym slips while they cavorted about playing netball. In the Upper Sixth I became a prefect and Deputy Head Boy with the perk of our own prefects' room again well heated in the winter by an open fire. For me the only down sides of being a prefect were firstly having to read the lesson in school assembly and secondly having to wear one of those ghastly silk tasselled prefect caps to and from school. To my knowledge no other school in the county had such outdated Corinthian styled tasselled caps. My friend Victor Wride suffered the indignity of having his cap pinched by the dreaded Marlborough School girls. When the cap was retrieved it had been "de-tasselled" - very Freudian!

After two years I managed to get three "A" level passes and decided that I had had enough of studying. The qualifications attained helped me to secure a career in H M Customs and Excise from where I retired some forty years later in the year 2000.

Je ne regrette rien.

PS To my knowledge none of the girls in my "A" level Arts Group are on the contact list or have ever been to a reunion; so where are you?

Marion Shorter, Pauline Batty, Sylvia Paris, Helen Chadwick, Benita Cruik-shank and Enid Albagli.

Girls' Assembly: the Truth Revealed

Val Rendell '57

David Helsdon asked the question Val answers it....

Girls' Assembly. *Girls' Assembly.* What went on behind the closed doors? What mysterious female secrets were exchanged? What esoteric advice was Miss Taylor passing on to the three hundred non-male persons in her special charge — persons ranging from little girls who had only just been parted from their dollies and teddies, to brazen buxom young women whose only interest was dolling themselves up and chasing teddy-boys?

I am going to disappoint you. It was mostly very dull, and the rest of it was slightly embarrassing. There was nothing at all about sex, boys, love, personal relationships and all the stuff that is now part of the syllabus from pre-school onwards. You boys shared our only education in the reproduction of the species, via the physiology of the rabbit. Not a good example, I would have thought, for any of us.

We were lectured about our behaviour, about wearing our school hats at all times, about not eating in the street, about not running in the corridors, about keeping the cloakrooms tidy. Most of the time, we were lectured about uniform. A Good Person would be asked to come and stand on the platform, and the various Correct Points of her uniform would be pointed out to us. How we all loathed the Good Person from then on.

I was at SGGS during the 50s, which was a very peculiar decade. (Brief interlude for social history.) The austerity of the 40s was over, the camaraderie and the make-do-and-mend spirit of the war years had faded. The swinging sixties were in the unimaginable future. An attempt was being made, especially in middle-class society, to re-create the lost world of comfortable respectable family life. But it never quite worked, because people had seen other ways of living.

This is encapsulated for me in the White Glove movement. Before the war, ladies wore gloves. Always. Miss Taylor tried to persuade her grubby untidy schoolgirls to start wearing white gloves with their gingham frocks and ankle socks. This was before the days of automatic washing machines. Nylon gloves appeared to solve the laundry problem, but they quickly turned a yellowish-grey, and in any case who would want to wear nylon gloves on a hot summer's day? In vain did the Good Person parade in Girls' Assembly in her white gloves and Juliet cap. Ladies no longer wore hats and gloves, and we were not persuaded.

To do Miss Taylor justice, there was a good deal of latitude allowed in the school uniform compared with other grammar schools in the area. We could wear a modest amount of makeup, and our dresses could be any style. But this well-meaning latitude only made us look ridiculous. Ankle-socks and lipstick do not go together. Lolitas we were not. Gingham only looks nice made up into a dress with a waist and a gathered skirt. This looks fine on a seven-year-old, not so good on her teenage sister. The fashion in the fifties was for circle skirts. Only a needlewoman of genius can make a circle skirt out of checked material, and it takes twice as much stuff. I tried to persuade my mother — who was a needlewoman of genius — to do this, and she refused on the grounds of economy. I shed many tears.

Do you remember the sack dress? It was the height of fashion in 1957, and someone had her dresses made in this shapeless mode. Hoist by her own liberal petard, Miss Taylor could only recommend a nicely gathered skirt, with a belt two inches wide, maximum. The fashion was for elasticated belts about five inches wide that pinched your waist as cruelly as a Victorian corset, but a by-law was created to forbid them. The Juliet cap was a well-meaning attempt to find a school hat that would please us, and it was chosen by democratic vote. But it looked extremely comic perched on top of a back-combed lacquered beehive hairdo. Or folded in half and pinned with hairgrips to accommodate a pony-tail. High heels were of course forbidden, but what about kitten heels? Or ballerina flatties, so low-cut that you could only walk in them by curling your toes under and gripping tight? The possibilities for transgressing the spirit of the school uniform, while adhering strictly to the letter of the law, were endless.

All this stuff about uniform; I told you that Girls' Assembly was dull. The embarrassing bit was about . . . yes, it was about Periods. In the 50s, in a mixed school, menstruation was the elephant in the room. Girls were always fainting, or bursting into tears, or having to leave the room urgently, or being unable to swim or run or do anything but moon about with headaches and stomach-aches - but nothing could be said as to why. (The same applied in the wider society.) The apparatus for dealing with a period was medieval — lumping great sanitary towels of cotton-wool that had to be burned after use. Our uniforms had no pockets, so where did you put a spare one? Only wicked sinful girls used tampons — or girls with wonderfully enlightened mothers. Tampons were never mentioned in Girls' Assembly. The little girls sat through this, open-mouthed. They were being introduced to the real world, the world not of Girls but of Women.

We had little preliminary twinges of feminism from time to time. Why wasn't there a Boys' Assembly? Why weren't the boys made to lose half their lunch hour in order to be lectured about wearing ties and caps and keeping the lavatories clean and tidy? **It wasn't fair**. It took us a while to translate complaints about unfairness into action. But that is another story.

I Was Ill the Day Mule Driving Was Taught.

Freddy Friedmann '57

The wind is blowing the tall palm trees outside my window as I look towards the sea. Here at home this is rare because even in winter the wind is not often strong and cold. This winter wind reminds me of when I attended SGGS from 1953 to 1957. That wind whistled through the cracks in our rattling windows on the top floor class room, which had once been the the the quarters of the servants. It was the wind that we had to endure when we trotted out in skimpy football uniforms, when the south pitch was iron -hard by frost. We weren't even allowed to put on pants.

Now that I am seventy and retired, memories are just as fresh. Memories of names are not as vivid as the faces because I can still check up on the old long school photograph.

I left school after an undistinguished career both in scholastics and sports and came to Israel to try and find any relatives that had survived WWII. I lived on a kibbutz where I worked hard and learned Hebrew. My first job was driving a mule team delivering food to the cow shed. SGGS had not prepared for this,or apparently I had been ill that day when mule driving was being taught. I also missed the lessons in cotton picking, haystack building, shovelling chicken manure and trawler fishing. The school dinners had stood me in good stead when it came to surviving on poorly cooked food. The dinner ladies made my stomach as strong as iron. I could digest anything except Prussic acid. Those meals of gristle and over-boiled cabbage had done their job well.

I have kept in touch with a few fellow pupils. Recently Margaret Anderson (Elders) informed me that at the last reunion they had talked about me a bit. Apparently I had beaten Mr. Short at wrestling in the gymn. I had forgotten that because I was much better at boxing. I had connections with Vic Wride, who is now a geologist., Gary Anderson who is now a painter, Andrea Cameron a librarian. Kathy Murphy retired on the Isle of Wight and Ken Johnson. A few years ago when I visited London to buy Laser equipment for my Physiotherapy Clinic, I found out that Ken Johnson was going to be the next President of the Isleworth Rotary Club. Being a Rotarian for the last twenty years, I phoned him up to congratulate him. He invited me to address his club, which I did with great pleasure. I told them that that when I played cricket for Drake House, I had always fielded at short leg which suggested healthy British humour,as my left leg was five centimetres shorter than my right. Ken invited me round for drinks after the talk and he gave me much news of other fellow pupils.

Other happy memories came from our Skiffle Group. It happened but few were aware of it but some of us formed a skiffle band called The Sinners. Jerry Gross and Tony Parton played guitars, Dave Turner was on drums, Vic Cornheim(not

SGGS) and your humble servant on washboard. We were enthusiastic but good we were not but we had fun and that was the point.

On retrospect, the education at The Black and White though not perfect in every degree, did encourage me to want to know much more and that I have done, having built up a large library taking up an entire room in my home. The school taught me fair play and sportsmanship, something which is rare in most sports especially professional events. I believe that it was due to the mind set of Mr. Brown. I do not think that most of the teachers were very good but it was the whole that mattered and not the specifics.

I am very grateful that I went to SGGS and met so many that gave me a good, safe start in life. There were very few days when I did not want to go to school.

"Partir, C'est Mourir Un Peu."

Pauline BATTY '57

Thoughts on the Move to Lampton Road
from Spring Grovian Magazine June 1959

At last, after many years of effort and persuasion, a new school has been built, and we are to leave the present " Spring Grove Grammar School. "Some of us will leave the old building with feelings of relief, and no-one can deny that the House is in many ways unsuitable for a school. This is very obvious in winter, when a gale howls round the walls, rattling and banging all the windows and causing doors to slam in a distant part of the building, shattering the hush that has descended on afternoon lessons. As the gale howls, curious pupils watch as a cleaner laboriously climbs the stairs to place a bucket which will catch the drips coming through the roof. Last year the defects were sadly more obvious when some plaster fell on the first floor, and when, at the "School Dance," rain even managed to seep through the roof in the hall.

Any who have suffered examinations in the hall in winter will not regret leaving. The door rattles, dismally in tune with one's thoughts, and blasts of cold air periodically remove papers from desks. The pupils sit huddled over their books with overcoats around their shoulders and miserable expressions on their faces. Although the hall may be cold, the form rooms can be even worse. The boy who sits at the back in front of the fire is seen in shirt sleeves with a beetroot-red face, while the unfortunate teacher paces up and down in front of the class in an effort to keep warm.

Lastly, many, especially the Staff, regret the lack of accommodation and the danger entailed in getting about. As one approaches the corner near Miss Richards's staffroom, one becomes cautious. Only the foolhardy go blindly on to be met in a head-on collision with a too-hasty little boy. Wise folk prefer to use the main staircase, for they know the perils of attempting to climb the back stairs at change of lessons!

However, the majority of us, if given the choice, would most probably prefer to stay in our present home. The two most important reasons for this are the fact that we have some of the most beautiful grounds in the neighbourhood, and that our school has a unique atmosphere.

There is little need to illustrate the beauties of our grounds; we shall appreciate them so much more when we no longer have them. So far, I have not seen so much as a tree in our new grounds, and the prospect is dismal.

The remarkably friendly atmosphere of school will be somewhat changed in a new building. There will be more pupils and extra staff, so that we are somewhat bound to assume the more impersonal atmosphere of a bigger school. This school will be new and modern. Never again shall we see a master braving the wind, gown flying as he hurries to the hut, or Mr. Lineham with a large black umbrella raised, hastening across the muddy earth to the pavilion.

With the loss of our grounds, we shall miss also what is left of beauty in the school, the heavy mahogany doors and the splendour of the music room; and none of us could fail to appreciate the artistic side of the Boy Prefects' Room, as we glimpse the football socks hanging up to dry in an inconspicuous corner.

However, we have to leave "Spring Grove." For some it will always have pleasant memories, for others, who have spent a short time here, it will occupy only a vague place in their thoughts. Nevertheless, we must look forward rather than backward with the hope that the " new school" will not be very different from the present one.

5 White 1955

Top row; Chris Plail, Hugh Leitch, Geof Hewett; Second row; John Sweetland, Richard Walker, Dick Harris, Walter Roebuck; Third row; Roy Yateman, Ken Johnson, Duncan MacIntyre, Graham, Don Watson, ?, Bob Poynter

Jill Ramsay, Peggy Evans, Audrey Minihane, Alison MacPhail, Janet Blight,

Daphne Cartwright, Olive Cutting, Barbara Adams and Celia Davis.

It's a Small World

Margaret Elders '57

Reading the "small world" comment about the Cedar of Lebanon at the Spring Grove Cemetery, Cincinatti brought to mind two examples of it in my own life. In 1961, as a young bride, I journeyed to Africa to join my husband. He was working in Northern Rhodesia as it was then called. I went by air, flying, if I remember correctly, on a Viscount. The flight took 22 hours and needed several stops en route to refuel at exotic sounding places, Rome, Malta, Benghazi, Khartoum, Entebbe and finally Ndala my destination. I approached the journey with some trepidation. It was my first long flight having previously only flown across the channel to Paris and that with friends.

You will, therefore, appreciate how glad I was to discover one of the other unaccompanied ladies was an OSG! Elizabeth Jackson was flying out to visit her fiancé and his family also in Ndola. Amazingly Lizzie's fiancé and my husband had become friends having met at the Sports Club. Both were waiting for our arrival in the old Nissen hut which was the airport building in those days.

The second "small world" incident happened some twenty years later. Natalie, our younger daughter, started her new school and befriended Victoria a class-mate. Soon the girls were inviting each other to their homes for tea and sleep-overs. Gradually the parents became friends too. One day Mary, Vicky's mother, and I discovered that we came from the same area. The inevitable question was, of course, was "where did you go to school?". Yes, you've guessed it. Spring Grove Grammar.

One evening Mary rang to say she'd hunted out the 1957 roll up photo. She'd found herself but couldn't spot me. Later, I rang her back, having found the

same photo to say that the tall, bean pole of a girl standing right behind her was me. Mary had an illustrious career at Spring Grove. As Mary Evans she succeeded Margaret Wilsher as Head Girl. There must be lots of small world stories out there among us OSGs.

Can you spot the bean pole in the photo extract - left?

I Should Be Doing Other Things!!

Helen Webber '57 (Lattimore)

I received my copy of the Spring Grovian Report and have spent valuable time today reading and thinking of school days, when I should have been doing other things!! My thanks to those of you who do this voluntary job - it gives a lot of us joy!

I joined the school in September 1952, starting in 1 Red, green Rodney house, and my first form master was Mr. Leitch. I met Mr. Leitch again at one of the recent reunions and was thrilled to have a chat with him about those days - I even think Peter Salter took a picture of us together and I noticed it on the website some while ago.

I was puzzled when reading the article in SGR 15, page 11, regarding Margaret Elders and Mary Evans. The Head Girl in the picture shown, two places to the right of Miss Ashcroft to my memory is Ann Waldron (good at cricket).

However, if you look at the 1957 'roll up', I believe that Mary Evans is ten places to the right of Miss Ashcroft and you will then see Margaret Elders directly behind her (two rows back).

I recall that Ann Waldron succeeded Margaret Wilsher as Head Girl and then Mary Evans, but that might be bad memory. They were all very nice girls, as I recall.

I really have loads of happy memories of 'Spring Grove' - perhaps my most important personal one is that I only went there because my older half brother, Kenny Matthews, was a pupil and I had attended a school fete with him. He left the school in 1952, just before I joined. One of his friends was Mike Stacey, who I was pleased to meet once again at the first reunion I came to. I have heard that Mike has sadly died since that time; he was obviously ill when we met.

Apart from him I don't think anyone else remembers my brother. He was very keen on cricket, and even helped coach the girls I understand!! He also made some frames for the Drama Club which were on one of the corridor walls and I was always proud as I walked by.

Very sadly, Kenny died at the early age of 28, from a form of muscular dystrophy. He had joined the Navy after leaving Spring Grove (..in Mr. Leitch's footsteps?). Again, he also said good things about Mr. Leitch to me, and his other favourite teacher was of course 'Dolly' Ransom. Unfortunately, I never had a lesson with her.

I can remember my brother (five years older than I) coming back to the school at Christmas time to a school dance. He was only keen to see some of his contemporaries, but my own friends were amazed at me being accompanied by such a good looking chap! He had been on an eighteen-month naval stint in the Mediterranean and was very bronzed. I have a photograph of us together when he was a first former, in his new SGGS school uniform!

Through these reunions, I have once again met one of my classmates, Maureen

Lawrence, now living in the West Country, and also an older girl, Jackie Simpson, who was my mentor at my very first job, at Rolex Watches, in Mayfair. Both Maureen and I went to Rolex, and she met and married her husband, a watchmaker. They are still together.

We had all been introduced to that company by Miss Williams, who took the Commercial Classes, and was a friend of Rolex's Company Secretary. We were very fortunate to have a grammar school that held commercial classes - it was unusual. Some of the girls were 5th formers and some were doing shorthand and typing courses after their 6th year A levels.

At the time, my stepfather was diagnosed with lung cancer, with only months to live, just as I was entering my GCE 'O' levels 5th year. I was told my plans to become 'a copy' of our Domestic Science teacher, Mrs. Margaret Webster, by going to university/college had to be abandoned and I was to go into an office!! What use would a university education be to a girl, I was told - much more useful to be a secretary!!

I did end up as Sec/PA to a director at Rolex and of course did get to meet the founder of that prestigious company, Hans Wilsdorf. I typed letters to some very important people, from Winston Churchill to Royalty, band leaders, very famous actors, etc. Rolex was a very happy company to work with.

I did feel somewhat cheated for not getting my university education, and becoming a teacher, but strangely it has worked out. I am still typing away and doing letters for all sorts of reasons, and it is also how I came to meet my husband!!

I could rattle on about Spring Grove for ages, and was pleased today to see Michael Gardiner's picture, with his contemporary, Alan Darg. Wasn't MG the guy who played the oboe - Jesu, Joy of Man's Desiring - comes to mind! Also I believe he directed a school play, based on Little Women, and I played Beth in that.   I think I had better stop now before I recall other school moments and fellow pupils. I have some notes to type out for my husband, on one of his voluntary jobs!! - and I have sewing to do for a daughter's directorial debut with a production of Pride and Prejudice at Hampton Hill Playhouse.

It has been lovely dipping into the past and thinking of those 'Happy Days'.

Under 15 netball '56/7(?)
Betty Greaves,
Carole Sheldon,   Gill Freeman;
Gill Stearnham, Valerie Stevens,
Sue Gardner,   Valerie Peskett

The Amazing Miss Ransom

Keith Lomas '57

There have been a few articles about Miss Ransom in earlier editions of The Spring Grovian and I expect it would be possible to fill up a complete edition on Miss Ransom herself and she was probably the most popular teacher at school.

After I left school, I was busy working for a qualification and then joined an international company and worked abroad and to my regret, I didn't keep in touch with old school friends and didn't hear news of the school. Then about 40 years later, one of those amazing coincidences occurred and I met Mrs Wade, mother of Colin Wade, who was at SGGS. She was down visiting a friend in our village in Devon. We kept in touch and I heard from her that Miss Ransom had taken up residency again in Hounslow having returned from working overseas. My daughter was living in Hounslow at the time and on one of my visits to see her, I looked up Miss Ransom, who was living in Lampton Rd. We met up several more times and she didn't seem to have changed at all. On one occasion, she came to dinner with us at my daughter's and I remember that she didn't stop talking from the moment I collected her in the car until I delivered her back home. When she retired from Lampton School, she travelled around and took up teaching again in a seminary in the Congo but had to leave when it was too difficult to live there because of the war and she was given half an hour to pack up her belongings and leave. By this time, she was approaching 90 years of age.

During one of our conversations, I mentioned that we had booked a holiday to visit China. Oh, she said, perhaps you could look up Albert, as if he lived in the next town. Albert turned out to be one of her pupils that she taught in the Congo who had gained a scholarship to China. She hadn't heard from him for some time but she had his address, which was the Peoples University in Beijing. I explained that I was on a guided tour of China, spending two days in Beijing being shown the Wall, Tianaman Sq and everything else of interest there before moving on to our next destination and even in the unlikely event of me having time to arrange a meeting, it was unlikely I would be able to track Albert down in Beijing. However, Miss Ransom had no doubts at all that I would be able to meet up with him and she gave me his last known address- a P O Box at the University, a letter and some money to give to him. I wrote a letter to him at the PO Box number and suggested that we met at 6.00 pm on the second day of our visit to Beijing at the hotel where we were staying. I hadn't received a reply back before we left for China and didn't hold out much hope of meeting him. 6.00pm came on the appointed day with no sign of him, then 7.00pm came and 7.45pm and I had almost given up any chance of meeting him and was due to rejoin the party for dinner at the hotel at 8.00pm. Just before 8.00pm someone came through the hotel door who could only be Albert. He was a tall, well built, black African, a member of the Hutsi or Tutsi tribe. He apologised for being late, due to the traffic. We had experienced the Beijing traffic during the day, so could sympathise with him.

Albert was full of praise for Miss Ransom. She had been instrumental in teaching Albert and helping him to obtain the scholarship to Beijing where he had gained BSc and MSc degrees in rocket propulsion and was currently trying to secure a place in a British or American university to study for a PhD.

I was able to bring a letter back that he had written to Miss Ransom and it was from him that I learned that Miss Ransom had died a year or two later.

Miss E.Ransom Was Something Else:

Chris Grant '58

I kept trying to peddle fast enough to catch up with her all the way through Belgium and Holland in the early summer of 1958.

It was a cycling tour, and there were days we just did do that all day. It was my first time away from home, and I was often terribly frightened, but I did it. Miss Ransom always appeared just about when I was about to burst in to tears.

We had bed bugs and the big silver balls of the World Fair in Belgium, and then we had the clean serenity of Holland (Thank You Lord for clean beds and flat roads at long last). I had five quid as spending money for 10 days, and my bike went wrong soon after we started. Miss Ransom lent me ten bob to get my bike fixed, and when I came home I never paid her back. It was a super trip, and one day we cycled past an airport as five Spitfires took off in formation - I doubt if many kids like me have seen that.

I did learn a bit of French - basically how to order a beer in Belgium and Holland. I came back home different than when I left, for Miss Ransom showed me how to explore. What a lady Miss Ransom was - for we were not little students with her - we were colleagues and friends. We explored together.

I love that woman, for she taught me how to teach. It was forty-five years ago, and I still can not keep up.

SGGS, Philately and Genealogy

Alan Sabey '57

S hortly before taking the 11+ my parents were asked to make three choices of schools if I passed the exam and three if I did not. My mother discovered that quite a lot of the parents of boys in this area had selected Isleworth Grammar School and my parents felt that a mixed school would be better for me. I passed the 11+ and got their first choice in SGGS. I seem to recall that before school actually started we attended a meeting in the School Hall to learn a bit about the school in advance. I seem to remember that there was a booklet as well. Everything from SGGS is long gone now so I can only rely on memories.

The first day at the school was a bit daunting as everything was new, but it did not take long to settle in. My first Form Master was Mr Leitch up on the top floor. Miss Hewitt and Misses Coulthard and Barr were Form Teachers over the five years I was there. My "house" was Drake and we had a red strip in our ties. Rodney house had green and Nelson house had blue. School uniform was purchased at Abernethies in Hounslow High Street.

I can recall waiting on the down platform at Isleworth station for the train to take us on our school outings. I can remember going to Southampton Water and to Cheddar Gorge. The memory is letting me down on the other places but no doubt someone will fill in the gaps. After the trip to Southampton Water, where we saw a number of the famous liners in dock, the photographs we took were displayed in the Art Room. I still have mine.

Incidentally Lawson Cockcroft looks after the archives of St. Leonard's church, Heston and I do the same for St. Mary's, Norwood Green. Lawson is a friend of our clergyman. What a small world!

I have tried to keep this gramatically correct in memory of Mr Lineham! What a wonderful teacher of the English language he was.

Sadly one Thursday afternoon I arrived home to be met by my mother at the back gate when I rang the cycle bell and once indoors was told that my father had died of a heart attack that morning while driving a London Transport bus in Greenford. He had been taken to the King Edward Memorial Hospital in West Ealing but had passed away in the ambulance on the way there. He was a month short of 45 and it came as a great shock to all of us as he did not seem to be ill. That summer we witnessed a foretaste of what was to come. He had driven the three of us and my mother's parents to Winchester so my grandfather could see his mother again as she was approaching her 100th birthday. While we were there, my parents took me to see the Cathedral and Dad collapsed in the High Street on the way back to their house. He recovered and we came home in the car and thought no more about it. Dad went to see the doctor who treated him for indigestion! Heart attack victims were not wired up to machines in those days.

The date was November 5th - yes, Guy Faukes day. I never bought fireworks again as a mark of respect and that night with the firework reminders remained painful for a good many years. Where I live is in the middle of an Asian community and Divali, spread over a number of nights, has taken the place of Guy Faukes with even louder bangs!

My achievements at school were not breathtaking but I persevered and remained in the A stream from 2A to 5A. Thus we were taught Latin by Miss Barr.

When it came to the 5th year and leaving in 1958, I had no idea what jobs there were out there and I knew I had to find a job as money was tight. The only male relative I ever saw was my maternal grandfather who was not in a position to advise me about jobs. I heard that someone was coming to the school to give advice on jobs and I waited... and waited... and waited but that did not happen.

Mr L T Brown, our wonderful headmaster, heard that I had been going to a number of interviews and not having any success and he called me into his Study. That was a privilege as the only other time I had been in there was when he taught us Scripture on one isolated occasion.

Mr Brown told me that he knew the Deputy Borough Treasurer of Heston and Isleworth Borough Council and would I like him to arrange an interview? Thus began my career in Local Government. I was in the wages office for 18 months, then a year in the general income office, moving onto the Rates Office which remained my career for the rest of my working life. Life at H & I B C in the Town Hall in Treaty Road was like a family where everybody knew everybody else. We merged with Feltham and Brentford & Chiswick Councils in 1965 and the atmosphere just went. I endured a year of the new Hounslow Council and realised that I was not going to get much further if I remained there so I applied for and got a job in the newly formed Rate Rebates section of Hammersmith and Fulham Council where I stayed for five years. Further advancement came with a job as a Recovery Officer with Ealing Council where I remained until the end of my career at quite a high level of responsibility.

Sadly my mother's last years were not good and she was in need of a carer, and I was that carer (frankly I found Social Services useless). I felt that for what she had done for me in keeping the home together after Dad died, I owed it to her.

She passed away in 1992 and my life took a new turn, a new chapter had begun. I was able to venture further afield than I was able to do for some time and I have had a couple of holidays in Australia and New Zealand. I have also been on cruises and coach tours including Istanbul where I walked in my paternal great-great-grandfather's footsteps as he was the Manager of a Small Arms factory out there, having been sent out form Woolwich Arsenal.

This year I have achieved another holiday goal and have had a week in St Petersburg and a few days in Moscow. St Petersburg is beautiful and I would go again despite having to pay nearly £100 for the visa. It is a photographer's paradise.

I returned to churchgoing again about eleven years ago and have become a Server, Sacristan and Parish Archivist. It was through the Serving capacity that I unexpectedly met up with Malcolm Measures at a funeral where he was a family mourner and I was a Server. Collecting and preserving things (as an Archivist does) fits in with my hobby of philately. This started when I was about eight or nine and Dad asked his brother-in-law for some spare stamps (the uncle was also a collector). The stamp collecting was put aside while at SGGS but was taken up again about 1968. I have achieved an International level Gold medal standard collection about the British Empire Exhibition at Wembley in the 1920s (the occasion of our first commemorative stamps). In addition to that I also collect items connected with the 1948 Olympic Games. Whenever there is a Summer Olympic Games these days there is a philatelic exhibition purely for Olympics, not other disciplines. This is part of the cultural side of the Olympics.

 In Sydney 2000 I entered my collection and won a silver medal and a major prize and recently it was entered in Beijing where I won a Silver-Gilt medal which looks about the same size as the medals won by the athletes. I am also interested in Thematic collecting where it is the subject on the stamp that matters not by which country and when.

Having sold the BEE collection but retaining the Olympics one, my interests have now turned to genealogy - the family tree. I had been interested in that since finding some family papers in 1968. Although I have done the trees of the four grandparents, it is my maternal grandfather's Lincolnshire ancestry which interests me the most. There are quite a few people researching their own branch of what has turned out to be one enormous tree with worldwide contacts. I am a member of the Society of Genealogists and of the Lincoln-shire Family History Society and committee member on the London branch. Earlier this year I went to Lincoln to present our Branch Report. I have found some distant cousins in Grimsby and go there a couple of times a year for a week of pure genealogy. This involves trips to the County Archives in Lincoln for the Parish Registers and to Grimsby library to search newspapers for obituaries and other notices as well as searching the other records that they hold.

The television programmes "Who do you think you are?" have brought more interested people forward. I have found some interesting bits of information in my researches over the last 25 years.

I am happy to answer questions on philately and genealogy through e-mail.

Last in the Line

Cynthia Harvey '58
(edited and approved by Gordon Harvey '46, and Malcolm Harvey , '53.)

When scholarship time came (that is what it was called then – not 11+) there was no second thought as to what my first choice of grammar school should be! If all went well I was to follow my two brothers to the Black & White School – Spring Grove Grammar. All did go well and in September 1953 I found myself in that same Music Room as Susan Gardner (see Spring Grovian February 2010). I was pleased to discover that several of my friends from Primary days were, like me, placed in form 1 Red and following the Assembly we were all marshalled up many stairs to the top of the building and Room 17 which was to be our form room with form teacher Mr Leitch. We were given our rather flummoxing time tables which suggested we were going to have to find our way around the school for different teachers and different rooms for our various subjects. As we started new lessons we were often asked if anyone had relatives who had been to the school and for a while I was able to glory in the successes of my two brothers.

Gordon had left the school in 1947 and after two years National Service and three years at Queen Mary College, London he had gained a first class Honours degree in mathematics. The Summer before I started at Spring Grove, he had married Maribel, who he had met during his National Service in Gibraltar, and had settled in Gibraltar as an Educator in the Admiralty. Brother Malcolm had just completed his O levels, acted as Best Man at Gordon's wedding, and was in the sixth form and a prefect.

With these two paragons ahead of me I suppose it was assumed I might carry on the family tradition of academia and I think for the first few years that was my ambition too. However, as time went by reality began to hit.

I had my reflected glory in the early days. I quite enjoyed the fame of having a brother who was one of those good-looking prefects who circled the school during breaks eyeing up the girls in the upper forms. My friends and I tried to make sure we were circling in the opposite direction so that we could meet up with them a couple of times. I am pretty sure that brother Malcolm had a rather different view of things from mine and his heart sank when he saw his little sister and her gang of giggling girls approaching. He was much more interested in seeking out a certain Pat Jarman!

My first setback was to find that, unlike my brothers, I was not very sporty, certainly not athletic. Both brothers took part in team games and Malcolm held the records for 100yd and 200yd sprints for many years. I managed to blot my copybook at my first race in preparation for Sports Day – 80yd skipping. With Malcolm and his fellow prefects looking on I managed to get tied up in my rope at the start of the race and finished last! I can see him now cringing embarrassingly on the sidelines. I redeemed myself a little later on as swimming was my forte and I managed to gain a few points for Nelson House in the school galas. I managed to pass my first year without a dreaded black star but early in my second year one came my way. I know for some pupils, black stars were received almost as often as school dinners but I had a quiet, well-behaved brother who had sailed through five years without one so mine came as a bit of a shock! I had almost forgotten about it when we had a House Assembly and by this time brother Malcolm was House Captain. I suddenly realised that my misdemeanour would be announced to all and sundry including the House Captain! I am sure that anyone looking at me that afternoon would have seen my discomfort as my face turned gradually redder. To his credit, Malcolm did not say anything to me or my parents and it was not until my report appeared that my mother knew. I just got one of my mother's knowing looks!

One of my initial ideas for a career was to be a teacher of the deaf, which would entail a spell at Teacher Training College, followed by specialist training. However, this was somewhat looked down on by Miss Coulthard who thought I "could do better than that and go to University". Not being very forceful, I went her way and set off on University interviews. The hard work with A levels took its toll and half way through the second year I had a big blip and nearly gave up. However, I persevered and was very pleased to achieve three creditable A levels - but not creditable enough to be accepted at University. Whilst all around me offered their commiserations, I must admit it was secretly quite a relief to me and I went on to work at Taylor Woodrow as a secretary which I really loved. An early marriage and family meant that I was not really a career person until later in life when my husband and I went into business owning and operating several toy shops now passed on to our children. My secretarial training, together with a good grasp of English grammar gained from my SGGS education, has been of great advantage in my work as well as a number of voluntary positions.

I sometimes regret not standing up for myself and going on my original path. Perhaps one of the faults of Spring Grove was that University was considered the ultimate aim and this might not be the best for some people. In the end, however, I suppose we all make our own way in life and now, in my later years, I am still able to fall back on the reflected glory of those brothers and mention their exalted careers in conversation when needs be!!

After his stint with the Admiralty, Gordon went on to attain an MSc degree and, with a Commission in the RAF, spent a number of years on the directing staff at The RAF College Cranwell, following which he became Head of Mathematics and Computing and later Assistant Principal at Wigan College of Technology.

Malcolm married Pat Jarman in 1959, soon after which they moved to live and raise their family in Canada where Malcolm had a long career in nuclear physics research and management with Atomic Energy of Canada (a crown company).

Recollections with Not a Little Nostalgia

Sue Gardner '58

When I passed the eleven plus in 1953 there was great joy in the family and no doubt as to which school I should attend. Dad was taken with the co-ed aspect as more suitable to prepare me for my future life in the real world. Mum was delighted that I would be going to her old school and was able to give me some insight into what I could expect. She attended in the '30s, her maiden name was Lillian Lawrence, having passed the appropriate exam of the day. She was one of the youngest of an impoverished family of ten children and my grandparents lacked the necessary wherewithal. Family history tells me she was sponsored by a local grocer so was able to take up her place. She remembered fondly the wonderful building and grounds and several members of staff then, one of whom was Mr. Callow who later taught me.

The following year my sister, Ann, also passed the eleven plus but nearly went to the Green School or Gumley House as being a different personality from myself it was felt she would do better at a single sex school. However she followed me to Spring Grove in 1954 which was just as well as things turned out. That year as some may remember my mother committed suicide, which was a very traumatic time for the family. The school was very supportive and staff encouraged all around us to "carry on as normal", exactly the right advice as dealing with sympathy would have been a burden too much. No counselling then, stiff upper lip and coping was the order of the day. I'm so glad it was.

In spite of that set back I remember my time at Spring Grove as a very happy one. I vividly remember my first day when all the newcomers were assembled in the music room, sorted into groups, red , white and blue, and then escorted to our new classroom. I was drafted into 1 Red and palled up with Jane Redstone, a friendship that was to last throughout our school life and beyond, until she emigrated to Australia and without her address we lost contact. Maybe one day she will appear on the friends reunited website, who knows? In the same year, although not in my class, Irene Williams and Elizabeth Grieves became firm friends. Betty (Elizabeth) and I have been in contact throughout the years and she now lives in my street. Irene and I are in touch at Christmas, she now lives in Norfolk.

Sadly my sister Ann, also took her own life in 1973 leaving a daughter, who was only an infant at the time. At the reunion in 2003 I was very touched to see an article on the notice board that Ann had written in the fifties for the school magazine. It was a very poignant piece and showed wisdom beyond her years. I sent a copy to her daughter who now lives in Holland. Reading the article that day I certainly felt the years fall away, taking me back to a time of security and stability we enjoyed at Spring Grove.

I participated quite a bit in the sporting activities, mostly athletics, tennis and netball. Betty, Irene and I were all in the netball team together, coached by Miss Phillips and Miss Hewitt. I also recall a stint in the gardening club held after school and supervised by Mr. Ridley (who looked like the notorious murderer Reginald Christie).

The word notorious certainly applies to another character whose path I crossed at Hounslow Heath Infants School, namely Francis Forsythe, nicknamed "Flossy". He passed the eleven plus the same year as me and went to Isleworth County for just one year. But schools were unable to change his attitude and he ended upon the gallows executed for having kicked a young man to death. He was a bully at 4 years of age, I know to my cost. It seemed inevitable that he would come to a bad end. Not so today when rehabilitation and early release into the community are the norm. Life was certainly more straightforward then. I still have my mother's form photograph; interestingly her form mistress was Miss Richards who was still there in my day. The values upheld by the school were mostly treated with respect and I am sure have supported most of us over the years; such a pity that they are no longer reinforced in society today.I was particularly pleased to read the articles by Jack and Marjorie Stammers in issue 15. We met at a recent reunion where they were very interested in some old school photos I had taken along showing myself at the school in the '50s and my mother there in the '30s. Mr Callow and Miss Richards were at least two of the members of staff who appeared in both! Marjorie was immediately taken with a photo of me in school uniform and was convinced that she recognized me. However as our paths could not possibly have crossed or overlapped at school I was sure she was mistaken. We conversed for a while and gradually discovered that she and Jack had lived opposite to me for several years. Here was the link then, she probably remembered me because we had been neighbours. How strange that one chance meeting – drawn together by SGGS- revealed many years later how close we were to each other in my childhood.

Another link is with David Helsdon who was a year above me at school. Meeting my then future husband Trevor in 1958, I was introduced to his best friend Martin who is David's eldest brother. Our friendship is still ongoing so I see David occasionally at family or social functions. Whenever we meet conversation inevitably turns to our memories of SGGS. I doubt our paths would ever have crossed but for my husband's friendship with Martin.

My first day at the school found me in the music room with new intake, waiting to learn which form, red, white, or blue we were assigned to. I recognized Irene Williams as we had spent some time together at primary school. She was with Elizabeth (Betty) Greaves who was known to her. It was reassuring to see at least one familiar face on such an important day for us all. Forms white and blue departed to places then unknown, taking Irene and Betty with them, leaving the remainder 1 red. It was then that I met Jane Redstone, lonely and distressed, having just moved to Harlington from Porlock in Somerset, and feeling totally bereft. She and I palled up and together with Irene and Betty, the four of us remained friends through schooldays and beyond. I still have photos of us all at Ruislip Lido.

My link with Jane was broken when she emigrated to Australia and I never heard from her again. Irene now lives in Diss, Norfolk and we are rarely in contact. Betty and I however are now living out our retirement in the same street in Ashford (Middlesex) and have very much kept in touch with each other over the years.

Finally another link I should like to mention is with Alan Sabey, also in print in issue 15. Sadly Alan and I both lost a parent while we were pupils at the school, a difficult thing to cope with so young. I am glad that he was able to share the experience of his loss with the readers, we were never encouraged to discuss our feelings at the time.

It seems that the wonderful SGGS still links so many of us, locally and world-wide. As with many others I shall always remember my link to the school and I feel grateful that my destiny led me through the imposing wrought iron gates at the entrance so many years ago.

With hindsight I'm sure my Dad was right; Spring Grove was the right school for me.

Sue's mother, Lillian Lawrence was also an OSG. 1925-1930.
She is third from the right in the front row in Miss Richards' Class photo.
1926(?)

Bulstrode Lad Takes on Spring Grove

Peter Salter '58

The article in a previous issue of the SGR from my former classmate Sue Gardner has inspired me to write something of my formative years, and maybe a bit more. So here we go!

Born in Fulmer, near that wonderful place called Slough (it's the place not the people in case you thought), I was fortunate enough to be educated privately until I was thirteen years old and which included five years at boarding school in rural Hampshire. Inevitably given the family circumstances, the costs of such an education became prohibitive, and of course the 11+ had passed me by.

My mother, who was not one to be obstructed by officialdom, trotted off with me in tow to see the Borough Education Officer, one Mr Bennett in the summer of 1954. She 'enquired' as to how I could get into the local grammar school, either Spring Grove or Isleworth County; she didn't mind which one, it was up to him to decide. I recall well Bennett telling her that it was impossible to get me into either without some evidence that this young lad would succeed in such an environment, and that therefore I would have to attend one of the secondary modern schools in the borough and that this would be somewhere called Bulstrode. Of course we had never heard of the place - such ignorance and what an eye-opener it would turn out to be!

Thus in September 1954 with a black blazer and polished shoes I travelled to Bulstrode, a day never to be forgotten as I joined its third year. The first few days were novel, to say the least, and one found quickly that this was a tough environment for one who had no knowledge of the hard areas of the Hounslow district, and what seemed to be little more than gang warfare in and out of the playground there. Towards the end of my second term ie March 1955, the yearly exams arrived and it turned out that yours truly shone beyond even the dreams of the Headmaster, Mr Dennis. Armed with that information my mother returned to speak to (not with) Mr Bennett and demanded a place for me at Spring Grove; she was thinking too of my sister Patricia who was at the Central and about to take her 13+. I think that Bennett was so taken aback that there and then he arranged for my interview by Mr Brown. So off we trotted, my mother wearing her lucky hat and a young lad somewhat bemused by the whole episode. The interview went well; my mother interviewed Mr Brown and he agreed that I would start at SGGS the next day which was the start of the summer term 1955. I joined form 3A which included folk such as Wendy Burns, Avril Clark, Mike Colman and Gordon Sadler who I have re-met at reunions. The end of year exams did not go well so LTB quite rightly held me back to do 3A again so I joined up with many of the folk who have been to our reunions and featured in SGR photos; one such classmate was Roy Schofield who I was to meet at work in the 1990s some forty years after we had been classed together - small world.

The years at SGGS passed by quickly, even though I ran slowly around the north pitch track, and never won any cross-country as the late Tony Richardson and Dave Pippard were always ahead of me - but it was fun. O levels in 1959 went well, and A levels too after Wallace Maylott, who was my next door neighbour in Jersey Rd., Osterley, persuaded me to "get a life" and switch to sciences. Thankfully I followed his advice. Leaving school in July 1960 I went off to the National Physical Laboratory at Teddington which I hated; ever tried getting from Osterley to Teddington and then night school in Kingston by public transport? So in 1961 the Met Office beckoned me and I never looked back. They sent me off to university for four years on full pay, paid for my books and my train fares to get to City University near the Angel. Armed with a 2.1 in Applied Physics I returned to the Met Office and followed an interesting career which took me to many places I had wanted to visit. This included scientific flights over the heart of Antarctica investigating the ozone hole - the US taxpayers funded those trips since I had been seconded to NOAA/NASA. Miss Richards was the inspiration to travel as much as possible through her geography lessons, and she was the only person who knew of my desire to see the biggest ice factory in the world, so thank you 'Miss' for those lessons, and to all the other SGGS teachers as well for shaping my life.

This is not the place to spell out one's career but it was an honour to meet and brief HM The Queen on a visit she made to my workplace, a surprise to meet similarly HRH The Prince of Wales another year, and a stroke of luck to crack a joke with HRH Prince Philip years later at the then RN College, Greenwich - he didn't appreciate my joke! Anyway this is how my two terms at Bulstrode turned out, and though I hated every day of them there is no doubt that it made me appreciate even more my time at SGGS where LTB and his staff moulded me into something that my mother had hoped for all those years ago when it seemed that Bulstrode was all I could look forward to.

Funny how things turn out isn't it? Especially when the lad's mother interviews the Headmaster!

Then and Now
Apart from their not being *quite* so close as they were forty years ago, they're still recognisable.
Prefects from 1960 & 43 years on.

Craig McArthur;
Sue Evans,
Peter Salter;
Cynthia Harvey,
Bob Venables.

SGGS and Beyond

Tim Leitch '58

I don't know what gets into folk at our time of life- perhaps the regret that we were not astronauts, TV foodie experts, world champions, and eminent scientists. Perhaps the desperate need for a Ferrari/ Harley or a Gucci outfit or even ride-on lawnmower have quietly passed by. Even the expat migration to Europe now doesn't seem such a good idea with all your funds in sterling!!. .

What I read in our splendid magazine is perhaps an indication of the time and era we all grew up in and the education and ethics that was the norm then.

We all seem to be content to reminisce on where we are today---bloody hell fire we are ONLY in our mid 60s and seem resigned to a period of self satisfaction and reflection. I have always viewed the Victorian work ethic we were instilled in as post war kids, has significantly held many back from doing what they believe in their hearts they should have done. I congratulate Frank Allen (Frankie McNeice P??) for being a rebel and following a talent (I also thank Mrs Hemming for her help at the last gasp in getting me through English language O level- as you can see it's not really improved).. How many of us who spent time in Twickenham coffee bars, dancing lessons (God forbid) and the wonderful smoke filled Eel Pie Island on Sunday nights, now look back at vintage news clips and disappear into a nostalgic haze of "why, oh why didn't I do this or that". Should I have joined a friend Dave Cousins and gone on tour with the Strawbs and written the song "State of the Union" a now pro Trades Union battle cry or become an Insurance salesman in Cincinnati USA. ...no too chicken.

I have only once ever applied for a job and that was the very first when the Careers master at SG let me know there were interviews being held by English Electric for Graduate Engineering apprentices. I was invited to Pall Mall in London to the mahogany marbled offices of English Electric and spent the whole interview talking to a pinstriped City Director of EE Co. on the merits of BMC series A engines (Mini) and the way to get 100 bhp from a litre without blowing the thing up. Nowadays the family shopping trolley with a turbo regularly achieves the unachievable of 1960. Ten happy years at EECo. and Imperial College in engineering with an honours degree, Chartered status and a multitude of specialist qualifications, I gave up making things and joined the Information age in the USA during 1970. That was when Britain lost its manufacturing base to the Far East and became a service orientated money launderer in the world economy. Banks never add value to anything; they take it. And that was where the pin fell out of Britain.

Had we known then, what we know now, would we have just buried our heads in the sand or made a break from the embedded responsibility ethic?

Now I have no regrets on anything I have done since, only that I was slow in seeing the trends, and that was down to the cross we all bear as the Victorian work ethic. The most flexible free thinkers I have ever worked with were those that were developing computer operating systems and software logic in conceptual models and then applying them to the developing integrated circuit technology that is in current day "chips". We will soon see phone type devices that are pure fantasy in Phone 4 Us at £49.99.

The thing that now holds up progress is the man in the street's assimilation of all the "things" that are around him. You all use about 5% of what Apple or Microsoft have given you on your PCs/mobile phones. Your kids will bridge the gap and use much more because they don't question the facilities any more than we do when we turn on the water tap. They use it for what it's worth without any preconditions or inhibitions.

Back to school days and I propose that although we may have been taught the moral standards of living in the 60s and thank goodness for that, we were constrained by our conservative past. I rest my case.

back row L-R, Tim Leitch , Peter Salter, John Harbour, John Baker
front row..L-R Bob Venebales,   Mick Shaw   Peter Creed

SGGS move to Lampton Road, Hounslow

50th Anniversary 25th March 2010

For some unknown reason I seem to have had an invitation to Lampton School to celebrate the 50th year after the move of SGGS from Isleworth. So proudly with old school reports/Degrees and prefects regalia I went on a dark March evening early in 2010.

I was surprised that I seemed to be only "Old" boy from Spring Grove GS in our year ('58) there, probably the earliest old pupil at the Lampton new school as it was, having only spent one year there in the Upper 6th, but that seemed to have missed the organisers.

A guided tour of much that I vaguely remember seemed not to have changed much. A few more classrooms and out buildings plus the ubiquitous and mandatory "Media Studies" studio that seems to be the in fashion for the "creative". God forbid…. whatever happened to traditional education? We seem to be saddled by the liberal dogmas of "equality" and mediocrity rather than "innovation and excellence".

A celebration ceremony; with reflections of the first years in Lampton and with the inevitable show of "rap" and "break dancing". Whatever next, but I suppose it's celebrating the "creative spirit" and acceptance of a social multi-language and cultural mix of pupils (probably about 1500 kids). Few reports of academic success were declared, after which I was expecting the celebration of some pupils being accepted on "X Factor" but not forthcoming.

I was left with a deep sense of depression and left early.

LTB would turn in his grave. Thank goodness for the reunions of the SGGS group and long should they retain those mixed memories of Spring Grove in Isleworth. Can I now stop biting my lip?

(Tim Leitch)

A Few Memories from My Salad Days

Val Bowers '59

I arrived at Spring Grove in September 1954, having just turned 11 and as green as little green apples. The very name Spring Grove was thrilling – images of lush woodlands with crystal springs bursting through. Well, not quite, but we did have superb cedars and a fountain.

The top floor classroom with open fire and draughty windows was to be my base for the coming year. The form master of 1 red was the delightfully young and ever cheerful Mr Arthur Chadband.

The following seven years just flew by with varying degrees of pain and pleasure.

I wouldn't have missed the daily assemblies for anything. Seated sedately in the front row of the hall just below the platform, we "first years" scrutinized each successive year pass down the centre aisle from front to back. Clutching satchels and taking their places, boys to the left and girls to the right. Eventually, the sixth formers, looking so very adult and sophisticated. Next the arrival on the platform of the prefects and the choir. Finally followed the two deputy heads, Kate Hemming and Bill Lineham, taking their seats at either side, front stage; then the footsteps of the Headmaster himself, Mr. L.T.Brown, as he took his place centre front; all three begowned and while we stood to attention. What drama!

Not all the memories are good. At the end of one of the assemblies, I believe it was in our first week, there was a disagreement about which way we should pass the hymn books for collection. Hushed whispers of "Not this way" and "Send them back that way" were flying to and fro. A sudden voice from above: "Stand up if you are talking". I promptly stood up, expecting the whole row to do the same. The voice summoned me to stand below His Headship, the eyes of the whole school boring into my back. Awarded four black stars and a detention, I learned that honesty is not always the best policy.

Was it one Christmas that someone decided to present Mr Chadband with a packet of hairgrips to control his unruly mop – to much laughter. There was also the morning he announced he had become a Daddy – the class erupted with cries of "Daddy-Chaddy". Unfortunately his attempts to instill in me an understanding of French verbs met with little success. I was relegated to "Delta".

Gradually I got the hang of it and worked my way up through the sets, through the gentle Mr. Read (Reid?), the enigmatic and somewhat intimidating Mr. Detsicas and, finally, to steer me through "A" levels, the charming Misses Coulthard and Barr.

One episode occurred that I'm not proud of. A new girl arrived with an unfortunate inability to pronounce her "r"s, they came out as "w"s. Her name Bernice Reed. We teased her mercilessly, asking her to repeat her name. If you should ever read this Bernice, my heartfelt apology. Kids eh?! One sunny day in the music room I was sat immediately behind Bernice. I was so entranced by the enthusiastic rendering of the Trout by Mr. Stuart Hart on the piano or, as he called it the "pee-ah-no-forteh". I was overtaken by the urge to grab hold of each of Bernice's lovely long plaits and pull her head from side to side in time to the music. Of course I was unable to see her face which probably registered excruciating pain – though I only tugged very gently! A sudden crashed chord and a voice boomed "That silly girl, stand up on your chair!" As one of the tallest in the class I towered above the seated pupils, suitably chastised until the end of the lesson.

One teacher I recall with fondness was Miss Di Clothier. Unkindly nick-named "Spring-bottom" she was a little lady who appeared to bounce along. We were all a bit wary of her at first, me in particular, as she taught my hated subject –Maths.

It was she who had the cracking idea of posing a question and demanding that we put our hand up or stand up. A real catch 22. If you hadn't a clue, like me, you had to gamble; stand up and risk humiliation or put your hand up and hope that she wouldn't pounce on you.

As I matured, I saw a softer, more human side of this lady and my fear of her ceased. My dislike of mental arithmetic, however, has never left me. I get by writing it down and taking my time. I enjoy sudoku – but that thy tell me is not maths.

In the SGR 10 in 2006, David Helsdon wrote that he'd always wondered what went on at "Girls' Assemblies". Well, they always started with Miss Taylor (Emily?) looking pained and addressing us thus; "Girls, it grieves me…" and issuing a long list of woes, from dropping litter to more serious misdemean-ors. One morning she decided to inflict retribution on those of us who had dared to "improve" our school uniform by the addition of a black or white elastic belt (showed off the waist to advantage we thought). After a good tongue lashing she insisted we removed said belts and hand them in until the end of the day. Protest was useless. We had to remain shapeless until we went home and retrieved our belts in school colours.

The two years of my sixth form were spent at the new Lampton School. I felt totally miserable at the change; the building was characterless and felt un-friendly. Many of my friends had left to join the world of work. I had to plough on in order to enter what was then called "Training College" (now "Colleges of Education" or are they all "Universities" nowadays?) Eventually I achieved my wish to be a Junior School teacher and loved every minute of the first five years. Then they moved the goal posts but that is another story. Dylan Thomas said, " The memories of childhood have no order and no end." I attend reunions whenever possible in the hope of recognising a few more "old faces" and, perhaps, recapturing a glimpse of my salad days.

The Cat Sat on the Mat

Chris Grant '59

I want to express a deep gratitude to Mr. Short our PT instructor. I was such a little guy, and basically useless in team sports. We were playing soccer, and I got the ball. The ball stuck to my foot for the first time. I took one, no two ...three antagonists and dodged them all. Boot it, and I did and scored. There was no applause because I was going the wrong way. Mr. Short came to me and said: "See me after school in the attic. You are quick, but soccer is not your forte. I am going to teach you to box, because you will need it", and he did using a glove on the end of a long pole. Mr. Short cared for all the kids, not just the stars.

I came up trembling before Mr. L. T. Brown more than one time. You got the silent treatment, but then he couldn't do it anymore and he would try not to laugh. Priceless moments when you fled, because he left your self-confidence intact while you scurried out with a major debt to pay in modified and corrected behaviour.

I also want to thank Hugh Leitch for filling us in on the last hilarious day of the Old Spring Grove. You taught me about Norman Arches, and why they do not fall down. Perhaps you remember I then went on holiday with a fancy camera in England and Wales and took all these pictures of arches and sold them for one penny a piece. I made three shillings and sixpence, and you had to give half the class an A. You gave me an A++. I probably owed you about eight pence in commission back then, but as I never paid you it is probably worth $15,000 today (given inflation). Please do not contact me.

I want to thank Miss Ransom, who peddled so energetically on her old heavy bike ahead of us on a cycling tour of Belgium and Holland so it would all be right when we kids checked in the YMCA. "Come along my friends" she said over her shoulder, "You are not tired yet!". But we were her friends. I wish I knew what happened to Miss Ransom.

Mr. Pearce, the best Math teacher I have ever known. Now why would I have trouble working out $2 + 2 = 4$? When I know that I know as much as he does. Mr. Pearce taught me that, because he knew Math was simple. I took that through some pretty advanced biostatistics at Harvard, but I still keep it simple. Spring Grove was wonderful. We were all so lucky to attend. Now we are all old farts, but all of us are that bit more mellow, that bit wiser, and that bit kinder because of our entire experience at Spring Grove.

I cannot remember the English teacher at Spring Grove, but I remember the homework.

Go away and write a poem. If you can not write a poem then write: "The Cat Sat on the Mat!".

I have battled with this for almost fifty years, and it is the best poem I have ever written:

The Cat.

The cat - sat - upon the mat.
He greeted me with a gentle purr
As I turned and locked the door
Behind me.
I said: "Hi, Cat!"
The cat - sat - upon the mat. Then he didn't do that.
He ran beneath my feet and
Jumped upon the counter top.
I demanded "Get Down!"
The cat arched his back, and
So very slowly turning
Gazed at me, then
With flick of his tail
Implied I was simply crazy ....
I pushed him off the counter top.
Landing light, tail high, he
Stretched and shrugged, then
Sauntered away.
No mistaking sublime feline haughtier!
So I sat and relaxed.
My table was laid,
It was the end of the day.
My meal was ready, and with a sigh
I spread my daily paper.
From absolutely nowhere that cat
Jumped up and sat ....
Precisely where I was reading.
Innocent turn of his head
and WE WERE EYEBALL TO EYEBALL!
I was so.. sorely... tempted.....
But it was me that blinked,
So I got up.
That Cat followed me,
And MY meal got cold
While I fed IT!

The real tragedy of Spring Grove is that you can never replace it. None of our grandchildren will ever know the awe of the music room or the Banksian room or the big trees outside. Nor walking in two centuries of history as, we did, in lining up the main stairs with the stained glass windows ahead. You can give kids the most modern school in the world, but you cannot give them history. History makes it real, and real stuff stays with you the rest of your life. It alters you.

Recollections from the Old School

Keith Lomas '58

I have enjoyed very much the articles in the Old Spring Grovian Reports which have transported me back to another age and my memories of my time at the old school may be of interest to others.

I started in the September 1953 intake and although I had never been near the school before starting, I knew a few people from the road where I lived in Heston, who had been there. These included Gordon Freke and his sister Enid- both several years above me, Lorna Pratley , Marie Heaphy and Jennifer Broad- ribb.

I managed to drift along at school, enjoying myself in most of the sporting events, particularly athletics where I twice won the County Long Jump title at Chiswick and broke the triple jump record at the White City. I was also selected to represent Middlesex in the All England Championships at Plymouth. Foot- ball, either on the South Pitch or on Greenhams field took up more time and what passed for Cross Country running, chasing round Greenhams again getting cold and wet. Another activity that I enjoyed was singing in the School choir- Mr Hart maintained a good standard and I have been able to join choirs throughout the years. Singing in the school choir, meant that you had to turn out for Speech Day and I remember prizes being awarded by Reader Harris, our local MP, Sir George Cribbett, D. Chairman of BOAC and Ruth Fitter, an actress. Another after school activity that sticks in my memory as achieving a high standard was the production of The Importance of being Ernest produced by Mr Blainey. Other events that I remember were Dick Pearce, Mr Maylott and Mr Misra wearing white coats and making a presentation about nucleur energy in the Physics Lab, Mr Ridley setting up a screen in the grounds to illustrate an eclipse of the sun and Miss King running a science club after school.

I don't have very much recollection of doing much work at school. I suppose because I didn't seem to do very much but I can remember going to the Odeon cinema on the corner of Havard Road to see the Conquest of Everest which occurred in my first year at School and School visits to Cheddar Gorge and Portsmouth.

By some stroke of luck, in the fourth year, it dawned on me that with O levels round the corner, unless I did some serious work I wouldn't pass any. I am sure this realisation didn't come from any teachers telling me that some serious effort was needed on my part and it's certainly not reflected in my Report book. Having read Rick Harris's article, I checked with my Report Book and it only contains the usual admonitions - 'Could do better'.

Whatever the cause, I pulled my socks up and did enough work to go up to the Fifth year and change from Mr Leitch's history class to Miss Taylor's and from Mr Howell's geography class to Miss Richards'. I can also remember being caught talking in Mr Maylott's Physics lesson and he asked me to define the emf. By some fluke, I managed to trot out 'It's the potential difference between the plates of a cell when it's on open circuit'. I don't know who was more surprised- he just muttered 'pay attention next time' and I escaped a detention.

I can't say that I found the teachers at school very inspiring but I achieved enough to get me over the hurdle of O levels and for that I am very grateful. I remember my time at SGGS as being very enjoyable there, with many happy memories in a different age from what is experienced now. I count myself very fortunate to have attended the old school; where else could we have had our chemistry lessons in a hut adjoining the tennis courts where the boys could see the senior girls playing tennis or having to walk to Hounslow for our swimming lessons in a swimming bath that was only just big enough for us to stand up in, let alone learn to swim?

Quite a few of the teachers came to school by bicycle as did a number of pupils. In an earlier recollection, somebody remembered Miss Coulthard driving a Fiat 500. By the time I was at school, she was driving a very stylish car, a Triumph Mayflower. Mr Titchener who was about six and a half feet tall, drove an Austin A30 , which he only just managed to climb into, Mr Bullough drove a Morris 8 convertible; Mr Hart drove an Austin Somerset and Mr Maylott drove an ancient Morris 12 but the most impressive was Mr Chadband's Talbot. The thought of bicycles brings back a smile when I remember an occasion when there was a bus strike and we were told to get to school as best we could. Proctor and Seaman managed to procure a tandem and cycled through the school grounds on it.

Probably in common with most others at school, I didn't have any idea of what I wanted to do when I left school. I had a conversation with Mr Leitch who threw out a few ideas and after school I set out to join the Met Office. This however was not for me and I remember looking at the Honours Boards at the back of the Assembly Hall. All the A level results were recorded there and, not so numerous, those pupils who had excelled and achieved degrees. There was never any chance of me going on to A levels or to achieve a degree but I remember a name on the Honours Board, Mr Millet, with the letters AC A after his name and I found out that this meant he was an Associate of the Institute of Chartered Accountants. This sounded interesting and I followed up what was required and became an Articled Clerk for 5 years while I qualified as a Chartered Accountant.

I used to wonder whether the Honours Boards from the old school were taken up to the new school and after I had qualified I paid a visit to the new school. I called on the Headmaster, Mr Lister. He was too busy to see me but introduced me to Miss Coulthard, who was my Form Mistress in my last year at the old School and I also met Mr Leitch, who said he would look into the status of the Honours Boards. I got the impression that they hadn't survived.

'60s - SGH & Lampton

8

SGGS - Isleworth to Lampton

A Teacher's View

Brenda Sweetland '52.

Like many others, I hold the memory of L.T.Brown in great affection. I remember particularly his campaign with the Local Education Authority for advancement of the promised move to more suitable pastures. At the Annual speech day, addressing the school and notable dignitaries, he never failed to remind the education officer that he was ready and waiting for the school to be relocated to his Promised Land.

Past pupils, and staff, all easily remember the detailed architecture and internal finishes of the old Spring Grove House. The magnificent entrance hall with central staircase, the wonderful oak panelling, stained glass windows, narrow stairways, open fires, non-standard classrooms and the dark rambling basement with its miles of hot lagged pipes! Also the lovely grounds and ancient cedar tree.

Moving to Lampton was goodbye to all that and the end chapter of a unique educational experience. The new, dull site at Lampton was depressing and traumatic by comparison. The building was modern and well designed, though clinical in its impact.

The Assembly Hall at the old school was woefully inadequate - not even large enough to accommodate the whole school - whilst that at Lampton was most impressive with balconies on three sides and a superb stage - a wonderful setting for morning assemblies.

Mr. Brown must have felt the move keenly, as the Headmaster's office-come-study in the new building was small enough to cramp his style, enthusiasm and mind.

The new school had only two staff rooms - a complete contrast to what everyone had been used to! Allocating them was no easy task. One faction wanted a communal workroom and a general staff room, another wanted segregated facilities for men and women. As usual, the segregationists held overriding influence and the male staff were housed in a small, dingy room on the ground floor, next to the Deputy Head's study, while the ladies enjoyed a spacious airy room on the top floor. It was also a resting-place for Miss Phillips' boxer Judy. Members of staff did not take kindly to enforced changes in amenities and services; their personal styles were cramped. Their loss of previous personalised arrangements for tea, coffee and conversation was regarded as deprivation!

The upside was the educational benefit gained by the use of modern specialist areas, the science laboratories and the fine home economics unit, the latter being a vast improvement on the "old cottage" where many of us met Miss Bromwich! The new facilities may have produced better results but weren't much fun! The P.E. department had fine facilities - it meant an end to country dancing in the cold, dark, damp loft with bowls to catch the water dripping through the holes in the roof! It was also goodbye to those appalling changing rooms in the cottage with open fire, dripping ceiling and plaster falling from the walls. We had a spacious gymnasium with easy access to courts and playing fields. The modern facilities must have been a great relief to the Headmaster and removed a great deal of his frustration and stress. However the overall impact for those who had moved from Spring Grove House was entirely negative, expressed by reduced identity, lack of 'ethos', a certain lack of professional freedom and the removal of access to an historic workplace. "Absence made the heart grow fonder", and this grew in intensity over time cementing the unpalatable truth that Spring Grove was not fully appreciated in it's heyday. Such is the hallmark of educational progress. On a more positive note. I can confidently report that the school caretakers, Mr. and Mrs. Voice, who were moved into a brand new family house at the new site, were glad to see the back of the old buildings. Particularly all those open fires that had to be cleaned, lit and stoked and the dust, coke fumes and filth generated by them. That is something that I shall never forget.

Perhaps the greatest miracle was that the old building never went up in plumes of smoke!!

Publicity Photo Lampton School Before Occupation

Isleworth to Lampton - the Pupils View

Janis Campbell '63

First impressions - arrived SGGS Sept.1958 after passing 11+ from Heath Juniors. Nearly 3 miles from home, meaning two buses (I bus and I trolleybus) to get there…Sister had been here 13 yrs before. I was very naïve, dressed in uncomfortable 'large' new uniform ("You'll grow into it!") from Abernethies. Navy blue blazers for girls- with Juliet caps. (I still have mine!) Black blazers and caps for the boys. Spring Grove House appeared a large imposing frightening building… lots of strange bigger children and grown-ups, the teachers. Luckily, lots of friends from junior class arrived too but we were all split up into 1 Green, Red, Blue and White.

First years were mainly classroom based on the ground floor for all lessons. No sets/streams for subjects at all. 1 Green (my form) with Miss Philips was in room 4 next door to the grand music-room which had the minstrels' gallery. All first year assemblies were held here, as the main hall wasn't large enough for everyone. We belonged to post war 46/47 baby bulge. Beautiful views to the west of the main building….a hockey/football pitch, a fountain, foreign-looking trees.. Remember art room and Banksian room. Told about the historical links with Banks, and Cook's trips to Australia – Captain, not Thomas. I remember Mr Hart's music room on left-hand front corner of the building. Remember the grand staircase and coloured windows and fireplace. Mr Brown always stood by this watching people file past in orderly fashion- keep to the left, no running, no talking…. I thought the Domestic Science rooms were in the basement, but my sister says they were elsewhere. We never actually 'cooked'-just made our hand-sewn aprons for future use! Also used the treadle sewing machines, sewing along lines of paper with no cotton thread in the spool to get straight lines!!

Never went upstairs much apart from going to the Library. Thought the Chem. lab was an awful smelly place…never discovered if there was a Biology Lab or a Physics one-these subjects were classroom-based. When it came to PE/Games, the Changing rooms for the girls were very pokey and primitive…spent a lifetime running up and down and jumping on the netball courts. Hated playing hockey on the front field, very muddy…knew it used to be a lake…Joined the gardening club, had a garden at the back of the school somewhere…The gym was all shiny and polished and can recall the 'usual' odour of bodies…Enjoyed wet games sessions when we had country dancing upstairs above the Chem lab in what was called "the Loft(?)" with Miss Sweetland. Don't remember where the loos were…perhaps I never used them? Often got lost going from classroom base to another building. Think we had school dinners in the main hall, but not too sure. Everything was on such a grand scale to a tiny 11 year old. Never realised there were so many pupils spread out in the whole school as the first years were kept very much to the ground floor.

My classroom had an old open-place fire at the back of the room, with a fireguard, but the heating was from radiators. ...Staff wore black gowns and put the fear of god into us...lots of rules to be kept...Mr Brown sometimes took us for French. Made us quake in our shoes....giving us rules and regulations for "Mens Sana in Corpore Sano". Being seen eating in school uniform in the street was verboten...so was not having the correct uniform. All items of uniform and PE kit had to be labelled, also exercise and text-books had to be covered and named. Gold stars, black stars, detentions, punishments (the dreaded cane) etc. We worked to a 6-day timetable-meant every Monday was a different day-very confusing. Homework was a new issue and I can still remember my mum writing notes to say I had spent hours doing it yet not completed the work...We were encouraged to be so conscientious.

I guess it paid off, as I got into one of the two 'A' classes in the 2nd year and was in top set for Maths-which I loathed (sorry Miss Clothier) - asked to go down to Beta with Miss King!

Just about got everything sorted about the rules, the building etc. when we moved to the new site at Lampton for my second year in '59. More confusion again...but this time in a nice new clean modern building.

1959-SGGS at the Lampton site.

Just one short bus ride away and not far from Hounslow West where I lived. Sometimes got a lift with dad going to work. A purpose-built 'box'...clean, concrete, flat-roofed, three storey light and airy building with lots of windows and extensive grounds for games etc. but Ralph says he remembers going to Greenham's fields back in Isleworth initially for football/games as the grass hadn't grown. Everything a school could need....two labs each for Physics/Biology and Chemistry, Library, Art and Craft/pottery rooms, Domestic Science room and Sewing room, Commercial room, Music room - this originally was at the front of the building but because the noise (!) was disturbing the nearby residents, Mr Hart had to move to the classroom on the opposite side of.

the building 2nd floor, corner room by the stairwell. Middle stairs by the main entrance were only to be used by staff, 6th form and prefects. Two other stairwells existed, but one couldn't cut through the library or Physics labs. Mr Brown told us he had wanted his lovely staircase from the old school put into the new building but it couldn't be accommodated. The main hall could hold everyone and had folding doors at the back, behind which was the dining room and kitchen. Main body hall floor was 'sunken' with a balcony around two sides. Stage was on ground level with curtains and lighting equipment for the productions etc.

First years based on ground floor…6th formers on top floor. Tuck shop held at break time each morning run by the caretaker's wife by the girls' loos/PE changing rooms' entrance. The Gym was fantastic, sprung floor, masses of equipment, wall-bars, ropes, etc. Absolutely brilliant and the changing rooms were out of this world…with showers! Imagine us coy 12/13yr olds making up all kinds of excuses not to have a shower…well at least until the shower curtains were put in! Rules were very strict…no girls and boys to be allowed in the gym together unless a member of staff was present! Everyone had wire cages to store PE gear and you had to have your PE kit in a PE bag with your name on it. If you lost your key for the cage and you hadn't given one to your PE teacher then you were stumped…Wonderful girls' toilets on the ground floor. Spent hours back-combing and spraying hair as was the fashion in the early 60's. Prefects regularly turfed out gaggles of girls from the loos especially when it rained….even though there was a large covered way outside the main hall. Large Technical Drawing area and woodwork room tacked onto the building.

School was built under the Heathrow flight path…No double, let alone triple, glazing in those days…Wonder we learnt anything at all as the teachers had to either stop talking or shout. Mrs Hemming was always asking us to do plane checks in lessons…Planes came over every 3 to 4 minutes some days.

When we were in the 6th form, there were 38 numbered rooms in the school and room 39 to us was The Black Horse at Lampton!

Masses of bike sheds available but difficult if not impossible to get round the back because they were in full view of the rooms of the Head, Secretary and Men's staff rooms at the front of the building.

The floor of the Main hall was shiny/unblemished/ 'sacred' and one could walk on it only in pumps/plimsolls. No outdoor shoes at all. If anyone (ladies!) wore stiletto-heeled shoes-even at a social occasion- you had to have those plastic protectors put on them.

The bare colourless walls in the corridors became scuffed and grubby with people having to hang their coats/keep shoes in them so they were gloss-covered in speckled paint. Classrooms were plain magnolia…rather lifeless…no trees or shrubs in the grounds although some were planted later and might have grown by now! All somewhat clinical and new as compared to the old house/school site. To us, we were part of the New school and somehow it was exciting growing up in a newly designed Modern school/world. It was the Swinging Sixties! Pop music era Beatles,trendy fashion.

We had everything we needed apart from a language lab which we believe Miss Coulthard finally achieved later on. New teachers came to the school, many just out of university. No staff ever seemed to leave the old school, old school photos bear this out. Whilst we were there, we had one of those long panoramic photos taken in our 4th yr. (Shame we didn't have class photos taken…as they do today). This was to coincide with Mr Brown's retirement.

New school scarf designed by Mr Bullough – lengthwise black and blue stripes with narrow white stripe in between-I still have mine! Girls were allowed to wear brighter blue jumpers/cardigans and grey skirts instead of navy. Blue or grey tights also. Same old style blue/white check material for summer uniform. To quote Mrs Hemming- "Not too many stiff petticoats girls, and belts are to be no wider than 2 inches". She also once said in a Spring girls' assembly "With the wearing of lower necklines, certain things have come to light." We think she was referring to necklaces (forbidden). White blouses with grey skirts were also introduced. Boys' uniform didn't change but everyone acquired binoculars…

We both stayed on into the 6th form. I was a prefect and Ralph was head boy from '64/65. I went to Brighton Teacher Training College and Ralph went to Leeds University to do Italian.

We still have school magazines - "The Spring Grovian"- dating from '58-65 (not'64) as well as several Prizegiving/Speech Day lists from the '60's. Also we have a photo of the new school - the one on the website.

Same shot as Page 140 taken in 1970

Mysteries At Spring Grove

Diane Higgs '60

Mystery No.1.

At the June Reunion at Spring Grove House, I met up with fellow classmate, Jean Furlong.. We sat on the steps of the terrace beneath Mr Hart's Room in the afternoon sunshine and reminisced about our schooldays at SGGS. Smiling because we knew the terrace was 'Out of Bounds'. Jean asked me if I remembered the rumour of a secret passageway leading to the Music Room via a door in the entrance hall. After trawling through my memory I vaguely remember something about this. Jean thought the passageway led from somewhere outside Mr Hart's Room to the 'Minstrel Gallery' in the Music Room.

Jean went on to say that one day, just before a half term, a boy had fallen through the door and by chance it had shut tight on him. The lad was locked in! His mother alerted the police when he failed to return home but rumour has it that he wasn't discovered until some days later!

Jean says that she remembers Miss Ransom taking her class up into the Minstrel Gallery via a stairway. Of course, after a glass or two of wine in the warm June sunshine, we simply had to find out! But sadly, after much prodding and tapping of the panelled walls in the hall we found absolutely nothing.

Can anyone else shed any light on this? Who was this boy? Is this secret doorway a fact or just a delicious rumour??

Mystery No.2

I left Spring Grove in 1960, but about 30 years or so ago I was passing through Isleworth and couldn't resist stopping my journey to take a look around the old school grounds. Like everybody else I was astonished at the awful vandalism of the 1960 planners but I eventually looked through the window of the Summer House. There, propped up against a wall, was the marble fountain from the Art Room. Someone had removed it and left it there to collect dust. Oh, I do wish I had tried to find out more about it but I hadn't a clue who to ask.....does anyone know what happened next?

The Searchers And Me

Frank Allen (a.k.a Francis McNeice) '60

It was late fifties and as rock and roll came in one window screaming and yelling so my education went quietly out another. All the dedicated tutoring in the hallowed and beautiful halls of Spring Grove Grammar School was a sad waste of time as I picked up a guitar and refused to put it down again. At the turn of the decade I left my seat of learning with nothing more than GCEs in English language, French and woodwork to justify my space in the classroom. Pathetic.

Almost fifty years on, with the publication of my second book, The Searchers And Me-A History Of The Legendary Sixties Hitmakers, I would like to think that dear Miss Hemming might have had just a little pride in the results of her long hours trying to instil in me the principles and the beauty of the English language. It is certainly something that she, or I come to that, could never have foreseen. And ironically it was that old devil rock and roll which precipitated my efforts.

Somehow, with precious little talent, I managed to make a career in music that has lasted for many decades more than I could have hoped and which shows no sign of ending. My first band, a skiffle group called The Ambassadors and formed along with former pupils of Spring Grove (Tom Hanlon, Jonathan 'Taffy' Evans and John Boterill) gave me the grounding and following a spell with Cliff Bennett And The Rebel Rousers I finally ended up as the bass player and front man with Liverpool based hitmakers The Searchers, albeit that they had achieved their initial chart success without any help from me.

In 1999, following the submission of a short article, I was asked to write a book and the result was Travelling Man, a humorous look at the touring side of the group. It sold well and has remained in print to this day. I stuck to what I knew and what I thought I could safely complete without making a fool of myself. Of course it was inevitable that diehard aficionados of the genre would want the complete biography, which Travelling Man most certainly was not.

I declined, mainly through not being at all sure that I was equipped for such an arduous and serious task. There were many things that I did not know about the band's history. They had been around for quite a few years before I came across them. But eventually I decided that if I wanted to call myself a writer, and I had most definitely got the bug by now, that I should take on the challenge.

In all I must have spent three years on the project some of which was in Spanish hotel rooms where I decamped to in order to avoid those annoying everyday distractions and other long hours in the National Newspaper Library trawling through microfilm of old Melody Makers and NMEs. It is a BIG book. Twice as long as my first effort it has ended up at over 440 pages and with more than 160 photographs. Maybe too long for comfort but I was only going to do this once and I didn`t want to leave anything out.

I covered my early life before music took over my life completely and naturally there are references to my days at Spring Grove where I idled my time until I left in 1960. Three archive photographs illustrate my days there. A shot of myself and Lyn Coleman at the front of the building to the left of the main entrance, a bunch of us goodness knows where in the grounds and a shot myself in my pristine new school uniform about to leave home for my first day at SGGS. The sharp eyed among you might spot that I am not wearing the horizontal striped tie of first year pupils. The early signs of a rebel perhaps? I have also reproduced those puny GCE certificates as a sign that my mind was not a complete vacuum.

Thank you Kate Hemming for your invaluable instruction during those formative years. I`m glad your time was not entirely wasted. Mr Sonji, bless him, actually encouraged me to make a solid bodied guitar as a woodwork project. It looked like a guitar but sadly would not play like one. But he understood my passion and I will be forever grateful to a truly lovely man.

I doubt that K Stuart Hart would have the same sense of pride in my endeavours. He was an immaculate man, not a thread out of place and a rigid and overly dignified manner and a plummy, precise pronunciation that could easily have been the prototype for the pretentiously vowelled Brian Sewell. Stiffly pressed striped shirts with white collars, a dark tie knotted to perfection and a beautifully fitting Prince of Wales check suit. I once went to him and said that one of my pals had told me that he liked Elvis Presley. K Stuart Hart looked down on me with a curdling look of contempt and without the remotest sign of amusement replied. 'Don`t be facetious boy.' I learnt very little about music from Mr Hart, although quite a lot about fashion. I just wish he could have seen the wider picture and that any appreciation of the arts, no matter how high or low, is infinitely better than none at all.

I hope that some of my fellow pupils who shared those days of fun, naivety and terror in deepest Isleworth will want to check it out.

The Searchers And Me-A History Of The Legendary Sixties Hitmakers
Published in hardback by Aureus (direct order only)
www.aureus.co.uk or www.thesearchersandme.com
The Searchers homepage www.the-searchers.co,uk

Mixed Memories

Richard Dawe '62

It always amazes me just how much Old Spring Grovians remember the school and its staff, as my own recollections are much less clear. I can recall the external appearance of this fine old building and its grounds, but I have no clear mental picture of the interior. I remember the Banksian Room and the infamous coal-scuttles, but that's about all.

My memories of the staff are equally vague, although certain characters made more of an impression on me than others. The diminutive Miss Clothier bullied me into a rudimentary knowledge of maths., for which I shall always be in her debt. The track-suited Mr Short left me with an abiding hatred of almost any sporting activity, and Mr Hart (the originator of the beehive hairstyle?) failed entirely to recognize what has proved to be a lifetime interest in music - I am now a part-time guitar teacher. Mr Cockroft and Mr Ridley taught me precisely nothing about Chemistry and Physics respectively; this has stood me in good stead throughout most of my adult life. I also remember my first form-master whose name, I think, was Mr Detsikas. He had sociopathic tendencies and was a stern disciplinarian, qualities rarely found in teachers today.

I was also a failed member of Mrs Shipton's String Class - the eponymous music tutor decided I was not destined to become a concert violinist after I left the instrument on a 657 trolley-bus.

On a more positive note, Miss Richards and Mrs Holman made Geography and Sociology fascinating, and Miss Coulthard did succeed in teaching me French although at the time she undoubtedly thought otherwise. Mr Lineham imparted a lifelong love of literature for which I shall be eternally grateful. I remember Headmaster Mr Brown as a real gentleman - indeed on his retirement Mrs Hemming described him as a "Scholarly Gentleman and a Gentlemanly Scholar", a clever use of the school's initials.

I read in the Spring Grovian about Frances "Flossie" Forsyte, who was hanged for murder. I lived in Standard Road, Hounslow, and Flossie lived just round the corner in Clare Road. He was a bully from an early age and it is no surprise to me that he came to a bad end.

The Journey from Hounslow Heath Infants via Hounslow Heath Junior Mixed to Spring Grove, then on to Lampton and finally Durham University was eventful, incident-packed, full of laughs and mostly enjoyable. I feel I had an excellent education overall, and I very much regret being such a trial to those responsible for it. I have lost touch with almost all my Spring Grove colleagues, although I still exchange Christmas cards with Pete Ellis, Colin Taylor and Philip his wife, Susan Norton as she then was. In the unlikely event that anyone else remembers me from those distant times I would be delighted if we could make contact.

One of my most vivid memories of school life was the dreaded school dinners. I particularly recall the gravy, which was of a gruel-like consistency with a very low viscosity. It had the unique quality of textile magnetism, attaching itself ineradicably to school ties and the lapels of school blazers. Its flavour was proportionate to its thickness, which meant that most of the time it tasted of very little. One of the regular desserts was steamed currant pudding or spotted dick. I remember we re-christened it Dunlop Tubeless, as we discovered it bounced to a surprising height when dropped on the floor. When thrown to the floor with considerable force the bounce was spectacular. Another timeless classic was semolina pudding with rose-hip syrup. If like me you hated semolina you just had the syrup. This left you staring in puzzlement at an empty plate with a pink smear in the centre.

When going through some old books, I discovered that in 1963 I won the Ann Lusher Prize for English. I had completely forgotten this - does anyone know anything about Ann Lusher, as I would be very interested to learn about her? Maybe you are even reading this yourself Ann, I do hope so.

I also remember Chemistry lessons with Mr Cockroft, especially the wooden benches with their Bunsen burners and the smell of gas and rubber. I charged in one day and flung my satchel on the bench. There was a loud crash as a new and expensive microscope fell to the floor. I think it was at this point that Mr. Cockroft realised that Chemistry was unlikely to be my life's work.

Another thing I vaguely remember was a school day-trip to the the Isle of Wight. I know we visited Osborne House and Carisbrooke Castle, and I remember Mr Detsikas patrolling the train corridors on the journey home, brandishing a wooden back-scratcher. Surely I cannot have imagined this - does anyone else remember anything more?

On a different subject, my father Ken Dawe is also an Old Spring Grovian. Ken was at school in the 1930's, and as he is now 90 I suppose it is improbable that there is anyone left who remembers him. Still, in that unlikely event I would be delighted to hear from any survivors.

Taking Stock

An unattributed view from "Spring Grovian" 1960

After two years in our present building, it is perhaps appropriate to look around and consider the advantages we have gained and what losses, if any, we have sustained, as a result of our transfer from the elegant serenity of Isleworth to the continual bustle of Lampton.

We have gained, at long last, a hall large enough to accommodate the whole school for its daily act of corporate worship, for the production of school plays and concerts, and for such internal social events as parties and dances, which make such an important contribution to one's school career. Its clean, bright colours and sparkling polished floors provide a striking contrast to the picture of the old hall, that survives in the memory of most O.S.Gs, the grimy cream walls, peeling blue paintwork, and the great, dusty girders, not to mention the even dustier floors.

Grouped around the old hall were the science laboratories and the gymnasium. No-one needs reminding of the small edition of the Crystal Palace, which served as a Biology Laboratory. Its north wall, made up of slabs of Icelandic lava, the hip bath, the vegetation hanging down and growing up from all sorts of unlikely situations, and threatening to engulf the young biologists, the extremes of heat and cold - all these impressions survive as part of "the good old days". Instead of this, we now enjoy clean laboratories, kept at a reasonable temperature all the year round. The provision of adequate facilities for specialist subjects just defies comparison. The handcraft and domestic science rooms are as modern and well equipped as any in the County, and represent our biggest gains.

The old Art Room, like so many other places in the old building, had "character". Probably the coldest place in any school at any time, its central heating pipes lay several inches thick in dust, way below floor level; (small wonder that Beethoven never smiled on us from his shelf, and the fountain never played!) In transferring to the new school, the art department has lost this "character" - the craft-room appears in "contemporary" guise - a constant succession of forms in diverse colours and assorted media parades across its length and breadth.

A few old favourites by O.S.Gs claim their places on the Art Room wall, but the experiments of the rising generations are closing in from all sides.

It seems, then, that from the material point of view, we have gained considerably as a result of the transfer. Our losses are much less tangible and no one seems able to state definitely, what is missing in our new premises. At Isleworth, we occupied a building that had been the home of Alfred Pears, and, before him, of Joseph Banks; the atmosphere of a 'home' persisted during our period of occupation, and staff and pupils worked together like members of one large family. The red brick house, set in its well-kept grounds, always seemed to be a friendly place, but a school is more than just a building, and though our present 'home' has rather a grim appearance, the Spring Grovian virtues of happiness and friendliness continue to flourish as of old.

The Beat Goes On

Dave Fittall '63.

I was interested to read Chris Curtis's comments regarding Thomas Hanlon's 'Beat Group Legacy' article from the December '05 publication. Sorry Chris – you're wrong on both counts! The late fifties/early sixties produced a plethora of aspiring Rock and R & B musicians and Spring Grove had its fair share – including me and a number of my fellow students. Along with Jeff Mitchell we formed 'The Sugarbeats' and, later, turned down the 'opportunity' of replacing The Stones at Eel Pie Island and the Crawdaddy in the mid-sixties – what if?

My term at the school stretched from 1957 to 1963 and Ian 'Mac' MacLaggan was in the same year, leaving at the end of the 5th form in July 1961. If I remember correctly, he was generally seen toting his guitar around – presumably easier than a keyboard in those days!

Frank McNeice was in the year above me, leaving in July 1960 as stated in Thomas's letter, so of course he was not at the school at the same time as Chris. Indeed Mac's school life only just overlapped with Chris's as he left as Chris was finishing his first year.

I remember our surprise – and pride? – when The Searchers introduced their new bass player Frank Allen – a guy from our school albeit with a name-change! Mac's fame with The Small Faces followed shortly after but another Spring Grovian who made it into recording was Mick Underwood, drummer with Mike Berry and The Outlaws – I think Mick also played with Cliff Bennet's Rebel Rousers.

My band played at the school dance in about 1964 with my brother Keith, also a Spring Grovian, on drums but at the previous year's dance the band – I think 'The Dreamers' - featured another classmate Stuart Mead. Stuart, who wanted to become an architect, was an extremely talented player and I often wonder what happened to him. Does anybody out there know?

Back to the Frank and Ian show! As many of you will know, Viv Syrett organised the 1960 'O' level (Frank's) reunion last May (04) and extended the invite to the '1961' year (mine and Mac's). Mac was actually in England at the time although was unable to make it but Frank did attend and appears on some of the reunion photos on the website.

From Frank McNeice (a.k.a Frank Allen of the Searchers) I got the latest OSG mag and enjoyed it very much although of course it was about earlier years in the main than my stay at Spring Grove.

While reading the letter from Anne Clarke (`54) I noticed some familiar names such as Ann Waldron (wasn't she head girl?) and John Botterill. John was one of
. the guys I formed a skiffle group with while at Spring Grove along with 'Taffy' Evans (you know, through all the time I knew him I never knew what his real

Christian name was) and Tom Hanlon. Tom was sadly killed in a road accident last year.

We used to rehearse at John Botterill`s house in Twickenham just around the corner from Kneller Hall. I am attaching a photo of our little musical group. We called ourselves The Ambassadors Skiffle Group and played in places like the Windmill pub in Bell Road (for ten bob between us), York Hall in Twickenham and the Red Lion Hotel in Hounslow. We were probably rubbish but we had a lot of fun and at least I did manage to make a profession out of it. Who was it said you can`t fool all of the people all of the time? Not true. I proved it. Check out our website :- www.the-searchers.co.uk

The lineup on the picture is Tom Hanlon back left on guitar, our washboard player whose name I can`t remember in front of him, Taffy Evans on tea chest bass, John Botterill on guitar and me on guitar far right at the tender age of around thirteen I would imagine.

A Vote for the L.T.Brown Cedar

Minnie Hill '60.

Reading articles in the SGR leaves me amazed at the memories and descriptions, especially of teachers, that I missed. I remember friends telling me of how wonderful Miss Ransom was but I hardly knew her. She looked sweet and full of kindness, I remember her face but that's all. There was Mr. Pearce (a good looking fella'), Mr. Stevenson (also good looking but a bit surly) and "Taffy" Howell, Mr. Ridley, Miss Pearson (domestic science)and Miss Phillips; all faces I remember but I had no real bond with any of them except the headmaster, Mr. Brown. Without him my life would be very different. He changed my world and even today whenever I have a difficult decision to make I consider what advice he might give me.

My life wasn't easy during my years at Spring Grove and for a very long time I drifted from one temporary residence to yet another. The 50s were hard times for the poor. Not enough food or sleep interrupted my homework and studying and bit by bit I failed in all subjects. I left with just an Art O level. Horrendous failure.

My last interview with Mr. Brown was poignant. He told me that I had wasted my time there but that he understood my difficulties. He had arranged for me to become a cadet nurse at the West Middlesex Hospital and he was confident that I could help people, especially children.

Wow! Someone with confidence in me!! He was right. I found another way to be and within two years I had passed several more 'O' levels and begun 'A' levels. As a student nurse and then a student midwife I had a zest for learning and study and I was determined from then on to be as good as I could get.

All of my career I have enjoyed. My contact with the human race has been mainly joyful. The majority of people are so very good and solid.

I wouldn't have encountered any of this without L.T.Brown. I never thanked him and I regret that; but for me he is a star. Before anyone believed in me, he did and I improved myself with him in mind.

I'm sure he watched over each and every one of us and really cared. He knew who could succeed but those that needed that extra push he pushed with gentleness.

Naturally, for me, the Cedar must be named the L.T.Brown Cedar if it is voted otherwise it would still be the LTB cedar for me!

The Beat Goes On

Chris (brother of Irene '60) Curtis
(Not the same Chris of the Searchers)

I have just been handed a copy of Spring Grovian by my sister, Irene, (1954-1960) who intimated to me that I might like to read the article on the back page of the December 1st Issue, by Thomas Hanlon, about the school's rock'n'roll heritage. I read with great interest about one Frank Allen, alias McNiece, of the Searchers. As an old Spring Grovian myself, 1960-1965, and a rock musician as well, I was surprised to read of one Ian MacLachlan from my school period. His name is actually Ian McLaggan, the Faces' keyboard player. Unless my memory is really beginning to play tricks on me at the ripe old age of 55, there was no-one of either of those names in my year. Fellow musician from my year, Graham Keedy, with whom I am still in touch will I'm sure agree with me on that. The only keyboard expert we had amongst us was my dear friend John Granger, now head of some school in Bournemouth, who was also out "On The Road" at the same time and on the same circuit as I was during the late 60s and early 70s. He doesn't remember a guy of that name either. I was bass player with a band called at first "Slow Dog" and later changed the name to "Wheels" playing clubs, colleges and tours as warm up band for the Strawbs, Fairport Convention, ELO, Manfred Mann's Earth Band and scores of others. My friend and also another bass player Graham Douglas, who lives just along the road from me, was in the year behind us and he doesn't remember the name either. So I think Mr Hanlon is mistaken in thinking that "Mac" Maclaggan was a Spring Grovian around that time. I have a feeling that the Small Faces were an Essex band in fact. That was where I met Stevie Marriott when I was working with a friend of his called Terry Reid. But that was in the days when Marriott was in Humble Pie. I may be wrong, but I don't think I am!

The Staff - 1958

The Staff

9

This chapter has been difficult to compile.

The backbone of any school, the staff, are the ever present figures in school life but it is only when we look back that we realise how little we know about them as "people" and their lives outside school.

There have been references to many of the staff in the previous chapters of pupils' memories but apart from these the only material that could be found was in past copies of the OSGA newsletters, usually marking retirement. The available newsletters are a random collection sent in by OSGs and nowhere near a complete set.

Sadly the later retirement tributes held little biographical detail. The list is by no means exhaustive. Some 120 staff taught at Spring Grove House. Most of those featured in this chapter taught at the school for over twenty years and several over thirty and some throughout the schools time at Spring Grove House. The exception was Bernard Joy, an international footballer and Olympian in 1936, who left to join the RAF in 1939 but returned to journalism rather than teaching in 1946.

With apologies for the omission of those who should have been included but for whom no biographical detail could be found.

Headmaster for 27 Years
of Spring Grove Grammar School

Mr. L.T. Brown M.A. (Cantab)

Mr. Leonard Theodore Brown, M.A., was headmaster of Spring Grove Grammar School for 27 years. Mr. Brown was a Scholar and Prizeman of Christ's College, Cambridge. His distinguished University career was interrupted by five years in the Intelligence Service in the First World War. After the war he returned to Cambridge and in 1920 was awarded 1st Class Modern and Mediaeval Languages Tripos, Parts I and II.

His first teaching post was at Haberdasher Aske's School, which he had previously attended as a pupil. Further teaching experience was gained at Sir T. Rich's School, Gloucester, and at Dulwich College, and then, at an early age, he was appointed Headmaster of Longton High School, Stoke on Trent. It was after three years in this appointment that he became Headmaster of Spring Grove Grammar School, in January 1935. He retired from this position in July, 1962, and in the following year he and Mrs. Brown retired to Hove.

Here his keen interest in education continued and for the last year or two he had assisted in the teaching of languages in a local girls' school.

Great headmaster

For his obituary Mrs. Hemming, senior mistress at Spring Grove Grammar School, wrote;-

"Mr. Brown will always be remembered with respect and affection by all who knew him. He was a gifted linguist and scholarly in many other fields too. A firm believer in the value of co-education and the development of the individual as well as the corporate spirit, he was an idealist with a practical approach to all problems. He impressed one with his dignity, his never failing courtesy and his unruffled manner.

He had integrity of character, an inner peace and a boundless fund of wisdom. He never failed to show tolerance and understanding: even in his most polished and gifted speeches, his friendly humour and love of mankind were obvious. He will be thought of as a great headmaster and a friend, always ready to listen, to understand, and to help."

Mr. Brown died suddenly on Sunday 23 January 1966 at the age of 70.

Spring Grovian - May 1942

Mr. A. C. P. Handover and

Mr. A. H. Aldersley

Mr. A. Aldersley   Mr. A.Handover

Of these two masters it can truly be said that they will live in the hearts of those who knew them. Both of them quiet, unassuming personalities, they exerted an influence which will go on for ever producing good in the world.

Mr. Handover had seen sixteen years' service in the School, and was universally respected. His infinite patience with the more backward pupils and remarkable conscientiousness in everything he undertook are fully recognised by those who worked with him as colleagues and by past and present pupils who were fortunate to attend his Mathematics classes.

In Swimming and Life-saving he rendered yeoman service, and in the latter connection we know that his work was of real national importance outside the School also. In the past he had also identified himself with all musical activities, instructing pupils in the violin classes and above all, conducting the operas which Mr. Varney produced.

Of the many tributes to Mr. Handover which have been written or paid, one of the most characteristic was from a parent contributing to the Memorial Fund—"He took such pains over the weaker pupils". To encourage the despondent, and to make the uncongenial congenial, are two of the greatest tasks of the teacher.

Mr. Handover excelled in both, as a large number of OSGs will know from their own experience.

Mr. Handover's enthusiasm on behalf of the Royal Life Saving Society gained him world wide recognition.

Mr. Aldersley endeared himself to all by his unfailing devotion to his work, his unflagging zeal, his kindly sympathy and his readiness to share in every activity of the School. No appeal for co-operation on his part in any matter whatsoever relating to its welfare went unanswered, and he put in many hours of his spare time and expended untold energy to its service.

Mr. Aldersley was, if anything, even more self-effacing. Nothing surprised him more than to be told how much many of us here owed to his teaching and to his personal example.

To the Science Sixth, in particular, he was a real friend, kindly, almost deferential, a true gentleman. To be able to understand adolescents so as to share their interests and win their confidence and friendship is a rare gift, and one which Mr. Aldersley possessed to the full.

He was appointed to the Staff in 1926.

Both died in 1941.

Mr. R.L. Callow Ph. D. M.A. B.Sc. B.D. F.R.G.S.

Mr. R. L. Callow spent over thirty years at Spring Grove, the last four as Senior Master. Mr. Callow's service to the school covers almost the whole history of the school itself. The school was opened in 1923, and Mr. Callow joined the teaching staff in the following year. He is recorded as Number 13 in the list of staff appointments, and how many changes in that staff he saw during his teaching career here may be gathered from the fact that the last appointment to the staff before he left was Number 120.

To estimate the number of pupils at Spring Grove who had the benefit of his teaching, one needs to deal in thousands. Most of those thousands of Spring Grovians will have known Mr. Callow.

In addition to his work as a Geography and Scripture teacher, his organization of the annual school outings and his active interest in the Christian Union were greatly appreciated. The scholarly interests and delight in study which character-ized his whole career were well illustrated by his choice of a leaving present, the Dictionary of Ethics and Religions.

A Memory of Mr Callow. - Ken Pearce.

When I arrived at SGGS in September 1955 as a fledgling schoolmaster, I was placed in a small staff-room with Mr Callow and Mr Barrett. Our room was immediately above the front door, facing the London Road. You'll recall that there was no Staff Room as such. The teachers were scattered around the building, two or three to a room. We did meet together at morning break though, in the Domestic Science Room!

Raymond Callow, the senior master, and George Barrett, head of Mathematics, had clearly known each other for years, but if I was in the room they referred to each other as "Mr Callow" and "Mr Barrett". First name terms in my presence would have been unacceptable.

Raymond Callow had lived in Brentford as a young man, and attended the Methodist Church there, but by 1955 he had bought a property at Hastings ready for his retirement. He went there every week-end, so it was arranged that he never taught the last lesson on a Friday afternoon. He left early to head for his coastal retreat. He lived with his sister, I think, and neither of them ever married.

He always wore a gown, and with his grey hair and slightly stooped head I thought he resembled a vulture when seen from behind. He did two things every day. He tackled the "Telegraph" crossword, and read a passage from the Bible in Hebrew. Who does that nowadays?

Raymond Leslie Callow, died in a nursing home at St. Leonards-on-Sea on 14th December 1972, aged 74 years

Ken Pearce

Mr F W Brown M.Sc. (Lond.)

Senior Mathematics Master 1925 – 1953.
Second Master 1941 - 1953

Mr.Frederick Brown was educated at Sandown Grammar School, Isle of Wight, and at the University College (now the university) of Southampton, graduating B.Sc. 1st Division (London) in 1913. His first teaching service at Newport Grammar School, Isle of Wight, (1914-1920) was broken by several years in the R.G.A. in the First World War. He had further teaching experience at the Lydney Grammar School (1920-1921) and at Steyning Grammar School (1921-1925). It speaks volumes for his tenacity and mathematical ability that despite the heavy strain involved in teaching he managed to continue his studies to such effect that by 1923 he obtained Upper Second Class Honours in Mathematics at London, no mean academic achievement even for a full-time student. Even after appointment of Senior Matematics Master at Spring Grove in 1925 he continued further studies, and by 1930 obtained the M.Sc. of London in the Principles, Methods and History of Science. This by no means exhausted his intellectual appetite for, as his friends well know, he was widely read in literature as well as science and had truly achieved a liberal education.

During the years preceding his appointment as Senior Master in 1941 in succession to Mr. Snaith, Mr. Brown had maintained a remarkable level of efficiency as a teacher and organiser of the Mathematics Department, and the consistently successful results in that subject over a long series of University examinations are a tribute to his untiring energy. But Mr. Brown was no mere specialist, seeking an outlet for his talents as a mathematician. He was a man of wide cultural interests: his conversation revealed a wealth of literary knowledge and a sound critical faculty. He identified himself with foreign travel and photography; and as far as the School was concerned, gave considerable assistance in games, and in those days could always be relied upon to turn out with other members of the Staff when they met the pupils at cricket and tennis. Perhaps the more sedate activity of the chess board constituted his favourite indoor recreation: it is a fact that his enthusiasm for the game made him an assiduous and inspiring coach for those countless pupils interested in it during his long career of teaching, and established the sound tradition the School now holds in chess.

In the double capacity of Second Master and Housemaster of Nelson, the same power of organisation he had shown as Senior Mathematics Master was readily apparent, and he devoted all his energies to preserving a high standard of discipline in the School and a live spirit of co-operation in House affairs. He supervised the morning assembly with a rod of iron, and once kept the boy's half off assembly behind demanding to know who was the author of a "horse laugh".

His gentlemanly yet firm manner, characterised by common sense and an unfailing humour and allied to sound scholarship, gained for him the respect of his pupils, and the many tributes paid to him on his retirement by Old Spring Grovians are evidence of his far-reaching influence as a teacher.

To those privileged to know and work with him for so many years his memory will be forever sweet. It is difficult to convey the remarkable combination of his qualities, but, fortunately the delightful memorial portrait of F.W. Brown by the gifted Art Master, Mr C. Bullough, cleverly caught much of the character of the man. Those lively enquiring blue eyes peering quizzically over spectacles well down on the nose, and, at second hand, you would enjoy the experience of hundreds of erstwhile Spring Grovians who felt the impact of that masterly yet truly gentle mind.

To generations F.W. Brown was known as "Basher" Brown; this was believed to be because of his habit of emphasising a point by "bashing" the board rubber on to the blackboard, often disappearing in the resulting cloud of chalk dust.. Certainly his generous physical proportions might well have inspired in the young some forebodings as to their fate should he have directed his energies in certain directions, but, in fact, of all men, physical violence was furthest from his nature. Others have even suggested that "Basher" was a corruption of "bashful," and, indeed, this may come nearer to the truth, for F.W. Brown was by nature extremely sensitive and reserved, ever considerate of the feelings of others. To a generous heart and a fine mind of high mathematical ability and liberal culture, add the highest integrity of character and a most unassuming modesty, spice all with a genial mirth, and there stands a great teacher, a loyal colleague, a faithful friend and a gentle-man. Under his charge the Mathematics Department grew steadily stronger and by the time of his retirement the record of successes by both pupils and ex-pupils was indeed gratifying. Many are the Old Boys of the Sixth Form who are deeply indebted to his inspiration; many, too, the less gifted mathe-matically who can testify to the patient, firm and yet ever kindly help they received. So beloved he was, alike by pupils, old pupils and all his colleagues, that all keenly cherished the hope of long and satisfying retirement after so worthy a career.

On his retirement in 1953 in his Speech Day address to the School, the Headmaster described Mr. Brown as a tower of strength to himself and to his colleagues, who had witnessed his untiring work and felt his genial com-radeship, and declared that he would be hard, perhaps impossible to replace. The more was the shock when this hope was so sadly dashed by his sudden passing three years later in 1956 at the age of 63.

Mr. G T W Barrett B.Sc. (Lond.)

From the Spring Grovian
- July 1965 on His Retirement

When Mr Barrett joined the staff in September 1928, the school was a mere six years old, comprising half the number of pupils it does today with very few in the Sixth Form. The Senior Mathematics Master at the time was Mr F W Brown whose portrait painted by Mr Bullough hangs in the school library adjacent to that of the late Headmaster, Mr LT Brown; and Mr Barrett came as Assistant Teacher of Mathematics. That the standard reached in this subject was a particularly high one was due to a large extent to the quality of the teaching of these two masters, later supplemented by that of Miss Clothier; and when Mr F Brown retired in 1954, Mr Barrett became head of the Mathematics Department. In this aspect of his work there must be countless Old Spring Grovians as well as many present pupils who owe much to Mr Barrett's teaching, and several may not as yet have fully grasped the fact that he has gone.

Even if the scope of his activities had ended here, his beneficial influence on the quality of the Mathematics in the school would still be felt, but Mr Barrett was also Form Master of the Sixth, a post he had held for twenty-five years at retirement, and one which gave him the opportunity not only of teaching his subject to Advanced Level but of helping to shape the character of those senior pupils, prefects included, with whom he daily came into contact. For the past fifteen years he had also been Housemaster of Rodney House, which afforded him an insight into a fair cross-section of the school; and his effectiveness can readily be appreciated from the fine record of Rodney House achievement over a long time.

Mr Barrett's association with the life of the school, however, extended beyond the classroom and he will be remembered for his continued interest in school cricket. He coached the First Eleven from 1929 to 1953, and during this period played with distinction in the Staff versus Pupils matches, besides umpiring regularly the Old Spring Grovians fixture. The school should be grateful to him for initiating a fund in the pre-war days for the erection of a cricket pavilion, the money being collected over a period of ten years. It was ultimately allocated to the purchase of the present scorer's box and sight screens. His love of sport did not end at cricket: he was a first rate tennis player and in his prime a formidable opponent in the tournaments that have become a traditional feature of the Summer Term activities. He could also combine mathematical proficiency with sport when he served for a long time as Chief Recorder at the school athletic and swimming events.

Mr Barrett was a master of outstanding personal qualities. In temperament he was amiable and equable, and his relations with pupils showed that he possessed an unlimited amount of understanding and patience. He was always ready to devote generous time to their individual difficulties even outside the normal timetable; no aloof, inaccessible figure, but easily approachable, he took a lively and kindly interest in their work. Yet such amiability was combined with a gentlemanly but quite firm manner where discipline was concerned. His clear-headed, orderly teaching enabled his academic successes to keep pace with the ever-increasing numbers of senior pupils. One prominent characteristic of Mr Barrett was a wisdom and power of judgment which he could bring to bear on any question involving a clear decision. He would express an opinion only after giving any problem calm, unhurried consideration.

It has been rightly said that houses retain the impression of the characters of their former occupants – an atmosphere, if you will – not directly due to their material surroundings. The school in general, and the Mathematics department in particular, will sense for a long time the influence of Mr Barrett's thirty-six years of service.

Miss E. D. Bromwich T.D.D.S.

Miss Bromwich was appointed in 1929, and in close association with Miss Walters became an integral part of school life in her several capacities of Domestic Science Mistress, Mistress in Junior Assembly and Form Teacher in the Lower School. A firm disciplinarian, she won the re-spect of her pupils by her complete understanding of them, her honesty of purpose and her whole-hearted devotion to their welfare. In her younger days she had given tireless assistance in their outdoor activities such as games and gardening, and the good of the School was without doubt her primary interest. Her spirit of service, high personal character and sound ideals did much to form habits of work and good conduct, and her influence on the School was far-reaching. She retired in 1949.

Miss E. D. Bromwich was gifted with boundless energy, living for the most part a healthy outdoor life, and her period of retirement seemed scarcely to have begun. Even when we heard that she had to undergo a serious and delicate operation, hopes were entertained of her ultimate recovery. Though she was not destined to enjoy a long period of happy retirement at Saxmundham with her companion, Miss Walters, it may be said of her with confidence that she has merited a more lasting reward and the welcome reserved for the just and faithful servant. Miss Bromwich died in July 1954.

Mr. W. Lineham MA

From the Spring Grovian – July 1965
on His Retirement

In 1928 Mr Lineham was appointed Senior English Master at Spring Grove Secondary School.

Graduating with honours in History at Leeds in 1924, his first teaching post was at Grange High School for Boys, Bradford, where he continued his studies, now in English, for his Master's degree, obtained in 1927.

In those days competition for grammar school assistant masterships was exceptionally fierce and any Middlesex vacancy attracted scores of applications. That Mr Lineham was selected for the post at Spring Grove from a field of about two hundred applicants, many of considerable merit, indicates the very high qualifications and attractive personal qualities which the Governors saw in him. The wisdom of that appointment has been abundantly demonstrated by his dedication to duty, his meticulous attention to detail, his outstanding ability as a teacher and as Head of Department, and by his marked influence as Senior Master on the general good discipline of the school. He was never willing to court easy or cheap popularity, yet his pupils or his colleagues will heartily agree that he has richly deserved the respect, high esteem and lasting affection with which he is now surrounded.

To Mr Lineham the school is indebted in many ways of which present pupils can have no idea. For over twenty years he edited the School Magazine and was responsible for the organisation of the School Library.

He assisted as producer or stage manager in several school dramatic and musical productions, in which he occasionally took one of the parts, and later organised and developed a really good orchestra, playing the leading violin in school concerts.

In these varied spheres, as in his leadership of Nelson House until 1957, Mr Lineham has given widely and effectively of his talents.

Colleagues, and pupils too perhaps, will greatly miss his crisply delicate sense of humour, often droll, ever entertaining, but never malicious; his unfailing courtesy, his wide scholarship. And who will not remember with envy yet with delight that beautifully formed, firm, regular handwriting, so completely characteristic of the man.

It may truly be said that his influence, no less than his service, has been an immense and continuous power in the lives of all who have been privileged to know him. We gratefully acknowledge that service and influence.

Mr. J. F. Cross M.Coll.H

From Spring Grovian December 1947

At Easter 1947 Mr. Cross retired after twenty four years' service. To many Spring Grovians, as well as to a number of his colleagues, Mr. Cross was something in the nature of an "institution," and the Head-master, saying farewell to him on behalf of the whole School, had to admit that it was completely impossible to assess his valuable services at their true merit, as there were so very few aspects of the School's life and history with which Mr. Cross had not been associated, not the least being his work for the Parents' and Teachers' Association.

All Old Spring Grovians were identified with him in some respect, and all of them without exception would readily renew their acquaintance with him and be certain of a very hearty welcome and a happy exchange of reminiscences. "Mens Sana in Corpore Sano" read the school motto and Mr. Cross certainly saw that the boys under his charge were " Corpore Sano".

Whether sprinting round the south pitch, nagged at on the North Pitch or urged in the gymnasium by the grey trousered and white sweatered Mr. Cross to "jump boy, jump, land on your toes, come along, come along, jump" , Mr. Cross saw to it that for short periods during the week at least, all boys at Spring Grove had a due ration of physical exercise.

His other activity was in the twin-roofed woodwork shop, where the mysteries of wood and the working thereof were imparted through two portions of the anatomy. The brighter ones absorbed these germs of knowledge through their ears, and the dull ones through their backsides. A three foot length of 2" x 1" pine wielded in expert hands can emphasize a point more effectively, and for a longer period, than any amount of hammering, however eloquent. Perhaps it was a dangerous practice, especially when his victim. was holding a razor sharp chisel near his nose. He had stock phrases; "Tools away lads" "Tip top work lad!" and, particularly, "Gather round this bench., lads" Then would follow a bloodthirsty tale beginning always thus - "This fool of a lad...." And, you know, he was right - they were fools. But science in the shape of impact adhesives has offered these "fools of lads" a second chance of making good. About to leave one class was commanded "Stay behind the biy with the plastic wood!"

A somewhat forbidding character of high standards and something of the English eccentric, for hobby he bred and showed rabbits. I am sure that many a modern semi-detached house is a better place to-day for the attentions of its O.S.G. occupants tortured and trained in primitive ways by Mr. Cross.

Mr. Cross entered the life of local government and for many years represented a ward in the Borough of Twickenham.

For his final years he lived in Sussex close to the.sea. He died in 1963.

Spring Grovian - May 1948

Miss E.H. Griffin M.A.(Lond)

Undoubtedly the most noteworthy event of the Spring Term 1948 was the retirement of Miss Griffin after twenty-three years' service as Senior Mistress of the School. To so many generations of Spring Grovians she has been such an integral part of school life that, in the words of the Headmaster, it would be most difficult to imagine the future without her presence on the Staff.

At the closing assembly, Miss Griffin was presented with a gold watch bracelet and a cheque as a small token of the affection in which she was held by the Staff and pupils, and in the course of his subsequent address the Headmaster paid a warm tribute to her as a most helpful colleague, praising her amiable temperament and friendliness and stressing the fact that, while she could be severe in dealing with misdemeanour, she was always eminently just in her administration of discipline. Above all, she was zealous and enthusiastic in her service to the School, and he would feel a very deep sense of personal loss in her departure.

In her reply, Miss Griffin thanked the School for its generous and handsome presentation, and recalled the hundreds of boys and girls who had passed through the School in the course of her many years at Spring Grove. For some weeks before that final assembly she had been dreading the idea of "the last time" she would be fulfilling the several duties of her position and visualizing how that "last time" would inevitably come when she must conduct the girls' assembly on Wednesdays, or ask a boy why he was not wearing his cap, or tell him to take his hands out of his pockets. The many generations of young people, however, with whom she had daily come in contact, had always made her realise the combination of youth and gaiety, and had forever kept her young in mind and outlook. She was profoundly thankful for that influence. While there would naturally be a feeling of sadness at her departure, the pupils should remember that,. although individuals go, the School lives on; and she recalled how singularly appropriate were the concluding stanzas of the Harrow School song " Forty Years On" in her present circumstances.

The affection and respect which Miss Griffin commanded had been remarkably expressed in a farewell party given in her honour by the senior pupils on the previous evening, to which members of the Staff and several Old Spring Grovians had been invited, while a similar function was held on the last morning of term in the Headmaster's study, attended by all the teaching Staff.

An appreciation of Miss Griffin by Mrs.Nancy D. Tomkins.

.. A lover of learning and all learned men: Wise in all doinges : Curtesse, to all persons; spewing spite to none : doing good to many : and... to me so fast afrend
...
—Roger Ascham's Preface to "TheScholemaster."

When I became a pupil at Spring Grove Miss Griffin was also "new," and yet such was her personality that already she and the School were synonymous in thought.

The School was young—just three years old, and lacking tradition, some of us were rather wild ; many's the time I had to report to Miss Griffin's Room on account of some escapade.

Her "dressings down" however, were never suppressive or conducive to fear; you were addressed with understanding, tempered wisely with degrees of sternness. You were aware of fairness and reason, and very often of a sense of having acted in an anti-social manner, but you never felt damned or outcast. There was always a place in the community for the trier.

The first apparent measure of Miss Griffin's influence for good was her ability to win the confidence of the critical.

Perhaps one of her greatest gifts to Spring Grove has been loyalty. By her example we learned to subjugate aspirations and little personal glories to the wider glory and success of the School. It was a proper lesson to learn, for in that boundless community beyond the School fences, common aims and common achievement play an indispensable part.

Unqualified success in teaching is probably more difficult to attain than in any other profession; more difficult but more worthy the attainment. It is difficult because the task is a dual one, combining teaching of a subject with the moulding of character, and worthy because the medium is the most exciting, most malleable, most quixotic of all clay, the youth of mankind.   It is no easy task to teach a subject to indifferent children, to dull laborious plodders, to the intelligent but lazy, in fact to a cross-section of pupils with occasional brilliance complicating the average intake. Less easy still is it to fashion a new generation, preserving individuality, nurturing traits that are strong, or creative, or quick with promise; discouraging the weakness of vanities, fears and hatreds, social jealousies and inequalities and littleness of mind and action.   It is most diffi-cult of all to do these things unobtrusively, by example rather than by exhorta-tion.

Miss Griffin succeeded. She has been the School's great teacher, correlating the school community with the social environment into which, in time, each child must pass.   Because she herself is a good citizen, vitally conscious of the individual's relationship to fellow men and women and to society itself, she gave to Spring Grovians the mental aptitude and temperamental exactness for good citizenship themselves. Her individuality inspires leadership in others, together with the will and the zest to lead full and useful lives to the utmost extent of their capabilities.

Now this School Magazine goes to Miss Griffin in her retirement, and for the first term in almost twenty-three years her ringing tones are no longer calling "Come in", from the room between the stairs. But her influence will not wilt like the beauty of the buildings, or her work break up like the mosaic of the Art Room Terrace. Her influence and work, the vibrant strength of her personality, the justice, truth and aesthetic inspiration, the friendship which Spring-Grovians have cherished down the years - these things are now a fundamental part of the tradition that is Spring Grove. Wherever in the world there are Spring Grovians - albeit unknown to many, there too is something of Miss Griffin.

A great teacher and a noble woman has finished her work for the pupils of Spring Grove but the association is immortal. May the years of retirement be as rich in, happiness as the school years were filled with service.

Nancy (Sterry) Tomkins (1926-32).

....and another tribute from Jean M. (Langton) Rhodes, (1933-1938)

"She possessed the gift of friendship"

It is to so very few that this gift is given and the loss of such a one is much more than a personal affair -the oommunity as a whole is the poorer.

Mrs. Wilkinson, or as she was better known "Griffy" - had this gift. To those of us she taught, it was not really apparent or appreciated during our school-days, but in the years to follow, this impression was corrected many, many times.

Personally, I shall always remember her first **visit** to my new married home, Griffy had retired and, on behalf of the University of London, was examining pupils for the ordinary and higher school leaving certificates. She had to visit our local Grammar School and wrote to ask if she could stay with us. I was petrified my headmistress coming to stay with us: Needless to say, she came and put not only myself at ease, but also my husband, who had tried to imagine his own Headmaster staying with us: We thoroughly enjoyed her short visit and she left leaving us much wiser people.

At Spring Grove Grammar School where, as Miss Griffin, she taught for over 20 years, she was French Mistress, and during the latter years - Senior Mistress. She was strict, and at times, unpopular with the pupils - but she could teach, and her influence has left its mark in the later life of her pupils. In the 1930's, one modern young miss dared to use make-up, she was immediately sent to wash it off;

When Griffy retired in 1948, she married and lived with her dearly loved husband near Swanage - but she never changed. We used to see her at the sea every year and always came away refreshed both in mind and s p i r i t . Children were her great joy, and even during her retirement she took a very keen interest and gave great help to her local youth organisations.

When in need of help or advice, one could always ask Griffy, she would have the answer. She had her own fixed ideas on most subjects, but could usually see the other's point of view.

> "A pleasure to meet, "An honour to know,
> "And so memorable to remember"

Miss B. D. Nash B.Sc. (Lond.)

At the closing assembly of the Christmas term 1947, the School had to say a regretful farewell to Miss Nash, who was leaving to take up an appointment at the City of London School. A term of over twenty years' service had naturally so identified her with Spring Grove that it seemed quite impossible to visualize the Banksian Room without her. In paying tribute to her in-valuable work over such a long period, the Headmaster, as in the case of Mr. Cross, confessed his inability to express in words how much the School was indebted to her, and how many hundreds of Spring Grovians had profited by her in-valuable help. With tireless energy, she had pursued her teaching in conditions of discomfort which those familiar with the glass-roofed Banksian Room under the tropical heat of summer suns or in the icy grip of winter blizzards could fully appreciate. Only a strong sense of duty and a hardy constitution could survive such trying conditions, but Miss Nash never complained ; on the contrary, all who were privileged to work with her and under her direction were conscious of an unfailing cheerfulness allied to thorough conscientiousness and high ability. Many old pupils now following notable careers owe her a great debt of gratitude, and their own achievements are a permanent testimonial to her tireless energy and effective teaching.

Mr. Bernard Joy B.Sc Econ (Lond.)

As an England International at Football and an Olympian in 1936, Bernard Joy was probably the best known of all the Spring Grove Staff . He joined the school in the early 1930s.

Born in Fulham, London in 1911, he studied at the University of London, playing in his spare time for the university football side at centre half. After graduating, he played for Casuals, where he eventually became club captain, leading them to victory in the 1936 FA Amateur Cup final. He also won ten caps for the England amateur team and was captain of the Great Britain football side at the 1936 Olympics in Berlin.

In May 1935 he joined Arsenal, then First Division champions. Joy mainly played as a reserve, only playing two games in his first season – he didn't make his debut for Arsenal until 1 April 1936 against Bolton Wanderers. Arsenal won the FA Cup that season but Joy played no part in the final.

However, he did gain recognition at international level soon after, when on 9 May 1936, he played for England in their 3-2 loss against Belgium, making him the last amateur to play for the national side; given the gulf in quality between the professional and amateur games in the modern day, it is exceedingly unlikely that Bernard Joy's record will ever be taken by another player. Although Joy was playing for Arsenal at the time, he was still registered as a Casuals player and he is recorded in the England history books as playing for them at the time, not Arsenal.

Joy continued to play for Arsenal, mainly deputising for the Gunners' established centre-half Herbie Roberts. Roberts suffered a broken leg in October 1937 and Joy took his place in the side for the remainder of the 1937-38 season, winning a First Division winners' medal, and then, with Roberts having retired from the game, on through the 1938-39 season (earning a 1938 Charity Shield winners' medal in the process).

With the advent of World War II, Joy was commissioned in the Royal Air Force where he was a PE Instructor, though he still turned out for Arsenal (playing over 200 wartime matches) and won an unofficial wartime England cap.

After the war he decided not to return to the teaching profession and moved into journalism; he was football correspondent for the Evening Standard and the Sunday Express until retirement in 1976. He also wrote one of the first histories of Arsenal Football Club, Forward, Arsenal! (1952), and other football books.

Hr retired in 1976 but still reported on matches for the Sunday Express.

He died in 1984, aged 72. His obituary in the Daily Telgraph concluded that the Press Box would miss the big, bluff, true soccer fan who provided the last link with game that, in his heyday, had been played and watched for pleasure.

A Tribute to Bernard Joy

Eric Beale 1935-40

Teachers are not always aware of the impressions they create on their pupils, or how they affect the pupil's future development. Bernard Joy was one of several excellent teachers on the Spring Grove staff, but he stood out because he was a man of many talents.

Everybody remembers him for his prowess on the football field. He had everything; height, strength, agility, wonderful co-ordination, endurance and above all he was a team player. But he wasn't only a footballer; he was also a pretty good cricketer and tennis player. And that wasn't all he was good at. He was an academic and his knowledge and interpretation of history was unrivalled.

Throughout my years at Spring Grove, he taught History and taught it well. Through him, I acquired a love of the subject which has stayed with me throughout my life, and enabled me to win the History prize and later to gain honours in Modern History at the University of Melbourne.

In his history lessons, I believe I hung on his every word. He made the subject enthralling and also taught us to look at events critically. I remember many of his sayings, and particularly this one: "All wars are stupid, but the Crimean War (1854-56) would be the most stupid of all." In the post-war years at the University of Melbourne, I made History one of my Majors, achieving Honours in Modern History. My essays on the English Civil War and 19th Century Europe, no doubt had their original inspiration from Bernard Joy's teaching.

He conveyed to me the important idea of never assuming the accepted version of events as being necessarily true. His knowledge of history was vast and he had the faculty of making historical events come alive. He was also a good disciplinarian though never a class room tyrant. In Form One, there was one boy who was a real trouble maker, to his classmates as well as his teachers. Bernard had him kneeling in a corner, crying his eyes out. There was no more trouble after that.

A pity really that he was never Sports Master. Once a week, he would stay after school to give the school teams some coaching, but because of his commitments to Arsenal, he was never able to attend our matches, which were played on Saturday morning. But he still took a keen interest in all of us aspiring young footballers. One Saturday, he took Ken Payne and myself up to Arsenal and gave us the best seats free to watch a top match. Even in those days, Arsenal were a dream team, studded with the top stars of the thirties.

It is most unusual that a man could be both an intellectual and achieve such high sporting honours.

To many of us, he was the great role model, and I heard of his passing in 1984 with much sadness.

221

Miss E. A. Taylor M.A. (Leeds)

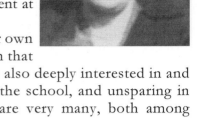

The school was fortunate in the devoted service given to it over a considerable number of years by many teachers, and never more so than in the case of Miss Taylor, who joined the Staff in 1931, became Head of the History Department in 1934, and was Senior Mistress from 1948 until her retirement at the end of the Summer Term, 1958.

Not only was she an enthusiastic teacher of her own particular subject, who succeeded in passing on that enthusiasm to many of her pupils, but she was also deeply interested in and concerned for the welfare of all members of the school, and unsparing in her efforts to promote that welfare. There are very many, both among present pupils and Old Spring Grovians, who will remember with gratitude her sympathetic interest in their problems, and her wise guidance.

Reported to have a "short fuse" her annoyance with pupils soon dissipated, and she always showed great interest in former pupils.

It is not only the pupils, past and present, who regard Miss Taylor with respect and affection. These feelings are shared by those who have been privileged to work with her: her efficiency as a teacher and organiser, her high personal character and ideals have won their esteem, and her warm friendliness, consideration and helpfulness have gained their affection, so that she has been to many not merely a valued colleague, but also a dear friend.

Her main interests were listed as Travel, Music, Literature, Theatre and Charitable Acts.

Miss M. E. Phillips Ling. Assoc. ,

Miss Phillips joined the Staff in 1930 after spending three years in Australia teaching at a college in Freemantle. She specialised in gymnastics in which she held high qualifications, but was also a form mistress and taught academic subjects.

Like her mother Miss Phillips was prominent in the Girl Guide movement, and was captain of the 1st Spring Grove Company just after the war.

She retired in 1966 having moved with the School to Lampton in 1958. After her retirement she was active in social work, particularly on behalf of the West Middlesex Hospital League of Friends and the Red Cross library service.

Her main recreation became bowls playing in the winter at the Hounslow and District Indoor Bowls Club and in the summer with Richmond Ladies Bowling Club which she captained in 1974.

Miss Phillips died in 1974.

In 1950 Spring Grove Grammar School lost the services, through retirement, of two masters whose names were famous not only in the School itself but also throughout the borough. In the case of each there was a record of more than forty years' teaching in Heston and Isleworth, and both incidentally were close friends during their boyhood days.

Mr. J. Owen Jones

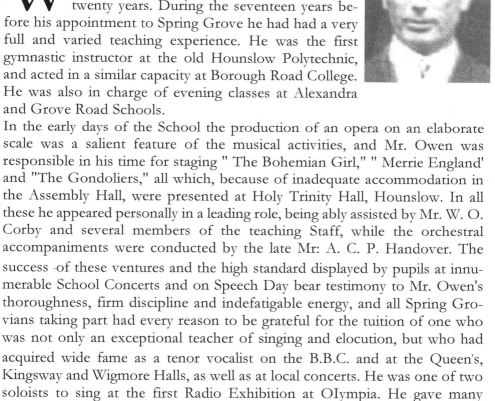

When he left Mr. Trevor Owen had held the post of music master at the School for over twenty years. During the seventeen years before his appointment to Spring Grove he had had a very full and varied teaching experience. He was the first gymnastic instructor at the old Hounslow Polytechnic, and acted in a similar capacity at Borough Road College. He was also in charge of evening classes at Alexandra and Grove Road Schools.

In the early days of the School the production of an opera on an elaborate scale was a salient feature of the musical activities, and Mr. Owen was responsible in his time for staging " The Bohemian Girl," " Merrie England' and "The Gondoliers," all which, because of inadequate accommodation in the Assembly Hall, were presented at Holy Trinity Hall, Hounslow. In all these he appeared personally in a leading role, being ably assisted by Mr. W. O. Corby and several members of the teaching Staff, while the orchestral accompaniments were conducted by the late Mr: A. C. P. Handover. The success of these ventures and the high standard displayed by pupils at innumerable School Concerts and on Speech Day bear testimony to Mr. Owen's thoroughness, firm discipline and indefatigable energy, and all Spring Grovians taking part had every reason to be grateful for the tuition of one who was not only an exceptional teacher of singing and elocution, but who had acquired wide fame as a tenor vocalist on the B.B.C. and at the Queen's, Kingsway and Wigmore Halls, as well as at local concerts. He was one of two soloists to sing at the first Radio Exhibition at OIympia. He gave many recitals of music and also of poetry, gaining personal successes in the latter in contests at Oxford University. At one period before the war, an interesting feature of the Summer term was a regular visit to the Taylor Institute, Oxford, of a party of selected pupils who, under his guidance, participated in competitive recitals of verse. Mr. Owen also gave distinguished performances in amateur operatic productions, notably in Gilbert and Sullivan staged by the Hounslow Operatic Society and later by the Donald Ford Light Opera Company. In recent years, in addition to his regular duties as Choirmaster at Bell Road Methodist Church, Hounslow, he formed the Trevor Owen Singers, who under his baton have achieved wide success. Amid all these activities he found time to serve on the Selection Committee of the Annual Borough Music and Drama Festival.

His breadth of activities was invaluable in his relations with pupils. He had considerable experience as a sportsman, having played cricket and football extensively with local clubs. He was also a member of Hounslow Swimming Club, in which he held the diving championship for some time. He had served in the Army as N.C.O. and officer during the 1914-1918 war. In the presentation ceremony for his retirement the Headmaster declared that Mr. Owen seemed to have learnt the secret of perpetual youth. It is certain that he brought an ardent enthusiasm and a vitalizing energy to everything he undertook, and it was obvious that this was by no means consumed when he came to the end of his long teaching service.

Mr. W.O.Corby

The School also bade farewell to Mr. W. O. Corby, and as in the case of Mr. Owen, will be much the poorer by his departure. In paying tribute to him, the Headmaster confessed his difficulty in recording everything that Mr. Corby had done, but from a wide range of activities he could recall the most outstanding. To manage the intricate finances associated with school dinners, the Parents' Association and the Christmas parties was a whole-time job in itself, while he would also refer to the careful preparation in expert penmanship of the countless certificates of merit awarded each year. As a teacher, Mr. Corby was held in very great affection by all those pupils fortunate enough to be in his classes. Perhaps his dominant quality was his "fatherliness" - a characteristic which many appreciated deeply, and one born of experience of family life and a thorough understanding of young people. Such an attitude on his part, however, never condoned laziness or slipshod work. Behind it was firm discipline. Everything he undertook was thorough and workmanlike, and efficiency and Mr. Corby were synonymous.

He was also keen on games, especially school football, and it can be recalled that he once even introduced Rugby football, in which he himself excelled, as an additional activity for those boys with sufficient aptitude and desire to form a Fifteen.

As in the case of Mr. Trevor Owen, his interests extended beyond the confines of School life, including work for his church, and the Vice-Chairmanship of the Local Youth Association. He was Secretary of the Hounslow Piscatorial Society.

In World War I he had also seen much service in France. His many activities, the Headmaster said, constituted true education, and should encourage the boys and girls of the school.

It was fitting, and a gracious gesture, that Mr. Owen should be on the rostrum at the farewell presentation to his colleague and friend.

Miss Ena Ransom B.A. (Lond)

It has been remarked before that SGGS was notable, among many other things, for the long service of some of its teachers. Miss Ena Ransom, who retired at the end of the Summer Term 1964, is one of the outstanding examples of this. She took up her appointment at the school in 1930 and was one of the few to serve under all its Headmasters.

Miss Ransom was a pupil at the Putney County Secondary School and continued her studies at King's College, London, gaining a B.A. Honours degree in French. During the course for her degree studies, she was awarded the Certificat Hautes Etudes Francaises, Toulouse, and subsequently obtained certificates of proficiency in other foreign languages awarded by English examining bodies.

After a few years' teaching experience, partly in London and partly in Austria, Miss Ransom joined the Staff of what was then Spring Grove Secondary School in September, 1930. She was appointed as a teacher of French, and has taught this subject throughout her career, but not exclusively. Her adaptability, wide interests and readiness to take other subjects was very helpful and much appreciated.

As a Form Teacher, Miss Ransom always established friendly relations with her pupils, who have been quick to appreciate her warmth of character and concern for their welfare, both in and out of school. She was enthusiastic and energetic in her approach to her work, always ready to organize visits for pupils both in this country and on the continent, to give freely of her time after school to any interested in a variety of activities, including the Stamp Club, which she ran for many years, and to give help wherever it was needed.

Miss Ransom's concern for others extended far beyond the school community. Her expressions of this concern are too numerous to detail, but at least two of them should be mentioned. For nearly two years in the late nineteen - forties she took up service with displaced persons in Austria, and latterly spent considerable time and energy on the collection of clothing and sending of parcels to missions in Africa. How much this activity was appreciated is evidenced by the grateful letters written by the recipients.

Both in and out of school, Miss Ransom's work was characterized by enthusiasm and energy and interest in the people with whom she came into contact. Her enthusiasm for the subjects she has taught and her unfailing interest in her pupils gained her innumerable friends. The friendly relationships established during school days lasted long after the pupils had left school.

Miss Ransom wrote about her early days at Spring Grove for the biography that Tony Evans, '36, wrote about his wife Betty, also '36, née Corby (daughter of the master Mr.W Corby).

"It was through Peter Corby that I found my Austrian refugees whom I brought out of Vienna the Easter before the war began and it's an event that I still don't understand, neither its origins nor how I was given the job to collect two people and finished up with eight or nine!!

We were a very International School at SGSS with connections both far reaching and detailed but how did it all begin? It certainly wasn't there when I joined the school in 1930 (what an age ago that seems!). It was a historic house, not a school, but it was a question of "We need a School: fees £5 a term to anyone (bright or retarded) whose parents can afford it. Where's a big enough building? O.K.let's have it".

"Under Mr. Wood we flourished. He was an individualist and catered for individuals not groups! One profited from the curiosity of the buildings and loved it! Games were incidental... THOUGHT AND REFLEXION were Mr. Wood's points; discipline was unnecessary as we were all in the topic of "Get Learning" and how you gave or accepted it was your business."

In 1948 Ena Ransom wrote an article for the Spring Grovian about
her relief work in Austria.

RELIEF WORK IN STRICKEN AUSTRIA
Ena Ransom

I'm going to write to tell you where I am and what I am doing. Can you imagine a large open field surrounded by mountains and pine trees? In this valley are put, in little groups, wooden huts in thirteen blocks, and in each hut are little rooms or parts divided off by cardboard where separate families live together, as families usually live, or they all share a hut like a dormitory. In each block are twelve huts, and never more than thirty people in one hut. We could have 5,000 people in Treffling Camp, but fortunately there are never that many.

Now who are all these people, and where do they come from? They consist of representatives from every nation on whose land war has been waged from 1939 to 1945. Some have been driven out by advancing troops, taken out by retreating armies, forced to leave by political groups, or have voluntarily left their homes, unwilling to live under men who profess a hated code. The White Russians and the Poles, the Silesian Germans, Latvians, Estonians and Lithuanians, and the Hungarians refuse to accept. Russian Communism; the same Germans will not go home to live `under the Poles; the South-Tyrolers don't know where they belong; some Roumanians and Bulgarians are not willing to return, and the Slav peoples, many of whom (e.g.., Chetniks) fought with the Allies during the war years, will not, under any consideration, return to help `Tito, and to work against their king Peter, now in exile in Switzerland.

So you see we are a very mixed "League of Nations," and usually get on very well together, as all are unwanted and homeless.

The Children go to school half the morning and half the afternoon. They learn lessons in German, and the 'Slavs and Hungarians have their own teachers for their languages. We are trying to run a secondary School, but we've no printed books, hardly any writing books, and few pencils. Do you realise that a pupil uses up a pencil in a month? He always writes with it, at school and at home, and. when it is worn down to half an inch in size, he can ask for a new one-if we have one! It's a marvellous excuse for leaving disliked homework—" Please I have no pencil! ".

All food is cooked in one of three huge kitchens. The hospital kitchen is for the sick, the nurses, the doctors and 150 very under-weight children (they vary monthly), the extra (zusatz) kitchen for those who work, and the children's kitchen for all those up to eighteen years of age. Any food that is sent to camp as extra gifts by the voluntary societies who are trying to help these un-fortunate people, is shared by the hospital and the children's kitchens, and used to bake extra white bread with cocoa and fruit in it for Christmas and Easter. There are five societies helping in Austria: the Quakers (F.R.S.), the Catholics (C.C.R.A.), the Jews (I.R.S.), the Save the Children Fund (S.C.F.) and the Salvation Army (S.A.).

Isn't it grand that so many different groups all realize how important it is to help anyone who needs it without thinking of race or creed? Of course it costs a lot of one, and that is why you'll always read appeals or hear someone (usually me) begging. These crowds have to be clothed, and what we get (worn clothing) doesn't last very long, so we need such a lot.

This summer we've used some khaki sacks (dull material, like army shorts) and made one garment for each person—dresses for women and girls, shorts for men and boys, and shirts as well for boys up to fourteen. They look very nice on, as the children are all so brown that the material matches beautifully.

In the summer no one wears shoes or socks because we're right in the country, and there are few stones to hurt. I wonder if I can explain where we are on the map? It takes exactly one hour in a 15 cwt. lorry to get to either Italy or Jugoslavia, it takes 36 hours to get from Hook of Holland to Villach with only three stops , where we get out to have a meal, Krefeld (Ruhr), Karlsruhe and Traunstein (near Salzburg). It's a very interesting journey, and a fine way to learn Geography, because one goes right through the "brown" mountains in Austria - the highest ones.

For breakfast they get coffee or tea (children have bread and butter too, when we get it). Dinner is soup, with meat and vegetables in it (if we've got any!) Supper consists of a kind of semolina pudding made of maize meal. It used to

227

be always possible to spread the bread with something, but in `the last six weeks it has been only dry bread, and not very appetizing, as it all has to be cut up the night before. I'm afraid things are going to be very bad this winter, as we've about 600 Germans in camp who want urgently to go home, but the permission to send them and the train in which they're to travel doesn't ever arrive. They don't seem to realise we'd love to get rid of them, and keep complaining that we're keeping them. Quite a number of things would strike you as odd, but I've got so used to them I don't notice it any longer : such a lot of people living in one hut with two stoves only, and a big pile of wood outside, inside or under the barracks, the same thing to eat every day; the cups and plates and saucepans all made out of old tins; the shoes made out of all sorts of bits of wood and material; the scarcity of combs (on an average one to about twenty people) ; the terrific heat in summer in a wooden hut, and the freezing cold and wind in winter, when gales sweep the valley, and the barracks are almost thrown over.

Worst of all the plight of the boys and girls of about 14, they have little chance to learn a trade, and the nearest Secondary School is twelve kilometres away. That means a walk of about three miles and then a bus, and that costs 11 Austrian schillings a day ! Very few can earn any money, and I put stamps on all the letters people bring to me to post. Unfortunately one can't change Austrian currency into English or Italian Lire, or one could buy things more easily.

I have about twenty intelligent boys here who would like to study, but by the time they leave here, it'll be too late for them to attend school again.

There is such a lot to tell you - but I must say thank you for all the packets you've collected so far for my camps - I hope you won't forget we'd be pleased to receive some more - even pins, needles, tiny bits of left-over stuff, or big blankets - just anything you can send will be gratefully received, especially for Christmas.

CHRISTMAS, 1947.

I had some lovely parcels from convents, my friends and schools, so we prepared to have an extra good Christmas. For a week in advance our kitchen staff baked all night, white bread with grated chocolate in it, and biscuits also with chocolate. All the children gave me a basket (or sack) with their name, age, and number of the hut. In each one we put a toy (or an article of clothing), 14 ozs. chocolate, a tangerine, (I'd been to Italy *just* to buy-these luxuries for them), 30 big sweets, 1-lb. of new chocolate bread and 1-lb. of biscuits. Father Christmas gave this out on December 24th. Then, in the night, at 11.30, everyone who could get into either Camp church or the village church, went. We were like sardines, and dozens of people stood in the cemetery, where a little light was burning on each grave. They couldn't even see the priest, but they knew it was " Heilige Nacht," and when the organ, violin, 'cello and choir rendered this carol, many homeless people remembered their homeland and families, and wept without shame. Everyone had a specially good dinner, provided through the work of the societies helping the D.P.'s, and then on the 26th we had a children's party. It was fun. I had six hundred children in a hall, and they'd never had a party before. We tried to teach them some games "Musical Rings", "Hunt the Thimble" (not a thimble, but 200 blue slips!), "Thief" and many others. We gave prizes, and then tea and cakes (cocoa and biscuits). The grown-ups had a dance in the evening. The school teachers had written a play and set it to music. It was acted by the children, and had to be repeated three times, as people couldn't all get into the theatre. We had a fine Christmas, and thank you all who helped us.

Then came the usual work again. It sounds as if everything is well with us, but think about some of these things. We have not one pair of shoes or boots, no nails and no leather to mend those which are worn out. I've given out fifty pairs of trousers among three hundred men some trousers are made of about fifteen to twenty-five pieces, that's all I've got.. We've no gloves and some men have to spend all day in the woods cutting down trees or chopping up wood. It's not very cold here yet; there's hardly any snow, but the ground is like iron in the morning and a sea of mud at midday, yet quite a hundred and thirty children have no shoes and no caps.

It's a queer life, because I never could have thought it would be so easy to get used to it. Some people have their families and children only about two hours' journey away, and yet cannot see them, or even get a letter from them. Their sisters and friends disappear, die or get married, and some have had no news of their husbands for five years, and even the Red Cross cannot find them. Children grow up never seeing a carpet on the floor, a cushion, curtain or tablecloth, not knowing what their father looks like, or what a town, road or a shop is.

They can't buy anything and see no use in learning about money, because it does not mean anything practical. The only things that matter to them are wood (for warmth) and food ! ! Can you imagine this?

Can you think of any boy of five who'd rather have a cap than a toy or football, or who can't use a knife to eat with at the age of nine? We have only spoons here--and if we get meat, we eat it as Henry VIII did, with fingers and teeth. The very worst of all is the problem of what is going to happen to all these people. Where will they be sent to next? Will they ever live in a real house again, and drink from a cup, or eat meat from a real plate with proper cutlery? Will they ever meet their friends and relations who are now lost somewhere in Europe or another time come soon when a letter will arrive from the East, from home? This is the worry of all adults and the older school children and explains the utter hopelessness in the faces of almost all.

You may meet or see pictures of some who've come to build a new life. These are the lucky ones. But many a mother sits in camp with six or seven children, a lost husband is "somewhere in Russia," and for her there's nothing.

That is why we do all we can to help them all with temporal gifts like food and clothing, so that they will realise that they do count, and that some people care what happens to them.

So again I thank you for your help, for the lovely parcels of clothes, pins, needles and toys that have been arriving and, hope you'll continue to help us, till the time comes when we can say our task is finished an all these people find a new home and begin again to believe that life is worth living.

ENA RANSOM,
Treffling Camp,
'0' Assembly Centre,
C i v i l Affairs (RE), Karten, Austria   December 1947

And finally John Young '53 has the last word on a remarkable lady....

Lunch with Dolly Ransom

There she was. Diminutive as ever (what did I expect?) and just as lively. My thanks to Keith Lomas for putting us in touch.

Dolly Ransom taught me parsing, and clause analysis. Thanks to her, I still know the difference between an adverb and an adjective. She also sacrificed a precious Saturday and took the whole class on a museum trawl in London. Culture for the masses.

Now, all those years later (in the 1990s), I had her to myself. Miss Ransom had an extraordinary tale to tell ... Over lunch in York I learned that she had retired from teaching at 60. Instead of tending her garden, she went to Africa. To be precise, she went to Ruanda. It seems that she was a devout Roman Catholic (I had no idea of this when she taught us). She linked up with a monastery and taught and cared for young people.

She knew several of those caught up in the terrible massacre and - now back home in UK – was doing all she could to organise help. We met only once. But it was very memorable.

I felt I was in the presence of someone with unusual charisma and (forgive the religious language) perhaps unusual holiness too.

Mrs. W. K. Hemming B.A. (Lond.)

The end of almost every school year saw the departure of some members of the staff, some to advancement within the profession, some to marriage and some to retirement. But for Mrs. Hemming it was difficult to think of her in any of those ways, for she had for some years been a distinguished successor to the former Deputy Head of the School; she had, for longer, been happily married to a man with whom she shared a common interest in education; and if it was meant by retirement knitting in front of the television, we have only to remember her skill at badminton and table-tennis to realise how ridiculous the thought could be.

Mrs. Hemming joined the school before the war as Miss Klarner and subsequently married another teacher at the School, James Hemming. There was in her room a photograph taken in 1934 of her surrounded by her form of Robins, Seagulls, Skylarks and Swallows (for so the Houses were called), the girls dressed in navy serge tunics and black woollen stockings.

When she retired the picture had changed, and so had Mrs. Hemming. She had grown older, of course, but what had not changed was her relationship with her pupils and theirs with her. In her farewell speech Mrs. Hemming reminded the School that it never grows old for the generations of school-children continually renewed themselves. It was Mrs. Hemming's great gift that she, too, had been able to change with the times, to understand new points of view and to sympathise with the problems of young people often bewildered by a rapidly changing society. From the girls of the School Mrs. Hemming expected, and obtained, a high standard of behaviour (adolescent girls being far more difficult to manage than are boys of the same age); but she was always ready to listen to reasonable explanations and her wise humanity helped to solve many tearful problems.

Especially, she always managed a happy compromise on the difficult question of school uniform. This may not always have been appreciated by some members of the lower school who, in the matter of fashion, had sometimes felt that nothing exceeds like excess. Sixth form girls, however, appreciated that within a reasonable conformity each was allowed to realise herself as an individual. And it was Mrs. Hemming's vigorous assertion of the fact that people are individuals that accounted for so much of her success.

Her loyalty to the School was unlimited. That after her resignation she should return each Monday afternoon for the benefit of the Upper VI members of the English Department was only what the school had learnt to expect of her , but few pupils can hope to know how much time and energy she spent on their behalf. Taking leave of her, the school wished her well, knowing that in the future her vitality would be expended in ever new and exciting interests, the most immediate of which was a journey round the world.

Perhaps it was no accident that she achieved this - like Phineas Fogg - in eighty days.

Miss E. M. Richards B.Sc. (Wales)

The school had long and devoted service given to it by many members of its Staff. An outstanding example of such service was in the case of Miss Richards, who joined the Staff of Spring Grove Grammar School in 1928, five years after the opening of the school. It is interesting to note that Miss Richards's number in the record of Staff appointments was 40, and that the last member of Staff to be appointed has the number 140. Miss Richards has thus seen many Staff come and go, and, of course, far more pupils pass through the school, in the course of her teaching career.

There are, indeed, thousands of pupils who have had the benefit of her skilful teaching. to which her great patience and deep sincerity and understanding have contributed so much, while over a hundred members of Staff have had the pleasure of working with her as a colleague.

Miss Richards was never one to seek the limelight: unassuming and quiet efficiency and thoroughness had been the outstanding characteristics of her work, and the keynotes of her wise direction of the Geography Department, and her valuable help in the teaching of Mathematics.

Her work as House Mistress has also made a considerable contribution to the life of the school, and many old pupils will remember with appreciation the care and thought which she devoted to the taking of the Junior Assembly in the old building.

But efficiency and care by themselves, while they command respect and admiration, do not necessarily evoke affection, and Miss Richards was most certainly held in both high regard and affection by Staff and pupils alike. For this, her kindly personality and readiness to help wherever help was needed were largely responsible. These qualities endeared her to the school, and when she retired from Spring Grove Grammar School, she carried with her, together with sincere gratitude for her long and valuable service to the school, the warmest of good wishes, and the assurance of a hearty welcome whenever she was able to visit the school.

Miss D. I. Clothier B.Sc. (Lond.)

Miss D. I. Clothier, who retired at the end of 1964, was an outstanding member of the Mathematics Staff of the school for nearly twenty years. Her pupils will long remember with gratitude not only the thoroughness of her teaching but also the very considerable insight and sympathetic understanding which she showed for their difficulties. To achieve such a combination, while always demanding utmost effort from her classes, has been characteristic of her very effective and successful teaching. Many candidates have reason to thank her for spurring them on to the efforts necessary for examination success. Miss Clothier has certainly understood how to get the best from her pupils, and has always been deeply concerned to act in their best interests.

Miss Clothier's concern for her pupils has by no means been confined to the classroom. It has been shown also in her work as a House Mistress and in her readiness to help with and take part in a variety of school activities. In addition, she has given generously of her time to organise and show programmes of films which she herself has made, some dealing with events at our own school, and some taking us much further afield. These delightful and interesting films have given pleasure as well as instruction to the pupils invited to see them, and have benefited various charities through the collections taken at the performances.

Miss Clothier's untiring efforts over many years for the welfare of the school have been greatly appreciated by colleagues and pupils alike. Her strength of character, integrity of purpose, devotion to duty and lively personality have won both respect and affection.

Return to Spring Grove

Hugh Leitch (1912 - 2007)

It was reading the earlier copies of the Spring Grovian report with so much interest and pleasure that finally persuaded me to make the necessary effort to attend the 2004 May reunion. My dear wife was rather anxious particularly about the journey involved. Before I left the flat she wondered whether, in view of my age and, as she said, my forgetfulness, she should put a label on me with my name, address, telephone number and next of kin! I treated her fears with the contempt that I thought they deserved and made my way confidently to Cromer station. The journey to Liverpool Street and Osterley was taken in my stride and was uneventful although I was rather later than I had hoped. Of course I well knew the way to school - I had done that walk hundreds of times. I forgot however that it was close on fifty years since the last time. I got lost somewhere south of the Great West Road and had to stop and look round to try to find where I had got to. Then a feminine voice rang out "Are you O.K? Can I help you?" Thank heaven my wife could not see me.   I told the kind stranger of my plight and, good Samaritan that she was, she took me in her car to the Harvard Road entrance. I thanked her for her kindness but still could not see the old school until I was shown the main entrance.   Spring Grove House seemed to be hedged in by ghastly new buildings. What vandalism!! Later that afternoon I was to see much more when I went out into what used to be the lovely grounds.   Where were the great cedars?   What had happened to the Banksian Room? It was all so depressing.

On entering the school I paused outside Mr. Brown's old room. There was only one person to be seen. Fortunately it was Vivien (Syrett) who may well have wondered who the old boy was and what he wanted.   I introduced myself and she very kindly ushered me into the throng in the Art Room and announced my arrival. I received a very warm welcome and, fortified by lunch and the odd glass of wine, the time passed all too quickly. It was such a pleasure to meet so many 'old' friends. I found that I could remember names but, of course, appearances had changed after fifty years. I joined Spring Grove Grammar School in 1951 as assistant History Master.

Why ? Was it just a job that came up at an appropriate time? Did you know of the school/ headmaster? Were you interviewed at the school?

Miss Emily Taylor was then Head of Department and also Senior Mistress. I remember her with great affection and respect – always kind and helpful, particularly to the 'new boy' in his first term in a new environment. Before that I had only taught in a Junior school in Greenford.

It took a little while to learn the geography of the old building. My staff room was on the top floor, a room that I imagine was part of the servants' quarters in the nineteenth century. I shared that room with Mr. Howell and Mr. Hart and we were later joined by Mr Bullough and Mr Ridley. There was no central heating of course but, in the old room, with a comfortable settee and a blazing fire in winter, any free periods could be pleasantly spent – marking of course!! I always felt rather sorry for poor Mr May, the caretaker, who had the job of regularly making up the fires in so many rooms. In the form rooms the staff were very well looked after. The teacher's desk was always the one nearest the fire.

There are so many memories. I well recall my very first day. I had to lead 5W down the wonderful staircase – in silence of course – and into the hall. While we all waited for Mr Brown, Mr. Hart and the choir began the short service with an introit. 'L.T.' announced the hymn, which was followed by two short prayers. He then gave a brief talk on one of the great religious reformers of the sixteenth century. There was a pause and he turned to a more mundane and serious matter. On his way to school he had had the misfortune to witness what he called "unseemly behaviour" on the part of a group of boys. This was to be deplored and all were reminded of the importance of good manners, courtesy and consideration for others. Mr Brown was a fine, scholarly Headmaster and his assemblies were always conducted in a very dignified and reverent manner.

The 'O' and 'A' level exams were soon to begin and I was asked to assist Mr. Callow and Miss Richards with the invigilation. This was a position I came to hold for the next twenty-five years. Mr. Callow was a pleasure to work with, nothing seemed to worry him, all small mistakes and minor difficulties could easily be put right. It was he who, at the end of the summer term when all the exams had finished, used to organise the school outings. I will always remember the one to Portsmouth and the trip around the Solent. It had been a most enjoyable day for me but only about ten minutes before the return train was due to leave I realised that one of my flock was missing. I was standing on the platform looking anxiously for the dear boy when Mr. Callow came up to me. I told him the problem and will never forget his nonchalant reply.

"Get on board Mr. Leitch - don't worry, he'll turn up somewhere."

I only hoped it would be at Isleworth! Mr. Callow was right – the wretch in question had joined his girl friend in another carriage.

I cannot remember when I first heard that at some time in the future the school would leave Spring Grove House and move into a new building with all modern facilities. Many of the staff looked forward to the change but for myself and a few others it would not be altogether welcome. With all its shortcomings we had become rather attached to the old house. The actual day when the school's association with Spring Grove House was to end came about in July 1959. As far as I can remember there was the customary end of term assembly and, shortly after that, school ended and everyone went home. However I do clearly remember that for four or possibly five male members of staff stayed behind, very disappointed that nothing had been said or done to mark the real importance and significance of the day. They were determined to make good this glaring omission and made their way to the History stock room to give the matter further serious thought. I'm lead to believe that the 'serious thought' was greatly facilitated by the quite accidental discovery of a bottle of Green Chartreuse hidden behind some volumes on Seventeenth Century European History. How that could have come about I do not know. It was then agreed by all that a glass should be raised to Sir Joseph Banks, the founder of the original Spring Grove House. It is, I think, quite possible that further glasses were raised and toasts proposed. Just before we were finally about to leave, one of the group said that as a last solemn act of remembrance, the school bell should be tolled. Apparently, but I can't vouch for it, that involved climbing out through the stock room window! The Bell was tolled – and heard, unfortunately, by Mr Voice the caretaker. He rushed upstairs to find out what was happening. I gather he was not pleased but all ended amicably and the four or five miscreants left the premises in good order – and spirits. I regret I cannot reveal names................

................**Happy Days.**

Hugh Leitch attended both the "whole school" and '60s reunions at Spring Grove House in 2004 and 2005, his 90th year. He died in 2007.

"Staff" at the '60s reunion 2005
Ken Pearce : Elizabeth Douglas :Hugh Leitch : Lawson Cockroft :
Tom Reynolds:

OLD SPRING GROVIANS' ASSOCIATION

10

Old Spring Grovians Association

Jean Langton ('38)

Jean's memories of the early OSGA & taking over as secretary in 1938.

The OSG Association was formed many years before 1938 – it began as a football club and during the pre-war years of the '30s the annual dinner was inaugurated. I was co-opted from the 6th form with Peter Rogers as Head Boy and Head Girl, to the committee of the OSGA, when Mrs Tomkins (née Nancy Sterry) and Mr. Terence Desborough were secretary and treasurer. I took over as secretary shortly after leaving school in 1938. War then came in 1939 and we were determined to keep the association alive.

We held a tea dance once a month in the School Hall throughout the winters. We couldn't hold evening dances because of the blackout – school curtains were not dense enough – but as the days lengthened we we held supper dances. We were only allowed ½lb of margarine for the sandwiches, cakes were in very short supply and milk and tea were rationed so we had to do all the catering and all the washing up too!!

The committee was ever changing; it was very difficult to keep up the continuity of office and to keep the threads of the Association together. They did a wonderful job during 6 years of wartime restrictions and we had invaluable help from Mr. Barrett and Mr. F Brown in keeping our books straight and giving us tremendous support in whatever we did.

We had a section in the school magazine as paper was also rationed, we were grateful to Mr. Lineham and Mrs. Hemming for this valuable opportunity to spread the OSGA news.

Every OSG in the forces overseas and with whom we could keep in touch, received each issue free (otherwise 1/- [5p]). We used to post towards 100 - I can't remember if it was monthly or not. We also used to write dozens of newsy letters abroad and the replies would be printed in the magazine. I felt this was a vital link between the Association and the OSGs in the forces – they would feel there was a welcome at the dances whenever they came home on leave. We had hockey, football and rambling clubs and tennis on the West Court (Polythechnic requirements permitting!) and everyone was welcome to come along and join in. When I retired as secretary in 1946 the Association flourished – with a bank balance, good membership and well supported hockey, football and rambling clubs. Sadly some members did not return and some were reported "missing". This was all especially poignant when we had been at school together, in the the same form and in the same form room. Everyone was special in those days.

The OSGA subsequently produced a magazine called The Echo. I was out of touch for some ten years due to marriage and the arrivals of the family – until I was invited to propose the toast to the Association at the Annual Dinner in March 1960 at the Red Lion. I had the privilege of being an Hon. Life Member of the Association, but this has long melted away into antiquity!

I am so delighted that the Association is back – my present involvement all stems from a chance remark by a classmate of mine. Sadly at a recent reunion there were only 2 or 3 of my year there, but of course we are all now in our twilight years!.

Since that meeting, I have had long conversations and the years have rolled away and I am delighted to be found again.

Stan Sach('46) was staying with friends when an old Middlesex Chronicle cutting was brought out which Stan thought might jog a few memories And he added a few of his own.

Fred Barnard Cup

Stan Sach '46

Thomas Heads the Winner for Old Spring Grovians

Beating Isleworth C.A. by the odd goal in three in Saturday's final. Old Spring Grovians became the latest holders of the Fred Barnard Memorial Cup.

Both teams were obviously handicapped by the bone-hard ground, and scrappy play was the general order of things. The Isleworth centre-forward took a chance to give his side the lead but the early reverse stirred the Old Boys into action. Steady pressure brought them their equaliser, Eldridge netting in a goalmouth scramble just before half-time.

After the change of ends Spring Grove kept the play well in their opponents' half and following a run by Eldridge to the corner flag, Thomas was on the spot to head a square centre into the net.

It was a well-deserved goal for Ken Thomas, undoubtedly the hardest worker on the winning side. Shots by Stan Sach and George Wilkinson scraped the bar. Old Spring Grovians can well feel proud of this first-year achievement in the competition sponsored by Hounslow and District League.

The above team included three "Guest" players, Ken Thomas (Right wing), Norman Dixon (Goal) and George Wilkinson. Other team members included, Eric Sach (Left Back), Geoff. Hughes (Right back), Stan Sach (Left half), Vic Eldridge (Inside left ?), Arthur Murray (Centre forward), Billy Hills, and Ken Keys, which leaves just one unaccounted for.

The game was played on Hounslow Town F.C.'s ground in Denbigh Road and our team secretary was Lionel Harbour, who after reading law and setting up practice as a solicitor conducted the conveyancing for my first house purchase.

Calling All OSGs

This was the article that Jean Langton put into the May 1944 Spring Grovian and gives a flovour of the OSG activities during the war.

Soon we shall see the end of the fifth year of war and the Old Spring Grovians' Association still existing, though not nearly so active as we should like it to be. However, present-day circumstances do not permit it to he otherwise, unfortunately, and many Of our would-he members are overseas. Do you ever think back on the days of 1940-41 when the Association, determined to beat the Luftwaffe, held tea dances from 3.30-6.30 p.m.? This helped a little to compensate for the lack of other entertainment, but there certainly was not the "excitement" about coming home at 6.30 as creeping in, well alter mid-night, removing one's shoes and carefully avoiding squeaky stairs, and then the next day hearing, " It took *you a* long time to come home last night "!!! So, when air raids were on the wane we resumed evening dances, though this year has been the most difficult. Owing to fog and the February "blitz", we had two cancellations and two other dances were failures. However, we now have Billy James and his Ballroom Orchestra, who will play for us until the end of July, and with a change of band (one member plays for Billy Cotton and Victor Silvester), we're hoping for a return of those enjoyable and friendly dances of a year ago ! So come along, bring your friends and have a good time.

Perhaps some O.S.G.s. have not realised that on the Sundays of the week-end after the dance (i.e., the fourth Sunday of the month) we nearly always go hiking or biking. We imagine this because we have so little support. Several members of the Committee take on the arranging of these days spent seeing the countryside, and it gives them little encouragement when only half a dozen people turn up. However, they are not dismayed, and will still carry on, and it is those who do not come who miss some grand fun - so now how about joining the party? If you'd like particulars of time and rendezvous, pay your sub. and be-come a member (2/- per annum). By the way, don't forget, this years membership card 1943-44 is invalid after July, so secure your new one 1944-45 in time for the September dance, entitling you to a 116 dance ticket instead of 2/-, and notification of all activities.

The record of O.S.G.s. in the Forces is very interesting and we have more than 250 boys and girls in the Services all over the world. Flt.Lt. Geoff. Pittman, walking along a dusty road in Rhodesia, thought he recognised the face of the boy walking towards him - he did; it was Geoff. Neil, a form-mate of long ago. They had a chat and passed on their separate ways! There must be many more encounters such as this; let's hear about them.

It may seem trivial, but it's interesting news for others, and if you want to get into touch with any Old Spring Grovians and don't know their address, let us know and we'll do what we can! Also, if you know of an O.S.G. abroad who would like the Magazine sent to him, send the address to us and it will be sent free

We now have the second generation at School. Ken Rothery and Phyllis Gooch were both O.S.G.s., and their little daughter, aged 11, has begun her school career at Spring Grove and is now in her first year.

We are very proud to claim as an O.S.G., Flt.Lt. Jack Kell, who last autumn was awarded the D.F.C. He was at Dunkirk and has taken part in raids on Stuttgart, Pilsen and Stettin, so we send him hearty congratulations from the Association.

"A Births and Marriages" column is included in this issue of the Magazine (and will be in future ones, too!), as we thought it would delight most O.S.G.s. to see who were the latest to enter bravely into the State of Matrimony and those who also had become parents of future, O.S.G.s.! The next edition of a "Scandal Column" is in course of production, so if you have any " tit-bits", send them along.

Once again we appeal for contributions for the O.S.G. section of this Magazine. It is very generous of the School Magazine Committee to allot us a portion for our very own, and we do thank them very much indeed, so now we want more and more news of the travels of Old Spring Grovians. We are happy to reproduce in these pages extracts from Eric Spong's letters from his prison camp in Germany to his home in Hounslow, and hope they will interest some of you.

May I, on behalf of the Old Spring Grovians' Association, wish all our boys and girls in the Services a speedy return and a safe journey home, and, until we all meet again, good luck to you all

JEAN M. LANGTON. Hon. Secretary.

OSGA 1945-60

Bud Cutting '44

Long, long ago there was an Old Spring Grovians' Association, an outfit with all the paraphernalia of a formal club, a Constitution, a Chairman, a Committee and even some features that don't begin with a capital C. Amongst the 600 or so members of our present, very informal, group of Spring Grovians, there may be a few at the maturer end of the age range, who remember the very early days of the OSGA. At the junior end there must be many in the full flush of middle age who were around as the Association withered away. But for me, the heyday of the OSGA was the period from the late forties to 1960 or thereabouts.

In the years following WW2 people who had been in the Forces were drifting back into civilian life, and many OSGs sought out old friends from Spring Grove, bringing about a rebirth of interest in the Association. At that time John Blandford was our enthusiastic and energetic chairman, Valerie Vidler was secretary and Jack Senior was treasurer. In 1950, Jack decided to move on, and Bill Osterburg, who was also a committee member at the time, was despatched

David Hunter '49 ; Hugh Rhys '48; Bud Cutting '44; Pam Neal '53;

Dennis Robertson '48:

Jean Raffe'48; Betty Phillips; Di Clothier:

to persuade me to fill the vacancy.   I think it was Gordon Collins who launched the newsletter,"The Echo", soon to be edited by 'Ginger' Johnnie White and Brian Woodruff.   Some years later, Hugh Rhys and David Hunter took over the editorship and gave the paper their own distinctive flavour.   I remember getting a letter from an indignant member who had decided to become an ex-member because, she claimed, many of the (very amusing) anecdotes in the Echo centred around local pubs and minor misdemeanours.   It lowered the tone, she said. The swinging sixties were a mere dot on the horizon.

A highlight of the OSGA year was the Christmas Eve Dance in the school hall. Men's cloaks were left in the physics lab and ladies' cloaks in Room 5, an illuminated cut glass globe hung from the ceiling reflecting light onto the dancers and music was provided by the Blue Ramblers band (or maybe not; I await a deluge of letters saying I'm wrong).   When the revelry ended, we adjourned to the Milford Arms.

Another regular feature of the year was the Annual Dinner, often held at the Red Lion in Hounslow.   The speech on behalf of the school was usually delivered by LTB himself and on one occasion he chose to review the various venues where the event had recently taken place.   He said, and I quote, "I was surprised one year to find myself at the Lion and Lamb" - a gentle hint to the committee that this was a step too far down-market!

Roads were still empty by today's standards but enough people in the fifties had cars to make treasure hunts a practical proposition.   Cryptic clues were devised by Johnnie W and Brian and those who had not got lost en route ended up at the Whites' house in Binfield to exchange stories of triumph and disaster.   During one hunt, Avril (the present Mrs Cutting – Ed.), as Hugh's navigator and clue solver, acquired a very large lump on her head, the result of an emergency stop. Could explain a lot......

One of John Blandford's bright ideas was the square dance team.   Eight of us were dragooned into appearing at various 'dos' to demonstrate how to do the Texas Star, for example. If a recent attempt to resurrect the idea is anything to go by, it must have been a hoot. It's a shame there were no video cameras in the fifties.

Then there were special groups that existed more or less independently of the OSGA, a serious football team(see Stan Sach's article SGR 5), badminton for beginners (OK, some players were pretty good!) and a Dramatic Society (see Margaret Sears' article in SGR4).

It was a near certainty that whenever the committee arranged an outside event, a river trip, a coach trip to Edenbridge on November the fifth or whatever, the weather would wreak havoc.   One of these events was a fete in the school grounds which took weeks to organise.   Right on cue, the heavens opened and wrecked the whole thing.   A fete worse than death! And with that dreadful pun, I must do the decent thing and stop writing.

Great Drama by Old Spring Grovians!

Cast of Blithe Spirit

Don Graham; Dave Owen; Brian Woodruff
Marjorie Reading; Eileen Forrest; Anne Lusher; Peggy ??; Brenda ??; Rita ??

Eileen Forest '47

It is very interesting to read people's memories in The Spring Grovian, but so far there has not been much mention of the O.S.G. Dramatic Society. We had had our appetite for drama whetted at School under Miss Johnson so when we left school a group of us got together and were joined by a number of other O.S.G'S who had just been demobbed after the war and we started a Dramatic Society. We bought part of a Barrage Balloon and used it to cover flats for scenery.

We were fortunate in being able to hold our rehearsals and performances at the school and we had the use of the former Summer House to store furniture and scenery. We used to gather there on Sunday mornings to make and paint scenery. We gave two performances a year, mainly of stock comedies such as Quiet Weekend and Quiet Wedding but also some of Priestley's "Time" plays such as "An Inspector calls." Personally the play I enjoyed most was "Blithe Spirit" because I was fortunate in having the plum, part of Madame Arcati. This photo shows the cast waiting to be made up . Have you any other memories of the O.S.G.Dramatic Society? If so, do share them with us.

Old Spring Grovians F.C. 1950's and 60's

David Helsdon '57.

Eileen Forrest's article in an earlier issue on the OSG Dramatic Society has finally prompted me to remind readers that the OSG had a well established and successful soccer club which played initially in the Hounslow and District League and latterly in the South West Middlesex League during the 50's and 60's.

The Club hit a particular high in the early 60's and the picture shows the first team in April 1964 having won the Hounslow League and Cup double for the first time in its history.

Standing left to right:- David Helsdon (Secretary), Peter Stubbs, Ted Watson, Owen Edmund, Eric Crook, Tony Strugnell and Bob Armstrong
Seated left to right:-
Keith Burnett, Hugh Mortimer, Ted Reid (Captain), Brian Green and Billy Gill

I am pleased to see that a number of these stalwarts are on our OSG contact list and have attended some of our reunions.

SPRING GROVE HOUSE

The research for this chapter was carried out by John Bloomfield, '54, from the Hounslow Library local history archives and WTC. They were published on his original SGGS website and are reproduced from the current www.springgrovegrammarschool.org.uk website.

11

Historical Dates and Events

John Offley was born in 1586, and was the oldest surviving son and heir of Henry Offley of Madeley (1536 -1613) by Mary, daughter of Sir John White, Lord Mayor of London. He was knighted at Theo balds on 25 April 1615 Sheriff 1616 - 1617. JP and DL. Struck off the Commission in 1632.

1635 - Sir John Offley owned a large house in Isleworth, shown on Moses Glover map. "Moat House"?

1645 - Sir John Offley built first house on the Spring Grove site

1754 - House sold to Elisha Biscoe, who demolished it and built Spring Grove House on the site

1776 - Death of Elisha Biscoe

1779 - House leased to Sir Joseph Banks for 21 years at an annual rent of £200 clear of taxes

1784 - Mail coach first appeared along road to London. Bristol to London in 12 hours. Average 9 mph

1808 - House purchased by Sir Joseph Banks for £6,000. Engraving shows lake in front of the house

1820 - Sir Joseph Banks dies, and is buried in St. Leonard's Church, Heston

1829 - Lady Banks dies. The property is bequeathed to nephew, Sir Edward Knatchbull

1830 - House purchased by Mrs Anne Fish, who lived there with cousin Henry Pownall and family

1834 - Mrs Fish dies, and Henry Pownall inherits the property

1838 - Andrew Pears snr., retires from the soap business

1850 - Estate sold by auction to property developer, Mr H D Davies

1862 - Pears factory moves to Isleworth

1886 - Spring Grove House sold to Andrew Pears. Estate extends to 20 acres

1892-94 - Andrew Pears rebuilt the house, adding a story, the music room, winter garden and conservatory; this cost £120,000.

1900 - Andrew Pears moved out of the house, to live in "Mevagissey House" on the London Road

1902 - House put up for auction but failed to achieve its reserve price

1903 - House proposed as new town hall but proposal narrowly defeated

1903 - House sold to Mrs Hossack, of Piccadilly

1905 - House auctioned and bought by Edgar Miller, Ph.D., of "Health House"

1906 - Eastern side of the estate (except drive and lodge) resold for development

1910 - House used as a private convalescent home and lunatic assylum.

1914 - House became a military hospital for the duration of the Great War

1922 - Estate bought by Middlesex County Council and house opened as Spring Grove Polytechnic

1923 - Spring Grove Secondary School established

1946 -   School renamed Spring Grove Grammar School

1959 -   School moves to new premises in Lampton; Spring Grove House becomes Isleworth Polytechnic

1967 -   Rebuilding of Isleworth Polytechnic is commenced, involving demolition of NW section of house. Two story, grey conctrete teaching blocks are built to within meters of the House's south and west walls the plan being to demolish the House as work progresses.

1969 -   SGGS, Lampton, becomes Lampton School when the London Borough of Hounslow establishes comprehensive education.

1972 -   Spring Grove House still standing: reprieved from demolition until Phase III, "date not yet fixed"

1976 -   Isleworth Polytechnic renamed "Hounslow Borough College"

1993 -   College renamed "West Thames College"

1996 -   Two-year refurbishment and restoration of house by the current owners is completed

2001 -   House still standing, and in full use as college administration centre First OSG reunion held.

2007 -   West Thames College Refurbishment begins.

Above;   19th Nov 2008; The new West Thames College Main Block starts to grow; the old South pitch cedar is to the right of the house;

Below;   May 2010; Demolition of the blocks, west of SGH, to the delight of the many OSGs who had been apalled by them when they returned to SGH for the OSG reunions.

The Story of Spring Grove House

Published in the Middlesex Chronicle on 3rd April 1959

At a time when a new Spring Grove Grammar School on the Great West Road at Lampton is nearing completion it is appropriate to publish this article on the history of the old building, prepared under the auspices of the Heston & Isleworth Schools Local History Society. The research was done and the article was written in 1957 by Mavis Bennett, then in the Lower VIth at Spring Grove Grammar School, assisted by Peter Morris and David Taylor of the Lower VIth.

The present building containing Spring Grove Grammar School was built in 1886 by a Mr Andrew Pears, the great grandson of the originator of the famous soap-manufacturing firm, whose firm is still situated in Isleworth, not far from the school. This building is, however, not the first to stand on this site, but in fact the third to do so. The earliest reference to the name Spring Grove is to be found in the mention of a house, belonging to a certain Sir John Offley, who lived from 1586 - 1647 and was Member of Parliament for Stafford from 1625 - 1626. This pleasant estate of trees and natural springs, inhabited by the Offley family for approximately a hundred years, is reputed to have stood upon Smallberry Green, which was then a common of around 41 acres.

Elisha Biscoe Esquire

In 1754 this property was bought by Elisha Biscoe Esquire, who also had a house and property at Norwood, to which part of the county his family belonged. Elisha Biscoe followed a very similar career to his father, Joseph Biscoe, who before his death in 1750 had been Deputy Chirographer to the Court of Common Pleas (this office was finally abolished in 1833). Elisha Biscoe's father and his wife, Elizabeth, were both buried at Norwood Church, Mrs Biscoe dying 19 years after her husband. Elisha Biscoe pulled down the then existing Spring Grove House and built another; and since the London Road, or the Great Western Road, as it was called, had become a turnpike, heavy traffic was beginning to use it, he erected a brick wall upon the south side to protect the estate.

Most of the owners of Spring Grove House have shown an interest in local public affairs and Elisha Biscoe was no exception; it is recorded that he built and endowed a school at Norwood for the education of thirty-four boys and six girls, residing in the parishes of Heston and Hayes and in the chapelry of Norwood. When he died in 1776 he also endowed a pension of £10 per annum on the retired schoolmaster and his wife, to be paid in quarterly payments, free of tax "for their subsistence by the owner of my Mansion House called Spring Grove"; no claim or payment, however, was ever made.

Upon his death he left a widow, Frances Biscoe, and was succeeded by his son, also named Elisha Biscoe.

Sir Joseph Banks

Sir Joseph Banks, an eminent naturalist, President of the Royal Society in 1778 and one of the foremost scientists of his time, "leased in 1779 and subsequently purchased Spring Grove, a house with extensive grounds at Smallberry Green, in the parish of Heston, Middlesex." By an indenture, dated July 30th, 1791, Elisha Biscoe (Junior) demised to Sir Joseph Banks:-

"All that capital Messuage or Tenement called Spring Grove House, situate and being at Smallberry Green in the county of Middlesex with the Household Offices, Barns, Stables, Outhouses, Yards, Gardens, Pleasure Grounds and Appurtenances thereunto belonging and also those four several Closes of Meadow or pasture land, containing by Estimation 14 acres; The Thirteen Acre Field containing by Estimation 13 acres; the Pond Field, containing by Estimation 10 acres and the Cold Bath Field (formerly Hangman's Close) containing by Estimation four and a half (more or less) situate, lying and being adjacent to the said Messuage or Tenement."

The Thirteen Acre Field and Cold Bath Field appear to have lain side by side to the West of the building, while the Pond Field lay to the South West of the building, between the turnpike road , already mentioned, and the two former fields. It is also stated in the indenture that when the said Elisha Biscoe should be enabled to make out a proper, good and sufficient Title to the Fee Simple and Inheritance....then it should and might be lawful to and for the said Sir Joseph Banks, his Executors and Administrators to become the purchaser thereof at or for the Price or sum of £6,000. Thus in 1808 Sir Joseph Banks bought the property freehold, after living there as a tenant since 1779, paying a rent of £200 yearly.

A painting of Spring Grove House of approximately 1797, a brick and slate mansion, by an unknown artist, is in the Viscount Wakefield Collection in the Guildhall.

At around the same time, in 1800, a survey of the estate was carried out by a certain D.Todd of Hounslow.

During his stay of about forty years at Spring Grove, which he used as his country house, Sir Joseph Banks, one of the most eminent naturalists of his time, encouraged the growth of science and pioneered some of the early experiments in Botany. He entertained many guests in his beautiful home, often including royalty and distinguished foreign scientists.

In 1770 Sir Joseph Banks had accompanied Captain Cook on his great voyage of discovery to Australia, a reminder of which is to be found in the border of rock formations around the present school building. Perhaps it is thus fitting that some of his early experiments were those with Merino sheep in 1785, which were to become a source of wealth to the new colony; these sheep experiments by crossing a native ewe with a Merino ram, imported from France, were said to have doubled the value and quantity of wool which the sheep carried. In 1710 sheep are reported to have weighed 28 pounds and by 1795 they had increased to 80 pounds; bullocks, with which Sir Joseph also experimented rose from 370 pounds to 800 pounds within the same period.

He also tried curing sheep diseases; he attempted a mercurial cure for sheep scab , the results of which were reported to the Royal Society of Arts, but although his method was a cure at one dressing in every case, a large proportion of the sheep were killed if it was used in wintertime. So he perfected the "tobacco-water" process and showed it to be easier to use, safer and with sufficient certainty of curing the disease.

He made many botanical experiments in the extensive grounds at at Spring Grove, among them one for getting rid of the Apple Tree Insect (Aphis Lanigera), which appeared in the area in July 1793, by cutting away all dead and diseased bark and painting the exposed areas with a mixture of sulphur and soft soap. And in 1791 he planted the seeds of a water plant from Canada (the Zizania Aquatica) on a pond at the House and so successfully introduced it that the whole pond was covered by 1804.

Like Elisha Biscoe, Sir Joseph Banks was interested in local affairs and in 1794 he carried out a census of the houses and population in the Parish of Heston for Daniel Lyons, a local topographer, having the means, in consequence of his residence at Smallberry Green in this parish, of procuring an accurate account of its present population as they existed in the month of July 1794.

The Spring

During Sir Joseph's possession, Spring Grove House became famous for the beauty of its ground, which contained many rare and beautiful plants, spread over a large area of pleasure gardens. Here Banks himself describes the miniature Lake and grounds: "the spring rises in a small grove within the precincts of Spring Grove, no doubt the origin of its name: this spring is carried by leaden pipes into the house, to which it affords an ample supply...... to this constant supply of fresh water, though it is very small, the great luxuriance with which water plants of all kinds suitable to this climate, succeed in the pond, is no doubt attributed...... In the middle of the basin (in the pleasure gardens) a small Island has been formed, by supporting a box of oak upon posts driven into the bottom; in the centre of this pond, the waste water is suffered to flow in the form of a spring, which rising into a large shell of the Chana Gigas, perforated for the purpose, imitates very well a natural spring and gives in hot weather the appearance of freshness and coolness, very pleasant to those who walk in the gardens". The grounds are also recorded to have held a tea plant, an American cranberry, which Sir Joseph helped to introduce, beautiful Magnolias and a splendid specimen of a Clanbrassiliana, another specimen of which is to be found in Kew Gardens. There were fine grafted Spanish chestnut trees sent by Sir William Watson from Devonshire and planted at Spring Grove in around 1783.

Besides several extensive kitchen gardens, peacheries and a gooseberry garden, there was also a conservatory with a vine - "the finest and best grapes cultivated in this country called Vest's Saint Peter's Grape" - which is said to have been first planted at Spring Grove in the year 1816 by Mr. Isaac Aldacre, gardener to the Emperor of Russia, who was no doubt one of Sir Joseph's scientific guests.

There were also strawberry beds at Spring Grove which occupied 5,645 square feet, even when the divisions between the beds had been deducted from the total area. It may also be noticed that it was on these beds that Sir Joseph renewed the old practice, which had then almost died out, of placing straw under the fruit to keep it clean and diminish the amount of evaporation from the earth, thus reducing the amount of watering which had to be performed.

Perhaps the crowning glory to 'Spring Grove's reputation at that time was that it gave its title to an apple, the "Spring Grove Codlin", which was first produced by Mr. Thomas Andrew Knight (1759 - 1838) and was extensively cultivated at Spring Grove. The apple was popular, until it was later superseded by newer varieties, since it was "ready for use in July, a season when London geese are probably better than at any other, but when the old English accompaniment of apple sauce was not possible to be obtained till Mr. Knight furnished this apple". Sir Joseph Banks died on June 18th, 1920, and was buried in Heston Churchyard. Even after his death, however, Spring Grove did not pass immediately from the horticultural limelight, for it is recorded that Dame Dorothea Banks sent the fruit of the Russian Globe Apple, produced from a plant received from St. Petersburg and cultivated at Spring Grove, to the Horticultural Society in 1821.Sir Joseph's widow continued to live at Spring Grove until her death in 1828, when she left the property to her nephew, Sir Edward Knatchbull, who in his turn sold the property to a Mrs Anne Fish in January 1830.

Henry Pownall

The year 1834 saw the death of Mrs. Fish and the subsequent purchase of Spring Grove by Mr. Henry Pownall. This gentleman was very interested in local affairs, especially in the form of improvements; he worked on many local committees during an era when radical changes were taking place, not only in local govern- ments and conditions, but also in national affairs. He worked with the Rev. Dr. Benson and Dr. Ralph Frogley for improvements to the town; 1829 saw the building of the Church of Holy Trinity, for the construction of which Mr. Pownall and others had worked; in 1830 he was a large contributor to the Hounslow Town School; and in 1849 he worked towards the introduction of gas lighting on the Great Western Road (London Road) through Hounslow. Mrs. Pownall also aided in local improvements and in 1859 Spring Grove Junior School was built at her own expense. Pownall Road and Pownall Gardens still commemorate this local reformer's name and work.

During the time he spent at Spring Grove, Henry Pownall spent a considerable amount of money on alterations to the Biscoe House in which Sir Joseph Banks had lived. The House was covered with Roman cement, a terrace was built along the south side and the main entrance was moved to the East side of the house. The grounds were nearly all made into pleasure gardens and it may have been at this time that many of the rare plants, with which Banks had experimented, disappeared. Inside the house Henry Pownall collected many beautiful pictures, among them originals by Morland, Bol, Perugino and Rembrandt, while in his new entrance hall he kept busts of famous people like Wellington and Pitt.

This Valuable, Freehold and Tithe Free Estate, was sold by Messrs. Winstanley, at the Auction Mart, Bartholomew Lane, on Wednesday, June 5th, 1850 at 12 o'clock. The fortunate buyer was Mr. Henry Daniel Davis who appears to have obtained a most desirable residence; since it -

"Is a most substantial and elegant structure, and has recently undergone extensive improvements and additions; it stands in the centre of delightful Pleasure Grounds on a verdant lawn, which sloped down to a fine Sheet of Water, and is supplied by never failing Springs rising on the Estate. It is approached from the High Road by a neat Lodge entrance and handsome Iron Gates and gravelled carriage drive through the Park to a handsome Stone Portico Entrance with a flight of Steps to the Halls, which are paved with Stone".

The house then also appears to have had six large major reception rooms, the smallest of which was a morning room 18ft. 6ins. x 18ft. 6ins. and the largest 26ft. 6ins. x 23ft. 6ins., a Drawing Room with French windows leading onto the West lawns. There was a large paved Entrance Hall with a stone staircase and stained glass window, as well as numerous kitchens, larders, cellars, servants' hall and butler's pantry. Upstairs there were five major bedrooms, the largest having a dressing room as well as being 20ft. x 18ft. 6ins., and seven servants' sleeping apartments. To the East of the House lay various outhouses for storing fruit and vegetables, carriages and harness. There were also five stables, a cattle shed, pigsties and poultry houses and two dairies.

The Cedars

In the grounds were two very productive kitchen gardens, peacheries, vineries, greenhouses, cucumber and melon pits, as well as a three-roomed gardener's cottage and a park which was of rich meadow and fine timber. The pleasure gardens too were extensive and varied with verdant lawns, American flowering shrubs, a sheet of water and a French flower garden. A broad terrace and gravel walks led by this paradise, disclosing a goldfish pond, fountain hermitage and Ice House; and, terminated by a grove of limes in which the spring arose, there was an avenue of magnificent Elm trees, some of which have survived until the present day. Older still are the Lebanon Cedars, said to have been the gift of the Duke of Marlborough to the Duke of Northumberland.

One must not omit the Holm Oak under the branches of which classes were taught in the early days of Spring Grove Grammar School. Many people will also remember the famous old cedar tree which blew down during a gale in 1952. It was replaced by a young tree, the gift of the School Secretary, Miss D.L. Ashbrook who always takes such a keen interest in Spring Grove and its pupils. Mr. Davis, who had lived at Thornbury House, now Campion House, died in 1898 at the age of nearly 80. He was in a great way responsible for the residential planning of Spring Grove, which altered it into a suburb for London's professional men and merchants.

In 1886, however, Spring Grove House was sold to Mr. Andrew Pears, great grandson of the inventor of the famous transparent soap, who formerly lived at Lanadron House, opposite his soap factory in Isleworth. Mr Pears pulled down the Banksian House and built at enormous cost the one which was the house to be occupied by Spring Grove Grammar School. This house was built partly on the foundations of the former house, of which there are few remains; only some of the elms survive at this time; none of Sir Joseph's rare plants (as far as it is known) are extant. There is a small ivy covered remnant, perhaps part of the old house, to the west of the present buildings, as well as the rock formation border of Sir Joseph's Australian souvenirs. Those are all that remain.

No Bathroom

It is amusing to note that, in spite of the lavish fittings, the architect did not see fit to install a bathroom. This was not because of any doubts in the mind of Mr. Pears as to the merits of his product, but rather to the contemporary fashion of using hip baths. The lodge of the estate, now in The Grove, bears the initials A.P. and the date 1893. Banksian Walk, now leading from The Grove to Harvard Road, was the original main drive to the house, Harvard Road not existing at that time. At the time of the completion of the house the grounds were more extensive than at present. The building faced a broad lake, now the south pitch, and two flights of white steps led to its verge, the tops of these being still visible. It is recorded that Queen Victoria asked her coachman to slow the horses of her carriage as she viewed "Mr. Pears' beautiful grounds". The larger trees in the grounds can have grown little since that time of Mr. Andrew Pears, and an impression of the past beauty of the grounds can still be obtained.

Mr. Pears held several social gatherings in the house and finally planned a grand garden party. Invitations were sent to local tradesmen, friends and a number of nobility in an attempt to overcome the class barrier. The tradesmen accepted but the nobility ignored the invitations. Realising failure in one of his major ambitions, Mr. Pears took up residence nearby in Isleworth and the house was left deserted. It became known locally as "Pears white elephant". Mr Pears inhabited his house for only a short time and, after he left it, the house remained empty until his death.

After many years of neglect the house was used as a hospital after the 1914 - 18 War, and later the ownership passed to the Middlesex County Council.

It became Spring Grove Polytechnic, the principal being Mr. C.A. Wood, M.A., who shortly afterwards was appointed Headmaster of the Secondary School which was housed in the same building, while retaining control of the Polytechnic classes in the evening.

The House Owned by Mr Henry Pownall
FOR SALE IN 1850

The House is a most substantial and elegant structure, and has recently undergone extensive improvements and additions; it stands in the centre of delightful Pleasure Grounds on a verdant Lawn, which slopes down to a fine Sheet of Water, and is supplied by never-failing Springs rising on the Estate.

It is approached from the High Road by a neat Lodge Entrance, handsome Iron Gates, and Gravelled Carriage Drive through the Park, to a handsome Stone Portico Entrance with Flight of Steps to the Halls, paved with Stone. The Accommodation consists of a Library, 20ft by 18ft, finished with Dove Marble Chimney Piece, communicating with A Gentleman's Room, used for Magisterial Duties, fitted with Presses, Dresser and bookshelves, Water Closet &c, and to which there is another Entrance.

A capital well-proportioned Dining Room, 28ft 6 by 19ft 8, with Painted Walls and deep Skirting-Board, enriched Cornice, and Black and Gold Marble Chimney Piece.

Drawing Room, 26ft 6 by 23ft 6, with Bow Window and French Sashes opening on to the West lawn by a flight of Stone Steps, and finished with Statuary Marble Chimney Piece &c.

Morning Room about 18ft 6 square.

Garden Entrance, spacious paved Hall, and wide Stone Staircase with Window of Stained and Painted Glass.

ON THE FIRST FLOOR

A capital light Bed Chamber, of the same dimensions as the Drawing Room, communicating with another Bed Chamber, 18ft 6 square.

A Bed Chamber, 17ft by 16ft 6.

Closet on the Landing, off which is a Water Closet;

Four Secondary Bed Chambers,

and a spacious Bed Chamber, 20ft by 18ft 6, with Dressing Room adjoining.

ON THE UPPER STORY *(sic)*

Are Seven Servants' Sleeping Apartments, Linen Room, and Housemaid's Sink on Landing

THE OFFICES

consist of

A lofty Kitchen with Boarded Floor, and fitted with Cupboards, Closet, and Dresser; Scullery, with Sink and Water laid on; Store Room over Kitchen, fitted with Presses and Dresser; a Small Room used as a Bathroom, and Servant's Bedroom, to which there is a separate Staircase.

In addition to the foregoing, in the Basement, is

The Butler's Pantry, fitted up with Presses, Servants' Hall with Sink and Water laid on, range of Larders,

Passage with Sink and Water laid on, and Force Pump.

Wine, Beer, Wood and Coal Cellars.

Entrance from the Yard to the Basement Offices.

Servants' Closet, &c.

A LARGE ENCLOSED CARRIAGE YARD,

A three-Stall Stable, Loft and Fruit Room over, Coach House, Brew House, &c.

Range of Carriage Houses, enclosed with Four Pairs of Folding Doors;

A Two-Stall Stable and Harness Room.

A lofty and cool detached Dairy, fitted with Slate Dresser and Shelves;

Slop Dairy, with Sink, and Water laid on;

Open Wood or Cart Shed;

Drying Ground, Poultry Houses, Pigsties, Cattle Shed and Stack Yard.

A capital Walled productive Kitchen Garden

Planted with a great variety of Trained and Standard Trees of the choicest description,

and fully Stocked and Cropped;

On the North Side of which is an extensive range of Peacheries, Vineries and Green House, and Water laid on in Pipes from the Spring.

Forcing Ground, with Pine, Cucumber, and Melon Pits; overlooking which is

A GARDENER'S COTTAGE
Of Three Rooms and Wash House.

ANOTHER FRUIT GARDEN PARTLY WALLED
The Pleasure Grounds
Are extensive and delightfully varied, and are laid out in verdant Lawns,
ornamented with luxuriant American Flowering Shrubs and Evergreens, mar-
gined by
A SHEET OF WATER

French Flower Gardens, broad Terrace and Gravel Walks, Gold-Fish Pond and
Fountain, Hermitage, Ice-House &c.

The general beauty being much enhanced by an Avenue of Magnificent Elm
Trees, terminated by a Grove of Limes, in which the celebrated Spring has its
rise, affording an abundant and never-failing supply of Water to the House,
Gardens and Lake.

THE SHRUBBERY WALKS
Extend round the Park, which is all rich Meadow, and very productive.

THE WHOLE ESTATE COMPRISES
33 ACRES 3 RODS & 8 PERCHES,
Be the same a little more or less.
The Land Tax payable for this Estate will be about £9 a year.

Possession may be had on completion of the Purchase.

By Direction of ANDREW PEARS, Esq., J.P.,
who is removing to Oxfordshire.

. Isleworth, Middlesex. .

Three minutes from the South Western Railway Station, with its excellent service of trains to Waterloo;
Ten minutes from Osterley Station on the District Railway, within half an hour's walk of the river Thames,
and only about two and a-half miles from Richmond.

Particulars, Plan, Views, and Conditions of Sale
OF

THE EXCEPTIONALLY CHOICE FREEHOLD

Residential Property

DISTINGUISHED AS

.. "Spring Grove House" ..

COMPRISING AN

IMPOSING MODERN MANSION,

TOGETHER WITH

Fine Model Stabling & Farm Buildings,

PLEASURE GROUNDS OF GREAT BEAUTY,

WITH

Kitchen Gardens & Extensive Ranges of Glasshouses:

Most pleasantly situate, on the High Road to Windsor (within nine miles of
Hyde Park Corner), some three minutes' walk from Isleworth Station, on the L.
& S. W. Rly., with its excellent service of trains to Waterloo in about 30 minutes; half-a-mile from Osterley Park Station, on the District Railway, and close
to Churches, Doctor, Post, and Telegraph Office.

The river Thames, with its Boating and Fishing, is within about half-an-hour's
walk; Richmond is only some two-and-a-half miles distant, whilst Syon House,
the historical seat of the Duke of Northumberland, and Osterley Park, the seat
of the Earl of Jersey, are both within about a mile radius.
The propery in all extends to some
20a. 1r. 16p.,
and is the well-known Residence of ANDREW PEARS, Esq., J.P.

Erected of red brick, some eight years ago, for the Owner's own occupation,
designed and built under an eminent Architect, is most luxuriantly and perfectly
fitted with every modern comfort and convenience.

It occupies an elevated position amidst its artistically laid out pleasure gardens,
and is approached from

A Picturesque Lodge,
guarded by a pair of exceedingly handsome ornamental iron entrance gates,
by a broad and well-kept carriage drive

On the Ground Floor.
THE IMPOSING ENTRANCE PORCH, supported by handsome monolithic
Marble Doric Columns, leads by a flight of marble steps to

The Vestibule
Having Mosaic Floor and Glazed Oak Doors, giving access to

Outer or Entrance Hall,
With Ornamental Marble Mosaic Floor, Oak Panelled Dado, and Glazed
Carved Oak Screen,
and pair of doors from which is reached

The Grand Inner Hall,
Having Oak Parquet Floor, Oak Panelled Walls, Handsome Tiled Fireplace.
with Mosaic Marble Curb Fender, Heavily Carved Oak Mantle-piece, and
Overmantel and Panelled Ceiling.
From whence ascends the

Noble Oak Staircase

Of easy rise, with Finely Carved Newels, lighted by Stately Stained Glass Window, and having Gallery Landing with richly Ornamented Ceiling. From the Hall there is a wide Corridor (in character with the same) leading to the Music Salon, and having Ladies' W.C. and fitted Lavatory Basin with Hot and Cold Water supplies.

Stately Dining Room,

Measuring about 30 feet by 18 feet (exclusive of bay, 7 feet 6 inches by 6 feet), with door to Serving Lobby, having Oak Parquet Border, Oak Panelled Dado, Handsome Enriched Ceiling, Steel and Brass Mounted Stove, with Tiled Hearth, Marble Cub Fender, and Massive Carved Oak Mantlepiece.

Ante or Waiting Room,

Measuring about 19 feet 6 inches by 9 feet 6 inches, with Polished Oak Floor, Register Stove, Mosaic Hearth and Sides, Marble Curb Fender, and Carved Mahogany Mantlepiece, and leading by double Mahogany Doors, lined with morocco leather, to

Cheerful Library,

Measuring about 20 feet by 19 feet 6 inches, having Polished Oak Floor, Large open Fireplace, with Ornamental Iron Panels at side, Mosaic Hearth, Marble Curb Fender, Finely Carved Mahogany Mantle-piece and erection of Mahogany Cupboards right and left of fire, one fitted with Shelves and Pigeon Holes, and the other enclosing an Iron Safe by Chubb & Sons.

Garden Entrance or Lobby,

Having Tiled Dado, Mosaic Floor, and opening to Glazed Porch with Mosaic
Pavement,
and leading by a flight of Marble Steps to Terrace and Gardens; adjoining is

Spacious Cloak Room,

Having Tiled Dado, Mosaic Floor, and Handsome Fitment of Double Lavatory
in
Oak and Sienna marble; also W.C. with Tiled Walls and Mosaic Floor.

The following Apartments all communicate and form
A Grand Suite of Entertaining Rooms,
COMPRISING
Elegant Drawing Room,

Measuring about 44 feet 3 inches by 25 feet 6 inches (in widest part), divided

by

fine
Ionic Columns and Pilasters, and having Polished Oak Parquet Border,
Two Handsome Brass Mounted Slow Combustion Stoves with Hand Painted
Tiled Sides and Hearths, Carved Marble Mantle-pieces, with Female Figure
Supports,
and Richly Carved Wood Overmantels. The Walls are decorated in Silk Panels
and the Ceiling, Walls, Mahogany Doors and Windows are all tastefully ornamented
in the Adams' style. This Apartment opens on to the Terrace and also to

Charming Morning Room,

Measuring about 23 feet 10 inches by 18 feet 9 inches, having Oak Parquet
Border, Brass Mounted Stove with Tiled Hearth and Sides, Massive White Mar-
ble Curb Fender and White Marble Mantel-piece; a pair of Glazed mahogany
Doors lead to the

Magnificent Music Salon,

Measuring about 34 feet by 26 feet 9 inches (exclusive of bay 11 feet 9 inches
by 5 feet 3 inches), and anbout 17 feet in height, lighterd by eight windows and
having Polished Oak Parquet Floor, Brass Mounted Stove with Tiled Sides and
Hearth, Massive Marble Curb Fender and beautifully Curved Mantel-piece and
Overmantel; above is the Minstrel Gallery, lighted by Two Stained Glass

Windows and approached by separate Staircase; the Walls and Ceiling of this apartment are most ornately decorated, whilst along the Frieze are some fine Frescoes representing musical subjects. A pair of glazed mahogany Doors give access to the

Splendid Conservatory,
OR WINTER GARDEN,

Measuring about 48 feet 6 inches by 28 feet 6 inches, heated by hot water, with Mosaic Floor, Ornamental Iron Staging, and Tiled Dado Walls, with Finely Carved Marble Reliefs by E.J. Van Weber, and containing

A delightful Smoking Lounge,
Decorated in the Saracenic style, with Mosaic Floor and Walls, and Painted Ceiling.
This Conservatory opens on to the Terrace, and also to the Billiard Room.

Handsome Billiard Room,

Measuring about 29 feet 6 inches by 18 feet, exclusive of recesses, with Stained Glass Top Light having Polished Oak Parquet Floor, Open Tiled Fire-place with Ornamental Iron back, Marble Curb, Richly Carved Mahogany Mantel-piece and Overmantel, Mahogany Panelled Dado with fitted Lounge Settees on raised dais, and Panelled Ceiling. A large Cigar Cupboard, finely fitted with Pencil Cedar, is a special feature of this room.

Adjoining is LAVATORY, with Tiled Walls, Mosaic Floor, and Two Lavatory Basins
with Hot and Cold Water supplies; also W.C. with Tiled Dado and Mosaic Floor.
Approached both from the Billiard Room and the Garden Terrace is the

Beautiful Palm House,

Having a Lofty Arched Roof and being some 75 feet in length, Heated by Hot Water, and Paved with Mosaic; at one end is a Gentleman's W.C. with Two Fitted Lavatory basins.

Walls, and approached by a separate Staircase is large BEDROOM for Menservants, with Hot and Cold Water supplies and separate W.C.

On Lower Ground Floor,

Approached by Two Staircases, having Luggage and Coal Lift to Top of House, and paved with wood block floor are, Coal Store, Bell Battery Room, Store Room, Boot Hole, Brushing Room, Three Wine Cellars, Servants' Hall with Pantry adjoining, Strong Room, Lavatory, W.C., Workshop, Box Store and Cellars, &c., whilst

Outside in Yard

Are Dairy with Glazed Brick Walls and Slate Shelves; Coal Store; Carpenter's Shop; Furnace Room, &c.

Capital Laundry

Including WASH HOUSE, fitted with Copper and Four Washing Trays, with Hot and Cold Water supplies; IRONING ROOM, with Stove and Ten Drying Racks; DRYING YARD; LAUNDRYMAIDS' APARTMENTS, comprising Sitting Room, Kitchen, Scullery, and Double Bedroom over.

The Mansion is lighted throughout with Electric Light (generated on the premises), the whole installation being duplicated so as to avoid inconvenience in the event of a breakdown, and is fitted with Electric Bells; the Hall and Principal Rooms are heated by Hot Water, whilst Gas and Company's Water are laid on. There is also a very large rain-water tank in yard with automatic electric pump to cistern in roof.

The Sanitation which is connected with the Main Sewer, is believed to be all that can be desired.

All the Internal Fittings, Woodwork, etc., are of exceptionally fine quality and character, whilst all the stoves have been specially constructed to burn anthracite coal, thus ensuring great cleanliness and absence of smoke, and the Mansion has been built with every consideration to artistic effect and convenience of plan.

The Excellent Model Stabling,

Situate at a convenient remove from the Mansion, and having separate entrance, is most substantially built, is exceptionally well-planned round a Large paved yard, is lighted by Gas and Electric Light, has Musgrave's fittings, and is well-appointed in every detail.

It includes FIVE-STALL STABLE; THREE-STALL STABLE; THREE LOOSE BOXES; HEATED COACH HOUSE for Twelve Carriages; CLEANING ROOM, with Sink, Copper, and Heating stove; capital HARNESS ROOM, with Glazed Harness and Bit Cupboards; above are LARGE LOFT, GROOMS' ROOM, FOUR CUBICLES, LIVING ROOM with Range. MEN'S WASH HOUSE with Fitted Sink and Hanging Cupboards.
Near the Stables are

Coachman's Cottage of Five Rooms,
Engine House, Dynamo House and Battery Store;
whilst almost adjoining are
The well-equipped Farm Buildings,
Comprising Fodder house, Wash-house, Cowshed for four, and ditto for two; range of Brick-built Piggeries, Two-Stall Stable, Slaughter-house, Brick-built and tiled Dutch Barn, Dog Kennel, and Open Cart Shed, with Lock-up Loft over.

The Delightful Pleasure Gardens
which are of an exceptionally attractive character, have been laid out in a most lavish and tasteful manner.
They are profusely adorned with fine old timber and choice shrubs and are intersected by gravel walks, and include wide-spreading lawns, herbaceous borders, ornamental fountain, old English garden, &c.
Full-sized Cement Tennis Court.

Ornamental Pavilion or Tea Room,

With tiled floor and roof, and fitted with Seats, Gas Stove and Cupboards. Creeper-clad Summer House, having mosaic floor, decorated walls and lighted by stained glass dome.
Special features are the fine clipped yew hedges and the shady shrubbery walk which surrounds the whole property.

The first-class Glass-houses

Include lean-to Peach House, two early Vineries, two early Peach Houses, two ranges of Pits, lofty span roof Stove House, two-division Cucumber and Melon Houses, two lean-to Forcing Houses, Show House, Tomato House, three-division Green-house, range of early intermediate and late Vineries, etc., the whole being heated by Three Stoke Holes with Six Boilers.

Two-Walled Kitchen Gardens.

Also Orchard, Fruit and Vegetable Garden and Several useful Buildings,

Including Two Potting Sheds, Bothy, with Mess Room, Scullery, and Bedroom, Bedroom for Five Men, Implement Sheds, Tool Store, Labourers' Mess Room, Vegetable Shed, and Three Brick-built Poultry Houses and Wire Runs attached.

The District of Spring Grove

The following extract is taken from the book **"And So Make A City Here"**
The Story of a Lost Heathland, *written by* **G.E. Bate,** Fellow of the Royal Historical Society, *and published by* **Thomasons Limited,** *of Hounslow, in 1948.*

The development of the district around Spring Grove House into a residential area began about 1850. In the June of that year we read that thirty-four acres of "Freehold and tithe free estate known as Spring Grove, situated at Smallberry Green on the Great Western Road between Brentford and Hounslow," was offered for sale. It was bought by Mr. Henry Daniel Davis, and he was primarily responsible for its development. Mr. Davis lived at Thornbury House, now known as Campion House, in Thornbury Road. He died an old man of nearly eighty years in 1898.

We can trace three stages in the development of Spring Grove as a residential area. The first, as planned by Mr. Davis, was to make it a place of residence for London merchants and professional men of the more wealthy class, and consequently the houses were on a fairly large scale with large gardens.

During the 17th and 18th centuries Isleworth had been a favourite place of residence for the aristocracy, it being only one stage out of London by horse carriage, but by 1850 most of the aristocracy had disappeared. At that time a network of railways was beginning to spread over the country, and a loop line with a station at Isleworth having been opened in 1849, the district was accessible from all parts by railway. This made it possible for a new class of people to reside outside the city in what was then pleasant open country.

The plan adopted by Mr. Davis was a much more liberal one than those which we find in the more recent developments of "desirable residential areas." The Grove and the broad open Osterley Road with their avenues of trees were intended to give dignity to the district. The "villa residences" which were erected, were well-spaced and varied in size and style. Instead of brick facings, most of them were faced with a special tile which had been invented and patented by the architect, Mr John Taylor, of Cheapside. These tile facings were also used for boundary walls where some of them have recently become detached and may be readily examined. They have stood the weather well for eighty years. The low pitched roofs, due to Italian influences in the designs, also form a marked feature of the houses built at this time.

At the entrance to The Grove from the nearby railway station two stone pillars still stand. They were placed there to carry lamps, and a livery servant was generally on duty at the spot to assist residents and visitors. At first the road was lit by candles and an old resident told me that he remembered these candles being replaced by oil lamps. Later gas and then electric lamps were introduced.

The Ordnance Map of 1864 marks, in addition to The Grove and Osterley Road, Thornbury Road, Church Road and Eversley Crescent. On a map made a few years before the sale of the land, in 1850, none of these roads is to be seen; the Spring Grove estate is shown, and running north by its west side is a lane marked "to Scratage."

The Osterley Road led on to Thornbury Common, and any intention to continue it has been frustrated, first by the construction of the District Railway, and then by the making of the new Great West Road. If it had been continued what a grand avenue could have been made!

Some of my readers will still remember the copse which was on the opposite side of the road to the church, and the stile and path through it to the Thornbury Road. Some of the large trees which grew in it still stand in the gardens of newer residences.

Spring Grove seems to have rapidly become popular. Commenting on this, a newspaper of the time states: "In locality it is singularly fortunate, having many charming walks and drives in its vicinity....... The great altitude (equal to that of the "Star and Garter" at Richmond) and its gravelly soil rank among the causes which have been assigned for its celebrity as an extremely healthy spot in the parliamentary records. The villa residences with which it is already studded, although only three or four years in existence, present many points of beauty and good taste."

Then came a setback. After a few years of prosperity its expansion ceased for lack of money; Mr. Davis left Thornbury House, and a number of other houses also became vacant. Probably one of the reasons which prevented merchants and professional men from maintaining these suburban residences was the acute trade depression of the 1870s.

It was, however, a passing phase, and Spring Grove revived. People began to return and a newspaper reported that "Much satisfaction is being expressed by the inhabitants of Spring Grove, in the fact that many large houses in the vicinity have been let, and it is hoped that this circumstance is an indication of a return to that prosperity which formerly existed in this pretty suburban retreat. Among the houses which have just been let is Thornbury House, formerly occupied by Squire Davis."

At this time there were a number of open spaces. Where the Central School and the trolley bus garage now stand was a meadow known as "The Poor's Meadow" the income from which was bequeathed, in 1632, for the use of the poor of the parish of Heston. On it, by the side of the Thornbury Road, was a pond.

The second stage in the development of Spring Grove followed the construction of the District Railway. Then were built many of the houses which we may call the "terraced houses," such as we find in Thornbury Road and College Road. These were much smaller than those built in the first period and were intended for a different class of resident.

The third phase came into full swing after the great war of 1914-18, when many semi-detached houses were built. Many of the old and larger houses were turned into flats, and in two cases large houses were pulled down and blocks of flats erected on the sites. One of these was the old vicarage on the corner of Osterley and Church Roads.

Soon after the war the Great West Road was commenced, and was formally opened by the King, in 1925. It cut across the last remnant of Thornbury Common. For over a hundred years it had been suggested that a new road be constructed to by-pass Brentford, but nothing had been done. Now that the time had come for its construction it was made to by-pass Hounslow as well as Brentford.

Vacant spaces were now rapidly filled with houses, but, fortunately, on the north side of the road, a sand and gravel pit had been made to get material for the construction of the new road. Now that it was of no further use it was partly filled with a clayey soil brought from the tube borings. This left an open site which the local council converted into a very pleasant park and rock gardens. One man who was prominent in the construction of these gardens was Mr. Councilor Heath.

Knowing the interest he took, and the work he did, in developing the parks, and also in the planting of trees in the borough, many would like to see his work commemorated. We often enjoy the fruits of the voluntary work of others without giving a thought to them or their work.

About the time that these gardens were constructed the Local Council also bought a piece of land nearer to the Thornbury road, on which was erected a branch library, and by the side of it a Bowling Green was made. This was a timely action, for very soon there was no further land available. With the building of the Secondary School in Ridgeway Road, the main building programme in Spring Grove seems to have been completed, and the whole of the area, which was open land a hundred years ago, has been utilized, but, fortunately, without the congestion so often found in some districts.

One wonders what will happen in the future. In some places we see the large houses which have served their purpose and are no longer required, pulled down, and on the sites semi-detached villas are erected. These are generally one type, monotonous in appearance and giving the impression of mass production. Let us hope that when the day arrives for reconstruction of Spring Grove, better ideas will prevail, and that it will remain a pleasant suburban district and worthy to retain the name "Spring Grove."

Spring Grove into the 21st Century

Reproduced from an article in The Independent

More For Your Money: Spring Grove, TW7

Published: November 2006

In contrast to Brentford's glorious and expensive 18th-century oasis, the Butts, and new luxury canal side flats, the Spring Grove conservation area is well hidden between the busy London Road and the even busier A4. It harbours a clutch of period and Arts and Crafts style homes on wide tree-lined roads in an area with swathes of green open space.

The spire of St Mary's Church (1856) dominates the skyline, and there are two historic buildings. West Thames College now occupies the listed Spring Grove House, erstwhile home of the Pears soap family and botanist and explorer Sir Joseph Banks. And, although for now boarded up, the Jesuit training facility Campion House, which closed in 2004, is tipped for residential conversion.

Spring Grove enjoys National Rail and Tube services, and Heathrow is nearby, although some homes are under the flight path.

Many buyers are young professional couples disillusioned by the higher prices in Chiswick and Ealing, Here they can get a cottage instead of a flat, or a large house instead of a small one. Many of them trade up after they start having children. More than 350 units, many of them flats and social housing, are being built on the former Brunel University site, and Try Homes has submitted proposals for 273 homes at Campion House.

A local residents' group is trying to prevent the developer from building too high, or too much.

They say, "We are not Nimbys and we don't oppose new flats, but this is a low-density family area with mostly three-storey buildings. We want the area's character to be preserved."

What is the property mix?

Mostly period houses and low-rise apartment blocks. The period homes were developed by Henry Davies in the early 1850s, primarily to house retired army officers in substantial villas.

Davies himself lived in Thornbury (now Campion) House, but his scheme was only partially successful in attracting military retirees.

What do flats cost?

A raised ground-floor studio in a large four-storey Victorian conversion near West Thames College has ornate cornicing, communal gardens and a shower but, alas, no bath; £159,950 at Churchills. An additional £10,000 buys a one-bed ground-floor flat in a modern block with communal gardens and allocated parking in the conservation area near Isleworth station.

What about houses?

If you don't mind having the builders in to spruce up a tired property, a three-bed, two-reception Thirties house with a garden and garage near Isleworth station; £265,000.

A three-bed detached house on Worton Way has three receptions, integral garage, off-street parking and a large (for this area - 60 foot) landscaped garden. It is near Hounslow town centre and Hounslow East Piccadilly Line; £435,000 at Townends.

(A check of the internet shows that the prices in January 2009 were remarkably similar to those quoted here for 2006. Ed)

How convenient are the transport links?

Spring Grove's southern section is convenient for Isleworth National Rail, and the north and east for Osterley and Hounslow East Piccadilly Line stations. Syon Lane National Rail is on the eastern edge. A good bus service links Spring Grove with Chiswick and Hounslow.

What about outdoor life?

In a word, excellent. Located between Syon Park and Osterley House, Spring Grove has numerous recreation grounds and a neighbour in Wyke Green Golf Course. It is near the Grand Union Canal, with its rustic footpath, and the Thames and Brent Rivers. Syon Park has a butterfly house, and steam and music museums are near Kew Bridge.

Shops and restaurants

A Tesco supermarket is located on Syon Lane, on the eastern edge of Spring Grove. Hounslow's large shopping parade is just to the west of the area , and more upmarket shops and restaurants are in nearby Chiswick, Kew and Richmond.

How do the local schools perform?

Spring Grove Primary, Star Road and Alexandra Junior School, Denbigh Road score well above average for English, Maths and Science, whereas Isleworth and Syon Secondary on Ridgeway Road scores below average.

Compiler 's note:- Sadly there is no longer the co-educational Spring Grove Grammar School. Apparently some of the pupils, there between 1924 and its move to Lampton in 1960, quite enjoyed themselves. Some, we hear, even had successful careers in later life!!

Sir Joseph Banks

12

Sir Joseph Banks

Peter Salter '58

Remember the Banksian Room, the Banksian Walk and somebody called Sir Joseph Banks? Who was he?

Sir Joseph Banks lived in the Georgian era, one of momentous change. Not a politician, but politically astute he had the ear of Government and Prime Ministers and leading members of many walks of life. Above all he was a loyal supporter and confidant of King George III.

Born on 13 February 1743 at home in Argyle Street, Westminster, he grew up with his sole sibling Sarah Sophia, on the family estate at Revesby in Lincolnshire. The Banks family was well-connected and wealthy. Young and genial, Joseph revelled in the rural life of the fens, which he would spend much effort later to drain, for the benefit of tenant farmers.

Joseph Banks received his earliest education at home under private tuition. Banks' father sent him first to Harrow at the age of nine and then Eton School which he attended from the age of 13 until 18,where he was a popular boy but the despair of teachers as he hated books. However at Eton he noticed the wild flowers and women picking plants for an apothecary; he paid them to tell him what they knew of them. Thus started his interest in botany, and the realisation that he needed botanical books to increase his knowledge; his teachers were delighted at this development. Banks went up to Christ

Church, Oxford in 1760 as a gentlemen commoner.

His passion for botany and dedication to Linnean precepts had developed to such an extent that, discovering that his Professor of Botany did no lecturing, Banks paid a professor, Isaac Lyons, from Cambridge to come to Oxford and teach him and his friends.

Banks did not take out a degree. He came down from Oxford in 1763 an independently wealthy man following the death of his father in 1761. Following her husband's death Mrs Banks moved to Paradise Walk near the Chelsea Physic Garden and Lee's nurseries at Hammersmith. This allowed young Joseph Banks to indulge further his interest in botany, and fish in the nearby Thames, and kept him in London (when down from Oxford) where he could further his knowledge of the natural world through direct contact with eminent people there, such as the naturalist Gilbert White. When Banks became of age in 1764 he became legally the owner of his father's several estates across England; thus suddenly a man of means he had to learn quickly the business of managing his many assets. He became well known in learned and social circles, and as an independent naturalist bought his way, in 1766, onto a fishery protection vessel, and was appointed naturalist for a journey to Newfoundland and Labrador; there he collected many plants and native artifacts before returning many later that year via Lisbon where he consulted with leading botanists. Although he did not publish an account of this expedition, he allowed others full use of his collection. On his return to England Banks found he had been elected, aged twenty-three, a Fellow of The Royal Society and the Society of Antiquities; clearly he had impressed London's scientific circle! During this time, government plans were made to better measure longitude through observing and timing the rare transit of Venus across the sun and included sending an astronomer on a RN ship to Tahiti. Banks saw an opportunity for him to be at the cutting edge of science and adventure; not for him the classical tour of Europe! By lobbying the Royal

Society and donating £10000 for the costs of taking his party on the voyage to Tahiti on what was to be James Cook's first great voyage of discovery, on board the *Endeavour* (1768-1771). Banks secured his passage as a gentleman scientist.

This voyage marked the beginning of Banks' lifelong friendship and collaboration with the Swedish naturalist Daniel Solander, one of Linnaeus' most esteemed pupils, and the beginning of Banks' lifelong advocacy of British settlement in New South Wales. The *Endeavour* had sailed into Botany Bay in April 1770 and proceeded up the east coast and through Torres Strait, charting the east coast of Australia in the process. During that global voyage of discovery, Banks and his party, which included his two dogs: obtained major collections of plants, insects and fish; made drawings of many specimens; and showed great interest in many disciplines of the natural world and anthropology. Many of these specimens remain in the Natural History Museum, whilst some of his geological specimens from Australia ended up at Spring Grove House. In Tahiti he learnt the local language, was tattooed there, and reportedly enjoyed the 'charms' of Queen Oberea. In Tahiti he observed the growth and abundance of breadfruit trees. The word 'kangaroo' was his phonetic spelling for the animal given it by locals. Perhaps above all his scientific work was his observation that the New South Wales he saw appeared ideal for colonisation. Banks returned to England a hero, and being a genial and knowledgeable man was the talk of the town, and in demand across London society including the King. He was an impressive and handsomely tall man, as shown in paintings of him by, for example, his friend Reynolds (it hangs in the National Portrait Gallery).

Frustrated in his attempt at a second voyage to the South Seas, again with Cook, Banks set off in July 1772 for Iceland, his only other venture outside Europe.

From this time, Banks was actively involved in almost every aspect of Pacific exploration and early Australian colonial life. It was planned to follow up Cook's first global voyage with a second beginning in 1772. Banks considered he should command it but was denied by the Admiralty. At this time Banks was keeping a young pregnant woman Miss B.....n; nothing more is known of her or child. In a pique of anger at not sailing again with Cook, and perhaps also to avoid gossip about Miss B.....n, he toured Iceland interesting himself in Icelandic culture as well as collecting geological specimens, some of which went to the Chelsea Physic Garden. Icelanders were much taken with Banks who made the first recorded ascent of Mt Hecla and in doing so discovered, by using Fahrenheit's thermometer, temperatures generally decrease with height.

In 1773 the King asked Banks to become a special adviser and Honorary Director of the Royal Gardens at Kew, the palace there being the King's favourite. In 1774 he was elected to the Council of The Royal Society, a sure sign that he was an authority to advance the cause of natural sciences despite an otherwise full life: developing Kew's gardens; managing his estates; developing further his herbarium and other collections; trying to complete his treatise on findings of his world voyage (not achieved in his lifetime); and at the same time meeting with (often through dining clubs), and corresponding with, the intelligentsia; touring Yorkshire; buying a London home at 32 Soho Square; and romancing a wealthy Kentish heiress Dorothea Hugesson – a workaholic and socialite of the first order!

He actively supported the proposal of Botany Bay as a site for British settlement. He proposed William Bligh to command two voyages for the transportation of breadfruit and other plants, including the ill-fated voyage on the *Bounty* which ended in mutiny in April 1789.

He married Dorothea Hugessen (1758-1828), daughter and heiress of William Western Hugessen in Holborn on 23 March 1779. They had no children. His home in Soho Square, no longer standing though a plaque commemorates it, became the focus and open house for his meetings with anybody in the world of science or travel. In the 1770s there was much debate in learned circles of the merits of different lightning conductor types; why such concern? There was a threat of war and thus need to protect strategic munition factories and warehouses such as the Woolwich arsenal. This vexed the King and, because the Presidency of The Royal Society was vacant, Banks as friend and confidant of the King, was recommended by The Society; the King agreed and was delighted, as must have been Banks as he saw an opportunity to become evermore influential in scientific circles at home and overseas. He was elected President of the Royal Society in 1778, a position he held with varying degrees of support, until his death in 1820. He remains the longest serving President in the history of the Royal Society, founded almost 350 years ago.

Thus he became a beacon for advancing scientific knowledge, and given his wealth was able to sponsor directly botanical collectors, and otherwise assist others, not so fortunate as himself.

It was opportune that Spring Grove House became available in 1779 for rent, since Banks could reside close to Kew whilst staying close to London. Thus Mr and Mrs banks, together with his sister set up residence at Spring Grove House, subsequently buying it and adding more land. They were happy and comfortable in their element there since Dorothea, Joseph and his spinster sister Sarah Sophia were country folk The ladies were proactive in developing a dairy farm there, collecting much porcelain and visitor's cards. Routines were established whereby visitors there were entertained according to the family's schedule of mealtimes. Visitors to Spring Grove there included Queen Charlotte and her children; it may not be too fanciful to suppose that Banks assisted in discussing collections for the Queen's garden at Frogmore, renowned to this day.

As Banks continued to develop Kew through collectors travelling the world, his own collection of specimens at Spring Grove increased likewise; his herbarium. It was very much, bring back specimens firstly for the King at Kew and secondly for moi aussi, particularly where plants and seeds were thought to be worthy of economic gain which was where Kew was headed. Conservatories were built at Spring Grove, a vinery and orangery established, raised beds made and strawberries and cranberries introduced from America, winter rice trialled (failed due heavy frost). Specimens of azaleas, rhododendrons, camelias, pelargoniums, lobelia, gladioli and climbing rose (Rosa

Banksiae) and monkey puzzle tree were planted alongside many others brought from across the world. These were happy times indeed at Spring Grove. The familiar cedar trees on the south and west pitches were gifts from either the Duke of Northumberland or Duke of Cumberland (probably the former in view of the proximity of Syon House). Banks wrote papers on plant diseases such as potato blight. He can be remembered also for his successful development of the Spring Grove Codling apple – an early maturing variety for use in eating goose so popular then in the summer months.

At Spring Grove House General Roy, assisted by Banks, conducted experiments leading to the establishment of the Ordnance Survey grid in anticipation of a secret network of munition stores across the country, located via the grid, ahead of invasion threatened by France; soldiers from Hounslow barracks were billeted there to guard equipment. Banks was as concerned as anyone about invasion but he maintained his heavy workload and full social life, being a regular member of many dining clubs. He was obviously held in great esteem being a coffin-bearer at the funeral of Dr Samuel Johnson.

Lt Bligh and the Bounty is worthy of mention; Banks advised the Government that Tahitian breadfruit plants could be grown in the West Indies to provide cheap and substantial crops for slaves working plantations there. The Bounty sailed in 1788 with Banks' two plantsmen, but few realised that amongst the mutineers was the gardener William Brown, subsequently murdered in the south seas. Doubtless Banks felt he owed Bligh a debt of honour and recommended he undertake a second voyage, and which was successful. Banks also secured for Bligh governorship of New South Wales; a poor choice as it turned out.

The late 18th century was momentous for Britain, especially the fear of invasion by France, the lost American colonies, whilst the colonisation of New South Wales began following Banks' advice to the Government. He had a role in choosing the governors of the settlement in New South Wales, founded in January 1788 with the arrival of the First Fleet. It was Banks who later recommended Bligh to succeed Philip Gidley King as the fourth Governor of New South Wales, Bligh's governorship ending in deposition during the Rum Rebellion in 1808. Banks corresponded with the first four Governors of New South Wales who, while they reported officially to the Secretary of State for the Colonies, also reported privately and therefore more intimately and openly to Banks.

Banks sponsored Matthew Flinders to circumnavigate Australia, 1801-03 which helped define the map of Australia. That voyage is an excellent example of demonstrating typical Banks' characteristics: use of his own money to increase knowledge; encouraging others in their difficult work; seeking no financial gain for himself; and showing his humanitarian spirit in organising a pension for Flinders' widow and child. The child became Mrs.

Petrie Flinders and a well-known Australian; another reason for regarding Banks as a 'founding father of Australia'.

Practically anyone who wanted to travel to New South Wales, in almost any capacity, consulted Sir Joseph Banks. He was the one constant throughout the first 30 years of white settlement in Australia, through changes of ministers, government and policy.

He intervened successfully with the UK Government on behalf of Icelanders whose welfare suffered greatly from the blockade of Danish shipping (Iceland was a colony of Denmark which supported France) by the RN during the Napoleonic Wars; for other reasons too, Banks is much respected in Iceland.

He had connections with Sir George Macartney's embassy to China (1792-1794), and with George Vancouver's epic voyage to the north-west coast of America (1791-1795).

He sent botanists to all parts of the world, including New South Wales, often at his own expense. Their collections were added to both Kew Gardens and to Banks' own collections. His collectors voyaged to the Cape of Good Hope (Francis Masson and James Bowie); West Africa (Mungo Park); the East Indies (Mungo Park); South America (Allan Cunningham); India (Anton Hove); Australia (David Burton, George Caley, Robert Brown, Allan Cunningham, George Suttor). David Nelson was sent on Cook's third voyage and Archibald Menzies was sent on Vancouver's voyage.

King George III had appointed Banks adviser to the Royal Botanic Gardens at Kew some time after his return from the Pacific. His informal role as governmental adviser on a range of issues was recognised in 1797 with his appointment to the Privy Council. He served as a member of the committees on trade and on coin. In his capacity as President of the Royal Society he was also involved in the activities of the Board of Longitude and the Greenwich Royal Observatory, the Board of Agriculture (founded in 1793) and the African Association (founded in 1788). He was also a Trustee of the British Museum.

In addition to the Banks family estates in Lincolnshire, Banks acquired his main London residence at 32 Soho Square in 1776. It was established as his London home and scientific base. His natural history collections were housed there and made freely available to bona fide scientists and researchers. Until his death, this house was a centre for the wider scientific community. He did not discriminate between British and foreign scientists. He was, in fact, influential in maintaining scientific relations with France, for example, during the French Revolution and the Napoleonic Wars.

In 1819 he was appointed Chairman to two committees established by the House of Commons, one to enquire into prevention of banknote forgery, the other to consider systems of weights and measures.

Honours flowed: a baronetcy in 1785, a Knight of the Order of the Bath in 1791, and Privy Councillorship in 1797. The latter involved further work including membership of the Committee of Coin and the development of copper coinage. There were other matters to attend to: commissioned as a Lt-Colonel he assisted in putting down the Lincolnshire riots in a humane manner in 1796. Expeditions continued to travel the world with his sponsored botanists; scientists caught up in war were assisted by him in returning to their home country; regular meetings with scientists and travellers continued at Soho Square; new societies were established and received his patronage eg the Royal Institution, and he was one of the founders of the British Library and a Trustee of the British Museum and Visitor to the Royal Observatory, Greenwich - working hard despite his increasing gout, he remained a hearty eater!

During the late 1700s British farmers were unable to export wool and thus forced to sell wool at home for little profit. The King and Banks recognised this, and believed one solution was to import merino sheep from Spain and cross-breed them with British stock. Banks had imported earlier two merino sheep from France (surprising given relations with France) and showed their excellent wool – imagine it, sheep at Spring Grove House! However Spanish law banned the export of merino sheep Banks therefore acted at the King's secret agent in the illegal import of Spanish merino sheep. The King's merino flocks swelled, so Banks was requested to have more to be imported from Spain and made available to reliable landowners; this he did conscientiously and thus merino/cross-breeds increased greatly in Britain. Some merinos were acquired and exported by the villainous Capt. McArthur to New South Wales, from which Australia developed its sheep industry.

The concept of transplanting Tahitian breadfruit saplings to the West Indies was no economic flash in the pan; Banks also arranged for other species to be transferred to different parts of the world eg pineapples, palm trees, mangoes and apples, and perhaps most famously for plants of Chinese green tea to be grown in India.

Noted earlier, paintings of Banks showed a tall handsome man but the painting by Phillips in The Royal Society chambers shows him in middle age as a bulky majesterial figure, resplendent in the red sash and insignia of the Bath Order, seated in Newton's chair and towering over proceedings. In the public galleries of the Natural History Museum is a sculpture of our man with a suitable Latin inscription which was commissioned by the British Museum and The Royal Society after his death; and there is a modern bust of him in the British Library in recognition of his part in its earlier establishment.

Banks enjoyed the company of, and correspondence from, people of knowledge and influence throughout his life. Apart from the King and Queen and British Prime Ministers, he was in contact with an impressive array of leading figures including: Linnaeus, Lavoisier, Gay-Lussac, Cavendish, Priestley, Crompton, Johnson, Wellington, Nelson and Emma Hamilton, Wilberforce, Watt, Gibbon, and Zoffany. This was some achievement for a man suffering increasingly badly from gout, such that in the last ten years of life he became almost confined to a wheel-chair and found difficulty in writing clearly; though he lost none of his enthusiasm and patronage of scientific endeavours. He is remembered by various geographical landmarks including: the Banks Peninsula in New Zealand proclaimed by Cook, the Banks Islands in Vanuatu named by Bligh, the Banks Straits in Tasmania named by Flinders, and Banks Island in Canada after its discovery by Parry, and of course by Bankstown now part of Sydney, Australia.

Banks' died on 19 June 1820. At his own request he was buried in an unmarked and unknown grave within St Leonard's Church, Heston. A commemorative plaque was placed in the church nearly fifty years later. Lady Banks died in 1829 and laid alongside her husband. After Lady Banks' death much of the Banks' estate passed to their nephew Edward Knatchbull. It was he who insisted that his uncle's letters be returned from the British Museum; they were sold later at auction - thus tens of thousands of Banks' letters were scattered across the world, but facsimiles of some are to be found on the Internet (eg www.nla.gov.au). Today his herbarium and zoological collections remain in the British Museum (Natural History Museum) with many of his papers and Cuban mahogany desk, whilst many of his books are in the British Library.

So why has popular history failed to highlight Sir Joseph Banks as a champion of scientific endeavour? Perhaps principally because he did not publish his findings from Cook's first global voyage and that he outlived all his peers and those he sponsored.

An Epistle from Oberea, Queen of Otaheite, to Joseph Banks, Esq.
London, 1774.

This supposed letter from Queen Oberea to Joseph Banks alleges amorous incidents between the two. It was purportedly translated by "T.Q.Z. Esq. Professor of the Otaheite Language in Dublin, and of all the Languages of the undiscovered Islands in the South Sea."
Published anonymously in six editions in 1774, it is now attributed to John Scott-Waring. A Rare and famous joke at the expense of Joseph Banks and his shore-leave at Tahiti: llustration from Frontispiece of Title doc.

> And were we gracious George thy gallant crew
> And had we – damn it – little else to do
> But turn thy great design of filthy farce
> And seek the wonders of an Indians A'___-
> DESIT
> With fronts unblushing in the public stew
> To search each crevice with a curious eye
> And seek EXOTICS where they <u>never</u> lie

Muriel Harris '49 tells us that her grandfather, Samuel George Short, wrote a book entitled **"Southall and it's Environs"**, published by 1910. This Passage about Sir Joseph Banks was taken from the chapter **"Heston and Hounslow"**.

The learned and accomplished philosopher Sir Joseph Banks lived close by at Spring Grove, for some time. He was a president of the Royal Society and founder of the Linnean Society and was in the habit of inviting distinguished men of letters and science, both foreign and native, to see him, thus making Spring Grove somewhat of a Mecca in the world of science.

Sir Joseph had the mortification of being arrested as a high-wayman, whilst searching for botanical specimens. The mistake was not discovered till he was brought before the magistrate"

Banks seen high up in Lincoln Cathedral

By Peter Salter ('58)

One of the jewels in this country's heritage is Lincoln Cathedral; famed for its west front, the 'Lincoln Imp', and of course the 'Dean's Eye' and Bishop's Eye stained glass windows in the transepts. But how many OSGs have noticed that Joseph Banks is commemorated in glass there?

The picture here was taken on a recent visit, and it was tricky capturing the image at the top of the particular lancet window! This window is in the Naval section of The Services' Chapel in the north transept. The view depicts Banks and the *Endeavour* together with his coat-of-arms; it is hard to read here but the caption says 'Joseph Banks lands at Botany Bay from the Endeavour'. Lower down the same lancet also depicts George Vancouver, and below him Flinders who was supported financially by Banks. There is at least one other tribute to Banks in the cathedral; see if you can find one when or if you are in the Lincoln area.

The Bounty

One reason for the fascination was Joseph Banks. He had not just returned to England with thousands of unknown and expertly preserved botanical specimens, professional botanical drawings and watercolours (as well as landscapes and ethnological studies) from his artists; Banks had also returned as the subject of romantic, even titillating stories. With his zeal for new experiences, he had thrown himself into Tahitian life, learning its language, attending burials and sacrifices and dances, endearing himself to its people, even having himself discreetly tattooed. The happy promiscuity of the Tahitian women was already well known from Wallis's reports and Banks's adventures on this front provided additional spice. Outstanding among the stories that made the rounds of London social circles was the tale of the theft of Mr Banks's fine waistcoat with its splendid silver frogging, stolen, along with his shoes and pistol, while he lay sleeping with his 'old Friend Oberea' in her canoe:

> Didst thou not, crafty, subtle sunburnt strum
> Steal the silk breeches from his tawny bum?
> Calls't thouself a Queen? and thus couldst use
> And rob thy Swain of breeches and his shoes?

The romance of Banks and Queen Oberea, broadcast in facetious verse and 'letters', helped ensure that the most-talked-about phenomenon to emerge from Cook's long, exotic voyage was Joseph Banks. To paraphrase one historian, Banks had no need to return to London with a lion or tiger - he was the lion of London. A few years after his return, he would make one more far-flung journey of discovery, this time a self-financed expedition to Iceland. In the course of his three rather eccentrically determined voyages, he had pursued natural history from Iceland to Tierra del Fuego, from extreme northern to extreme southern latitudes - a range unmatched by any naturalist of his day.

With these travels behind him, Banks purchased a London town house in fashionable Soho Square and settled into the sedate but stimulating routine he was to maintain until the end of his life. In 1778, he was elected president of the Royal Society - and would be re-elected annually for the next forty-two years - and he was raised to a baronetcy as 'Sir Joseph' in 1779. On his return from the South Seas, he had been introduced to King George, who also shared Banks's enthusiasm for natural history; Banks had been appointed botanical adviser to the King, and the two men became enduring friends. From their conversational strolls together were laid the plans for what would become the Royal Botanic Gardens at Kew, an enterprise made successful by

Banks's energetic enthusiasm and dazzling connections with botanists and collectors throughout the world. This dedication would continue from his appointment in 1775 until his death. Banks's nearby villa, Spring Grove, and its extensive land became a model of experimental farming, another interest he shared with the King. The stud stock of Spanish merino sheep, which he had acquired with much difficulty and bred at Spring Grove, was, with the royal stud, which he also managed, the foundation for the growth of the British export wool trade in the next century.

But mostly what occupied Banks, apart from his duties at the Royal Society, was his correspondence. In his town house, with his fine library and unique collection of specimens, beautifully mounted in cabinets of his own design, he was furnished with much of what he required for his further researches. The rest came to him from the eager outside world. Reports of the prodigious appetite of a cuckoo raised by hand, and of the tonal qualities of Tahitian wind instruments; descriptions of battles between spiders and flies; introductions to promising students of botany and natural history; queries about prospective African expeditions, proper methods of raising ships from riverbeds, the correct authorship of'God Save the King"; reports of unicorn sightings, of the later years of the famous German Wild Boy and his fondness for gingerbread; descriptions of destruction done to wall fruit by insects, the superiority of olives to other oil-producing trees; gifts of newly published treatises, specimens of seed, of insects, of fighting flies and remains of the spiders they had conquered - all streamed into 32 Soho Square. The kangaroos, opossums and plants that would so inconvenience the Gorgon in 1792 were all destined for Joseph Banks.

His correspondence, most of it now lost, is estimated to have comprised anywhere from 50,000 to 100,000 letters. His correspondents included great names such as William Pitt the Younger, Lord Nelson, Benjamin Franklin and distinguished scholars of many nations. But there were also captains who offered interesting specimens from their travels, farmers and a letter forwarded from a schoolmaster giving testimony that he had seen a mermaid.

Anywhere in the world, everywhere in the British Isles, people noted curious phenomena, came up with curious questions, observations or theories and thought, 'I'll write to Joseph Banks.' When Samuel Taylor Coleridge wanted 'hashish', he contacted Banks. Without straying far from London and his well-managed Lincolnshire estates, Banks knew everyone, and everything. Studiously apolitical, he was respected and trusted by most parties. Few British expeditions of discovery of any kind, whether to Africa or Iceland, were mounted without consultation with Sir Joseph Banks. In Banks's correspondence is mirrored the British eighteenth century, with all its energetic, questing optimism, its daz-; zling sophistication and its occasional startling innocence; an age in which geographical and scientific discoveries surpassed anything previously dreamt of, and yet an age in which it was still, just barely, possible to believe in mermaids and unicorns.

2000 and on...THE REUNION YEARS

13

2000 and on....First Reunion

By the middle of 2001 the web sites organised by John Hore, '51, and John Bloomfield, '54, and press advertising by Pam (Neal, '53) Isom had enabled over 300 former pupils to get in touch with each other via the SGGS websites or snail mail. Several got together for mini reunions with their own groups of friends. Pam, John Hore and Avril (Acott, '53) Cutting decided that the time had come to organise a reunion. The newly restored Spring Grove House was booked, catering organised, invitations issued and the anxious wait for enough OSGs to book and make the event viable began. 120 OSGs took up the invitation and were able to come to on Wednesday 19 Sept, 2001.

The day began at 11.30a.m, co-organisers Pam and Avril welcomed early arrivals in the music room with coffee and biscuits.

Brian Isom and Bud Cutting had produced several notice boards and a small wine and soft drinks bar had been set up. Although there were seats, most preferred to just mingle and search out their old school friends, helped by the name tags worn by all. Recognition was not easy after nearly 50 years but there was no mistaking the genuine affection being shown when long lost friends found each other. Chattering voices echoed around the art room and way up into the glass roof. There was a brief pause to enjoy a buffet lunch in the old room 5. After the light rain stopped, some moved out onto the terrace to stroll around the corner to the west pavilion, which is now the caretaker's lodge. Several small groups roamed around the main building and were able to take a peek into rooms 3B & 4 which are still classrooms.

Around 3.30p.m. goodbyes were said, the organisers reviewed a successful day and were left to ponder the question, shall we do it all again next year?

A Hounslow Chronicle reporter covered the reunion in the 27 Sept. 2001 edition. **The number registered with the reunion site continued to increase week by week.**

Following the first reunion several year groups decided to hold their own mini reunions. The '58/9-ers held two reunions in Camberley either side of Christmas 2001.

Wednesday 28th November 2001 - a momentous day or rather evening when a group of past SGGS pupils gathered at the Duke of York pub in Camberley to meet for the first time in 42 years. A couple of us agreed to meet for a beer, but this gathered momentum until the following eleven came along: Doreen White, Dick Lawrence, Alan Sabey, Colin Mackay, Mick and Jane (Halligan) Shaw, Rod Sewter, Bob Venables, Jerry Gross, Keith Lomas and Roy Schofield. Jerry's wife, Di, also came along and Doreen's daughter insisted on accompanying her - in case we had all turned into axe murderers! I think she was quite disappointed that we were all apparently quite normal.

Nine of us were from the class of 1958/59, Jane Shaw was three years later and Jerry one year ahead. One feature of meeting in a pub was that we had to spot the ex SGGS people from the rest of the clientele. That was not so difficult once the numbers reached critical mass but was quite interesting for early arrivals. Bob Venables, Jerry and Di Gross and Mick and Jane Shaw have kept in touch over the years but for the rest of us this was the first meeting since leaving school. There was much reminiscing of school days, with many memories being triggered by the conversation, as well as a great deal to talk about.

Top Row: Colin McKay, Keith Lomas, Jerry Gross
Middle Row: Alan Sabey, Lesley Booth, Roy Schofield, Rod Sewter, Bob Venables, Jane Shaw, Peter Salter, Steve Randall
Bottom Row: Cynthia Harvey, Maureen Oswald, Mick Shaw, Doreen White, Gillian Sternam, Doris Chapman

February 10th 2002 saw 18 Old Spring Grovians gather at Mick and Jane Shaw's house. People came from many places, but Lesley Booth set an unbreakable record by coming from Australia.

After 40 years everyone was clearly delighted to meet up again. The house was full of small groups of people reminiscing about life at school, the teachers, what the school had meant for them. Later on the conversations turned to life after school and the careers people had pursued.

Late in the afternoon someone noticed a smell of burning and after much searching it was noticed that Mick Shaw had hung two of his old school caps over wall lights. As daylight faded lights had been turned on and Mick's was quietly smouldering and just about to burst into flames. Fortunately little damage was done to the cap.

Jane and Mick were thanked for their generosity in opening their home and ensuring that the day was a resounding success. Smiles were very definitely the order of the day. As Keith Lomas said a few days later, "How do we beat that"?

1951-2 Mini-Reunion:- On 27 February 2002 ten OSGs enjoyed a pub lunch together at the Kingfisher in Chertsey.

John Hore, Margaret Newton, Anne Fowler, Eric Crook, Edna Seymour, Brian Martin, Jean Capel, Francis White, Brenda Sweetland.

Peter Bush (right) should have been on the end of the photo (left) but the volunteer photographer who took "the full group" managed to miss Peter out.........at least that's the story John told!...

Bottom :- **2002 Reunion Class of '53.**

Back Row: Enid Faint; Margaret Daniels; Brian Isles; John Young; Avril Acott; Ray Pearce; Mabel Spindler; Pam Neal;

Front:- Wendy Spring; Sylvia Wilkinson; Rona Hodkinson; Maureen Drake; Shirley Butterfield; Merrill Thewliss; Joan Lainson:

More than 200 Spring Grovians Meet Again at May 2002 Reunions

May 11th – years '59-60　　　　**May 18th – all years '25-59**

Two reunions were held in May 2002 at the old school building, Spring Grove House. Following last year's successful first reunion for many years Pam Neal,'53, Avril Acott,'53 and John Hore, '51, organised a second full school reunion, on the 18th May 2002, which was attended by 155 Spring Grovians spanning the period from 1930 to 1963. Sadly the numbers at the school are limited which meant that once again there were several who would have liked to attend who couldn't be accommodated.

Vivien Syrett contacted as many '59-60s Spring Grovians as she could for a reunion at Spring Grove House on May 11th 2002. Her group were hunted down and many had to be "persuaded" that they'd enjoy it! (some with very little time to get used to the idea!)

Some time after the event, Vivien still hadn't really come to terms with the happenings of that day. What she said then sums up very well the feelings of many who were attending a reunion for the first time, both this year and also last year .

Vivien said, "I bet you think that, after two weeks, I'm able to sit back and reflect on the events of the 11th .... Wrong!

To my surprise (and relief!), the day was brilliant! There was the sort of buzz of excitement rather like the first day of term after the summer holidays - rather than a gap of 42 years! Very few had kept in touch with ANYBODY else, yet, in no time at all, everyone was chatting and laughing as though they'd only seen each other the day before in school. This is, perhaps, what surprised me (and everyone else!) most.

Despite most people admitting they'd had nervous misgivings before coming, it was remarkably "easy" in the end, and everyone was so glad they'd not chickened out!"

The 11 May reunion was "year" specific and there were worries that the turn out may be lost in the size of the rooms but in the event there were sufficient people to avoid "rattling" in the building and so they were able to have lengthier conversations and a casual freedom of movement!

There were also video messages from some who couldn't attend, that were set up in the "Cloakroom" with showings throughout the day. Many groups "talked back" to those on the screen as they were speaking and burst into spontaneous applause at the end. It was described as "another example of the incredible spirit of camaraderie amongst peers which marked the day."

The only downside was the reaction of Spring Grovians who were returning to Isleworth for the first time for decades. Many had a real sense of outrage and an

almost physical pain when they saw the insensitivity of the awful buildings so close to the South entrance and West terrace.

Feedback from both reunions has been highly complimentary - with words like "magic" or "magical" used surprisingly often. The reunion experience was described as "some sort of surreal, magical time-warp!"   Most seemed to be amazed at how much others remembered about them, all convinced before they'd arrived that nobody would remember them and vice-versa!

Returning to the "real world", many could not believe how few photos they had taken because they were so caught up in the whole thing. Similarly, they could not believe they didn't even get round to asking what people did, or even if they were married, had children etc. because most conversations seemed to revolve naturally around "do you remember ..?" stuff!

Many of the journeys home were spent trying to remember who said what to whom or recall events that others remembered so well that were still lurking in the unlit depths of memory. Some reported not sleeping at all on the Saturday night remembering events-school concerts-plays-silly jokes-nicknames etc.. It seems that all of us, when talking to others, describe Spring Grovians in their fifties plus as "boys" and "girls".

Spring Grovians' good fortune was put into perspective by Penny O'Hare, (the admissions secretary who doubles as our "dinner lady") et al who work at West Thames College (present occupiers of Spring Grove House), who have so often been regaled about how it used to be that they were all very jealous of the schooldays we all seem to have enjoyed so much - AND received a decent education to boot!

It seems that there are still questions unasked or unanswered and people finding us (and being found); so you non-attenders so far, take heed of the forgoing and join for the 2003 "season" which is now being planned...

Girls of '52 : - Beryl Wood, Val Stobart, Angela Jenkins, Jill Wagner,
Margaret Newton, Margaret Wilsher, Sylvia Harmer, Jean Neale,
Edna Seymour, Audrey Simpson, Sheila Beale.

- 2002 Reunion Reactions -

....or some answers to "Howozit 4 u ?"

I had a lovely day and was so happy to meet three of the boys (men!) from my particular form 1948 (Red) who had news of some of the others.   But what happened to the girls? I remember them all! and where they sat in class. "Outsider" friends of my sister Val and myself are completely bemused by our affection for our school.   I think it has to be due in no small part, to the building itself which retains much of its atmosphere despite the efforts of developers and "improvements" .

The reunion brought back many happy memories of my schooldays – there must have been some bad ones but we don't remember those do we?

I didn't sleep at all on Saturday night remembering events – school concerts - plays – silly jokes – nicknames etc. and so many people who, although we must all be in our seventies, I shall always remember as "the boys and girls" from school.

Heather (Steel) Gunn 1948

I had a magical day on Saturday. I say magical because it allowed me to slip back in time some fifty years and wallow in nostalgia for a whole day. The old school building may now be hemmed in by concrete and glass but the spirit of the school survives unrestrained in the lives of the friends I was reunited with on Saturday.

Peter Looker 1954

I'm amazed how much some people remembered and it was wonderful to tour the old house again – it seemed so much smaller than I had remembered!   But the old staircase and music and art rooms still looked wonderful,and it was a nostalgic and wonderful day.

Barbara (Jenkins) Harrison 1960

Another memorable reunion. It was just great seeing so many new faces not to mention being reunited again with those from the previous get together. I hope we have another reunion – if we do please put my name down – I'm hooked now!

Sheila(Witcher) Beale 1952

Another splendid day at the 'old' school. It was wonderful to meet so many old friends who are rapidly becoming new friends. We appreciate enormously all the tremendous hard work which you have put in to get us to this point. Now you are the victims of your own success - how are you going to cope with the vast numbers that want to gather together. No doubt you will be as inventive as always.

John Young 1953

I really enjoyed the second reunion. If possible, it was even better than the first.

Maggie Seymour 1956

What a great day we had, and hopefully there will be more. I certainly enjoyed myself and Peter and I were very pleased to meet you.

Carrol Baldry 1957

Such a good turn out of OSGs so good to meet up again and especially to meet people who couldn't make it last time.

Jean Capel 1951

Just a quick note to say how much I enjoyed Saturday's event. Meeting so many old faces I had long forgotten. I will watch the web site should you decide to have another.

Chris Grimes 1956

I really enjoyed the day on Saturday and it was lovely to meet up with old friends.

Olive Cutting 1955

I really enjoyed meeting up with so many old friends. To be able to see around the school again was just magic. I liked all the pictures too, and shall be taking some copies...when I learn how!

Enid Faint 1953

What can I say? In the words of Cole Porter "What a swell party". I haven't had such a laugh in years. It really was like a time warp for although I've kept in touch ....I haven't actually **seen** anyone over the years. But it was as though we still knew each other so well....the general banter and joking was as good as ever. My only regret, on reflection, is that I should have asked people what they had done with their lives...had they married, had children? It was so nice to see them that the questions just didn't come out...ah well, perhaps next time!

Michael Hutchings 1960

The whole day was magical. The building just as I remembered it and the restoration work has been carried out superbly. But the greatest pleasure was meeting the people again. For the majority of our "lot" this was the third or fourth meeting and we are now all very comfortable in each other's company but it was great to see so many new "old faces".

Roy Schofield 1957

It was amazing how easily everyone picked up from where they had left off years ago. I must admit that I was a bit apprehensive before I walked in but within five minutes I was chatting to people that I recognised straight away.

Sue (Carter) Davies 1960

'50s Fellows at 2002 Reunion

Back Row: Peter Looker '53; Ron Cotterell '54;   Ken Cutting '51; John Young '53;
Ray Pearce '53; Ron McNeill '51;

Middle Row:
 Jim Young '54;John Hore'51;Brian Martin '51;   Eric Crook '51;Frank Williams '53;
   Front Row:- Tony May '51;   Ian Issaac '51;   Brian Isles 53' ;

Hugh Mortimer; Viv Syrett;
        Colin Wade; John Kiley; all '60

Val Pryke; Fay Twining;
        Brenda Sweetland;   all '51

Jean Raffe '48; Rene Townsend '48;   Douglas Roberts (1) '37;
Sylvia Cheeseman '46; Bud Cutting '44   Brian Woodruff, '42; Douglas Roberts (2) '37

The Sister Pryke:-

Marie '47; Valerie '51;
        Sylvia '57; Julie '55;

Late '40s OSGs that Lunch

Bryan Shepherd, John West, John Coppin, Mrs. Coppin, John Ward, John Huffell David Andrews,

Jean Raffe, Gordon Freake Dennis Robertson, Renee Townsend, Mrs. Huffell.

On Wednesday December 4th 2002 Spring Grovians from the late forties, together with their wives, met for lunch in Hertfordshire. This was a very creditable effort as some came from Dorset, Hants and Kent, although curiously no-one hailed from Hertfordshire! The White Horse was selected for proving easy to find being only five hundred yards left along the A404 from J18 of the M25. Even so someone contrived to drive straight past, didn't you John! Memories of a drive through the weather of a typically miserable winter morning were soon dispelled on being presented with coffee by a roaring log fire. As each newcomer arrived there were introductions followed by gradual recognition. Small groups formed to catch up on the past, then disperse to reform anew with different members. So much to say. So many rekindled memories.

Lunch arrived, seats were taken, but the chatter continued a pace. Although crackers were pulled with the vigour of youth, sadly maturity reasserted its will. Only one paper hat went on and then but briefly. Courses were taken, the plates were cleared, then after coffee and mince pies it was time to think about home. There was general agreement that the time had been well spent with everyone hoping to meet again in a more central location sometime next year.

Bryan Shepherd (1948)

'55-'56ers Now Do It Regularly!!

David Clarke, Isabel Stevenson, Colin Geere, Dick Pearce, Tommy Hanlon , June Thornton, Ken Johnston, Olive Cutting, Ann Morgan.

Reunion 3 - May 17th 2003 - What a Superb Day!

What a superb day it was again, this being my third reunion at the dear old school. I was delighted to see more "new" old faces from my year and other years and also to meet up again with other now more familiar regular attenders.

It was great to see Audrey Simpson who had come over from Canada as she was a fellow pupil from infant school. I had not seen her since 1952.

Whoever organised the "guest appearance" of the sports trophies did Jean Neale and myself a favour as we were able to have our photos taken holding the Junior athletics cup that we won jointly in 1948 - was it really 55 years ago?

The ambience of the reunion was second to none, the buffet was excellent and as for the organisers of the day they need a special accolade for all their efforts.

I understand that there will be another reunion in 2004, so come on everyone let's make it a good one.

I'm grateful to everyone who made this day so special for me.

Sheila Beale, '53.

'57-59ers Got It Together on 7th June 2003

Lesley Hall (1959)   and   Peter Salter (1958)

Over 130 former chums and colleagues from the late *'fab fifties'*, together with friends from the early *'swinging sixties'*, and some of our teachers from those times, were reunited at Spring Grove House on what was a glorious June day. For the 58-ers it was their fiftieth anniversary year of starting at SGGS, while for the 59-ers it was their sixtieth birthday year. The organisers: Carrol Baldry, Lesley Hall, Mary Pollock, Rosemary Jervis, Peter Salter and Barbara Wren, had a lot of fun putting this event together – not least finding and reuniting folk who came from as far afield as Australia, South Africa, USA, Canada, Spain, Switzerland, and Isleworth(!) That sense of fun spread to all who came to visit the scene of their formative teenage years.

Many came with a mixture of some trepidation, curiosity, anticipation, and excitement. The common unspoken questions on entering the old school seemed to be: *'will they recognise me'*, *'how to greet former chums'*, and *'do they really want to meet me again?'* It took only seconds for any to ice to melt away as arrivals stood and took in the vista of the entrance hall (we can still hear the 'oohs' and aahs' from those looking in astonishment at the main staircase, stained glass windows and the fireplace there; not much appreciated in school time) filling with so many smiling and happy faces. There was amazement all round with so many folk instantly recognisable; many have definitely been using the right face-cream!

The banter (matching at times aircraft noise from overhead) was non-stop. The gossip and reminiscences from schooldays was as if we had just turned up for a new term of school lessons, but mixed with snatched news of life-histories; quite surreal for many guests and perhaps emotional for others. For some at the reunion, there were perhaps goodbyes that had not been spoken previously, for others the realisation that though they had moved on there was now a rare chance to rekindle new or old friendships and share experiences in slower time after the day's dust had settled.

And how wonderful to see again some of our teachers. Messrs Lawson Cockcroft, Ken Pearce, Tom Reynolds and Bill Songi came along and quizzed us on our careers - and surely were not disappointed at what they heard. Unfortunately Hugh Leitch, Stuart Hart and Cliff Bullough were unable to attend so they will have to hear about the day secondhand . It was a pleasure not only to meet with our mentors, but also to say a proper 'thank you' to them, and to all their colleagues, for their hard work and earlier advice in our education. We all realise, now if not during our schooldays, that SGGS was a family school (we found that at least twelve of the three key years had married other Spring Grovians and five of these couples came along to show how and why they did it); and the reunion like other reunions at Isleworth further showed this by the shared enjoyment of all those present.

Photos galore were taken, a selection of which accompany this report, but the memories will be also inside the hearts and minds of guests.

Guests were heard to say:

'A lovely day to share memories'; 'Another one please, soon'; 'Would not have missed this for anything'; 'Great to see you all again'; 'Surreal feeling, seeing all those faces again'; LT Brown would have smiled at the way everybody greeted each other, girls and boys hugging joyously'; 'A day of nostalgia'; Memories came flooding back'; 'Fun fun fun, as was always'; 'Saw faces that I'd thought I'd forgotten'; 'My head will be spinning all the way home'; 'Really glad I came'; 'Good times – great memories'; 'Come and see us, we are living so close to you'.

The most difficult thing for the organisers was to tell guests at the end of the afternoon that they really had to leave; and as far as is known nobody got left behind, but the search of the basement was only pretty casual – so who knows! Will there be a re-run of this special event? We can certainly find more people who have been 'hiding' all these years but will need a bit of help. It seems that there is a demand for one in a couple of years' time – we'll see.

Front: Jean Innes, Rosemary Jervis, Gillian Ford; - Next back: Irene Curtis, Mary More, Les Sears, Frances Bacon, Keith Burnett, Hilary Mayes, Alan Benfell; - Next back: Pat Balderstone, Sylvia Power, Carol Pitfield, Mary Pollock, Brenda Hunt, Jacqui Sewell ; Next back: Beryl Steels, Peter Skinner, Barbara Wren, Carol Hughes, Neil Murgatroyd, Lesley Hall, Viv Jefferies, Jean Scrivens,Carole Sheldon, Anne Scrivens, Valerie Bowes: - Top: Tom Reynolds (staff), Michael Dean, John Beecham, Jenny Broadribb, Martyn Hirst :

Anita Craft, Roy Schofield, Sue Gardner, Tony Meadley, Norman Bennett,
Gill Stenham, Irene Williams, Roger Seaman, Liz Grieves.

Jean Innes;   Lesley Hall;   Mary Pollock; Jenny Broadribb;   Irene Curtis
Gillian Ford; Rosemary Jervis

Keith Lomas, Peter Creed, Malcolm Measures, David Cogman, Alan Sabey,
Bob Venables

"60th Birthday" - '60/61 Reunion May 2004

1961 Group (l-r) Jo Sisman, Pat Sherwood, Sheila Smith, Ann Pizzey, Lesley Ryan, Jeff Mitchell, Jane Halligan, Mike McKay, Roger Jones, Barrie Chessell, Terry Munro, Keston Harper, Lesley Maylott, John Carr, Peter Meadley, Geoff Overd, David Fittall.

Building on the success of a reunion in 2002, a second one for ex-pupils from O-Level year 1960 was held in the Music and Art Rooms of the old school on 22nd May, 2004. Ostensibly marking our collective 60th birthdays, it was a wonderful day, greatly enjoyed by all. The weather was warm, so was the company and, of course, the venue was as special as ever! The number of ex-pupils from O-Level year 1960 located currently stands at an incredible 128, and over 70% have now taken the opportunity to meet up with their peers at one or both of our year reunions. Many present had made strenuous efforts to be there from all over the country, and overseas - Bob Armstrong from Australia, Bob Freullet from Indonesia, and Sue Forey and Janet "Gyppy" Stretton from Canada.

Among those joining us this time were a sizeable group of ex-pupils from 1961 who will now "spread the word" about reunions among others in their year, and we were also delighted to meet again five former members of staff, all looking very well. From his amazing collection of memorabilia, Mr.Pearce shocked us this time by bringing his mark books for our year, together with the comments he'd made on our reports!

There was an especially warm, spontaneous burst of applause at the appearance of Mr.Leitch, who was attending his first reunion. Now in his 90th year, he looked marvellous and was on great form.

After the reunion, about 50 of us moved on to the Town Wharf in Old Isleworth to continue reminiscing.

Helen Protopapadakis, Sue Forey, Jean Furlong, Diane Waite, Sandie Gibson, Margaret Gaunt

250 OSGs Meet at Spring Grove House in 2004

Walking through the school gates on a cool bright October morning there was the usual frisson of excitement as the school holds so many happy memories . It is such a joy to return to the old school and meet up with former school friends. Up the steps to the east door and into School. Past Miss Ashbrook's Office (do you remember the red-ish hair piece?) and the Head's room into the main entrance hall and that wonderful staircase. Such memories. Greetings from Pam, sign in, oh there's ..... hugs and "it's so good to see you" .."tea and coffee in the Music Room". So the day began for most. Into the Art Room, more faces, just who is that? Look at the list of who is coming, especially from your year and the joy of meeting up with old school friends. Whilst reminiscing, we wonder that the School in this building produced such lovely people - what was the magic? It spanned so many years; 1924 to 1959. The photo boards provided lots more interest and reminiscing. "Have you seen the photo of the cricket/hockey team?" - "Mr. Leitch is here!"

Mr Hugh Leitch who taught history came all the way from Norfolk to join former pupils and it was a pleasure to chat to him about his experiences teaching us, as according to Mr Leitch, it seems, we were quite a nice lot!

The usual splendid buffet and accompanying wine encouraged a really convivial atmosphere, and it can safely be said that everyone had a thoroughly enjoyable time eating, relaxing and chatting.

"There are more chairs in Room 5, shall we sit in there?" and so on. So many half asked questions and half heard answers as people come and go between groups. Some sadness too that several who had intended to be there had not been able to make it on the day.

Photos, more tea and coffee, and all too soon it's time to go and we still haven't managed to speak to old "what's his name" - "We must keep in touch.", "See you next year?" and it's all over.

It has been said by several of the guests that our Reunion on 2nd October was the best yet. There were quite a few OSGs for whom this was their first Reunion, and it was very lovely to share their delight in being in the old building again. This also meant that more old school friends were reunited and the memories came flooding back. Incidentally, the ladies who provide the tea and coffee for us, really enjoy "our day". They have said that they wish they had been a part of our School as we are such a great bunch of people, now isn't that nice, and true! This year 172 people from places as far away as the U.S.A , South Africa, Australia, Northern and Southern Ireland and Scotland gathered in the former Art Room, Music Room and Room 5. Old friendships were renewed, news exchanged and we were able reminisce about the "good old days".

So another great day - many requests for another one "soon"...

Avril (Cutting) Acott and Mabs (Taylor) Spindler ('53ers)

56 years on - the 5th year '48 met at the Octoberfest 2004

There had been some mini reunions in the past, but this time the '48ers came back to life with twenty odd being in attendance. The biggest group at the reunion were the '48ers. More had been expected and we are indeed sorry for those who were unable to make the reunion, but sincerely hope there will be future opportunities.

One of the mini reunions was held for the benefit of Colin Tuffield. Colin, having lived in Melbourne, Australia, for the past 40 odd years, surfaced via e-mails and the lines were red hot involving half a dozen of us trying to make a date for the 2nd October. Colin had been planning a 7 week visit to Chicago, Geneva, Frankfurt and about 6 other locations in the UK. Being an old (and I mean old as he was 1 year older than most in the 5th form) employee of Quantas he was able to obtain cheaper air tickets but the start and finish dates were dictated by Quantas. It looked doubtful that Quantas would be kind enough to enable him to attend the main reunion so it was planned on an either/or basis that on the 26th September Colin would be given a mini. The welcoming committee to comprise Vera Heath (nee Newton), Doug & Marlene Lygo, Dennis & Pam Hoare, Ken & Lyn Munday and of course myself and my wife May. However, it was not really surprising knowing Colin of old that his final travel plans would have him in the UK for both of the dates. However, it was decided to go ahead with the mini thus giving us all the chance of having two sessions. I'm sure the 2nd October 2004 will remain in the memories of those who made the journey to Isleworth for the splendid reunion, for a very long time. Many had travelled from overseas and from all over the country and most of the '48s were attending the reunion for the first time. What a time we had mulling over old times and recalling various aspects of school life in the years gone by. In my case I was asked "Do you remember the Harvest Camp in Hereford when we had to can plums as the harvest was not ready?", "Do you remember the cartoon you drew of Basher Brown and the consequences that went with it?", "Remember when you were passed over the heads of the crowd at West Ham football ground when you felt unwell?", "Remember getting a detention when a bunch of us went through a gap in the fence to go and see the Moscow Dynamo's?", "Do you remember upsetting Muzz when you accidentally damaged the shelf in front of the wood-plane cupboard?" How memories came back after 56 years is truly amazing, many of us were unable to recognise each other but thanks to the name tags they were sufficient to overcome the apparent senior moments.

There was a lot of talk on subjects such as heart bypasses, arthritis, diabetes, high blood pressure, cholesterol levels, Brentford and Luton football clubs and two participants were heard to claim having achieved records for obtaining the most Black Stars in any one year.

I was reminded that although being christened Eric I had various nicknames in the early years, such as Ecky and Eggy but for the life of me I can't recall why. Can anybody help me? However, I eventually became Rick and it has been with me ever since.

I even had the pleasure of meeting Eric Beale; Eric had provided an article in Issue 5 of the Spring Grovian Report. Eric's 5th year was 1940 the same as my brother Ron and he thought long and hard and "Yes", he believes he did remember my brother. I will now try and find out from my brother in South Africa if his memory is sufficient to recall the 40's.   Rick Holt, '48.

The '48ers
Back row, Bryan Shepherd, Hugh Rhys, Peter Bennett, Mike Whillock,Ken Munday,
Rick Holt, Doug Lygo
Centre row. Left to right. Dennis Hoare, Heather Gunn, Colin Tuffield.
                              Dennis Bailey, Mike Sloman
Front row.   Mrs Bennett, Pat Child, Vera Newton, Jean Cave-Abbott and Jean Hirst.

The '51ers
Fay Twinning, Joan Morey, John Hore, Shirley Turner, Margaret Dobell, Philip Fox,
Heather Campbell, Roy Julian & Shirley Wheddon.

'53ers - mainly Blue:- Mike Grassley; Colin Coleman; - ; - ; Mabel Spindler;
Jim Young ('54) Brian Isles; John Young; Rita Cox; Ray Pearce; Avril Acott;
Pam Neal; Reg Day; Bob Mott;John Stevens:
Front; Margaret Daniels; Shirley Butterfield; Rona Hodkinson; Enid Faint:

Peter Linford,(Australia)
Barbara Adams (Sth Africa),
Hugh Leitch, Myrtle Atkins (USA)

Barbara Adams, Mike Campling,
Dick Pearce, Dave Clark

Doug Lygo; Sylvia Cheeseman;
Tony May

Heather Campbell; Jill Wagner;
Edna Seymour

OSG Siblings at the 2004 reunion
Gordon '45, & Cynthia '58, Harvey;   Sheila '52, Eric '40 & Tony '47, Beale

Nearly 400 OSGs Meet at SGH in 2005

L ike a bottle of vintage port, the OSG reunions back at the old school go on getting better with each year and this, the fifth big reunion, was the best yet. On Sept 24th, 150 OSGs and some spouses from all school years came together in the former Art and Music rooms.

Peter Salter (1958) and friends organised a very successful reunion for the 1957/58/59 years only on 14th May.

Vivien Syrett (1960) organised a 1960/61 reunion on 3rd September.

A Ton of Success back at School

Lesley Hall, '59, & Peter Salter '58.

O ne hundred folk came from around the world to reunite at school on May 14th with their pals and long lost classmates from the late '50s and early '60s – some fabulous 'young' swingers. Roger Fry and Neil Murgatroyd wore their kilts to represent the 1959 Scottish Branch of the Old Spring Grovians!

For the organisers, Rosemary Jervis, Mary Pollock, Barbara Wren and ourselves the day was the culmination of efforts to find some 'new' old faces who had been hiding all these years since leaving school; we even found an Angel (Arthur) from the class of 1958!

Three of our former mentors made it back to school again: Lawson Cockcroft, Hugh Leitch and Ken Pearce.

Delighted to meet some of our teachers again; all of us should feel confident that they were satisfied with what they saw and heard from their pupils from fifty years ago. It was a pleasure to offer Hugh Leitch advance 90th birthday greetings for his big day in late 2005, and to give him a bottle of Scotland's 'finest' to help that day along.

Outdoors, the east wind ensured that Heathrow's aircraft steered well clear of school, so it was even more pleasurable to be in the old place without having to break off the craic every half minute due to flights overhead.

Roger Fry; Peter Salter; Michael Dean; Peter Stubbs
Rosemary Jervis; Lesley Hall; Barbara Wren; Mary Pollock; Pat Salter

1960 (+/- 1) Reunion 4th Sept 2005
Vivien Syrett '60

The weather was kind once again for a 1960 Reunion held on 3rd September 2005 to mark 50 years since our joining the school in 1955. Helping to "celebrate" this occasion were staff members and former pupils from nearby years, mostly 1961 and 1962. It's amazing how every reunion has its own distinctive flavour according to the particular mix of reunion regulars and new faces present, and this one was a good one enjoyed by all.

For O-Level year 1960, this was the third attempt in four years to get everyone from the year together at the same time! Unrealistic, of course, but we can claim a certain degree of success. Of a total of 129 1960-ers tracked down, 122 were theoretically available to attend a reunion (taking no account of health problems or geographical location etc.). Life being what it is, it's remarkable that 76% of them have taken the opportunity on at least one occasion to make the pilgrimage back to school for a reunion!

Those from 1961 were celebrating their 60th birthday year and, for some, it was their second reunion in the year, having also attended the one in May, but we were also delighted to welcome "new" faces such as Ian McLagan who had been able to engineer a little detour on his way back home to the States after a trip to Germany.

A few pupils from 1962 were able to attend their first reunion - a trickle which we hope will become a future flood!

No reunion report would be complete without mentioning our wonderful staff - clearly Spring Grove was as special to them as it was to us. Messrs. Pearce, Cockcroft and Reynolds looked amazingly well and always interesting to talk to; we were delighted to meet Mrs. Douglas, attending her first reunion, who had no idea that just two words -"soused herrings" - were sufficient to bring forth a rash of memories even today! And what can we say about Hugh Leitch, nearly 90?! Having cut his teeth on our May 2004 reunion, he has now appeared in marvellous form at five of them!

As usual, time seemed to fly by with still so much to say, so about 30 continued reminiscing at the Town Wharf in Old Isleworth where it was still warm enough to sit outside on the riverside terrace.

1961 ers:- Mike McKay : Peter Meadley : Dianne Basham : Ian McLagan : Alan Worrell : Roger Jones : Barrie Chessell

....and finally the reunion once more for anyone who attended secondary school at Spring Grove House.

In August Derek Hale, '53, was casually flipping through Saga Magazine when he was surprised to read an ad. saying he was being sought by a Mrs Isom !! He phoned the number and as a result arrived back at Spring Grove House on 24th Sept. for the first time in fifty two years. He sent this account of his return.

After making contact with Pam and receiving details of the OSGs get together I drove to Isleworth in anticipation of reliving some wonderful memories; however the mood changed when turning into the car park and being faced with ugly, characterless Lego-like blocks of concrete, obviously designed by some architect's technician with an inborn hatred of anything elegant and beautiful!! His father probably failed the 11 plus and waited years for revenge through his talentless son.

After this initial shock I entered the main hallway and in so doing, a wonderful time machine! Those little girls in short socks and blue check had grown into elegant ladies. Not too many fellas but there was Pearce and the ever smiling John Young. I won't mention all the 'girls' by name except to mention my lack of surprise to see Merill Thewlis and Sylvia Wilkinson together as inseparable as they ever were.

Wandering the corridors was wonderful except for being unable to enter our old classroom from which we heard the roar of the crowds from Twickenham (on the Universities' match day) and where we all stood at the windows in amazement as we watched the maiden, and only, flight of the Brabazon that giant of the skies.

Then to wander round outside, horror of horrors! Where the magnificent trees, the lawns, the terraces? Where the soccer pitch? Where the hockey pitch, the long jump pit, the little sports pavilion and the tennis courts? But most of all where the Banksian Room which, I was told, was the first part of what was intended to be total demolition, before some right minded person stopped the Philistines?

Over 100 OSGs from a wide range of years were gathered in the Music Room. Some who were at the school before the war to the ones who made the move to Lampton. What a visit, what an experience, what memories, a wonderful day.

Below:-Marie Walker, Barbara Holloway, Jean Ridley [all '51];   Jean Rixon, Jeane Neale, Angela Jenkins, Edna Seymour [all '52]

Whole School Reunion 2006

It has long been my ambition to visit Spring Grove House again, but until we went onto the internet in February 2005 I didn't have any idea that reunions had already been underway for a few years. Unfortunately I couldn't make the 2005 reunion but very quickly put my name down for 2006. At last I was going to see the school and old school friends after 53 years. I had a little sense of foreboding as we drove up Harvard Road and into the car park entrance by the old hockey pitch, parking the car on the tennis/netball courts. Having been warned that building work had been carried out some years ago I thought I was mentally prepared, but I admit to feeling quite devastated when I saw "our school". What had they done to it? To my eyes what had been a very majestic building was now just a little island in a sea of concrete and glass. My feeling of sadness soon changed when we went into the Harvard Road doorway bringing back memories of going in that entrance in September 1948 on my first day at the new school!

Once inside the doors everything seemed the same as I remembered it - that lovely staircase and stained glass window, and beautiful panelled foyer, I could now forget the monstrous buildings outside.

Down the corridor to the Music and Art Rooms to meet up with old classmates, it was great to see everyone after so long. Fantastic also to see that Mr. Leitch had made the long trek again from Norfolk. We were able to have a good look around the building, going down the stairs to the basement, bringing back memories of school dinners eaten down there before the new canteen was built. Then up the "back" stairs to have a look round - so many memories. Back downstairs to the Music Room and a lovely buffet lunch, more chat, more looking at old photographs.

I for one went home very happy that I had mingled with old friends and sat again in Room 5, my first form room in 1948. At least Miss Bromwich was not there to admonish me for talking after the 'silence bell' -or maybe she was!!

Ann Wood '53

After reading the magazine over the past 3 years Michael '52 and I, '53, decided that we would travel to Spring Grove House after some 50 years and see if we could recognise some of the people of our age, once in our year at School.

In 2005 we took Michael's sister Margaret to look at Spring Grove House from Harvard Road. We were sorry to see our dear old school almost hidden from view by the new West Thames College. We entered this year past Miss Ashcroft's office and of course L.T. Brown's to view the memorable stairs and stained glass windows, the Music and Art rooms almost unchanged.

Michael had brought his autograph book containing many ditties and signatures from those who left in 1952 and some signatures of the Head and Teachers. The autograph book proved to be very interesting to those of 1952 and perhaps a little embarrassing. Michael also found his school tie, which needed a few running repairs before it could be worn.

We were pleased to see so many of our old school friends there, some hardly changed at all and many who became recognisable as we chatted. What a marvellous feat of organising the day it was. We had really been persuaded by Ann Wood to come and how pleased we were we had made the effort.

Due to some sterling detective work by Pam Isom, who had gone through copies of the Middlesex Chronicle to find Old Spring Grovian marriages and then followed up all the Marie Lewis's (Heaphy would have been easier), Ann Wood and I have been reunited and have picked up where we left off almost 53 years ago.

Marie Heaphy '53

Left:- Marie Heaphy;
Pearl Middleton, Ann Wood;
Margaret Daniels,
Joan Watkins (all '53)
Below:- Ken Munday,
Ken Johnson, Avril Acott,
Pam Neal, Eric Crook,
Jean Guggiari, Jean Dickson.

'48ers :- From left back - Peter Bennett, Ken Munday, Rita Tebbutt, Doug Lygo, David Andrews: Front - Mike Sloman, John Huffell, Vera Newton, Hugh Rhys, Daphne Bannister, Heather Gunn, Colin Tuffield.

Whole School Reunion October 2007

OSGs from around the world and with 5th form years ranging from '37 to '60, met up at Spring Grove House in early October. Numbers were depleted this year. The '53ers had held their 70th birthday bash in London earlier in the year. The '58/9s reunion spread its year range wider than originally planned to trawl in some extra support and the '48ers were hit by a variety medical problems. We must study the sporting calendar more closely before organising the next one; we've had one on cup final day and this year's was World Cup rugby semi final day with England in action. Jean McNeill and Anne Clarke, both '54, travelled from New Zealand and Australia respectively but sadly there were only five others from their year there to greet them. There were 120 in all, our senior boy was Alfred (Jack) Stammers, '37, and senior girl was his sister Marjorie, '42.

A slow start this year, Pam was asked if we'd got the right day as no-one had appeared by 10.30, she looked extremely worried but gradually everyone turned up.

Once more a lot of noise as groups got chatting and a great spread again provided to keep energy levels up.

We had an interesting presentation from WTC principal Thalia Marriott on the redevelopment of the Spring Grove House site which was greeted by universal approval by the assembled OSGs and is detailed later in this newsletter.

And then the dispersal, the caretaker (in our parlance) had trouble throwing out the last three girls, Sylvia Cheeseman, Jean Raffe, and Heather Gunn. Shown leaving

REDEVELOPMENT of the WEST THAMES COLLEGE SITE AROUND
SPRING GROVE HOUSE

The recent reunions at Spring Grove House have given us the opportunity to revisit the place where we spent, and it seems most of us enjoyed, our senior school years.

Many had left the area at or soon after the end of their school days and not previously been back but on their return all were appalled at the way in which the historic house had been surrounded by hideous 1960s buildings.

At the **October 2007** reunion West Thames College principal Thalia Marriott [pictured right] kindly volunteered to give a short briefing to those present (below) on the redevelopment to the site to be undertaken by West Thames College. These met with the universal approval of the OSGs present. It was following this briefing that the Waite cousins, Dianne,'60, and Sandra '57, (left) suggested that the OSGs should present a tree for the landscape project when the refurbishment of SGH was completed and the idea for the L.T.Brown Memorial Cedar Tree was born. The idea was enthusiastically supported by Thalia and the project committee also gave their support so the fund was started.

2008 Reunion

Another successful reunion was held at Spring Grove House in October. This year there was a good, if more diverse attendance with, sadly, not so many from the usually well supported years '48 - 54. But it was a noisy, happy gathering, as ever, with probably more inter year mixing as a result. Marjorie Semple, Principal of West Thames College, (pictured below) kindly briefed us on progress of the redevelopment work to Spring Grove House and the site. Happy day - the bulldozers were about to move in!

John Blight, Brian & Bernice Stevens, Barbara Wilsher, Clive Spokes, Dorothy Stewart & Tony Willis.

Cranes Seen at Spring Grove House

Following our briefing at the October 2008 reunion we heard that cranes had been seen at Spring Grove House. Thinking they were probably not the type that nest in chimneys, checks were made with the WTC principal, Marjorie Semple. She confirmed that they were not the feathered variety but aiding the construction of the first buildings, including the new Sports Hall, Learning Centre and Atrium which are going up very rapidly and the work is on course to be completed by Easter 2010.

We had offered the services of the OSGs who would happily have demolished the buildings that had been build round SGH. The chosen bulldozers however- did a pretty good job.

The photo above was taken on 8th October 2008, 4 days after the reunion.

Above and below, same view, mid March 2009

2009 Mini Reunions

'53ers Mini Reunion - Pam Neal '53

A recipe for making 56 years vanish in a flash - sit 3 friends down, with coffee and a stack of old photographs! Whilst Margaret [Daniels] and I had met up again at various reunions, neither of us had seen Jean [Carter] since we left school in 1953 [or 1952 in Margaret's case].

Jean was "found again" last Autumn and although it was too late for her to come to the October reunion, a coffee morning in Bournemouth seemed a good compromise. What we didn't realise was that we had chosen to meet on the coldest day of the year, with a bitter wind coming off the sea, but it didn't cool our enthusiasm. Hopefully Jean and her cousin Audrey [Rowland] will be able to come to this October's reunion. So, why not join us and turn back the clock - there can be few more enjoyable ways of passing the time.

A Pie, A Pint and An Old Bell

The Annual Re-Union of the 5th. Form 1954 was held at The Old Bell at Grazely, south of Reading on the 6th November 2008.The following came along and had an enjoyable time.

David Hutchinson, David Gregson, Paddy o'Neill, Alan Darg, Michael Gardiner, Janet Griffiths, Carol Treherne, Pat Whetstone, Wendy Butlin, Freda Booker and Bryan her husband and Joe Catlin.

John Catlin is the front man and in contact with 33 old members of the 5th. Form spread throughout the world.

Below:-David Hutchinson,David Gregson, Paddy O'Neill , Alan Darg,

Michael Gardiner:

Above - Carol Treherne & Freda Booker -   Joe Catlin & Paddy O'Neill;
Below- Wendy Butlin & Pat Whetstone;   Mike Gardiner & Janet Griffiths,

'55ers Reunion

Margaret Evans, Ken Johnson, Daphne Thornton, Sylvia King,
Keith Lomas, Avril Acott, Pauline Williams and June Thornton all met at the
Old Fire Station, Waterloo on 10th December. Ken Johnson organises these
drink/lunch get to-gethers a couple of times a year. New old friends are always
welcome, for more details contact Ken Johnson.

200 OSGs Attend 2009 Reunions

The Organisers of the June 13th reunion were delighted to meet up with 116 OSGs and staff on a glorious day at the old school in Isleworth. The need to recruit more from adjacent years for '58/59ers reunion to go ahead meant a few less for the "whole-school" reunion in October but over 120 OSGs turned up on the day, with several who have only just found us. The general consensus was that although there were a few years that were, not surprisingly, poorly represented there was more intermingling between years and hopefully more friendships will result.

W. Thames College Principal Marjorie Semple again attended to brief us on the refurbishment process and although the campus is very much a building site, progress can be seen and news that the concrete block on the "West Lawn" is next in line for demolition brought the biggest cheer of the day.

Sylvia Cheesman '45, '53ers - John Young, Pam Neal, Ray Pearce, Avril Acott

'58/9ers 50th Anniversary Reunion
June 2009

Organisers of the June 13th reunion were delighted to meet up with 116 OSGs and staff on a glorious day at the old school in Isleworth. Quite a lot of new 'old' faces shared the day with former school pals. It was good to meet up with members of the Blight clan, Creed siblings, Sternham and Jervis sisters, and the Beecham brothers, and to greet the married couples Conroy-Chantler and Perrow-Hayward and Warne-Hart again.

Folk came from afar; Bob Garnham m'57 from New Zealand, Lesley Booth '58 from Oz, John Harbour '58 from the US just for the weekend, Jackie Warne '63 and husband David Hart '60 from Denmark, '59ers John Beecham and Roger Fry from Bonnie Scotland, Ray Dent '62 from Wales, and from many other places in between.

Staff members Muriel Hosking, Ken Pearce and Tom Reynolds no doubt were delighted to see and hear of successful lives and careers of guests, and which were shaped by them and their colleagues all those years ago. It was pleasure to thank them all publicly for everything that they did for us some fifty years ago before we set out on our life journeys.

Above :-John Harbour; Arthur Angel:
                              :- Richard Lawrence; Rosie Lawrence; Roy Schofield
Below :-Gill Sternham; Mervyn Jones; Lesley Booth:
                              :-Mick Shaw; Keith Lomas; Bernard Hunt

The milling throng....twice

October Reunion 2009

What can be said that hasn't already been said? The Reunion last October was most interesting, I think that as time goes on, we are forgetting the difference in the years we were at Spring Grove and greet each other as old friends and family. Certainly the atmosphere was wonderful. As usual seemingly endless teas and coffees were prepared and served by our honorary OSGs Penny and not Veronica this time but Annie, and of course the wine. I certainly haven't forgotten to mention the wide variety of delicious food prepared and supplied by Lizzie. The other staples are the photo boards with the odd letter prepared and set up for us by Pam and Brian.

Inevitably some of our older friends are unable to come now but we were delighted to see two old school friends from '53, Audrey Rowland and Jean Carter. Marjorie Semple (the Principal) also came along after lunch to talk about the progress of the new buildings. Having been to the topping out ceremony last May and meeting some of the Architects, Builders and Staff, I am very enthusiastic about the plans – almost wish I was a bit younger so that I could study there too.

Finally, thank you to all who came to make it such an enjoyable and successful day and to those who couldn't make, we missed you. Avril Acott '53

Inaugural Meeting of Club 80

Stan Sachs '46

Stan Sach, Phil Marshall, Gwen Paige(Mantel), Peter Wotton, & Eric Badby

The date of our reunion was Tuesday 6th. Oct. at the Old Mill Hotel, West Harnham, Salisbury, where we gathered for afternoon tea followed by dinner in the evening. We have called ourselves 'Club80' as the object of the get together was our actual or impending Eightieth Birthdays, having joined the school in 1941, all in the same first year class. The five were : Gwen Mantel (now Paige) with husband Geoff, Peter Wotton with wife Danni, Phil Marshall with wife Cath, Eric Badby with wife Joan and yours truly-Stanley Sach with wife Sylvia.

There was much reminiscing as is usual, and it was a great pleasure to meet the husband and wives of our old friends. After a leisurely breakfast we made our journeys homeward as far as Sussex, Buckinghamshire, Surrey, Dorset and Twickenham. We know there are a few more eligible '46ers out there who could join our club.......but they must hurry up !!

Cornish OSGs 2009 Reunion

In the late summer in Cornwall Alan Sabey caught up with Peter Creed, Les and Sheila Sears and John and Lorna Seater. The Cornish Branch of OSGs.

They spent several days travelling around that part of the country and, although the weather was disappointing it did not put them off or spoil their get together.

They all met up on the Sunday for a pub carvery lunch where the red wine and the beers flowed very nicely!

It was a very pleasant break to get away and catch up with old friends. and revive memories.

L to R - Peter Creed, Sheila and Les Sears, Lorna and John Seater, Alan Sabey

OSGs En France

Three '58 ers met up at the beginning of March in the French medieval village of Thuir, in the Pyrenees Oriental Dept at the home of Lesley Booth. Susan Jackson drove over for the occasion from her base at Trie sur Baise in the Haute Pyrenees and Keith and Sheila Lomas —ex Gumley House, travelled down by Eurostar and TGV from their home in Kent.

The meeting had been planned for some time but awaited a suitable occasion when the ladies were not commuting from Australia for us to get together. The occasion presented itself when Lesley announced she had bought a house in Thuir. We talked about all those things that OSGs talk about when they get together and put the world to rights.

Our return journey was disrupted by the weather. The worst snow storm to hit that part of France in 50 years disrupted all road, rail and aircraft travel but it didn't dampen our enjoyment, we still found things to talk about, surviving on plentiful supplies of bagettes, cheese and wine.

REUNION 2010

Our Reunion on Saturday 2nd October was lovely. Very relaxed with "old" faithfuls and some very welcome new ones as well. We are so impressed with the affection that OSGs who live in other continents hold our school that they are prepared to spend effort, time and money to travel to be with us. Thank you all who have travelled far over the past ten years to join us and for all the shared memories.

Saturday held an extra treat for those interested, as the Principal of West Thames College, Marjorie Semple, took groups on a guided tour of the new and fully operational Theatre, Atrium and Sports Hall Building. "Very impressive", "wonderful facilities", "so different from our day", etc. just some of the comments overheard from returning viewers. Before the tours started, Marjorie told us that the building works were slightly ahead of schedule and all being well, the other new buildings will be handed over in the summer holidays next year.

The landscapers will plant L.T.Brown Cedar this winter in order to get it established before the unveiling of the plaque of dedication next September, a year earlier than originally expected.

The Sept. 2011 reunion will be the last full school reunion that we will organise. After so many happy reunion memories, we think it better to go out on a high and of course if anyone would like to pick up where we left off, we will help. We will still maintain our Contact List and the web-site, and as long as you send in copy, our Editor will carry on with the SGR & website.   Avril Acott

Jeane Neale;Ann Yateman; Ray Pearce;Edna Seymour;

Margaret Wilsher; Angela Jenkins

Top :- '48ers in force.   Peter Salter Margaret Pursey
2nd Row:- Margaret Spicer; Sheila Beale; Guest; Rosemary Higson:
Above; Peter Bennett; Edna Seymour; Rick Holt; Joyce Bennett: David Andrews
Below L, "Senior girl for the day" - Marjorie Stammers'42; with sons.
                        Below R,   Tony Beale;   Eric Sachs

L.T.Brown Cedar Planted Dec. 14th 2010

The idea that a cedar tree should be donated for the landscaping to complete the refurbishment plans at WTC and SGH was suggested by the Waite cousins,Sandra and Diane ('57 & '60) at the 2007 reunion. From the founding of Spring Grove as a school there was a Cedar of Lebanon tree at the South West corner of Spring Grove House. A heavy snow fall caused the original tree to collapse on Tuesday, January 2nd. 1951 at 11.00a.m.

The fund was started and the first donation from Betty Collins '47 was made on the 12th Dec 2007. We have had 168 donations and raised £3,306.28p.

The Landscapers asked us to have the tree on site for planting in Dec 2010, so John Catlin '54 and Ray Pearce '53 met at Majestic Trees in St Albans to view and select a tree. Genuine Cedrus Lebani were not in plentiful supply and we had a choice of just 3 trees. We chose one and, following negotiations with Majestic Trees, they agreed to let us have it at trade price. This enabled us to purchase an extended care warranty which will involve an arborialist visiting the site 5 times during the growing season and effectively gives us a two year guarantee on the tree. The balance was used to buy the dedication brass plaque (below) unveiled at the 2011 reunion. We hope that all OSGs who have

contributed think that the money has been invested wisely. The tree was planted three years after the first donation almost to the day Dec. 14th 2010. A small group of OSGs (left) braved the December chill to watch the planting.

After the shock of seeing the awful '60s concrete blocks surrounding the house at the first reunions, all will be delighted that the WTC refurbishment programme has replaced them with new buildings that compliment and display the old house to advantage.

L to R:-
Bud and Avril Cutting; John Coppin;
Marjorie Semple, WTC principal;
Kathy Barrett; Ray Pearce;
John Catlin and Pat Whetstone.

There is a 5 minute video of the actual planting on the website
www.springgrovegrammarschool.org.uk

Spring Grove Grammar School

Isleworth

Roll of Honour
WWII

1939-1946

Debt of Honour - WW II Old Spring Grovians

By Peter Salter '58

Ohe thing which struck me as quite strange whilst a young lad at Spring Grove was the absence of any memorial to those Old Spring Grovians who made the supreme sacrifice during the Second World War; particularly odd when I knew that Isleworth County honoured their boys who were killed. I have often wondered why this might have been.

After much research, together with help and encouragement from several seniors, the list below has been drawn up as an attempt to right a wrong, especially as we approach sixty years since the end of the war.

Sgt (Pilot) Charles Cunningham **Adams** RAFVR, 605 Sqn; **21.5.1943** Age 21. Grandcourt War Cemetry, Seine-Maritime, France

Sgt (Pilot) Frederick Thomas **Allen** RAFVR, Sqn? **:12.5.1943** Age? Feltham Cemetry

Pil Off Norman Lewis **Ballamy** RAFVR, 44 (Rhodesia) Sqn: **15.6.1943** Age 21. Runnymede Air Force Memorial

WO II (CSM) David Geoffrey **Barden** Int Corps, Unit?: **25.6.1946** Age 23. Taukkyan War Cemetry, Burma. See notes below.

Sgt (Obs) John Leslie **Barden** RAFVR, 101 Sqn: **31.1.1943** Age 24. Amsterdam New Cemetry, Holland. Brother of David G Barden

Wren Hazel Mary **Batten** WRNS, HMS Assagi: **12.2.1944** Age 23. Chatham Naval Memorial

Sgt Albert Robert George **Boothby** RAC, Recce Regt: **19.1.1944** Age? Minturno War Cemetry, Italy

Fg Off (Obsvr) Richard Job Thomas **Brown** RAFVR, 39 Sqn: **30.11.1942** Age 26. Catania Cemetry, Sicily

Spr Charlie **Buckland** RE, 255 Field Coy: **18.4.1945** Age 34. Faenza War Cemetry, Italy

Spr Charles Samuel **Burge** RE, 172 Field Coy: **5.3.1943** Age 25. SFAX War Cemetry, Tunisia

Sgt (Air Gnr) Charles Frederick **Castle** RAFVR, 228 Sqn: **5.9.1942** Age 27. Twickenham Parochial Cemetry

Pte Sidney Arthur **Chennel** 1st Airborne Div, 3rd Bn Para Regt: **17.9.1944** Age 18. Arnhem Oosterbeck War Cemetry, Holland

Sig Richard Frederick Walter **Collier** Royal Corps Signals, Unit?: **29.5.1940** Age 23. III Corps unit?. Dunkirk Memorial

Tpr Frederick William **Donhou** RAC, 6th RTR: **21/22. 11.1941** Age 21. El Alamein Memorial, Egypt

Cpl Cyril Albert James **Eckert** 6th Airborne Div, 13th Bn Para Regt: **23.8.1944** Age 22. 13th Bn Para.
Ranville War Cemetry, Calvados, France. See notes

L/Cpl Stanley George Thomas **Eckert** 6th Airborne Div, 9th Bn Para Regt: **6.6.1944** Age 19.Ranville War Cemetry. Brother of Cyril AJ Eckert

Sgt (Obs) John Hartas George **Garrick** RAFVR, Sqn?; **31.5.1942** Age 24. Eindhoven (Woensel) General Cemetry, Holland

Sgt Alexander Joseph **Giles** RAF, 144 Sqn: 21.7.1940 Age? Runnymede Air Force Memorial

Lt Ernest Walter **Gill** RA, 306 Bty 27 Searchlight Regt: 28.12.1943 Age 32. Khayat Beach War Cemetry, Israel

Sgt (Pilot) John Eric **Goodrich** RAFVR, Sqn?: 1.7.1942 Age 26. Kidlington Burial Ground, Oxon

Tpr Cecil John **Gough** RAC, 13/18 Roy Hussars: 15.2.1945 Age 24. Reichswald Forest War Cemetry

Sgt William Roy **Govett** RAF, 50 Sqn: 16.4.1941 Age 20. St Leonard's Churchyard, Heston

Sgt Leslie Charles **Gray** RAFVR, 150 Sqn: 9.6.1942 Age 21. Runnymede Air Force Memorial.

Cpl Gerald Percival Seth **Harris** 1/4th Bn Essex Regt: 6.4.1943 Age 31. SFAX War Cemetery, Tunisia

Cpl Stephen George **Harrold** 6th Bn Queen's Own Roy West Kent Regt: 26.10.1944 Age 29. Santerne Valley War Cemetery, Italy

Flt Sgt (Nav) Ronald Patrick Grenville **Hill** RAFVR, 44 (Rhosesia) Sqn: 31.3.1944 Age 23. Durnbach War Cemetry, Germany

Rfn Ernest John **King** 9th Bn Cameronians : 8.2.1945 Age 25. Reichswald Forest War Cemetery

Pil Off Horace Gordon **James** RAFVR, 145 Sqn: El Alamein War Cemetry, Egypt

D W **Jean** RAF: 5.7.1942 Age 27: 1941 No info available from War Graves Commission

. Sgt (Air Gnr) Erod Gordon **Johnson** RAFVR, 101 Sqn: 31.3.1944 Age ?. Hanover War Cemetry, Germany

Shipw'ht Walter Thomas Charles **Jordan** RN, HMS Barham: 25.11.1941 Age 21. Chatham Naval Memorial

Sgt Victor George **Knighton** RAFVR, 150 Sqn: 8.11.1941 Age 22. Runnymede Air Force Memorial

Flt Sgt (Pilot) Arthur Walter **Lynch,** RAFVR, Unit?: 5.7.1941 Age? St Leonard's Churchyard, Heston

Sub Lt (A) Derek John Theobald **Marais** RNVR, HMS Sparrowhawk: 22.9.1940 Age 21. Lady Old Churchyard, Orkney

Fg Off (Pilot) Victor **McConnell** RAFVR, 83 Sqn: 11.4.1944 Age 23. Schoonselhof Cemetry, Antwerp, Belgium

Air Fitter (A) Norman Frederick **Matthews** RN, HMS Landrail: 30.1.1942 Age 21. St Leonards Churchyard, Heston

L/Sgt George John Lionel **Meadows MM,** Royal Canadian Regt: 15.12. 1944 Age 22. Gradara War Cemetry, Italy

Flt Sgt (Nav) Wilfred William Murdoch **Milne** RAFVR, 248 Sqn?: 11.4.1944 Age 23. Heston & Isleworth (Hounslow) Cemetry

Sgt (Air Gnr) Edward Henry John **Morgan** RAFVR, 576 Sqn: 17.6.1944 Age? Arnhem (Moskova) General Cemetry, Holland

Sgt Jesse **Morris** RM, HMS President III: 11.4.1943 Age ? Portsmouth Naval Memorial

Flt Lt (Pilot) David William Hew **Owen** RAF, 102 Sqn: 20.5.1940 Age 22. Hamegicourt Churchyard, Aisne, France

Plt Off (Pilot) Leslie William **Parfitt** RAFVR: 16.7.1941 Age 29. Jonkerbos War Cemetry, Gelderland, Holland

Sgt (Pilot) Herbert William **Parry** RAFVR, No 1 PRU: 19.6.1941 Age 19. St Helen's Churchyard, Benson, Oxon

Flt Sgt (Air Bomber) Francis **Pinch** RAFVR, 49 Sqn: 8.5.1944 Age 20. St Doulchard Cemetry, Cher, France

Surg Lt John Wade **Rhys** RN, HMS Glowworm: 8.4.1940 Age? Portsmouth Naval Memorial. See notes

Sgt (Pilot trainee) Ronald George **Rider** RAFVR, Unit?: 29 4.1942 Age? Harare (Pioneer) Cemetry, Zimbabwe

Flt Sgt (W Op/Air Gnr) Robert **Sadler** RAFVR, 635 Sqn: 4.6.1944 Age 23. Downham Market Cemetry

Pte Eric Desmond **Sansom** RASC, Dunkirk retreat, Unit?: 22.5-11.6. 1940 Age 21. Paluel Churchyard, Seine-Maritime, France

Flt Sgt (Pilot) Eric Vernon **Sansom** RAFVR, Sqn?: 23.10.1941 Age 26. St John The Baptist Churchyard, Colerne, Avon

Pil Off Desmond Wallace **Skipper** RAFVR, 101 Sqn: 28.9.1943 Age 22. Cambridge City Cemetry

LAC (Nav trainee) William Herbert Frederick **Smale** RAFVR, Unit? : 15.9.1942 Age 19. St Jean-sur-Richelieu Cemetry, Quebec, Canada

Flt Sgt Leonard Edward **Small** RAF, 84 Sqn in retreat ahead of Japanese: 12.3.1942 Age 20. Singapore Memorial

Flt Sgt (Nav) Eric William **Spriggs** RAFVR, 15 Sqn: 21.6.1944 Age 22. Heston & Isleworth (Hounslow) Cemetry:

Ord Smn Herbert Herbert Godwin **Stokes** RN, HMS Jason: 27.8.1944 Age 19. Portsmouth Naval Memorial

Lt Arthur Norris **Stone** 5th Bn? Royal Berks Regt: 20.1.1945 Age 29. Nederweert War Cemetry, Limburg, Holland

LAC Peter Charles **Turland** RAF, Unit?: 2.5.1945 Age 23. Unit? Labuan War Cemetry, Malaysia

Pte Terence James **Twohig** RAPC, Unit?: 26.10.1942 Age 23. St Leonard's Churchyard, Heston

Ass John Edward **White** RN, HMS Charybdis : 23.10.1943 Age 24. St Peter Port (Foulon) Cemetry, Guernsey

Sgt (Air Bomber) Eric George **Wyatt** RAFVR, 103 Sqn: 28.4.1944 Age ? Vevey (St Martin's) Cemetry, Switzerland

In addition the following nine losses are believed to be OSGs:

Sgt (Flt Eng) John James **Eaton** RAFVR, 66 Sqn: 2.12.1943 Age? Berlin 1939-45 War Cemetry, Germany

Sgt (Air Gnr) Peter Norman **Ellis** RAFVR, 161 Sqn (Special duty): 14.2.1945 Age? Cambridge City Cemetery

L/Cpl FJ **Ferguson** Royal Corps Signals, Burma P&T Sigs: 24.6.1946 Age ? Taukkyan War Cemetry, Burma

Sgt (Air Gnr) Ronald **Greenwood** RAFVR, 76 Sqn: 4.6.1942 Age ? Bergen General Cemetry, Norway

Sgt Charles **Kelly** RAFVR: 28.6.1941 Age ? Runnymede Air Force Memorial

Sqn Ldr Peter **Nixey** RAF, 214 Sqn: 20.6.1942 Age 22. Ommen General Cemetry, Overijssel, Holland

Flt Lt (Pilot) David William Hew **Owen** RAF, 102 Sqn: 20.5.1940 Age 22. Hamegicourt Churchyard, Aisne, France

Sgt William James Henry **Robb** Royal Fusiliers, 9th Bn City of London Regt: 12.9.1943 Age 26. Salerno War cemetery, Sicily

Pil Off (Pilot) Alfred Victor **Snelling** RAFVR, 78 Sqn: 9.6.1941 Age ? St George's Churchyard, Middleton St George, Durham

It may be thought perhaps insensitive to make any remarks about individuals listed above, but the following is meant as a symbolic tribute to all those brave and gallant young people cut down in their prime:

John Rhys was a great sportsman, and brainy too (just like his brother David). He went on to become a doctor after qualifying in double quick-time at Guys Hospital before being called up to serve in the RN. He was appointed Medical Officer of *HMS Glowworm*, a ship which is famed in the annals of British naval history. She was the destroyer, which fatally shot up by the German cruiser *Hipper* in the Nowegian Sea and without any serviceable guns or torpedoes left to fire, damaged her adversary by ramming her before sinking with the loss of most of her crew. The captain of *Glowworm* was awarded the VC posthumously. The Barden brothers' lives were commemorated by their parents' endowment of the Leslie Barden Prize for Geography and the David Barden Prize for French. David won a Kitchener Scholarship as well as another major scholarship to Christ's College Cambridge to study modern languages (LT Brown's very own college and faculty); but after one year he joined up, and whilst training undertook some teaching at Spring Grove before going to the Far East where he died from influenza after the war had ended. A third brother Arthur, and sister Gladys both served their country well and survived the war.

Stan and Cyril Eckert (see photo) were paratroopers; Stan jumped and landed in Normandy just after midnight on 6th June 1944, followed shortly by Cyril. Later that day Stan wrote a poignant letter to his mother whilst sheltering in a ditch. Sadly he was killed shortly after this, but the next day a Royal Marine Commando found his body and forwarded the letter to Mrs Eckert. The letter is on display in the Merville Battery Museum near Ranville in Normandy, though much faded. Stan and Cyril are laid to rest in graves close together, alongside many others from the Parachute Regt, in the Military War Cemetry, Ranville.

Hazel Batten, the only young woman from our school known for certain to have been lost, drowned near Durban in unknown circumstances but which cost several other Wrens their lives, and which may have been as result of a tragic accident close to the beach.

There were many other brave men and women in uniform from our school, but who came home; some had surprising adventures, one such was Roy Baxter (1938). Roy was a Sgt aircrew member on a Wellington bomber which crashlanded behind German lines in Libya in July 1942. All six crew got out, and with their emergency water walked back 180 miles (yes 180!) over the next nine days back to the Allied lines to fight another day – and they did. This story hit the national newspapers at the time and was reported later in the *Middlesex Chronicle* who made much of it with a headline akin to 'local boy goes for long walk in the desert'.

If anybody can assist in determining the veracity of the 'additional' nine names at the list end above, please contact me. Finally, I am grateful to those OSGs who were very patient with my questions of certain OSGs, and especially to Dennis Collins (1938) who generously made available his researches into those who gave their lives.

The Commonwealth War Graves Commission does not list Peter Gibbs; Jack Handscombe (1941) wrote to me with details of Peter Gibbs. Peter left school early and went to sea..In 1941 his ship was torpedoed in the Atlantic; luckily he was rescued after surviving two weeks in a small boat. Later that year, whilst supervising cargo operations on his new ship in Liverpool docks, Peter was knocked into the ship's hold and killed. Jack told me that he and his pal had a drink in *The Winning Post* at Whitton only a week or so before the accident.

There may still be other names to surface of those young people from our old school who made the supreme sacrifice. May they all rest in Peace.Comment: on reflection I think now we have to assume that there was no memorial at school simply on account of the great number who were lost; LT Brown and the staff of the day would have been devastated at its size. Readers will recognise the large number of young men who served in the Air Force, many were in Bomber Command which lost some 50, 000 aircrew. Several of our young men are buried in St Leonard's Churchyard, Heston, the resting place of Sir Joseph Banks and his lady.   May they **Rest in Peace.**

An environmentally friendly book printed and bound in England by
www.printondemand-worldwide.com

This book is made entirely of chain-of-custody materials